THE AMERICA
OF CARL SANDBURG

Carl Sandburg on visit to Washington for Civil War centenary observances; he celebrated 85th birthday with new volume of poems. *A Washington Post photograph by Ellsworth Davis.*

THE AMERICA

OF

CARL SANDBURG

By

HAZEL DURNELL, M. A., Litt. D.

Lecturer in American Literature
The University of Geneva, Switzerland

With a Foreword by
GORDDEN LINK

THE UNIVERSITY PRESS OF WASHINGTON, D.C.

Library of Congress Card Catalog No. 65-17638
Printed in the United States of America

To the Memory of my Husband

ACKNOWLEDGMENTS

Grateful acknowledgment is made to the publishers of the following works of Carl Sandburg from which seven poems and sundry fragments or excerpts have been used by permission of the author and identified in the *Bibliography* and *Notes* sections:

HARCOURT, BRACE AND WORLD, INC., 757 Third Ave., New York, N. Y. 10017

From *Complete Poems*—four fragments and two excerpts from the "Foreword"; ten fragments and eleven excerpts from various sections; five fragments and nine excerpts from the volume *Good Morning, America;* two fragments and five excerpts from the "New Section"; and three poems ("Buffalo Dusk," "A. E. F.," "Helga").

From *Always the Young Strangers*—seven fragments and eight excerpts.

From *Abraham Lincoln: The Prairie Years*—four fragments and five excerpts; from *Abraham Lincoln: The War Years*—nine fragments and six excerpts.

From *Remembrance Rock*—four fragments and eight excerpts.

From *Home Front Memo*—six fragments and seven excerpts (two excerpts copyright by Museum of Modern Art).

From *Wind Song*—two fragments and one excerpt.

From *The American Songbag, Chicago Race Riots* and the "Foreword" of *Early Moon,* one excerpt each.

HARPER AND ROW, PUBLISHERS, 49 E. 33d St., New York, N. Y. 10016

From "Foreword" by Carl Sandburg to the volume, *To Turn the Tide* by John Fitzgerald Kennedy—one excerpt.

HOLT, RINEHART & WINSTON, Inc., 383 Madison Ave., New York, N. Y. 10017 (For Works published by Henry Holt & Co.)

From *Chicago Poems* (1916)—eleven excerpts and twelve fragments (also acknowledged under *Complete Poems,* above) and one complete poem, "Fog."

From *Cornhuskers* (1918)—nine excerpts and twelve fragments (also acknowledged under *Complete Poems,* above) and three complete poems, "Early Moon," "Upstairs," "Southern Pacific."

THE MODERN LIBRARY, INC., 457 Madison Ave., New York, N. Y. 10022.

From "Foreword" by Carl Sandburg to the Special 1921 Edition of Whitman's *Leaves of Grass*—one excerpt.

TIME, INC., Time & Life Bldg., Rockefeller Center, New York, N. Y. 10020

Carl Sandburg's "Chicago Dynamic" speech, published by *Life,* November 4, 1957—two fragments and three excerpts.

Acknowledgment is also made to the following publishers for the use of fragments or excerpts from works by contemporaries of Mr. Sandburg:

HARCOURT, BRACE AND WORLD, INC.

From Rebecca West's "Introduction" to *Selected Poems of Carl Sandburg*—two excerpts and three fragments.

From Louis Untermeyer, *Modern American Poetry* (1936)—one excerpt.

HOLT, RINEHART & WINSTON, INC. (For works published by Henry Holt· & Co.)

From Russell Blankenship, *American Literature as an Expression of the National Mind* (1931)—one excerpt.

From Robert Frost, *Complete Poems* (1929)—five excerpts and four fragments.

ALFRED A. KNOPF, INC., 501 Madison Ave., New York 10022

From Llewellyn Jones, *First Impressions* (1924)—one excerpt.

THE MACMILLAN CO., 60 Fifth Ave., New York, N. Y. 10011

From Bruce Weirick, *From Whitman to Sandburg in American Poetry* (1924) —one excerpt.

From Edgar Lees Masters, *Spoon River Anthology* (1915)—four fragments.

From Edwin Arlington Robinson, *Collected Poems* (1921)—five excerpts and four fragments.

OXFORD UNVERSITY PRESS, INC., 417 Fifth Ave., New York, N. Y. 10016

From M. L. Rosenthal, *The Modern Poets* (1960)—two excerpts and five fragments.

PANTHEON BOOKS, INC., 22 E 51st St., New York, N. Y. 10022

From Boris Pasternak, *Dr. Zhivago*—one excerpt.

SIMON AND SCHUSTER, INC., 630 Fifth Ave., New York, N. Y. 10020

From Max Lerner, *America as A Civilization* (1957)—one excerpt.

FOREWORD

In more ways than can be briefly enumerated, Carl Sandburg has played a constant and dominant role in my existence. There was even a time when I cultivated a long cowlick and made what amounted to a minor career of reading his poems in an abandoned imitation of his style before college classes and women's clubs throughout the country. It is, I suspect, because of this personal identification, rather than any slight contribution to the literature in the field, that the honor falls to me of presenting a distinguished, perhaps even definitive, study of Carl Sandburg and his personal America. Here is the book that I have dreamed of writing myself for nearly forty years.

Hazel Durnell is the kind of literary historian who makes her readers wish they had done this page or that passage themselves. Reading *The America of Carl Sandburg,* I found myself thinking back through the years, measuring by my own experience the impact that the poet has been having on people across our own land and abroad virtually since his first appearance on the literary scene. What was Mrs. Durnell doing when first I met Carl Sandburg, I found myself wondering. Arithmetic supplied the answer. She was a young Phi Beta Kappa housewife in Ohio writing essays—on Carl Sandburg and his contemporaries. She already had been head of the Department of Modern Languages at Franklin College and I was just breaking into newspaper work by way of afternoon and evening assignments. But we both, like thousands of others, had received impetus and inspiration from *Chicago Poems and Cornhuskers,* from *Smoke and Steel* and *Slabs of The Sunburnt West.*

Halfway through Mrs. Durnell's manuscript, I laid it down to relive a past that she suddenly made vivid. Thirty seven years had not dimmed the scene. A story had broken in the old Brooklyn *Standard Union* that had everybody working overtime. Curiously enough, all I recall about it is that it was responsible for City Editor McCarthy's act of desperation in sending the paper's seventeen-year-old cub reporter to cover a major appearance by Carl Sandburg and his guitar. Having raised a mustache for this job and having carefully cultivated both the upturned front brim of battered felt hat and the generally cynical posture of the era's city room, I nevertheless gave way to frenetic excitement at my first meeting with the man whose poetry I had been aping for some two years. I was so assiduous in my questioning (and Mr. Sandburg was as always so kind) that I was able to outlast all of my grown colleagues in the post-program interview.

Mirabile dictu, an hour after the lecture-recital was over, Carl Sandburg and a new assistant were on a hunt through the proverbially damp cellars of Flatbush following leads in a grubby notebook. And the trail led to many old songs, some in manuscript, that were to end up in *The American Songbag.* The adventure was continued the following day in an area where the cellars were knee-deep in water. It would not make sense to the present generation that ten years later my wardrobe still included one pair of trousers, carefully uncleaned, bearing for all to see the watermarks of literary history. Nor that, having stayed up all night to write my story, I managed to attend my morning classes at New York University before reporting to the poet's hotel room for the second day of glory.

It need hardly be said that my term paper in Sophomore Literature at the University was on Carl Sandburg. Blithely entitled "Carl Sandburg's Philosophy of Life," it was written with the quiet assurance and forgivable dogmatism of one who treasured a secret cache of letters from the poet, himself. It had two passages conceivably worthy of quotation.

As he himself admits, "I guess you'll find my philosophy sort of muddled." It is not muddled so much as it is, like his life, variegated. His is the philosophy of the common man, with occasional flights up the two-step ladder to Babbittry. His is the philosophy of the out-thrust jaw and indignation resigned; and sometimes there is the low-hung head and resignation barely indignant.

And then, reminder of the Great Adventure:

But we might go on indefinitely coining phrases descriptive of Sandburg's multi-faceted philosophy. It would be well, now, to take Sandburg's own advice, given once [one year earlier!] to an eager, if callow, representative of the press who had the temerity to quiz him on his philosophy of life. The poet had just given one of his unique song and poem recitals and was still hugging to his Middle-Western bosom the inevitable Sandburg guitar. In a tone that made the instrument quiver against his chest like a thing alive he cried, "When a man has written seven books, the chances are there's something between the lines that tells about his slant on life. Have *you* gone through those books?

This jejeune contribution, published the following year in *The Poetry Review* of London, had one passing distinction; but it remained for Hazel Durnell, in *The America of Carl Sandburg,* to point out that it was the first published analysis of Sandburgian philosophy to appear in a British journal.

Six years after its appearance, I was at George Peabody College for Teachers, in Nashville, Tennessee, teaching a writing course and working for my Ph. D. My correspondence with Mr. Sandburg had waned. Suddenly I received a telegram:

MEET ME UNION STATION THURSDAY NINE-THIRTY. GIVING WAR MEMORIAL AUDITORIUM PROGRAM. PROTECT ME FROM DOWAGER DAMES.

HIRAM CORNHUSKER

So it came about that for almost a full glorious week I secreted Carl Sandburg in my graduate dormitory room while he was getting ready for his program. Together with Ralph Wickiser, the Illinois artist, who was also a part-time instructor, we stayed up far into the night discussing the "New Poetry" and singing songs to the accompaniment of the famous guitar.

Three memorable events followed. First, I was summoned to the office of doughty Ida Z. Carr, Dean of Women and behind-the-scenes administrator of the campus.

"Mr. Link," she said, "there have been numerous complaints about the noise emanating from your quarters."

"The 'noise' to which you refer," I replied with, I thought, considerable dignity, "was made by Mr. Carl Sandburg and his guitar."

"Mr. Link," she cried, drawing herself up to her full five feet, and seeming almost as wide, "kindly do me the favor of not adding prevarication to your other shortcomings."

Next, came the dedication of the War Memorial Auditorium, with Carl Sandburg as the main feature. It was typical of his warm, thoughtful nature that he managed to have me sit on the platform and to dedicate the program to his host.

Finally, and most important of all, Mr. Sandburg was the guest of the Peabody Poets, a group of which I was the faculty sponsor. We sat at the side of the room while the president, Mae Mills, made the introduction. A heavy elbow nudged me in the ribs.

"Gordden," he said, "that's the prettiest, little Southern girl I've seen on this trip; why don't you do something about it?"

"But, Carl," I objected, "she's just a baby."

"Son," he replied, "there's only one cure for youth and that's age. She'll get bigger."

He was so right. The following January she was just big enough and we were married. No further documentation is necessary to support the statement I have frequently made that Carl Sandburg has been the most important single influence in my life.

These were the memories that came to mind while Hazel Durnell made Carl Sandburg and his times take almost tangible shape. Despite her formidable scholarly weapons, she has managed to keep her subject alive. The essentially homespun Mr. Sandburg might claim that the adornment he least wants or needs is the scholarly footnote. He did not have to fear, while this stupendous piece of scholarship was being sweated out, that either he or his America would be obscured or obfuscated in the process. Both the man and the country of which he has become so convincingly the symbol emerge warm and broad and alive, as if they had never been subjected to the act of documentation.

Anna Lenah Elgström, the distinguished Swedish critic who edited Sandburg's poems in the Swedish edition, has written of Hazel Durnell

that she "pictures Carl Sandburg as poet, historian, and human being, bu.
she also depicts the America which is reflected in his writings; in both
respects her description is richly faceted, profound, and enthusiastic without, however, excluding a critical sense of nuances." In the same way
that impact is lost in translation, even from such lucid writing as Mrs.
Elgström's, there is considerable diminution in any description of the
kind of work Dr. Durnell has done on Carl Sandburg. *The America of
Carl Sandburg* must be read and studied and then re-read for a full appreciation of its scope, its depth, and its intuitions.

It is not sufficient for a scholar like Hazel Durnell to arrange for the
use of a carrell in a great library and to check out the references in
Reader's Guide. To trace the influence of his Scandinavian heritage upon
Sandburg's writings, she went to the University of Stockholm for the study
of Scandinavian literature. There she achieved an insight into the spiritual
kinship of Sandburg with Ibsen, Engström, Tegner, and Selma Lageröf.
Along with her University studies and her discussion in depth with such
critics as Annah Lenah Elgström, she did special research in the University Library and in the Royal Library of Stockholm. She also did research
at the University of Uppsala which had awarded Sandburg an honorary
degree of Ph. D. *in absentia*.

Her studies took her to the University of Geneva, which has a collection of Americana and where she is now Lecturer in American Literature; to the University of Illinois, which is planning to construct a special
room to house Sandburg manuscripts; to Galesburg, Illinois, where she
investigated source materials at Knox College and made the acquaintance
of Mrs. Adda George, founder of the movement to organize Sandburg
Birthplace, Inc. It was through Mrs. George that she was able to copy
the first small volumes by Carl Sandburg—privately published by his
English professor.

Mrs. Durnell's interviews with Carl Sandburg and, as I know from
personal experience, with virtually everyone who ever had any contact
with the poet, are models of this subtle research tool. It was during one
such discussion, for example, that Mr. Sandburg revealed to her his fondness for the works of Hugo and Villon and their influence upon his own
writings.

If there is source for information or insight in a study of Carl Sandburg
that Hazel Durnell has not explored, I have been unable in the past year
to uncover any indication of its existence. During this time, *The America
of Carl Sandburg* has been on my desk—a now-tattered Zerox copy of
the manuscript. There is hardly a page that has not been changed or
amended since first I saw it; I have laboriously kept up with the author's
progress through innumerable telegraph, telephone and postal messages.
To Mrs. Durnell there is nothing static about the act of scholarship.

Somewhere along the line she decided to eliminate a quotation from
Frederic Amiel of Geneva with whose ideal Sandburg seemed to be in

accord: "The reader desires in a poet something more than a juggler in rhyme and a maker of verse; he desires in him a painter of life, an observer, a friend, a fellow-creature, a being who thinks, loves, has a conscience, feels passion and repentance." To these goals, she pointed out, Sandburg has aspired; this definition, she thought, aids in the understanding of the social poetry of Sandburg. Nor did she retain the words of President John F. Kennedy: "As poet, story writer, collector of folk sings and biographer [Sandburg] has expressed the many-sided American genius." But the truth of these statements is still made manifest in her book.

The America of Carl Sandburg might well be called a study in depth. The author analyses unconscious Scandinavian influences on Sandburg's thinking, conscious French influences, and the effect on his writing of Lincoln, Emerson, Emily Dickinson and other New England writers, and, of course, Whitman. She discusses early problems of overcrowded cities which Sandburg knew in his youth and the movement for social and economic reform in which Theodore Roosevelt and Woodrow Wilson took the lead. She evaluates the social critics in the Middle West, principally Edgar Lee Masters and Carl Sandburg, and the poetry that grew inevitably in this climate.

This book depicts Sandburg as a social conscience and a voice of national awareness, reflecting the impact of World War I following his return from covering Norway and Sweden for 390 American newspapers. Thereafter, it shows the growth in scope and depth of Sandburg's writing, both in poetry and prose, through the years of the Depression. Here Sandburg is shown championing the cause of collective man as the shaper and maker of human destiny. Through his poetry, which is essentially moral in function, and which was shaped to reach varied audiences, Sandburg, as the author points out, achieved identification with the fighting struggle of urban existence, with the social and political currents of national life, and with the economic problems of the common man.

Dr. Durnell elaborates a significant contrast with the style and approach of Robert Frost who also aimed at democratization of poetry.

There is considerable stress on the Lincoln influence. The author believes that the moral and humanitarian attributes of Lincoln democracy are fundamental characteristics of Sandburg's writings. She maintains it was inevitable that Sandburg, through the magnitude of his interpretation should become the literary embodiment of the Lincoln tradition. And she is convinced it follows that, in the public mind, he has emerged as a national symbol and the most eloquent voice of democracy in America today.

In a special university program Mrs. Durnell once gave an interesting summary of America's critical response to the Lincoln biography. There seemed to be general agreement, she said, that aside from the monumental story of Lincoln, these six volumes aid in the understanding of some of the very serious problems of the American experiment; that these problems, put to the test of internecine war, throw light on the question of slavery and the racial issues which affected the nineteenth century; that Lincoln's wisdom and opinions—his supreme defense of democratic principles—help to explain to our troubled generation the origins of many disturbing tensions; and, finally, that Carl Sandburg intensifies our consciousness of the social structure of our nation.

In this context, it would be appropriate to offer one passage from *The America of Carl Sandburg:*

A wide humanitarianism, a moral earnestness, a broad insight into features of American life that are significant in the evolution of the nation and an abiding faith in democracy are distinguishing features of his work. In interpreting the feelings and aims of the people the social poetry in its varied fusions of voice and mood, in its less disciplined form, does not comply with conventional literary standards, but nevertheless achieves an important pragmatic significance by its appeal to the common consciousness. With its sympathetic analysis of human relations and its identification with the currents of national life it is addressed to the American conscience and to the potential existent in the American people.

It is through such statements as this that Mrs. Durnell supports her contention that Carl Sandburg's work "represents a form of literary nationalism in its comprehensive conception of the American story."

The America of Carl Sandburg is the study of my old friend that I have been wanting for nearly forty years to write. I should be very proud to have written it. It will be the touchstone for any future scholarship in Sandburgiana.

GORDDEN LINK
Poet in Residence
Anne Arundel Community College

Severna Park, Md.
August 15. 1965

PREFACE

This book is the outgrowth of work done for a doctorate which was received in 1963 from the University of Geneva, Switzerland; and I remain profoundly grateful for the direction of Professor H. W. Häusermann and for the helpful criticism of Dr. Edwin Pratt and Dr. Raymond Tschumi during those earlier years.

Much of my research was carried on in the Library of Congress in Washington, D.C., and to the officials of the Library of Congress I express my gratitude, for they made available to me a study table on an upper floor of the Library where books and periodicals could be kept undisturbed; and I wish to state my appreciation of the personal interest and helpfulness of the librarians of Hendersonville, North Carolina, and Asheville, North Carolina; and of the kindness of officials of the Royal Library in Stockholm and of the Carolina Rediviva Library in Uppsala, Sweden. Sincere thanks are also due officials at the United Nations Library in Geneva and the *Bibliothèque Publique et Universitaire de Genève.*

Many individuals not connected with libraries have aided with research. First and foremost among these individuals, I respectfully acknowledge my debt of gratitude to Mr. Carl Sandburg for the honor accorded me by personal interviews. At the University of Illinois I owe thanks to Professor Emeritus Bruce Weirick for the courtesy of an introduction to personnel of the Department of English Literature; and to Professor Henning Larsen for his generosity in giving me a copy of his award speech when the honorary Doctor of Literature degree was conferred upon Mr. Sandburg by that University in 1957.

I wish to express my gratitude to Mrs. John E. George of Galesburg, Illinois, for her letters of suggested aids to research; to Mr. Ralph Newman, proprietor of the Abraham Lincoln Book Shop in Chicago, for his advice and counsel and for the loan of collector's items from his collection of Sandburgiana; to Mrs. Anna Lenah Elgström in Stockholm, Sweden, for her personal assistance with interviews; and to those who assisted with Swedish translation and with gifts of Swedish newspapers and magazines pertaining to my subject; to the Newspaper Enterprise Association in Cleveland, Ohio, for photostatic copies of articles written by Mr. Sandburg as a war correspondent in Christiania, Norway, and Stockholm, Sweden, in 1918-1919.

Events occurring since 1963 have made certain additions and revisions advisable and continuing research has brought new material to light. For recent advice on the Lombard years of Carl Sandburg I am deeply appreciative of the assistance of Professor John C. Weigel, of Lombard College and, later, of the University of Chicago.

For generous permission to quote from his books, further acknowledgment of my debt to Mr. Sandburg is due, for he had kindly said: "You may use anything I have written." This cooperation was of immeasurable assistance, for his works contribute importantly to a more perceptive understanding of our changing society. In this connection, I have elsewhere acknowledged my gratitude to Mr. Sandburg's publishers, Henry Holt and Co.; Harcourt, Brace and World; Crosby Gaige; and Charles Scribner's Sons.

Emerson said of Abraham Lincoln, "He is the true history of the American people in his time"; and in many and varied ways the life and writings of Carl Sandburg reflect a long period in American social history. His monumental biography of Lincoln, which is without doubt his masterpiece, is a comprehensive survey of the early nineteenth century and of the Civil War period; it presents a candid portrait of the finest traditions of a free people incorporated in the Lincoln story. His autobiography in *Always the Young Strangers* portrays the society of a rapidly changing America in the late nineteenth century; and his poetry delineates the vast changes brought to the twentieth century by the Industrial Revolution, increased immigration, the rise of the great cities, and the tragedy of two World Wars. Yet he has retained a firm faith in the people and in the ever-renewing vitality of the nation. His life has been a full and significant one, and his writings mirror human experience in a growing America destined to be lifted to an important place among the world powers. It is not without reason that he has been referred to as "the Lincoln of our literature."

The late Adlai Stevenson, Ambassador to the United Nations, wrote of his old friend:

> Carl Sandburg is the one living man whose work and whose life epitomize the American Dream. He has the earthiness of the prairie, the majesty of the mountains, the anger of the deep inland seas. In him is the restlessness of the seeker, the questioner, the explorer of far horizons, the hunger that is never satisfied. In him also is the tough strength that has never been fully measured, never unleashed, the resiliency of usefulness which wells from within and which no aging can destroy.

It has been a richly rewarding experience during the past ten years to observe the influence across the nation of such a man as this, to note in Europe the impact of his image, and to detect, studying his works in depth, the heartbeat of humanity.

August 26, 1965   H. B. D.

CONTENTS

PART I

CARL SANDBURG AS CITIZEN AND WRITER

PART II

CARL SANDBURG INTERPRETS AMERICA

PART III

AMERICA AND CARL SANDBURG

Illustrations

PART I

CARL SANDBURG AS CITIZEN AND WRITER

I

SWEDISH ANCESTRAL BACKGROUND

Carl Sandburg's parents were Swedes who had joined the great expanding wave of European emigration to the United States of America in the nineteenth century. Economic privation forced them, as it did thousands of others, to leave their homeland and to begin life afresh in a new country. They left a venerable nation which has been characterized as " a modern democracy on ancient foundations. " * For many centuries Sweden had been predominantly an agricultural country. In its southern province of Skäne the rich earth was tilled by the inhabitants at least four thousand years ago. But agricultural development had been slow because of a shortage of land due to the entrenched privilege of a land-owning nobility. The industrial revolution was late in arriving, hydro-electric power non-existent and the wealth of the copper mines was near exhaustion; and while iron from the mines had not been depleted, there were as yet no railroads through the Arctic wilderness to transport the remaining supply. Repeated crop failures, a little past the middle of the nineteenth century, brought a continuing threat of famine.

In view of all these economic and political conditions, when news arrived from America of rich land in the Middle West which could be bought for a dollar an acre, and of the Homestead Act (1862) which under easy conditions granted land free, many of the proud but landless Swedes who loved their country but wished to be economically independent, chose to emigrate to that region of the United States. They came, they saw, and after conquering the hardships of the language barrier and after achieving other difficult readjustments, they settled. As Swedes, too, they brought their particular national temperament, a compound of their sincere, devout

---

* Ingvar ANDERSSON and Others. *Introduction to Sweden*, p. 11. Published by the Swedish Institute, Stockholm. 4th edition. Printed by Almquist & Wiksells, Uppsala, 1956.

Lutheran faith, innate serious-mindedness, sense of responsibility, civic virtue and tradition of disciplined freedom.

The first permanent settlement by Swedes had been made in 1638 at a spot on the Delaware River which is now called Wilmington. This settlement was already a fully organized community with farms, schools, mills, churches and local government when William Penn landed to begin the colonization of Pennsylvania and the founding of the city of Philadelphia in 1682. *

A few nineteenth-century immigrants from Sweden had arrived in the Middle West before our Civil War, but the great wave of Swedish immigration occurred after the war. ** In one of these post-war groups coming to America in the early 1870's was August Sandburg, who had saved enough money from working in a distillery to pay his passage to America. After working for a few months in a cheese factory in Herkimer, New York, he went on to Galesburg, Illinois, to join a cousin, Magnus Holmes, who had lived there for many years.

With another group, from Apuna, Sweden, came a young, blue-eyed, fair-haired girl, Clara Mathilda Anderson, destined to meet August Sandburg in Bushnell, Illinois, where she had found work in a hotel making beds and helping in the kitchen. Young August had come to Bushnell with the railroad gang with which he worked. They met—and on August 7th, 1874, were married and set up housekeeping in Galesburg, Illinois. In spite of the difficulties which had caused them to emigrate, these two retained a deep affection for their native land and for the language of the country they had left behind. As time went on, they learned to speak the language of their adopted homeland, but they never relinquished their love of the mother-tongue. They read their Swedish Bible regularly, and subscribed to a weekly paper from Chicago, *Hemlandet*, the Swedish expression for Homeland. Both were humble people with a staunch and unwavering moral code and an innate sense of thrift intensified by the necessity of frugal living; they were both devout members of the Swedish Lutheran Church and were exceptionally industrious, honest, trustworthy persons endowed with the native love of cleanliness and a pride in work well done.

Thus the Sandburgs' family life retained a strongly Swedish flavor; but it partook also, of a cosmopolitan atmosphere, for among the various nationalities represented in Galesburg were English, Scottish, Irish, German,

---

* At the waterfront in Wilmington, Delaware, is an important black granite monument given to the state of Delaware as a gift from the school children of Sweden to commemorate the landing of the Swedish immigrants in 1638.

** A very thorough and interesting study of the Swedish emigration movement to the United States in the mid-nineteenth century is presented in detail in the volume *The Emigrants*, by the Swedish author Wilhelm MOBERG.

See also: *Americans from Sweden* by Adolph B. BENSON and Naboth HEBIN; the foreword is written by Carl Sandburg.

See also: *Old Swedes Church Descriptive Bulletin*, issued by Old Swedes Church of Wilmington, Delaware.

Italian and French. Approximately 3,300 of the 20,000 inhabitants of Galesburg were immigrants from Europe.

Pioneers from New England and their children owned much of the town property and had established the framework of politics, religious denominations, the three colleges and the public schools. * Pioneers had also come from New York, New Jersey, Pennsylvania, Ohio, Kentucky and Tennessee. But the cosmopolitan spirit brought by the foreign born also became a power in the intellectual development of the community; for the assimilation of the immigrant has been one of the great strengths of the American nation.

In the eastern part of the United States an expanding economy based on textile mills and factories was developing; in the South agriculture was slowly regaining shape out of the ashes of the institution of slavery and the plantation system; and civilization was pushing westward into Indian territory and into the prairie. Between the California Gold Rush of '49 and the Oklahoma Land Rush of '89, a vast wave of pioneering expansion —the greatest in American pioneer history—spread westwards. The years following the Civil War required building activities of all kinds. The 1870's became the period of railroad building to open new territories for settlement. The Bessemer steel processing plants of Pittsburgh now were able to produce steel from iron ore and to build the rails for the increasingly important railroad system; while to meet the needs of steel production came the development of the coal and oil industries of Pennsylvania and eastern Ohio and the copper and iron ore industry of the Great Lakes regions. Machinery for tilling the soil and for harvesting crops was being manufactured, and this machinery made possible expansion and further development of the rich corn lands of the Middle West. The increase of corn permitted an ever increasing production of pork. The wide prairie grazing lands supplied food for great herds of cattle; into the prairie town of Chicago this produce was brought to market, and Chicago became a stock market center which was destined to become the greatest railway center on earth within a few decades.[1]

When America was one hundred years old the anniversary was marked by the Philadelphia Exposition in 1876. All nations of the civilized world were invited, and here the rapid development of America was shown to the older nations of the earth. The United States had excelled in the expanding

---

* Galesburg is unique in its origin. It was founded in 1837 by eastern pioneers who had come a thousand miles to establish a college which would inculcate Christian principles in the midwestern prairie which was being opened to settlers. The idea was conceived by a Presbyterian clergyman, the Reverend George Washington Gale, and Sylvanus Ferris, a New York cheese maker, gave financial aid to the settlers in establishing new homes. Most of these 200 early settlers came from the Mohawk Valley of New York with Dr. Gale, who had helped to raise both funds and volunteers for the founding of the college and city. Thus the city was literally built around Knox College which was an act of faith destined to be very influential in the history of Galesburg by continuing to provide higher education.

Galesburg has remained a cultural community, for Lombard College and Browns' Business College, both founded at a later date, gave the city the distinction over many years of having three colleges. Lombard was, however, merged with Knox in 1930.

field of mechanical inventions, of farming implements and industrial and agricultural machinery. The friendly interchange of ideas in progress was of great benefit both to America and to the countries who sent representatives to the Philadelphia Exposition.

With industrial, agricultural and economic improvement came a desire for greater development of the arts and education. An appreciation of the arts and a growing consciousness of the cultural side of life arose. The Art Institute in Chicago was established in 1879.

In literature, the West and the Middle West rose to prominence at about the time that the first transcontinental railroad was completed. In the Far West loomed the names of Mark Twain, Joaquin Miller and Bret Harte. In the Middle West William Dean Howells distinguished himself in the literary field. This Ohio youth was to be later acclaimed the Dean of American Letters. In the East, Walt Whitman was writing and revising the poetry contained in his volume entitled *Leaves of Grass*.

To the foregoing geographical background and literary milieu there was to come another writer who in twentieth-century American letters would have his special claim to fame.

II

CHRONOLOGICAL SURVEY OF SANDBURG'S LIFE AND LITERARY ACHIEVEMENT

A. EARLY LIFE IN GALESBURG

Carl Sandburg was born January 6, 1878, in a small three-room frame house on Third Street, in Galesburg, Illinois.[2] As said, this prairie town had come into existence only forty-one years earlier; and in the 1870's it had developed into a railroad center because of the crossing of rail lines coming from Chicago.*

We know from Sandburg's autobiographical writings that his parents were humble, pious and imbued with Swedish tradition. They were strong people and were determined to succeed. The father was puritan in type and hard-working to the point of physical exhaustion. He gave his son some of his own political consciousness as they went together to listen to Republican speeches and Republican band music. The father had absorbed the political tradition of Lincoln; and his son followed in this tradition.

Carl's mother was possessed of a warmer, kindlier nature, patient with her children, giving generously of maternal affection, believing that " with thought and love in the home so much can be overcome."[3] She, too, endowed her children with spiritual values and with a high moral code illustrated in her unwavering devotion to the Swedish Lutheran Church. Commentators on Sandburg's home background agree with the poet himself that his mother had an inner grace and bright radiance, a religious devotion and a deep interest in her children, her friends and neighbors which combined to produce in her a loving and lovable character.

In 1882 the family moved to a larger home on East Berrien Street, where young Carl was to pass the formative years of youth. Here he grew up in the company of other Swedes and of New Englanders, Germans, Irish, and Italians; they played together and they understood each other. Economically, life was difficult for the Sandburg family; though the father was the personification of honesty, sobriety, tireless industry and faithful application to duty, his working hours were spent at the forges of the Chicago, Burlington and Quincy Railroad shop, ten hours a day for only

---

* The site decided upon for Knox College and the city of Galesburg was the center of a vast fertile prairie; thus farming has always been, and still is, one of the greatest assets of the community. Yet industry also arose due to the selection of Galesburg as a division point by the Chicago, Burlington and Quincy railroad. The Santa Fe railroad was also built through the city, but the Burlington (or " Q, " as it is locally referred to) still ranks as the city's major industry employing 2500 men today. Cross-country freight trains are here broken up, switched, re-arranged and dispatched in six different directions.

fourteen cents an hour. On this, the family was fed and clothed, the home paid for and some of the hard-earned dollars given to the Swedish Lutheran Church.

One of the small boy's earliest memories of the Berrien Street home was of the Swedish Bible. He relates: " It was the first book that dawned on my mind as a book, as a thing made of paper and, on the paper, black marks your eye could pick off from the page and you could say the words that lay there on the paper. This wonder came into my life when I was four years old. It was winter, cold outside, and winds howling. Mary and I heard father by the light of a small kerosene lamp read a chapter. What he read I have forgotten and couldn't have remembered the next day because I didn't understand it. But I recall several times that week going to where that book lay on the top of a bureau. And I opened it and turned pages and held it near a window and had my wondering about how those black marks on white paper could be words your eye would pick off into words your tongue could speak... *Gud* meaning ' God ' or *evangelium* meaning ' gospel. ' I asked my mother to point out these words for me so my eye would know how spoken words look when fastened down in black on white paper. She put her finger on those words and I had a dim beginning of learning to read, a hazy understanding. I took comfort in mother saying it would be clear to me when I started to school and learned to read." [4]

Sandburg tells in *Always the Young Strangers* of his early school years, his first attacks on the alphabet, then in the second year on arithmetic and spelling and some geography. By the time he reached the fifth grade, he had begun to read books in the school library, other than texts or required reading. The first extracurricular books to which he turned his attention were the *Young Folks' Cyclopaedia of Persons and Places*, and the *Young Folks' Cyclopaedia of Common Things*. One Friday afternoon in the winter of 1889 he was permitted to take home from the library the first volume of Abbot's *The History of Napoleon Bonaparte*. He read it alone, wrapped in an overcoat and seated at the window of his third floor garret. By Sunday he had finished the first volume, and the following week he brought home the second volume.

In the sixth grade this avid young reader became absorbed in the history books of the library, such as *Napoleon and His Marshals* and *Washington and His Generals, The Boys of '76*, which he read many times, *The Story of Liberty, Old Times in the Colonies*, and *The Boys of '61*, to learn of the Civil War. He read also *Huckleberry Finn* and *Tom Sawyer* by Mark Twain and some of Charles Dickens' works. Eugene Field and Longfellow were read in school and his first taste for poetry became apparent; Gray's " Elegy in a Country Churchyard " he memorized; but the history books were his private reading material.

As a young boy he saw some of the old-time pioneers and first settlers who had helped to found Galesburg. He saw them at the Old Settlers picnics, at County Fairs, at celebrations and occasionally on Main Street. In his boy's mind he tried to picture " them standing where there wasn't a wall or a roof on Main Street not yet a street—no streets anywhere and no houses. There they looked around and decided where to clear for the first row of houses, the Public Square, the Church, the blacksmith shop, the general store—and the college to be the focus of light and hope for the youth of the coming generation. They saw their little town rise to be a place and a name where before there had been silence broken only by wild-animal cries." [5] Some of these old-timers he saw; others he heard about; and he was to grow up with their children and grand-children.

In the seventh and eighth grades it was *A Brief History of the United States* that left its imprint on the inquiring mind of the boy, consumed by the desire to learn much, much more, over and beyond the ordinary curricular subjects. Yet it is important to note that he was an active, strong, athletic boy who engaged in healthy outdoor games with the other boys of his crowd. In baseball young Carl Sandburg excelled; and he hoped some day to make a minor league team, until in a practice game one day, while running at top speed, his right foot was seriously cut in the instep by a broken bottle. The four stitches required to close the gaping wound put an end to all professional baseball ambitions, but the game never lost a great fascination for him. This interest in athletics played an important part in Sandburg's later career.

B. EDUCATION IN THE DIFFICULT SCHOOL OF EXPERIENCE

After the close of his eighth grade schooling in 1892, such education as this promising young scholar could secure had for seven years to come from outside the school room, from reading books, magazines and newspapers by himself, from learning in the school of experience, from listening and watching tradespeople and many others as he worked at various and sundry jobs. For economically the Sandburg family had reached the danger point; and the youth had to turn with all his energies to any jobs available to help add to the meager family income. Hard Times and the Panic of 1893 were at hand.

From an early age, and while still able to attend school, he had worked at small jobs on Fridays and Saturdays to earn money. At home, too, he had always assisted with the family garden and household tasks, such as bringing in coal, carrying out ashes and carrying pails of water from the wooden pump outdoors into the kitchen for family use.

When eleven years old, he cleaned out the second floor office of a real estate firm each morning before going to school. This was his first regular paying job. Each Friday was pay day—and each Friday he received his week's pay—" twenty-five cents of United States money, a silver quarter of a dollar." [6] At the age of twelve he worked after school as a newspaper carrier, delivering about fifty copies of the Galesburg *Republican-Register* to regular subscribers. A little later he delivered in addition the Chicago morning papers, earning thereby seventy-five cents a week, plus one dollar a week for the afternoon deliveries of the Galesburg papers. From the Chicago papers he tried to absorb something of the questions of the Tariff and Free Trade, which then were subjects of public discussion; and from another Chicago paper which he delivered he read of Oliver Wendell

Holmes and of a boy who had visited with the poet. He so liked the portrayal of Holmes that he silently resolved to read his writings.

At the age of fourteen he walked two miles to work each day to deliver milk for a man who had two milk wagons, one of which the youth was permitted to drive.

Then, in October, 1892, tragedy struck the Sandburg family a devastating blow. Two of the younger brothers, Emil, aged seven, and Freddy, aged two, were stricken with diphtheria. The doctor was unable to cure them, for the miracle of modern medicine in the treatment of diphtheria was then unknown, and Emil and Freddy died less than one half hour apart on the third day.

Hard times were upon them. The father's work day had been shortened to four hours a day—as had other railroad shop men's time; and now the month's pay check was less than sixteen dollars. Young Carl's twelve dollars a month milk delivery pay was needed to meet the family expenses. By 1893 hard times had become a major economic catastrophe which was to go down in history as the Panic of 1893. So little food could be obtained that the Sandburg family learned to eat bread spread with lard sprinkled with salt. A neighborhood food coöperative came into being, each family contributing to the utmost. The Sandburg garden yielded potatoes. Perhaps this coöperative spirit may have been a portion of the foundation upon which was built the youth's faith in the goodness of common people.

Young Sandburg took a job as a porter in the Union Hotel barbershop at three dollars a week, plus occasional small tips. To the hotel came lecturers, show people, minstrels, actors. The youth watched them all and helped them whenever he could. One of his early thrills was seeing the singer Eddie Foy in the shop one day, and brushing his clothes and receiving an ever-remembered tip of two nickels. Then followed, in succession, another milk delivery job, a job as a tinner's helper, a job washing bottles in a pop bottling shop, a job as a potter's helper, and as water boy for a construction gang, as a boathouse assistant, as ice-house helper and stage-hand at the auditorium where, as an assistant, he was privileged to see many famous stage personages such as James O'Neill and Al G. Fields. Young Carl helped with horses at the race-track; and when circuses came to town, rose at four in the morning to water the elephants in order to earn a pass to the circus.

While we do not know from his writings of any particular strains he underwent in his adolescence, we do know that he had his " bitter and lonely hours moving out of boy years into a grown young man." [7] He longed to see the world. In 1896 at the age of eighteen, he made his first trip to Chicago, having in his pocket one dollar and fifty cents and a railroad pass to Chicago. By eating frugally and availing himself of cheap sleeping quarters, he stretched that dollar and fifty cents so as to enable him to see Chicago for three entire days. He visited the Eden Museum, saw two variety shows and walked through Marshall Fields and many other large department stores; he looked at the buildings of the Chicago *Daily News* and of the *Tribune*, newspapers which he had sold throughout the years; he watched the Elevated cars, stopped in at the Board of Trade, walked out to Lake Michigan, and saw for the first time in his life " water stretching away before his eyes and running to meet the sky." He walked for miles and "never got tired of the roar of the streets, the trolley cars, the teamsters, the buggies, surreys and phaetons, sometime a barouche with a coachman in livery, now and again a man in a saddle on horseback."[8] He returned to Galesburg penniless but richer for the experience of having seen a little of another world outside his own.

This trip was a significant experience in the life of Carl Sandburg. After his return to Galesburg he longed to be again in Chicago's crowds and roaring traffic and to see again the beauty of the shimmering water of Lake Michigan. He had wanted to go into the offices of Victor Lawson, publisher of the Chicago *Daily News* and the *Tribune*; but he had been unable to think of anything he might say if he should be admitted to the offices. However he had enjoyed his first insight into the activity of the great city. These facts are evidence of the incipient trends toward journalism and cosmopolitan city life that were taking shape in the young man's mind.

In 1897, at the age of nineteen, young Carl, overcome by this same searching spirit of restlessness, decided to see the West. With three dollars and twenty-five cents in his pocket and with no baggage whatsoever, he bade his family good-bye in June after telling them of his expectation, boarded a boxcar of the freight train standing near the Galesburg station and headed West on what was to become a memorable and important trip. As he crossed the Mississippi River standing at the open side door of the box car of the freight train, his eyes swept over the Father of Waters " with a sharp hunger that the grand old river satisfied."[9] This " hunger " was a manifestation of his insatiable appetite for learning, for seeing, for studying and finally for providing food for his mind and thought and soul. Through the alchemy of adaptation, he was soon to transform these experiences into poetry.

Young Sandburg left the freight train at Fort Madison, Iowa, spotted a small steamboat on the Mississippi and obtained employment from the captain, helping the crew unload kegs of nails, and they sailed down the river past Burlington, Quincy and finally Keokuk. He had determined before saying good-bye to his parents that he would travel as a " gaycat,"[10] as a man who hunts work hoping to find eventually a job to his particular liking.

At Keokuk he left the boat, sleeping that night near a canal and having his first experience with a hobo who offered him a roast beef sandwich, one of several this professional knight of the road had secured as handouts. Not caring for the company of the hobo, he obtained a job at blacking stoves the next day, and the following day hired himself out as a waiter at a small lunch counter. Always hoping to better his situation, he again boarded a freight train to cross half the state of Missouri, stopping at Bean Lake where employment with a railroad section gang was given him. After two weeks he hopped another freight train going to Kansas City where he worked as a dishwasher in a restaurant; from here the harvest fields of Lindaborg, Kansas, beckoned; and as he went westward through Kansas via freight car, meetings with tramps, panhandlers, and even petty thieves were inevitable. The Kansas wheat harvest provided work and funds for further travel until he came to the Rocky Mountains and Denver, Colorado, where a hotel offered a dishwashing job. After two weeks here, young Sandburg felt he had had enough of the West and headed back East to Galesburg, again via freight, arriving there richer by fifteen dollars and a great wealth of experience acquired through hard work, especially in the Kansas wheat fields and with the railroad section gang—richer also by greater self-respect and with greater hope for the future. He had acquired a measure of self-confidence and was not afraid to face whatever struggles life might hold in store for him. His trip West had extended from late June until mid-October.

Some commentators have referred to Sandburg's trip West as one of the most famous and significant trips in modern American literature. But the greater part of what we know of this trip comes from Sandburg's recollections as set down in the autobiography of his first twenty years. We must therefore bear in mind that they were memories of a poet of seventy-four, who long since resolved the quandaries of his younger days and whose main interest in the past was the light it threw on his subsequent development. This is not just emotion but recollection of " members who moved in a miniature drama "; [11] it is the reminiscence of a particularly forceful, matured mind. Allowing for this, however, it must be admitted that graphic impressions remained to the poet, and memories of feelings that could very well have outlasted the years and distortions of memory. Although Sandburg was like many other young men in wanting to see the country, it is clear that his reactions to it, and the aspects he seized on show unmistakable signs of keen sensitivity and a pictorial imagination that fixed scenes in his mind for years to come, together with a lyrical appreciation and gifts of expression, a sharp gift for the observation of life and a keen sense of the pathos of the human situation.

Sandburg's sensitivity to this last aspect—the human situation—is made evident by his sympathy for the vagrants whom he met on the freight trains. In his mind they were a direct reflection of the period known as Hard Times. In writing of these vagrant workers he states :

" Newspapers said the country was pulling out of the Hard Times, more factory chimneys smoking, the full dinner pail and the promised McKinley prosperity on the way. Yet there were still many men out of work, many men who had left their homes hoping for jobs somewhere. You could see these men riding the boxcars and sitting around in jungle hangouts." [12]

Of Larned, Kansas, he wrote that there were " empty houses here and there. People had moved away because of conditions, Hard Times. On one corner stood a big ghost hotel empty of travelers, no business; and here and there on Main Street a place once open for customers but now spiders and cobwebs had taken over." [13]

Sandburg saw in his trip a kind of poetic odyssey. The above illustrations show some of the roots of his later development.

Back in Galesburg he again turned to delivering milk, but as he drove the milk wagon he eagerly read each day in the Chicago *Record* the two-column lectures written by University of Chicago professors on questions of history, government and literature. A little later came a better opportunity—that of learning the painter's trade.

But suddenly there came a complete change in his life when, on February 15, 1898, the U.S. battleship *Maine* was blown up in the harbor at Havana, Cuba. As a result the United States soon declared war on Spain; and on April 26, Carl Sandburg offered his services with Company C, Sixth Infantry Regiment of Illinois Volunteers, and was accepted.

Thus it was in uniform that for the first time in his life he saw the city of Washington, where his regiment was given physical examination by a surgeon. There was little time to roam around but some of the regiment walked out past the Washington home of Abraham Lincoln before going to Falls Church, Virginia, for military training.

On July 11, six companies of the Sixth Illinois boarded the *Rita*, a Spanish ship captured by the United States Navy; on the evening of July 17 they arrived at Guantánamo Bay, Cuba; the next morning brought news that the battle of Santiago had been fought; the ship was ordered to Puerto Rico and upon arrival the troops were immediately marched to a field near Guánica, thence to Yauco and on to Ponce. Young Sandburg proved to be a good soldier and enjoyed the companionship of regimental life, and his keen, alert sensibilities eagerly absorbed the new sights and experiences, placing them in proper mental pigeon-holes to be drawn upon when the right time would come. Before leaving Illinois with his regiment, he had promised the editor of the Galesburg *Evening Mail* that he would attempt to write to that newspaper his impressions of the Spanish-American War; and accordingly he sent back long letters describing regimental life in Cuba and Puerto Rico. These letters were published and may therefore be considered his first assignment as a newspaper reporter. The war, however, was soon over and the troops were transported back to New York.

Young Sandburg arrived home in Galesburg after his soldiering, with a firm determination to go to college; and in the autumn of 1898 he enrolled at Lombard College in Galesburg for classes in Latin, English, public speaking, drama, elocution and inorganic chemistry.[14]

C. COLLEGE LIFE AND EXPERIENCE; THE TURNING POINT IN THE SANDBURG CAREER

Carl Sandburg entered college at the comparatively late age of twenty without a formal high school education, which had been denied him by force of circumstances. Yet he had privately read his sister's high school text books and as much else as time and conditions would permit; and college entrance requirements were less rigid then than now. A fire-department job would help him with expenses and the college had awarded him one year's free tuition because of his Spanish-American War services. At last he was to get the higher education which he had so fervently desired.

In May of 1899 young Carl was the Spanish-American War veteran designated by his Illinois Congressman to take the examination for West Point Military Academy in recognition of his services in the War. (In America such an appointment is an exceptional honor for it is officially extended only to young men of superior intellectual promise, of excellent character and unquestioned patriotism. To the few chosen it offers the opportunity of a college education at West Point, subsequent appointment as a commissioned officer, and a career in the Armed Forces.) Years later Sandburg wrote: " I went to West Point, being a class-mate of Douglas McArthur and Ulysses S. Grant III—for two weeks—returning home and to Lombard College after passing in spelling, geography, history, failing in arithmetic." [15] The poet Amy Lowell later described his failure in arithmetic as " most fortunate for American literature." [16]

Lombard College, founded in 1851, was an institution with liberal traditions. The old college records are incomplete and do not disclose Sandburg's complete curriculum. But while he was a student there from 1898 to 1902 the college exerted a strong influence on his thought processes, his interest in history and social science and his interest in literature. The most formative influence upon him during his college life was, however, the deep personal friendship with Professor Philip Green Wright.

(a) *Professor Philip Green Wright*

Professor Wright is best known for his studies in tariffs and economics which made him internationally famous. At the same time, however, he was a poet, a biographer, an excellent English instructor, a man of intense social consciousness, an advocate of social reform in the early 1900's and a man possessed of political optimism. An admiring student wrote of him in 1934: "Those who knew only the economist of later years for his distinguished researches on sugar tariffs and vegetable and mineral oils can have only the faintest notion of what his extraordinary mind, coupled with his quiet enthusiasm and gentle, encouraging friendship, meant to those of us who, as his students, came under his amazing spell." [17]

Professor Wright had almost daily contacts with young Sandburg during the latter's four college years and helped, by his inspiration, to shape the young man's career. Three students including himself organized a " Poor Writer's Club " [18] and discussed with the literature professor their efforts at composition. Carl Sandburg became editor of the college paper at the age of twenty-three, and editor of the college year book at the age of twenty-four, contributing to them many of his student literary productions. In the classroom, Carlyle, Shakespeare, Kipling, Emerson, Whitman and Ruskin were among the many writers studied and analyzed. This was Sandburg's first contact with a mind attuned to poetic appreciation. For this reason, Professor Wright's poetic outlook was one of the strongest influences on the young student's literary career. There is an amazing unanimity on this point.

C. E. Van Norman of Galesburg (the owner of the book company which bears his name, and also of a splendid collection of Sandburgiana), pronounces Professor Wright to have been " a fine teacher and a man who greatly inspired Sandburg." [19] So mutual was the admiration of professor and student, that in one of Professor Wright's publications, *The Dial of the Heart*, (1906) young Sandburg is the honored writer of the foreword. Mr. Van Norman considers this publication, which presents a lesson of

" wider charity and a deeper sense of brotherhood," [20] as establishing the influence of Philip Green Wright upon his pupil—both " inextricably woven together in printer's ink." [21] Professor Wright's reference in his book to poets in all eras who feel " world current flowing by and reveal its direction and destiny " [22] may seem almost prophetic of the twentieth century distinction of his pupil.

Quincy Wright, Professor of International Law at the University of Chicago, son of Professor Philip Green Wright, has known Sandburg since the Lombard days when the young man was frequently a guest in the Wright home, whether on Sunday evenings, when Professor and Mrs. Wright entertained students inclined toward literature, when the Poor Writers' Club met with Professor Wright to discuss their own compositions, or when Sandburg helped with the printing press in the Wrights' basement. Professor Quincy Wright refers to Sandburg's interest in poetry and literature as " inspired by my father during the Lombard years and further stimulated by a job as assistant to the Mayor of Milwaukee and for many years as reporter on the Chicago *Daily News*." [23] Alan Jenkins, pastor of the Central Congregational Church of Galesburg, refers to the elder Professor Wright as " Sandburg's literary and spiritual mentor as well as his first publisher.... Wright was the kind of English teacher who could creatively listen, who aimed not to prescribe subject and form but simply to encourage individuality and aptness of expression.... While Wright instructed in prosody, verse analysis was always subordinated to literary appreciation." [24]

But literature and poetic appreciation were not the only fields in which Professor Wright influenced young Sandburg. In political theory and economic theory he also left a deep impression on his student's mind, and helped him to see humanitarian horizons as a goal. Alan Jenkins stresses Wright's social consciousness which became a part of his teaching: " In Wright Sandburg rejoiced to find a campus apostle of economic reform... Wright was among those who were learning to see Lincoln as not only exemplary but as representative and prophetic; as not only a shaper of the ' American dream ' but as one of its products. Wright's early academic career coincided with the first great period in Lincoln research and writing. He had been doing graduate work at Harvard (1886-1887) when the Lincoln biography by Nicolay and Hay began running serially in *Century Magazine*. He was in his second year at Lombard (1894) when the same writers brought out their two-volume *Complete Works of Abraham Lincoln...*; thus, by the time Sandburg enrolled at Lombard, his English teacher was teaching Lincoln, the man.

" One surmises that the full extent of Wright's influence on Sandburg will never be known, that it is indeed beyond the reach of Sandburg's own introspection, that such chronicling can at best only vaguely symbolize an influence that went soul-deep, affecting motive and desire." [25]

A member of the Lombard class of 1908, John C. Weigel, writes: " Through him [Wright] I first gained a picture of the real Abraham Lincoln, the kind of human being Carl Sandburg has given us in *Abraham Lincoln: The Prairie Years*. As I read it, Carl Sandburg, I wondered if even you

— 14 —

know how much of Philip Green Wright shines through in the rare beauty of your precious book." [26]

To Carl Sandburg went the honor of being invited to write the biography of his English professor upon the latter's death, for the *Dictionary of American Biography*. And in a memorial brochure, written by Sandburg and others for the Wright family and for their private distribution, the poet affirms : " Philip Green Wright will always be a momentous figure to me.... I had four years of almost daily contact with him at college, for many years visited him as often as possible, and there never was a time when he did not deepen whatever of reverence I had for the human mind.... He was at home in either the utilitarian fields or in the realms of the ethereal and insoluble. He was a great man and a teacher. " [27]

During the summer vacations in his college years Carl Sandburg sold stereoscopic views for the well-known firm of Underwood and Underwood, and these selling trips took him to various parts of the country. In New Jersey his sympathy was drawn to the young boys working in a glass factory under conditions which today would be unheard of. His social sensibilities, already developing at Lombard, became aroused at the labor conditions in these glass works at Millville; and accordingly we find in his first published volume, *In Reckless Ecstasy*, both prose and poetry of protest.

As a speaker, too, he had developed considerable power by this time. In addition to writing and editing, the youth took an active part in the college debating club, the Erosophian Society; and as a senior student he won the annual oratorical contest, his subject being " Ruskin : A Man of Ideals."

Sandburg's interest in music was inherited from his parents. In this direction too, his college years show evidence. He attended all the free concerts and took an interest in student musical activities. He played a leading part in one musical extravaganza, *The Cannibal Converts*, written by Professor Wright and produced at the Galesburg Opera House.

During his first year at Lombard he earned his expenses by working as janitor and as callman in the Galesburg fire department; in addition to these jobs, his duties included ringing the college bell for classes. In the bell-tower were books belonging to the overcrowded college library and these he read between bells; most of them were theological books,[28] but everything he read gave him some knowledge to be stored away for future use.

Sandburg was still quite young when his first books were written; these were later published privately by Professor Wright on the printing press in his home. The three volumes were entitled *In Reckless Ecstasy*, *Plaint of a Rose*, and *Incidentals*. Professor Wright added prestige and dignity to the first volume, *In Reckless Ecstasy*, by writing the foreword, for he instinctively believed the poems in it foreshadowed great promise.

Professor Wright says of Sandburg, in his introductory preface to this little volume : " He had seen a great deal of the world; some of it, I believe, from the underside of box cars, traveling via the Gorky Line to literary fame. The boys called him the ' terrible Swede '; not such a bad characterization, after all; for it is a quality of this old Viking blood that it enables its possessor to land on his feet in any and every environment, and this the students found out, perhaps a little to their surprise. The 'terrible Swede,' as captain of the basketball team, led them to a series of remarkable victories, and when the time came for electing the editor-in-chief of the college paper, then also, for this most coveted honor in their gift, they could find no one more fitting than this young descendant of the Norsemen. My own association with him was on the literary side. He, together with two other incipient geniuses, Brown and Lauer, constituted an extremely informal organization which met Sunday afternoon in my study for literary refreshment. At these meetings we read, for our mutual edification and criticism, our own productions in prose and verse and any other sports of the spirit which we happened to run across during the week. Very delightful, very innocent and refreshing were these meetings, where our minds wandered the free fields of fancy and imagination." [29]

The above characterization by Wright is proof that a poet may also be an active participator in life.

(b) *Sandburg's College Writings*

There is much in Sandburg's *Reckless Ecstasy* which reveals his basic philosophy and outlook. A paragraph from this little volume also serves to explain the harshness of the Chicago poems to come a decade later:

" It is often the case that ideas which cannot be stated in direct words may be brought home by ' reckless ecstasies of the language. ' It is fear of the accusation of obfuscation that drives writers to the reckless ecstasy... There are some people who can receive a truth by no other way than to have their understanding shocked and insulted.... There are thoughts beyond the reach of words, and these the seers transmit only by lurid splashes of verbiage, that cannot be gauged by common-sense but must be sought out by the spirit of sublimity in us. I try to express myself sensibly, but if that fails, I will use the reckless ecstasy. As Kipling has one of his untamed children of the forest say, ' I will be the Word of the people.' Mine will be the bleeding mouth from which the gag is snatched. I will say everything." [30]

Reflecting the young student's sympathy with the poor, and with human suffering, is a poem entitled " Pulse-beats and Pen-strokes " selected from the little volume *In Reckless Ecstasy.* * This poem is imitative and immature; yet Professor Wright recognized in it the seeds of talent and encouraged its publication. The poem also reflects the influence of the social optimism of the English professor:

> " The cogs and the wheels, they hum and whirl
> Paying their bond to human brain;
> They card the wool, they hammer the steel,
> They utter no cry of joy or pain....

---

* It should be stated here that the college poetry was written under the name of Charles A. Sandburg, the youth then preferring the anglicized form of the name " Carl "; however, he later reverted to " Carl. "

The hovels shall pass and the shackles drop
The gods shall tumble and the system fall;
And the things they will make, with their loves at stake,
Shall be for the gladness of each and all." [31]

In the above lines we sense the influence of Browning and Emerson, that though a man's reach should exceed his grasp, he should ever have before him as a guiding star his great ideal " to rouse to thought the things to be; O star ! inspiriting, marvelous star." [32]

The following quatrain from *In Reckless Ecstasy* illustrates Sandburg's choice of words, his methods of expression : forecasts for us a tendency toward more forceful verse; and in a manner, prepares us for the more powerful strength of the free verse of his later poems :

"I do not gild my words with Attic salt,
You think; and yet that's surely not my fault;
I would be fresh as winds that sweep the sea.
And pack my words to last like God's basalt." [33]

In some of the other poems in this book we note the use of philosophical themes—unexpected in one so young—such as in the poem " Complacency. " Yet never was complacency permitted in the personal make-up of this young poet. Rather, he was beginning, by 1902, to appeal to the hearts of men who read, as in the poem " Pity " :

"I am Pity, and on my brow is written ' Pause '.
The gush of blood is an awesome sight
And ere I stab, I pause,
And pausing, sheathe the blade.
I do not leap headlong
While Anger and Resentment ride the heart.
The ignorant who gloat at desecration of their own,
All those who grope and stagger where the light is not,
And those who cannot read and therefore maunder o'er
the passport others bless,
For these do I knock on the hearts of men who read." [34]

These writings were not published in book form until after the close of Sandburg's college career. *In Reckless Ecstasy* and *Plaint of a Rose* were published in 1904; *Incidentals* in 1905. But the fact that Professor Wright chose to be the publisher and thereby to prolong the period of " mutual edification and criticism " is one of the most significant testimonies to Sandburg's gifts at that age. This also shows the maturity of the student whose college life came later to him than to many young men in the ordinary run of events. But these formative years had given him a basis of learning and had inspired him with a hunger for further learning.

Lombard College proved to be the turning point of his career, for it enabled him to work with his brain as well as with his hands. It brought into sharp focus all his previous experience as a boy with a working class background, as a soldier, as an immigrant's son eager to identify himself with his country; and it did this through close contact with Professor Wright, whose influence first set Sandburg on the road to giving expression to his humanitarian sympathies and lyrical feeling in the medium of poetry. It likewise set him on the road to a conception of politics that intellectualized his father's political interests. The little volumes published at this time show him to be a lyric poet—but a poet with a passionate interest in human condition, a poet of social protest, though on humanitarian rather than political grounds.

D. IN THE FIELD OF JOURNALISM

Sandburg's college career however was never formally completed. Circumstances forced him to leave college in 1902 after four years of study and to return to his work with Underwood and Underwood, although he still lacked a few credits for a degree. (In 1927, after the publication of several volumes of poetry and of *Abraham Lincoln: The Prairie Years*, Lombard College and Knox College, a sister institution in Galesburg, each awarded him an honorary Doctor of Literature degree).

While traveling over the country selling the stereoscopic views, he was able to read, in his spare time, writers such as Emerson and Tolstoy, whose works were then much in the foreground. His later writings show, too, that with his awakened social and political interests these experiences developed him rapidly as an observer of human nature and as a commentator on and critic of the social scene. His understanding pity went to the poor, namely those compelled to work in factories and mills for wages far too low. He had tasted long and bitterly of economic difficulty himself during the years of the Panic and its aftermath; he had felt the pinch of frugality, knew the toll it exacted, and felt deeply moved whenever and wherever he saw the similar struggle of others before adequate labor laws had been enacted.

The desire to write was becoming more and more deep-seated, yet necessity demanded that he earn enough to live. Accordingly during the first two years after college he deliberately undertook a succession of writing jobs in addition to his sales work with Underwood and Underwood. For a short time he wrote local items for the Galesburg *Daily Mail*; then for six weeks he was police reporter for the New York *Daily News*; and for a brief period he wrote in Chicago for *Unity*, a magazine of the Unitarian Church.

Gradually journalism became his career. In 1907 he became associate editor of the *Lyceumite* in Chicago. For this magazine he prepared brief biographies of eminent personalities who were lecturers and entertainers for the Lyceum and Chautauqua circuits, which were then much in vogue as a medium of entertainment throughout the country. On these circuits traveled actors, musicians, preachers, Congressmen, Senators and lecturers. As associate editor of the magazine, Carl Sandburg was given the opportunity of addressing, from the platform, an annual meeting of the International Lyceum Association. His speech, which he devoted to Whitman, was so well received that he was invited to deliver the same address several times, in Pennsylvania, in Indiana and in Michigan. His success as a public speaker led to a change in his work. While speaking and writing as associate editor of the *Lyceumite* in Chicago, he met Winfield P. Gaylord of Milwaukee, Wisconsin, who offered him a position as a writer and speaker for the Social Democrats in Milwaukee; thereupon in 1908 young Sandburg severed his connection with the *Lyceumite* to go to Wisconsin.[35]

Milwaukee was one of the first cities in which civic and social consciousness became of special significance during the presidency of Theodore Roosevelt. These were the days when the President was wielding his " Big Stick " in political and social reform, the days when gigantic trusts and monopolies were flourishing. We recall President Theodore Roosevelt's administration as a period of " trust-busting. " The idealists of the Republican Party were determined that their party " should represent the will, not of crooked political bosses and corporations, but of the rank and file of the people, in the spirit, not of Mark Hanna, but of Abraham Lincoln." [36]

On the Democratic side, William Jennings Bryan of Nebraska was the greatest orator of the period and his " Cross of Gold " speech had made him nationally famous. Carl Sandburg studied closely the social democracy of Bryan, the theories of Lincoln and those of Theodore Roosevelt, who was speaking vigorously against special privilege, high finance, and Tammany interests. The political and social philosophies of the Social Democrats of Milwaukee were much to Carl Sandburg's liking; and it was here that he began to take an active, propagandist interest in politics; he became a part of the national and civic reform movement for decency in government and improvement in labor laws. Association with the reform movement against entrenched privilege was characteristic of many serious-minded men of the period. " Almost every notable figure in the Progressive era, whether in politics, philosophy, scholarship or literature, derives his fame from his connexion with the reform movement." *

" Omnivorous curiosities, idealism, deep sympathy for the oppressed, hatred of social injustice and abuse of power " [37] had been among the characteristics attributed to Philip Green Wright by Sandburg; these characteristics may be seen in Sandburg himself, as he wrote, spoke and labored in behalf of political and social reform.

While in Milwaukee he met Miss Lilian Steichen, a Phi Beta Kappa graduate of the University of Chicago, and sister of the photographer, Edward Steichen. Miss Steichen and Sandburg were married June 15, 1908.

Because of his prominence in the government reform movement, Sandburg was invited to take the place of the editorial writer of the Milwaukee *Daily News* during a vacation period. One of his editorials concerning the new Lincoln penny, which he described as the coin of the common people, brought wide and favorable comment. In 1909 he was given a position on the Milwaukee *Journal* as City Hall reporter; and it was at City Hall that he met the Social Democratic candidate for Mayor of

* Allan NEVINS and Henry Steele COMMAGER, *America; the story of a free people* Oxford, Clarendon Press, 1943, p. 358.

Milwaukee who, upon election, asked young Sandburg to become his private secretary. Although he had numerous contacts with politicians in the Mayor's office Sandburg did not choose to make politics his career. He preferred to voice political and social criticism through his writings and speeches, and in order to do so he returned to the field of journalism. In 1912 he joined the staff of the Milwaukee *Leader*. [38]

In 1913, *System: the Magazine of Business* in Chicago offered Sandburg the associate-editorship. This was a trade journal published for office managers. Here he learned not only the viewpoints of executives and industrial leaders, but also a filing system which was to be of very real assistance in the tremendous task of compiling and filing material for *The War Years*. Here he also learned to appraise the opinion of management, while not losing sight of the viewpoint of labor.

The interchangeability of early twentieth century party politics should be noted here. Many of the civic and social reforms for which the liberal Social Democratic party of Wisconsin had fought were taken up by the two major parties, Republican and Democratic, and incorporated in their platforms; and under the energetic and constructive leadership of Woodrow Wilson many of these reform issues became law. The Clayton Anti-Trust Act, the Adamson eight-hour labor law, the Federal Trade Commission Act, the Federal Reserve Banking System, the Underwood Tariff, the income tax, farm relief and child-labor laws were enacted. But by no means should all the credit go to Wilson; much credit must be given to the liberal wing of the Democratic party and to the Progressives of Theodore Roosevelt persuasion; in fact, an entire generation of reformers had laid the groundwork for these long overdue achievements. Carl Sandburg was a part of that movement, not out of contempt for democratic society, but out of indignation toward oppressors, out of pity for the oppressed and out of a sincere desire to aid in the amelioration of the common lot. In view of the varied political currents and cross currents he preferred to leave the waning Social Democratic party in 1917, and to become an Independent voter, as Philip Green Wright had done before him. Nevertheless, even as an Independent, he gave his fullest support to Wilson's policies during World War I and to his fight to help save democracy as a way of life. This political independence he maintains to this day, although during World War II he declared himself solidly behind President Roosevelt in the conduct of the War against totalitarianism.

The Chicago *Daily News*, a large and important newspaper, offered Sandburg a staff position in 1917. He was to be prominently identified with this leading city publication for many years.

E. First Published Volume of Poetry: Chicago Poems

Along with his newspaper work, Carl Sandburg had been quietly working on poetry, writing and re-writing it. If we except the privately printed college poems, Sandburg's first impact on the public as a poet can be said to date from 1914, in which year a few of his poems appeared in *Poetry* magazine.

Influence of Harriet Monroe

In the field of poetry, 1912 had marked an important date; for in that year Harriet Monroe founded in Chicago the magazine entitled *Poetry: A Magazine of Verse*. The founding of *Poetry* magazine was the spearhead of the renaissance in American poetry. And the establishment of this literary periodical was the elemental core from which radiated a new enthusiasm instilled in the early twentieth-century poets, and a renewed public interest in poetry. Miss Monroe felt that American poetry should treat of contemporary American life in new and freer rhythms. At a later date (1917) * she edited, with Alice Corbin Henderson, an important anthology, *The New Poetry*, which contained poems by new writers allied with the movement; it also clearly stated the aim of the movement:

" We wanted to get rid not only of rhetoric but of poetic diction. We tried to strip away everything that was artificial, to get a style like speech, as simple as the simplest prose, like a cry of the heart." [39]

In the pages of Miss Monroe's magazine many poets gained their first recognition. Her publication played a vital part in the future of Carl Sandburg; for when his first poems were printed in *Poetry* magazine in 1914 their revolutionary style and subject matter immediately made them a topic of discussion among the readers of verse. And these few published selections brought Sandburg his first literary prize—one hundred dollars, a half share of the Levinson Prize for Poetry. This prize was established by Mr. and Mrs. S. O. Levinson of Chicago for *Poetry* magazine with the provision that the winner be chosen by the staff of that periodical.

However, Sandburg's recognition by Harriet Monroe did not mark the beginning of his use of free verse as an artistic medium. Some of his college productions showed that this style was there in outline, although other of these earlier productions were written in rhyming verse. Yet when his poems began to appear in *Poetry* magazine, he was given a specific stimulus, as he came into close contact with a number of other writers employing the same experimental methods in style and subject matter. His ideas modified and crystallized as he sensed the ascendency of parallel poetic drives.

Nevertheless, when Sandburg's productions were first published in Miss Monroe's magazine, the little poem " Chicago " produced consternation and shock at the unrestrained frankness of his appraisal of the city; although followers of the political reform movement saw the power of this unfettered verse. This initial reaction was, by and large, confined to the literary public. Over a diversity of opinion, the name of Carl Sandburg rose to prominence in the world of poetry and many magazines began publishing his poems—magazines such as *The Literary Digest, Bookman, Current Opinion, The Nation* and *New Republic*.

---

* A second edition consisting of 640 pages was published in 1923 by Macmillan and Co., New York. A third edition consisting of 775 pages was published in 1932.

Miss Monroe recognized the strength and promise of Sandburg's free verse poems, and she and other officials of the magazine urged the publication of his first collection.

Chicago Poems

Sandburg's volume of poetry entitled *Chicago Poems* was dedicated to his wife and published in 1916. Its 73 pages were divided into several sections entitled *Chicago Poems, War Poems, The Road and the End, Fogs and Fires, Shadows,* and *Other Days* (1900-1910).

The first section was especially remarkable for its powerful evocation of the vital forces that made up this great city then in the throes of industrial reorganization and plagued with corruption. In harsh, bold, violent language he laid bare this city as the

> " Player with Railroads and the Nation's Freight Handler;
> Stormy, husky, brawling,
> City of the Big Shoulders... "

The strong and forthright accusations of social evils and industrial disorganization that followed raised a storm of protest and shock among many readers, even though tempered with lines such as:

> a ... " city with lifted head singing
> so proud to be alive..." [40]

Few poems in the English language express so much in so few lines; for precision of word selection, powerful, magnetic phrases, and harsh metaphor build the lines into a unified structure of architectural strength and descriptive power.

Sandburg's use of free verse immediately opened him to attack by the traditionalists. He was not a member of the Imagist group headed by Amy Lowell and Ezra Pound, but he was in broad sympathy with at least two of their guiding principles:

(1) " To use the language of common speech, but to employ always the *exact* word, not the nearly-exact, not the merely decorative word.

(2) " To create new rhythms—as the expression of new moods—and not to copy old rhythms, which merely echo old moods. We do not insist upon ' free verse ' as the only method of writing poetry. We fight for it as for a principle of liberty... We do believe that the individuality of a poet may often be better expressed in ' free verse ' than in conventional form." [41]

Sandburg shared their search for a new and more forceful instrument of language, forged from the common experience of men. John M. Synge's expression of this point appealed to him so much that he quoted it in 1950 in the foreword to his volume of *Complete Poems:*

" '... When men lose their poetic feeling for ordinary life, and cannot write poetry on ordinary things, then exalted poetry is likely to lose its strength of exaltation, in the way men cease to build beautiful churches when they have lost happiness in building shops.' " Then follows Sandburg's own profession of faith and poetic dedication :

" Poetry and politics, the relation of the poets to society, to democracy, to monarchy, to dictatorships—we have here a theme whose classic is yet to be written."

Along with the new emphasis on drawing both subject and language from everyday life, Sandburg rejected the use of rhyme, a measure which he defended in the words of Oliver Wendell Holmes as a " capitulation to the necessity of introducing allusions, in place or out of place, in order to produce rhyme. Can there be imagined a more certain process for breaking up all continuity of thought, than this miserable subjugation of intellect to the clink of well or ill matched syllables ? " And Sandburg concluded : " The fact is ironic. A proficient and sometimes exquisite performer in rhymed verse goes out of his way to register the point that the more rhyme there is in poetry the more danger of its tricking the writer into something other than the urge in the beginning.

" Perhaps no wrong is done and no temple of human justice violated in pointing out that each authentic poet makes a style of his own. Sometimes the style is so clearly the poet's own that, when he is imitated, it is known who is imitated. Shakespeare, Villon, Li Po, Whitman—each sent forth his language and impress of thought and feeling from a different style of gargoyle spout. In the spacious highways of books major or minor, each poet is allowed the stride that will get him where he wants to go if, God help him, he can hit the stride and keep it." [42]

In some of the *Chicago Poems* rough, unpolished diction alternates with an impressionistic thumbnail vignette technique, each vignette constructed in a disorganized form and designed to contain very little rhythm, each registering a brief characterization of human personality such as we find in the rough lines of "Jack, " or in the delineation of " Chamfort. " They contain a consonance of style and substance intended to communicate the idea expressed in the poem " Personality " which represents the musing of a police reporter in the Chicago Identification Bureau as he scans the thumb prints before him—each thumb print a brief but identifying impression. The police reporter sees the ensemble of these records as a picture of milling masses of humanity whose feet crowd the earth in search of room to stand. The sum of the short character sketches by Sandburg presents an impressionistic picture of the motley population of the seething, half-formed metropolis.

In certain poems can be sensed a *rythme manqué*, as in " The Shovel Man " and " A Teamster's Farewell, " and the effect hovers between that of poetry and prose; but behind it is deep feeling and a talent for sketching character portraits with a few strokes of the pen.

With this brisk, forceful delineation of the industrial life of Chicago, sometimes tinged with bitterness at the inequalities of life, there is at the same time, a moving tenderness or lyricism. We need only quote the description of the " Fish Crier " whose " face is that of a man terribly glad to be selling fish, terribly glad that God made fish, and customers to whom he may call his wares from a pushcart." [43]

Not all of the Chicago poems are a criticism of the city's social circumstances. In refreshing and pleasurable contrast is the sensitive, subtle poem " Fog, " probably the best known in this volume. Its airy fantasy, grace and pleasing imagery instantly won recognition for the author as a master of metaphor and figurative speech.

Others of the Chicago poems are of such beautiful lyricism that they have been set to music. In " Lost " we find a tender lyric quality, a delicate imagery, soft metaphor and depth of feeling. The haunting loneliness and wavering unrest of harbor life in the poem present an emotional appeal. In " Monotone " there is beauty of phrase and image :

> " The monotone of the rain is beautiful,
> And the sudden rise and slow relapse
> Of the long multitudinous rain.
>
> The sun of the hills is beautiful,
> Or a captured sunset sea-flung,
> Bannered with fire and gold." [44]

In " Nocturne in a Deserted Brickyard, " Sandburg sketches " amid fluxions of yellow and dusk a wide dreaming pansy of an old pond in the night " [45]—where some see only bricks.

In a general delineation of the facts of the industrial system Sandburg, in the *Chicago Poems*, also turned to the role of social historian. In particular, as with Emerson (to be discussed separately) he espoused and ennobled the commonplace, giving value to aspects of universal appeal and at the same time holding up for public consideration the covetousness of unthinking or selfish men, especially the misuse of power by some of the industrial magnates. He took Emerson's plea for treatment of common themes, of trades and manufactures, for frank portrayal of many men to its furthest point in poetic development. At the same time in reply to those who see in him a chaotic, cacophonous prose, he developed the image as a vital tool of his art; he explored meaningful and arresting rhythm patterns, exercised a gifted control of words and developed a technique of swift pen stroke vignettes that set his thought in graphic form. With all this his shock images were set in a varied pattern of mood; his love of nature in smooth lyric lines and beauty of phrase. At the very least the *Chicago Poems* were recognized as arresting and topical; it is no exaggeration to claim that in them Sandburg achieved stature as a dynamic, controversial painter of an America developing in material growth more rapidly than in spiritual growth.

F. CORNHUSKERS (1918)

In the second volume entitled *Cornhuskers*, we see poetic improvement from the standpoint of artistry, sensitive perception and restrained treatment. The subject matter is changed, the expression diverted from a raucous criticism to a gentler and more musical tone. In this second volume we note the influence of Sandburg's Swedish background more than in any other volume of his poems. Carl Sandburg's mother was still living in 1918 when this volume was published. That Sandburg had studied Swedish history and literature is evidenced by the poem " Charles XII of Sweden, " which had been published privately in the slender booklet entitled *In Reckless Ecstasy*. In this poem the young collegian referred to Charles XII as *Immortal Swede:*

> " Ne'er have I seen a royal one like thee,
> No purpled one so prodigal of thrones,
>
> . . . . .
>
> The panoply and pageantry of sceptered ones you scorned,
> The banquetings, the heraldry and pomp
> Foreswore for common soldiers' fare,
> That you might be intented
> On the frozen, wind-swept prairies,
> In a palace lit by everlasting lights." [46]

This almost unknown poem, which may be seen only in a few collectors' volumes, demonstrates the influence of Swedish history and foreshadows as well the Sandburg love of things belonging to the common man.

The second volume depicts a Sandburg grown in poetic stature, more accomplished in delicate perception of beauty, broadened by experience, mellowed by time and wider knowledge of people, a lover of the land, a staunch patriot. The grass of the prairie, the call of the wild duck " woven in greens and purples, " the " phantom of the hunting dog, " the " marching corn, " the " mocking birds over the marshes and uplands " have given him a " song and a slogan " [47] as he sings of prairie life in joyous melody. Whereas in the first volume his mood had been one of protest, whereas he had been defiant and even contemptuous of misuse of wealth, we now find not only an exultation in the soil, but also a profound consideration of world events, a deepening appreciation of what America means. His poetry is now the voice of a son of the prairie, and it sings of " an ocean of tomorrows, a sky of tomorrows "; [48] it is not only the voice of the people of the cities, but also of the prairie farms, with greater beauty incorporated in his gentler and more lyrical lines.

The technique here includes more imagery, more repetition and contrast, a greater sweep. In the earlier poems of this group we find tones of greater poignancy, greater joy in nature, and in life close to earth; the subject matter is more comprehensive.

In this second volume, Sandburg's verse exhibits more of a pastoral quality than in any other volume. In the long poem, " Prairie " and in several of the shorter poems such as " Loam, " " Hemlock and Cedar " and " Falltime, " Sandburg's poetry compares with the pastoral poetry of Robert Frost. Both poets, in employing their pastoral vernacular, display creative energy, strength of phrase and thought, and a sensitivity to life and nature; and a tinge of mysticism now pervades the Sandburg lines, as evidenced in " Illinois Farmer " and " Early Moon. " Greater optimism for the future, a song for the dignity of labor, a love of the great outdoors, characterize such lines as :

" Have you seen a red sunset drip over one of my cornfields, the shore of night stars, the wave lines of dawn up a wheat valley ? " [49]

During the First World War Sandburg gave his services on the lecture platform for patriotic purposes; and we find a serious analysis of democracy in his writing. War poems in the latter part of this second volume convey the patriotic spirit of America. Sandburg indicts the Hohenzollerns with verbal violence in " The Four Brothers. " The poem " Grass, " as a sardonic judgment of the hideousness of war, is one of the best known in modern American writing. A memorial poem of 1918 contains a reverent tribute to the war dead :

" The gray foam and the great wheels of war go by and take all—and the years give mist and ashes—and our feet stand at these, the memory places of the known and the unknown, and our hands give a flame-won poppy—our hands touch the red bar of a flag for the sake of those who gave—and gave all." [50]

Before Carl Sandburg left Chicago for Stockholm as a war correspondent, this volume, recognized as the best book of poems published in the United States in 1918, had won for him his first Pulitzer Prize for Poetry.

G. WAR-TIME CORRESPONDENT IN STOCKHOLM AND RETURN TO FAME AS A PULITZER PRIZE WINNER

National recognition as a journalist had come to Sandburg in his staff position with the Chicago *Daily News* because of his writings on cultural, civic and political events in Chicago. In 1918, the Newspaper Enterprise Association elected him to represent it in Norway and Sweden as a special war-time correspondent. From Scandinavia he sent to America cable dispatches and regular newspaper correspondence. His articles from Stockholm were published by a syndicate of 390 American newspapers. In his capacity of war-time correspondent, he sent not only straight war news, but interpreted conditions in Europe, such as the rise of Bolshevik control of Russia and other situations anxiously watched by the Western world. In his journalistic endeavor, Sandburg studied closely the European philosophies motivating the people of whom he wrote. (These journalistic writings will be presented later in the thesis under *World War I*).

After completing his assignment in Scandinavia, Sandburg returned to his newspaper work in Chicago and to the publication of another volume of poetry.

H. SMOKE AND STEEL (1920)

The third book of poems entitled *Smoke and Steel* is dedicated to Sandburg's brother-in-law, Col. Edward J. Steichen, " painter of nocturnes and faces, camera engraver of glints and moments, listener to blue evening winds and new yellow roses, dreamer and finder, rider of great mornings in gardens, valleys, battles ! " [51] The poems of the third book reflect the tragic impact of World War I upon America, and the will, the vision, the inspired strength of the nation in its determination to aid in achieving victory. There is a correspondingly greater assurance of rhythm and style of expression.

This third volume exhibits a wide spectrum of moods and subject matter; but particularly does it stress the greatness of the human lives and the human spirit involved in the war effort. These poems convey to the reader how closely Sandburg was identified with the American scene, how clearly he reflected the import of questions before the nation as scenes changed.

Among the poems dealing with the mystery of life may be mentioned " Boy and Father, " in the lines of which the tenderness of the Sandburg nature and the feeling for religion are apparent. The poem " The Mayor of Gary " had been written in 1915 concerning industrial and social conditions then existing in Gary, Indiana; but it had not been included for publication until 1920, in this volume *Smoke and Steel*. In it we again see the challenge to human conscience, the irony, the social protest which had characterized the early *Chicago Poems*.

These poems serve to show the variety of the themes of Volume III, from the pathos of the long, powerful poem " Smoke and Steel " to the imagery of the very short ones containing brief portraits of landscapes such as " Steamboats turn a curve in the Mississippi crying in a baritone that crosses lowland cottonfields to a razorback hill." [52]

There are also character studies, such as we see in the tragic disillusionment of " Clean Curtains, " which, as " white prayers in the windows," [53] symbolize the efforts and the frustrations of life in the crowded tenement districts.

Notable among the many nature poems are " The Wind Sings Welcome in Early Spring, " " Sand Scribblings, " " Harvest Sunset, " the poem " Just Before April Came " in which " frogs beat the air with a recurring thin steel sliver of melody." [54] One of the best-known war poems is " Crimson Changes People " which interprets the disillusionment following the war :

> " Did I see No Man's Land in your eyes
> And men with lost faces, lost loves
> And you among the stubs crying?
> Did I see you in the red death jazz of war ? " [55]

In *Smoke and Steel* the poet is himself a painter of war-time nocturnes and faces as he portrays humanity bearing " scars of fire." [56]

I. SLABS OF THE SUNBURNT WEST (1922)

The fourth volume, *Slabs of the Sunburnt West*, published in 1922, is dedicated to Helga, the youngest daughter of the Sandburgs. With this volume there enters an element of historical pageant, as the expansion westward is evoked and the broad view of a moving, changing population is brought to life, rather than individual representatives. With surer, firmer touch Sandburg follows the theme of the prairie and the frontier, the extension of the nation and the founding and growth of the city of Chicago, evidenced by the first long poem, " Windy City, " which traces the development of Chicago from the days of the pioneers.

In this fourth volume the reader discovers a wider vision, the fresh strength of a more panoramic viewpoint; he finds the long poems more illustrative of primitive American culture, the short poems more philosophical, sometimes sardonic, sometimes optimistic—but through it all runs a spirit of national consciousness, a sense of evoking America. Sandburg's growing preoccupation with the frontier characteristics and developments that distinguished the expansion of the nation are assuming the nature of a national vocation. America is his theme. Among the best known of the short poems is " Washington Monument by Night. " " And So Today " is a tribute to the Unknown Soldier buried in Arlington National Cemetery across the river from Washington. An evocation of the " sandstone slabs of red " and the " gates of the great American Desert " [57] is contained in the concluding title poem. The story of the Forty-Niners and the many early migrations which paved the way for civilization,

> " is scribbled on the panels
>   of the cold gray open desert.
>   ... on the big sky blanket over the Santa Fé trail
>   it is woven in the oldest Indian blanket songs." [58]

Sandburg now commanded the respect of the American poetry-loving world, not only of the professional classes but also and still more significantly, of ordinary, private citizens. Accepted he was by fellow poets and literary circles. Amy Lowell, for instance, in 1917 had referred to him as a " propagandist " for the industrial classes, whose literary endeavor had " not yet stood the test of time "; [59] yet she had so changed her impression of him that she publicly dedicated a poem to him.

" To Carl Sandburg "

" Today I saw a country I knew well but had never seen,
A country where corn runs a mile or more to a tree-line,
A country where a river, brown and bronze, streaked green with the
    flowering heads of water plants,
Slips between a field of apples and a field of wheat.

. . . . .

So I have seen the man's country, and heard his songs before there are
    words to them.
And the moon said to me : ' This now I give you ', and went on, stepping
    through the leaves.
And the man went on singing, picking out his accompaniment softly on
    the black-backed guitar." [60]

J. OTHER FORMS OF LITERARY ACHIEVEMENT

(a) Children's Stories

Like other famous men Sandburg has many sides. The range of his writing widened considerably after his return from Stockholm, for the range of his experience and of his sympathies broadened; to his writings several new vehicles of literary expression were added, and came to fruition about the same time. Upon his return to Chicago he found his three little girls, Margaret, Janet and Helga, rapidly growing up and asking for stories; and he answered by inventing fairy tales—not of kings and queens and princes and castles—but of people and things set against an American background—fairy tales of the Village of Cream Puffs, the Village of Liver and Onions, of the Wedding of the Rag Doll and the Broom Handle, of Potato Face, of Corn Fairies, of Pigs with Bibs on. His children so enjoyed these improvisations that before long he was prevailed upon to write down the stories and to publish them in book form for the delight of other children. One volume was published in 1922 under the title of *Rootabaga Stories*, in 1923 came the second volume entitled *Rootabaga Pigeons*. The charm of these children's stories has been well expressed by Frank Lloyd Wright, the nationally known architect who included in his autobiography a letter to Carl Sandburg concerning the *Rootabaga Stories*. One paragraph of the letter reads :

" All of the children that will be born into the Middle West during the next hundred years are peeping at you now, Carl—between little pink fingers, smiling, knowing in their hearts they have found a friend." [61]

To achieve success in fantasy for the young is very difficult; but Sandburg has done so, not only because of his love for children but also because he himself was young at heart. There are morals to be drawn from his fairy tales, such as the vanity of striving for wealth rather than for character building, as found by Slipfoot in *Rootabaga Pigeons*; or of the value of ideals and dreams such as those of the White Horse Girl and the Blue Wind Boy who could look beyond high hills and tough rocks across " blue water as far as the eye could see. And far off the blue waters met the blue sky." [62] For Carl Sandburg is one of the " fireborn " (a phrase from Swedish folk lore) who understands the path of struggle but also the "blue" of happy imagination.

(b) Collector and Interpreter of Folk Songs

Love of the folk song and love of history and the children's story are the product of a mind which was a compound of love of the past, of history, of the beautiful and the pathetic, and which built an atmosphere of popular tradition. In this sense folk songs are fully a part of Sandburg's presentation of America.

Since folk songs are closely interwoven with everyday life they become an interpretation of human affairs and manners as preserved in oral

Study before television program, "A Visit with Carl Sandburg," in a series of filmed conversations with the elder wise men of our time. *Photograph by European Picture Service.*

tradition. Carl Sandburg saw the significance of folk songs in the interpretation of the American frontier as it moved from New England and the
east coast across the continent. To him these songs were human documents
which shed light on earlier periods of American existence.

The English colonists had brought many ballads to the New World, and
these supplied a pattern for the early American folk songs which reveal the
heroism, the tragedy and the comedy in the seventeenth and eighteenth
century American life. As the pioneers carried the early ballads westward
there was a continuing need for folk songs in the undeveloped sections of
the country. This fact helps explain why the old ballads were handed down
by word of mouth and why new ones were gradually added to the old.

But by no means must folk songs be considered as the exclusive posses-
sion of the pioneer, the adventurer, the uneducated or the illiterate. Many
famous Americans have prized these ballads for their historical worth.
Woodrow Wilson not only prized them as sociological studies but also
sang them; Theodore Roosevelt encouraged their preservation; Abraham
Lincoln was fond of them. A separate section in the Library of Congress
in Washington is given over to a systematic filing of them and contains
valuable recordings, for a vital part of the social history of the nation has
been incorporated in folk songs.

Sandburg developed a system of musical shorthand to set these ballads
down on paper as he heard them sung in his travels across the country.
By the 1920's he had collected several hundred folk songs. In 1926 he
published *Songs of America*, a small booklet of eleven pages; this was,
however, only a preliminary work for the large 495-page volume entitled
The American Songbag which was published in 1927. This volume contained
the words and music of nearly 300 ballads accompanied by his personal
explanation of the character and setting of the selections. (He was to
publish a third volume in 1950). Because of his active interest in collecting
and interpreting early ballads Sandburg became known as a distinguished
folk song anthologist, and as the father of present-day interest in American
folk music.

The poet says of his *American Songbag:*

" The book begins with a series of Dramas and Portraits rich with
the human diversity of the United States. There are Love Tales Told in
Song, or Colonial Revolutionary Antiques: some of them have the feel
of black walnut, of knickerbockers, silver shoe-buckles, and the earliest
colonial civilization. Out of the section of Pioneer Memories, one may
sing with the human waves that swept across the Alleghenies and settled
the Middle West, later taking the Great Plains, the Rocky Mountains, the
west coast. The notable distinctive American institution, the black-face
minstrel, stands forth in a separate section. Mexican border songs give
the breath of the people above and below the Rio Grande. One section
contains ballads chiefly from the southern mountains. Two powerful
Great Lakes songs are given, ' Bigerlow ' and ' Red Iron Ore, ' either of
which may yet rival the song of the Volga boatmen; the quaver of rare
Irish lilts in ' The ould Sod. ' A little series of exquisite musical fragments,

light as gossamer mist, are grouped under the title ' Lovely People. ' The book closes with a list of spirituals called ' The Road to Heaven.'

" A wide human procession marches through these pages... It is a volume full of gargoyles and gnomes, a terribly tragic book and one grinningly comic; each page lifts its own mask. It is as ancient as the mediaeval European ballads brought to the Appalachian Mountains; it is as modern as skyscrapers."*

Sandburg's poetry lectures were often concluded by requested folk songs, and verbal explanation of the songs. (These poetry lectures have taken him to over two-thirds of the State Universities of the country and have included audiences of as many as 3,000 people at the University of California).

The only singing lessons the poet ever had were from a choir singer in Galesburg—but in his singing lie emotion, character, mood and lyric feeling. The great underlying reason for his interest in folk songs is the essential folk-quality he finds in them—the same grass-roots folk-quality he has tried to instill in a portion of his poetry. The fact aids in understanding the ragged, broken and uneven lines of Sandburg verse; for careful analysis reveals that in many instances this effect is deliberate—in other instances the spirit of the lines has meant more to Sandburg than the rhythm; and here I am reminded of the Glasgow address of T. S. Eliot on " Music in Poetry" :

" It would be a mistake to assume that all poetry ought to be melodious or that melody is more than one of the components of the music of words. Some poetry is meant to be sung; most poetry, in modern times, is meant to be spoken—and there are many other things to be spoken of besides the murmur of innumerable bees or the moan of doves in immemorial elms.

" Dissonance, even cacophony, has its place : just as, in a poem of any length, there must be transitions between passages of greater and lesser intensity, to give a rhythm of fluctuating emotion essential to the musical structure of the whole; and the passages of less intensity will be, in relation to the level on which the total poem operates, prosaic—so that, in the sense implied by that context, it may be said that no poet can write a poem of amplitude unless he is a master of the prosaic." **

The spirit and rhythm of early America have been introduced into certain poems through the poet's knowledge of folk songs, particularly in *The People, Yes.* Folk songs, however, have influenced the spirit of the poems more than their rhythm. We sense the music of loneliness and unrest in the rhythm of the poem " Lost, " the music of quiet beauty in " Nocturne in a Deserted Brickyard "; the music of Polish folk song in " Picnic Boat "; the music of the Hungarian accordion in " Happiness "; the sadness of mournful music in " Cripple "; the music of autumn cornfields in "Theme in Yellow "; the music and rhythm of the waves in " Young Sea "; the

---

* In Foreword to Sandburg's *American Songbag.*
** T. S. ELIOT, *On Poetry and Poets.* London : Faber, 1957, p. 32.

crash of steel and flash of molten metal, the explosions of flame and crackling sparks in " Smoke and Steel "; the musical sounds of summer in " Silver Wind "; the music of the Psalms in " Glass House Canticle. " To this poet there is even a music in silence. Some of his poems have been set to music. (A brief account of these may be found in the notes). [63]

Professor Allan Nevins of Columbia University, New York, says of Sandburg:

" The breadth of the prairies is in Carl Sandburg and his work. Poetry, novel, songbook, biography, history, children's stories, folk tales—he has written them all in superbly human terms. He is the nearest approach to the *minnesinger* America has ever produced." *

Sandburg endeavored to interpret his love for the folk-quality and spirit of America, whether through the medium of the lyrics to be read and to be spoken, through that portion of his lyrics transcribed to music, or through his personal singing of American folk songs.

Carl Haverlin, president of the New York Civil War Round Table and of Broadcast Music, Incorporated, New York City, edited and published in 1950 Carl Sandburg's third collection of folk songs entitled *The New American Songbag*. Mr. Haverlin writes of the poet:

" All of the time all of us felt good because here in our offices for a little while was a man who had heard America sing. In bayou, or in cool logger's ways and in the prairie sun, he had heard America singing. Here among us was a singer who knew our great broad sprawling teeming tempestuous stern beautiful land—and a man who had heard our people sing—yes ! " **

" People singing; people with song mouths connecting with song hearts; people who must sing or die; people whose song hearts break if there is no song mouth; these are my people." [64]

Thus Sandburg's systematic search for folk songs speaks of a sense of vocation or dedication as does his espousal of the cause of the common people of America in his poems. His collection is a piece of historical or sociological documentation as deliberate in its own modest way as the more ambitious biographical study of Lincoln in another.

K. ABRAHAM LINCOLN : THE PRAIRIE YEARS (1926)

As early as the first World War, Sandburg had become greatly interested in writing of Abraham Lincoln, whose character he had always admired. His formative years of childhood and young manhood had been spent in the Lincoln country. Galesburg was not far from Springfield where Lincoln practiced law. Around young Sandburg were Galesburg citizens who had

---

* Allan NEVINS, in a letter of tribute on file in the Pack Memorial Library at Asheville, North Carolina.

** Carl HAVERLIN, in the *Journal of the Illinois State Historical Society*, Winter, 1952; page 387.

known Lincoln and those who had seen him when the famous Lincoln-Douglas debate took place in 1858 in front of the Main Building on the Knox College campus. Sandburg refers to his boyhood impressions as follows : " At the front of Old Main many times I read on a bronze plate words spoken by Lincoln and Douglas some thirty-four years before I stood there reading those words. They stay with me and sometimes I would stop to read only those words that Lincoln said to twenty thousand on a cold, windy October day : ' He is blowing out the moral lights around us, when he contends that whoever wants slaves has a right to hold them.' I read them in winter sunrise, in all the weathers of the year." [65] The Sandburg mind was eagerly receptive of Lincoln lore, legend, history and writings even in the days of his youth, and that influence so deepened with the years that the poet decided to write the story of Lincoln " because he felt Lincoln was being lost to the nation's youth." *

In 1926 his two-volume work *Abraham Lincoln: The Prairie Years* was published, bringing instant and nation-wide literary fame and financial remuneration that ran into tens of thousands of dollars. Now Sandburg became not only a nationally recognized poet, journalist, humanist and social critic, story-teller for children, collector of folk songs but a writer of excellent prose. Both his poetry and his journalism contributed to *The Prairie Years* and resulted in a sympathetic and illuminating study which is in many places a prose poem. The biography was (and still is) widely read; and Sandburg achieved increased distinction in the literary world.

However these volumes were only the beginning of his prose writings on Lincoln. Sandburg said : " The more I got to love the companionship of this man the farther I went in my job." ** Many years of further intensive Lincoln research were to come. The public interest in his *Prairie Years* was so wide-spread that in 1927 Sandburg published for young people *Abe Lincoln Grows Up*, which was taken from the first part of *The Prairie Years*, and dealt with Lincoln's life prior to the Springfield years and prior to his entry into the national political scene. Thus Sandburg carried out his original plan of portraying, as a model for American youth, Lincoln's strength of character in the face of struggle and adversity.

L. GOOD MORNING, AMERICA (1928)

With the publication of *The Prairie Years* Sandburg struck a chord that was all-American and capable of appreciation by the entire reading public. His distinction in the literary world brought him an invitation from Harvard University to read some of his poetry before the Phi Beta Kappa society.

In 1837 the poet Emerson had been invited to address this same Phi Beta Kappa chapter at Harvard, at which time he delivered his famous lecture on " The American Scholar. " Such an invitation to Carl Sandburg

---

*Frederic Hill MESERVE, in *Journal of the Illinois State Historical Society*, Winter 1952, p. 337.
** Ibid.

proved the heights to which he had risen in the critical esteem of the literary world by 1928.

Sandburg read a new poem " Good Morning, America, " at Harvard, and was awarded an honorary membership in Phi Beta Kappa, the honor society of the College of Arts and Science. Such an award was recognition of him as a poet of national stature and as a writer who had made a specific contribution to American literary tradition.

" Good Morning, America " is the long sixteen-page title poem of Sandburg's fifth volume of poetry which was published in 1928. The poem presents a diversity of form and effect. It varies between refined lyrical eloquence and undistinguished diction; between good rhythm and inferior rhythm in the proverbs and folk-sayings; between a projection of the ideal and that of the real. Yet these variations are not without deliberate, constructive intention and effect. Here again, skill and craft have been concealed by a considered use of flat, halting passages. The style must be studied carefully in the context of the overall impression which Sandburg seeks to give. The greatest merit of " Good Morning, America " lies in its moral force, and its idealization or re-evaluation of aspects of life commonly accepted as undistinguished. This for Sandburg, as for Emerson before him, is the summit of national poetry, to appreciate the distinguished aspects, of course, but also to recognize and restore to its proper value every constructive activity at all levels of society.

In " Good Morning, America " the poet eulogizes the creative power of those who built bridges, railroads, churches, cities and all the things that have gone into the development of a great nation. He writes of the desire for religious freedom in the minds of those who founded America :

" Facts are phantom : facts begin
With a bud, a seed, an egg.
. . . . .
And so, to the pavilion of the four winds
Came the little one they called America,
One that suckled, struggled, toiled, laughed, grew.
The little new republic had its swaddling cloths,
Its child shirt, its tussle to knit long bone joints.
And who can read the circle of its moons now ? " [66]

In poetic pageant we review with Sandburg the pictures of the colonists riding horses to Boston or to Richmond and we catch a glimpse of early America, of nineteenth-century America, and finally of the America lifted to a position among the World Powers during the present century.

But with the admonition that " morning goes as morning-glories go " [67]; that Spain, Rome, Greece, Persia each took her turn at leading the civilizations of the earth long before America came of age, the poet bids us look " into the storm of human hearts and see if somewhere in that storm there are sacred hearts taking a bitter wages of doom, crimson-plunged hearts of the Redeemer of Man. " [68] He bids us consider well the lessons of the past before the time that could bring " twilight, sundown, gloaming "— and a fate that could bring " the hour of writing ' Good night, America,

sleep and sweet dreams!'"[69]   Yet with this qualification, he has a vision
of the particular future he sees for America, when we " make new propellers,
go past old spent stars and find blue moons on a new star path," [70] and he
voices his fervent supplication :

> " Sea sunset, give us keepsakes,
> Prairie gloamings, pay us for prayers.
> Mountain clouds on bronze skies—
> Give us great memories.
> Let us have summer roses.
> Let us have tawny harvest haze in pumpkin time.
> Let us have springtime faces to toil for and pray for.
>
> . . . . .
>
> Moonlight come down. . . meet every bird cry and every
>   song calling to a hard old earth, a sweet young earth." [71]

The poem is a celebration of the greatness of America and it is also a
plea for tolerance and humanitarianism.

It contains the finest qualities of Sandburg poetry and also a deviation
from nobility of philosophical thought and expression to the realm of the
vernacular in homely proverb, lingo and slang. Sandburg reverts to slang
in the midst of this poem to include in it not only the intellectual, the
historian and the statesman—but also those whose lives and culture represent
the less literate, the less privileged elements of society. His theory is
comparable to that of Whitman who said : " Slang profoundly considered, is
the lawless germinal element, below all words and sentences, and behind all
poetry, and proves a certain perennial rankness and protestantism in
speech. . . Language, be it remembered, is not an abstract construction of
the learn'd, or of the dictionary-makers, but is something arising out of the
work, needs, ties, joys, affections, tastes, of long generations of humanity,
and has its bases broad and low, close to the ground. Its final decisions are
made by the masses, people nearest to the concrete, having most to do with
actual land and sea." [72]

America is not an abstract, chauvinistic theorization, however, but an
organic composite that Sandburg manages to make us perceive in the
numerous sensitive, miniature poems that reveal in telling images details
that are a part of the larger context. Plants, bird life, nature are reminiscent
of both Thoreau and Emily Dickinson as sketched in such lines as :

> " In the morning eyes of the brown-eyed Susans,
> in the toadflax sheaves, smiling butter-and-eggs,
> in the white mushrooms sprung from air into air
> since yesterday morning, since yesterday evening,
> in the corn row corridor walls of cornstalks—
> the same southwest wind comes again, knowing—
>
> How the field people go away,
> the corn row people, the toadflax, mushroom, thistlebloom people
> how they rise, sing songs they learn, and then go away,
> leaving in the air no last will and testament at all." [73]

In this poem Carl Sandburg, as a lover of outdoor life about him, places thoughts and action in his cherished " field people " who leave not even " a cricket's hut for counting its summer heartbeats, or a caught shimmer of one haunted moonray to be passed on "—" the running southwest wind knows them all." [74] This personification is continued in many poems of the American landscape. Among the portraits of human personality are " Sarah's Letter to Peter " and " Broken-Hearted Soprano "; we are also given the poem of the " Couple, " a study of domestic love and contentment which may reflect the love and devotion of Sandburg's parents.

In general, this fifth volume may be regarded as an evocation of American history and a presentation of the American landscape and of the growing things native to its soil. The nature poems show that Sandburg turned, as did Thoreau, to the life of the fields and woods, to the movements of the great rivers and little streams, to the habits of birds and flowers, of oaks and poplars and elms, to the fall of rain and snow to learn what lessons they had to teach. He sifted through his fingers the sands of the Mojave Desert and pondered on the lesson of its history; he looked into the vast abyss of the Grand Canyon in search of the meaning of its great age and depth and saw the ancient story of flame and fire and ice; he saw it as a memorial to Time, as a witness to the short pilgrimage of mankind endowed with faiths enduring through fire and bloodshed. He brought us close to the natural beauties and the values of the American environment.

After the publication of *Good Morning, America,* Sandburg returned to his Lincoln research. The task of preparing the first two volumes of the Lincoln biography had been stupendous but not nearly so stupendous as the one on which he was now embarked—*Abraham Lincoln: The War Years.* Thirteen years of effort were to go into *The War Years*—and the compilation of material took him into nearly every state in the Union. It became necessary to bolster his finances in that period to support a family of five. To help with travel expenses, he gave lectures on poetry and programs of the folk songs in his collection, carefully adjusting his public appearances to localities which might possess more Lincoln material. During the long period spent in writing the Lincoln biography, Sandburg crossed the continent many times. As his contacts broadened, his viewpoints broadened and he became more conservative in his political outlook; his associates came more and more to include judges, governors, historians, college professors, librarians and newspaper publishers. He became an intimate friend of Governor Horner of Illinois, of Professor Joseph Warren Beach of the University of Minnesota, of Eugene Meyer, publisher of the Washington *Post,* of Oliver R. Barrett, wealthy Chicago lawyer and Lincoln collector,[75] (Sandburg was later to write a book on the Lincoln collection of Oliver Barrett)—and of executives of great prominence in the industrial world. He was seeing life from new angles and his many friendships were contributing more and more to a universality of perception. Although still with the Chicago *Daily News,* he was permitted to allocate about three months of the year to lectures and recitals of folk ballads, all the while gathering data for his monumental undertaking of *Abraham Lincoln: The War Years.* In 1929 he published a brief biography of his brother-in-law, *Steichen the Photographer*. This contained forty-nine photographs by Steichen, reproduced in what was then the new Knudsen process. Because of the great expense involved the edition was limited to 925 copies. In 1932 appeared *Mary Lincoln: Wife and Widow*, a biography of Abraham Lincoln's wife.

So immense was the task of *The War Years* that in 1932 Sandburg felt it necessary to leave the Chicago *Daily News* and move with his family away from Chicago to the quiet of Harbert, Michigan, where, in a remote home overlooking the lake, he could write in seclusion.

But his seclusion could not prevent him from feeling deep concern for the tragic economic dislocation and financial calamities of the Depression period of the 1930's. Hungry men without jobs, idle factories, the transition from national prosperity to financial panic, the insidious currents of subversion attempting to penetrate America—all these events so disturbed him that he took up his pen to write his strongly defensive affirmation of popular democracy, *The People, Yes*.

M. THE PEOPLE, YES (1936)

This is a volume of considerable importance in Sandburg's representation of America and its people, filling as it does 180 pages comprising 107 sections. In the foreword, Sandburg himself characterizes *The People, Yes* as follows :

> " Being several stories and psalms nobody would want to laugh at
> Interspersed with memoranda variations worth a second look
> Along with sayings and yarns traveling on grief and laughter
> Running sometimes as a fugitive air in the classic manner
> Breaking into jigtime and tap dancing nohow classical
> And further broken by plain and irregular sounds and echoes from
> The roar and whirl of street crowds, work gangs, sidewalk clamor,
> With interludes of midnight cool blue and inviolable stars
> Over the phantom frames of skyscrapers." [76]

In style, this volume is of mingled and multiple cadences, beginning with rhythmic verse, later changing to "irregular sounds and echoes" from the streets in which the poet " gives back to the people their own lingo." [77] This lingo is at times composed of slang and phrases often too coarse for some readers, of primitive folk-sayings and proverbs, of superstitions and popular beliefs which are affirmative of democracy; yet there are passages of beautifully phrased, deep wisdom, of great truths. In the less regular, less literary sections, we find popular beliefs set forth in the language of the less literate, for Sandburg wished this volume to be expressive of all classes, all types; he wished it to be expressive of the substantial people " who go back to the nourishing earth for rootholds," [78] for it is these substantial groups which form the underlying basis of democracy.

Much of the 180 pages is not poetry at all—or even free verse; and much of the section of proverbs, folk expressions and yarns is far beneath the Sandburg level. They contain an accumulation of clamorous sounds, irregularities and combinations which, in their great length, detract from the style and form of the volume as a book of poetry. Yet they do not diminish the political and social worth of this volume portraying the processes of democracy.

The People, Yes contains Sandburg's criticism of democracy's short-comings; but far from being sophisticated, academic, embittered or cynical, it rings out as a stout-hearted and heavy-fisted defense of the democratic way of life. The Marxist and Fascist theories of Communist clubs had attracted a certain amount of support during the calamitous chaos of the 1930's. The answer to the claims of these subversive elements must be, in the poet's opinion, representative of the long history of nations moving toward established constitutional self-government. It must be a blending of varied individualities, a mingling of varied human emotions and ideals, failures and successes, projected into a dream of hope, a dream of solidarity, a dream of progress.

> " Once having marched
> Over the margins of animal necessity,
> Over the grim line of sheer subsistence,
>   Then man came
> To the deeper rituals of his bones,
> To the lights lighter than any bones,
> To the time of thinking things over,
> To the dance, the song, the story,
> Or the hours given over to dreaming... " [79]

As an American book, *The People, Yes* occupies a celebrated position. As originally published in a separate volume, it was much more impressive than when included in the volume of *Complete Poems*. In the separate edition the reader accepts in prose form and at face value the proverbs, folk-sayings, the yarns and memoranda (even in their over-abundance), studies them, follows their interpretations of human emotions and interests; suddenly he finds the volume lifted above the crudity of vernacular speech to lyric poetry, while such portions as the elegiac Lincoln sections and the last twenty-five sections raise the tone to a new and higher level.

Few writers, if any, have defined with such artistry the elements of democracy as Sandburg in his lines :

> " The people is a polychrome,
> a spectrum and a prism
> held in a moving monolith,
> a console organ of changing themes,
> a clavilux of color poems
> wherein the sea offers fog
> and the fog moves off in rain
> and the labrador sunset shortens
> to a nocturne of clear stars
> serene over the shot spray
> of northern lights." [80]

Sandburg maintains the case for democracy against totalitarian guardian-state regimes that claim to represent the interests of the individual, regimes disguised under the name of democracy but effectively removing power of choice from the common man. Sandburg paints a picture of the vital force of a people in many different shades but qualified by the inherent dignity of man in his work, family, friendships and responsibilities. He also paints with touches of irony other anti-social selfish aspects; he has never lost sympathy for the " souls driven into paths too steep for them, for the hulks of broken men." [81]

N. ABRAHAM LINCOLN: THE WAR YEARS (1939)

Following the publication of *The People, Yes*, Sandburg returned to his Lincoln writing. Inspired by the magnitude of his subject, driven by determination and will power, he worked on the magnificent portrayal of Lincoln in *The War Years* until it became the largest and most detailed account of that period ever given to literature.

In 1939 the four volumes were at long last completed and within a few months twenty-nine thousand sets of *The War Years* had been sold.

The biography of the wartime Lincoln attracted the attention of the entire academic world; and so universal was the acclaim of *Abraham Lincoln: The War Years* that it brought Sandburg doctoral degrees from many colleges and universities, including Harvard, Yale, Dartmouth, Rollins, Lincoln Memorial, New York University, Augustana and Uppsala in Sweden.

The completion of this monument of research and sensitive prose established Sandburg firmly in the field of American literature. The work was crowned with the Pulitzer Prize for History and by election to membership in the American Academy of Arts and Letters. Later, in 1952, it won for him the award of the Gold Medal for History and Biography by the American Academy of Arts and Letters, the highest honor within that society's power to bestow.

O. SECOND WORLD WAR JOURNALISM AND PUBLICATIONS

During the Second World War, Sandburg devoted practically all his literary production and his platform engagements to denouncing the inherent evils of the Nazi regime—and of totalitarianism. His deep patriotism exalted the American form of democracy, the personal freedom and independence which he prized so much. Here again he reveals his interest to be basically humanitarian and political, a tendency that only strengthened as he grew older.

During the war he was asked by newspapermen and Washington officials to undertake an unusual journalistic task, that " of studying quietly the swift changes which Washington is too close to for analysis." [82] Thus once more he, the recipient of two Pulitzer Prizes, became a nation-wide newspaper reporter—this time given his own freedom of choice in submitting one article each week for syndication throughout the United States.

His pamphlets, some of his major speeches and a portion of his columns, poems and legends during the Second World War years were published in 1943 in a 300-page volume entitled *Home Front Memo*. Also in 1943, he published *Storm Over the Land*, a profile of the Civil War taken chiefly from *The War Years*. This is a volume of 440 pages which offers the story in abbreviated form.

In 1944 Sandburg published in collaboration with Frederick Hill Meserve (distinguished collector and connoisseur of Civil War photographs) a volume of 126 pages entitled *The Photographs of Abraham Lincoln*.

Also during the war, he began another phase of writing that required nearly five years of research and serious effort—the writing of a 1,067-page novel *Remembrance Rock*, vast in its 350-year historical span, far-reaching in its interpretation of European events leading up to the founding of the Colonies and replete with analyses of the crises through which the young Republic passed.

P. MOVE FROM MICHIGAN TO NORTH CAROLINA; PUBLICATION OF FIRST NOVEL

By 1946 the Sandburg family decided that the severe winters of Michigan were not desirable for the writer's health. Therefore Mrs. Sandburg began to look for a new home in a kindlier climate. In Henderson County, North Carolina, in the lovely, wooded, residential town of Flat Rock, immediately adjacent to Hendersonville, was found the desired location. The Sandburgs bought a beautiful white, colonial homestead, well over a century old, and situated in a 245-acre estate. This interesting home had been built in 1833 by Christopher G. Memminger, who in the 1860's was treasurer of the Confederacy under Jefferson Davis. Here, in their mountain retreat, the Sandburgs live today in quiet happiness and the writing goes on almost continuously.

One reaches the home by a beautiful winding road, through an aged forest of towering pines. The entrance to the private drive is marked by stone pillars covered with ivy and green lichens.

The house itself is situated on a hill and surrounded by stately white pine trees and large boxwoods, southern shrubs and a semi-formal flower garden; and it overlooks a vast expanse of forested area and a smaller area of pasture land. Directly in front and at the foot of the hill is a lake which on two sides is bordered by tall forest trees. The vista beyond the lake is breath-taking. Standing on the dignified pillared porch, the viewer sees the mountains of North Carolina and, on a bright day, the blue outline of Mt. Mitchell, the highest mountain in the eastern United States. Says Sandburg: " The skyline here has as much mystery and infinity as Lake Michigan." [83] This former Memminger estate was once proposed as a capital site for the Confederacy, when the southern states considered moving the Confederate seat of government from Richmond, Virginia, during the Civil War.

Most of Sandburg's novel, *Remembrance Rock*, published in 1948, was written at Connemara Farms, the name given the Flat Rock estate. Just as his earlier years had been a preparation for the Lincoln biography, so had his life span been a preparation for the novel. His early life as the son of Swedish immigrants who came to settle in a little city which had been founded on a new frontier only a few decades before their arrival, his life in cosmopolitan surroundings in a period which saw the greatest mass immigration to the New World, his long study of history, his many travels across the continent, his wide acquaintanceship with men of many trades and professions—all these factors provided the groundwork for this novel. Sandburg had been a part of a changing scene in a rapidly changing continent; and *Remembrance Rock* was the sum of all that he has learned and lived—a poet-historian's interpretation of the American story. With this epic portrait he donned the robe of a national pageant painter.

In 1949 came his *Lincoln Collector: The Story of Oliver R. Barrett's Great Private Collection.* This is a 344-page volume detailing and interpreting the diversified collection of Lincoln letters, documents, relics and related materials which the Chicago lawyer had gathered over a period of sixty-three years. The many illustrations and the thoroughness of historical interpretation make of it a treasury of Americana of the Lincoln period.

In 1950 Sandburg combined and published all of his volumes of poetry under the title *Complete Poems*. This large volume of over 800 poems won for him his third Pulitzer Prize. In addition to the poems of the six volumes which have been discussed, this collection contained a section which included poems of World War II. Outstanding is " The Man With The Broken Fingers, " a poem two pages in length, published separately in 1942. So deep an impression did it then create on the reading public that the author received inquiries as to whether it was war propaganda or actual incident. The author's informant had been a Norwegian lieutenant who related the incident as told to him by the son of the tragic figure of the poem, who had submitted to allowing his ten fingers to be broken one by one, then his arms and shoulders, rather than divulge the names the German Gestapo wanted. Death was the inevitable result; but the story of this war-hero now lives in poetry and " throws a shadow, down from the spruce and evergreen timbers of Norway—and across Europe and the Mediterranean—to the oasis palms of Libya. " His death as a patriot was " a quiet step into a sweet clean midnight." [84]

Another important poem of this last section is " The Long Shadow of Lincoln: A Litany " based on the President's Message to Congress, December 1, 1862. The words of Lincoln in that Message to Congress during the Civil War were so far-reaching that they were applicable during World War II. Sandburg's poetic tribute to President Roosevelt, whom death claimed April 12, 1945, is a poignant expression of personal loss and of the mourning of the nation. Thus the war is reflected in both the subject matter and the mood of many of these later poems.

In 1950 he also published a one-volume biography of *Abraham Lincoln* " for those who haven't the time for the entire six volumes." [85] The one-volume edition of 430,000 words is condensed from the six-volume biography of 1,800,000 words, but it has also some new additional material which has come to light since the publication of the original biography. (As an example, the Robert Lincoln collection in the Library of Congress, opened for inspection July 24, 1947). In 1953 Sandburg published *Always the Young Strangers*, autobiographical in nature, delineating his life up until 1898 and interpreting Swedish immigrant life in Galesburg, Illinois, in the last two decades of the nineteenth century.

In the autumn of 1957 was published a Sandburg anthology entitled *The Sandburg Range* containing representative selections from his tremendous literary output. These selections encompassed his writings as poet, biographer, historian, novelist, troubadour, autobiographer and storyteller for children. It conveys to the reader, in abbreviated form, the broad sweep attained by Sandburg through the incessant labor of his long years as one of America's foremost literary figures.

Though now an octogenarian, Sandburg's literary pursuits continue. He is at work on another book, a sequel to *Always the Young Strangers*, to be entitled *Ever the Winds of Chance*. And poems continue to appear. It is especially significant of this poet's interest in youth that his recent volume entitled *Wind Song*, which appeared in October 1960, is a selected list of his later poems (and sixteen new ones) dedicated to "dear young folks." This is indicative of his belief that in a properly instructed rising generation lies the wisdom of tomorrow. To these young people he commends the prayerful, terminal stanza of " Good Morning, America "; he invests them with a knowledge of the importance of stability and strength of character as in the poem " Wind Song ":

" Long ago I learned how to listen to the singing wind and how to
 forget and how to hear the deep whine,
Slapping and lapsing under the day blue and the night stars:
 Who, who are you? " [86]

He endows them with faith and a sense of responsibility in such lines as:

  " Knowing so well you are going far,
  knowing your great works are ahead,
  ahead and beyond,
  yonder and far over yet." [87]

He tenders them his affection in the concluding dedicatory lines:
" I sign this book for you saying love and blessings: may luck stars ever be over you." [88]

At his Connemara Farms home, the poet takes regular exercise in order to retain his sturdiness of health, for he well knows the direct relationship of physical well-being and efficient literary endeavor.

Sandburg's industry in writing, his keen analysis of social, political, moral and economic questions continue, as does his unwavering interest in all kinds and classes of people. His memory of books and people is remarkable.

He has been the friend of many thousands. In all walks of life he has met and talked with people—the bootblack, the harvest hand, the section hand, the fisherman, the waiter, the barber, the soldier, the industrialist, the bookseller, the clergyman, the writer, the publisher, the banker, the lawyer, the historian, the college professor and the college president. We catch a glimpse of the universality of his friendships when Mrs. Sandburg says of him: " Mr. Sandburg is interested in everything and has been interested in everyone he ever met. He likes people." [89]

Sandburg has the loyal devotion of an understanding wife, and the love of three daughters, Margaret, Janet and Helga (now Mrs. George Crile, Jr.) and a writer in her own right, living with her family in Cleveland, Ohio. Even though a young author, she has already published two novels, *Wheel of Earth* and *The Owl's Nest*. Her father says: "she will probably write novels throughout her life." [90]

As we have already seen, Sandburg has been the recipient of many literary prizes and honors. In his home lies a wide array of medals and awards for literary achievement. There lies the Medal of the Royal Order of the North Star sent from the King of Sweden in 1953; there lies the Gold Medal of the American Academy of Arts and Letters; alongside it is the Silver Jubilee Award of The Limited Edition Club:

> " To Carl Sandburg
> Who Has Been Named One Of
> Ten Living American
> Authors Whose Works In
> The Years 1929-1954 Are Most
> Likely To Become Classics "

Of special significance however, is the fact that, when the American Exhibition was held in Moscow in 1959, the United States sent as a cultural ambassador Carl Sandburg, to represent American ideals to the Russians. He was officially chosen to take part at the formal opening of the Exhibit.

On the way home from Moscow Sandburg went to Stockholm. There he was popularly acclaimed by many thousands. He was also welcomed by King Gustav VI who awarded him a second royal decoration—a gold medal bearing the words *Litteris et Artibus* in recognition of literary achievement.

Sandburg is a member of The National Institute of Arts and Letters, of the American Poetry Society, of the Authors League of America, the National Press Club of Washington, the Michigan Authors Association, and of many other organizations.

Many colleges and universities have awarded him honorary degrees. In 1957 Professor Henning Larsen, of the University of Illinois, read the citation when that University conferred an honorary Doctor of Literature degree upon Sandburg. This portrays succinctly and vividly the life span and attainment of Carl Sandburg and conveys a knowledge of the high esteem in which Americans hold him and something of the legendary veneration in which he is now clothed:

" Son of the prairie, product of the Melting Pot, Sandburg is in flesh and blood what we like to think America and American. Born in 1878 in the then small prairie town of Galesburg, of Swedish immigrant parents, he learned early the struggle of the common worker; but he learned also, from hardy and upright parents, courage, honesty and respect for his fellow men. This made him the poet of the people.

" The story of his life and success is not unlike that of Askepot (the boy-Cinderella of Scandinavian folktale) who rose from the ashes of the hearth to win the princess and half the kingdom. Newsboy, janitor, milk-driver, dishwasher, hobo, soldier and student; reporter, poet, story teller, lecturer and singer of songs, biographer, novelist, historian... from the wrong side of the railroad track to the head of the writers of today... a leader for all times.

" For his deep knowledge of America, for his interpretation thereof, for the richness of his person in word and in work, for the way he is of us, above us, and for us as a poet, biographer and historian, we wish to make him a member of this University and in honoring him be honored in turn." *

---

* From the official citation prepared by Professor Henning Larsen of the University of Illinois. A copy of the citation was given personally to the writer of this study by Professor Larsen.

III

LITERARY INFLUENCES

In discussing the literary influences which helped to shape the pattern of Sandburg writing, it is impossible to include all of them, for Sandburg's reading is not restricted to American literature but includes literary masterpieces of many countries such as England, Scotland, Ireland, France, Spain, Italy, Norway, Sweden, Russia. He is not unacquainted with Chinese and Japanese literature; he hopes to find time in the future to write of Hokusai of Japan together with Engström of Sweden. In the discussion of influences, I shall begin with Abraham Lincoln as the most important of all.

A. ABRAHAM LINCOLN

Carl Sandburg in 1956 made the statement: " The chief influence on my poetry was Abraham Lincoln. I have him soaked in my blood and brain and bone." [91]

While American democracy has been the animating principle of Sandburg's writing, Lincoln, as the symbol of democracy and as the poet's personal ideal, had the deepest influence on his poetry — and on a vast portion of his prose. In the words of Sandburg:

" Lincoln foreshadowed something. The people took him as a new figure of hope for them. This hope ranged around wider freedom, political and economic, for the common man. It might be long in coming. But Lincoln held the lights and the high torch for it." [92]

" In Lincoln's mind was a constant searching around the question, what is justice? an inexorable exactitude, a scrupulous care... Lincoln's personality was wider in range, had more colors and shadings — than any other man in our history. He had a sense of human tragedy, a feeling for the lives of those who toil without being requited, for the victims of an inexplicable fate." *

" He believed that ' Improvement in condition — is the order of things in a society of equals.' " [93]

The above statements reveal some of the fundamental characteristics of Lincoln which influenced Sandburg both as a man and as a writer. In the brief review of the *Chicago Poems* already given, the Lincoln influence is clearly shown in the subject matter and mood, in the humanitarian pleas for economic improvement of the lot of the industrial worker. The principles of Lincoln may be seen as the underlying motives of many of the early poems; however, as the poetry grew in volume, Sandburg took

---

* Frederick Hill MESERVE, quoting Carl Sandburg in *Journal of the Illinois State Historical Society*; Winter, 1952, p. 338.

Lincoln himself as a theme to illustrate the ideals of democracy, for " Lincoln had a deep-rooted faith in the people, loving and understanding them with all their faults and failings. " [94] We therefore, find much of Lincoln in Sandburg poetry — particularly in *The People, Yes.* In this volume he quotes Lincoln on many pages and writes of him on others :

> " He was a mystery in smoke and flags
> Saying yes to the smoke, yes to the flags,
> Yes to the paradoxes of democracy,
> Yes to the hopes of government,
> Of the people.... " [95]

In *The People, Yes* is the challenge to democracy as set forth in the words of Abraham Lincoln :

" As I would not be a *slave* so I would not be a *master.* This expresses my idea of democracy. Whatever differs from this, to the extent of the difference, is no democracy. " [96]

Many of the shorter Sandburg lyrics are expressive of the same fundamental principles. His Phi Beta Kappa poem, delivered at William and Mary College in 1944, was devoted to the sixteenth President.

Sandburg has been a long-time friend of Adlai Stevenson (ever since his meeting with Mr. Stevenson's father, whom he interviewed while collecting material for his first two volumes of the Lincoln biography, *The Prairie Years*). In a speech at Stevenson's inauguration as Governor of Illinois, January 1949, Sandburg gave a further assessment of the influences that Lincoln exerted on him :

" When you go through the speeches and letters of Lincoln, you may find the word ' responsibility ' about as often as you find the word ' freedom. ' He wanted freedom for all men, everywhere. He has become a world figure, in a certain sense adopted by the whole Family of Man because of what he represented in the name of human freedom. And yet we will have to go far to find any human struggler as keenly and sincerely weighted down by the burden of personal responsibility that he assumed on his own, as a volunteer, as a citizen free and willing. " [97]

However, the Lincoln influence must not be considered solely as a human, political or idealistic one. From the literary viewpoint, some of the Lincoln speeches and writings are at the root of his literary expression at its clearest and finest. Sandburg writes of Lincoln's literary style as follows :

" Abraham Lincoln had many styles. It has been computed that his printed speeches and writings number 1,078,365 words. One may range through his record of utterance and find a wider variety of styles than in any other American statesman or orator. And perhaps no author of books has written in such a diversity of speech tones directed at all manners and conditions of men.

" This may be saying in effect that the range of the personality of Abraham Lincoln ran far, identifying itself with the tumults and follies of mankind, keeping touch with multitudes and solitudes. The free-going and friendly companion is there and the man of the cloister, of the lonely corner of thought, prayer, and speculation. The man of affairs before a living audience is there, and the solitary inquirer weaving his abstractions related to human freedom and responsibility....

" The fate of man, his burdens and crosses, the pity of circumstances, the extent of tragedy in human life, these stood forth in word shadows of the Lincoln utterance, as testamentary as the utter melancholy of his face in repose. And in contrast he came to be known as the first authentic humorist to occupy the Executive Mansion in Washington, his gift of laughter being taken as a national belonging.

" Three short pieces from his pen are kept as immemorial possessions of the American people, each keyed to a high tragic note. These are the Letter to Mrs. Bixby, the Gettysburg Speech, the Second Inaugural....

" The Lincoln vocabulary ranged from the plainest of street vernacular to archaic Anglo-Saxon terms... His influence on the styles of other speakers and writers has been vast. The extent of it is incalculable." [98]

Sandburg, in *The War Years*, lays stress on Lincoln's word power, his simple, direct eloquence in speech, his forthright, incisive yet magnanimous thought expressed in documentary form. He quotes the impression of the orator, Charles Sumner, concerning the Lincoln state papers as being " in weight and pith suffused with a certain poetical color, recalling Bacon's ' Essays, ' having unconscious power without form or apparent effort, arising from no model, but springing directly from the man himself. " In all his shelves of books, said Sandburg, " Sumner could think of nothing past or present with which to compare Lincoln's public-affairs writings. " [99] Sandburg presents the chief of the telegraph office in Washington as saying : " No ruler of millions, since King David the Psalmist, has clothed great thoughts in sublimer language. " [100] And Charles Francis Adams Jr. is heard to say of the second inaugural address : " That rail-splitting lawyer is one of the wonders of the day. Once at Gettysburg, and now again on a greater occasion, he has shown a capacity to the demands of the hour which we could not expect from orators or men of the schools. The inaugural strikes me in its simplicity and directness as being for all time the historical keynote of this war... Not a prince or minister in all Europe could have risen to such an equality with the occasion. " [101]

Steeped as he was in Lincoln's writings, thought, letters and style, Sandburg naturally absorbed much of the style and manner of the President's expression. The directness and eloquence of Lincoln at his best are often reflected in the elevated style of Sandburg in *The Prairie Years* and *The War Years*; while the diversity of the Lincoln language " directed at all manners and conditions of men " is a very vital part of Sandburg's biography — enabling the reader to see and hear Lincoln as he actually wrote and spoke in life. The " high tragic note " is masterfully employed by Sandburg in his portrayal of the human condition and of the national crises of the 1860's. It is sincere, direct and without the slightest trace of melodrama — a truthful statement of fact enriched by deep sympathy.

In his biography of the President, Sandburg made this statement concerning Lincoln's influence over the people : " None threw a longer shadow than he. " [102] No one has cast a longer shadow over the Sandburg code of ethics and literary vision than Abraham Lincoln. Sandburg, Lincoln and democracy are words closely associated in the American mind.

B. Ralph Waldo Emerson and other New England writers

Whitman is generally admitted as having exerted considerable influence upon Sandburg. However it seems to the writer of this study that no one who is prepared to admit this could seriously discount the influence of Emerson, the New England intellectual who, a generation before Whitman, had called for American literature of a truly national character. In fact, the first important literary recognition of Whitman as a poet was by Emerson, whose prestige had long since been acknowledged; and Emerson, prior to Whitman, challenged America to accept a new concept of literary values.

This concept together with a redefinition of the idea of the scholar was given in a famous address, " The American Scholar " delivered by Emerson before the Phi Beta Kappa Society of Harvard University on August 31, 1837. The poet Lowell recognized this speech as " an event without any former parallel in our literary annals, " and Oliver Wendell Holmes pronounced it " our Intellectual Declaration of Independence." [103]

Carl Sandburg in his youth was an ardent reader of Emerson, whose literary productions were then being given great prominence. We are told by his friends of his fondness for Emerson, and he himself confirms the fact in the autobiography of his first twenty years, *Always the Young Strangers*, when he states :

" I met people in Galesburg who were puzzling to me; and later when I read Shakespeare I found those same people were puzzling him. I met little wonders of many kinds among animals and plants that never lost their wonder for me, and I found later that these same wonders had a deep interest for Emerson, Thoreau, and Walt Whitman. " [104] At college too, the study of Emerson was given special classroom attention by Professor Philip Green Wright.

When we consider at length the Emerson address on " The American Scholar, " we see many parallels in the literary concepts and thought processes of Emerson and Sandburg. Emerson chose to illustrate his concept of the scholar by the use of a fable derived from the ancients — a fable declaring that the gods of antiquity had divided Man into individual men of specialized skills in order that combined use of these skills might benefit Man, in the same manner that the hand is divided into five fingers, and therefore better fitted to perform its functions. The fable, though old, presents a doctrine suited to modern times — that there is One Man present in each man only partially or through one faculty. Man has become men, each individual endowed with a special talent. But only the combined talents of men present a true picture of Man. Man is not

an engineer, or priest, or professor, or soldier, or scholar, or farmer —
but the sum of all these functions; (however, in the divided state of society,
these functions remain distributed).

In his address on " The American Scholar " Emerson wrote :

" In the distribution of functions, the scholar is the delegated intellect.
In the right state, he is Man Thinking. In the degenerate state, when
the victim of society, he tends to become a mere thinker, or the parrot
of other men's thinking.

" In this view of him, as Man Thinking, the theory of his office is contained. Him Nature solicits with all her placid, all her monitory pictures;
him the past instructs; him the future invites. Let us see him in his school
and consider him in reference to the main influences he receives.

" (1) The first in time and the first in importance of the influences
on the mind is that of Nature. Every day, the sun; and after sunset,
Night and her stars. Ever the winds blow; ever the grass grows ...
[Could this quotation be the inspiration of the title of Sandburg's second
volume of autobiography now in preparation, *Ever the Winds of Chance?*]

" (2) The next great influence on the spirit of the scholar is the mind
of the Past — in whatever form, whether of literature, of art, of institutions, that mind is inscribed. Books are the best type of influence of the
Past... Each age must write its own books; or rather each generation
for the next succeeding.

" (3) Action is with the scholar subordinate, but it is essential. Without
it thought can never ripen into truth. So much only of life as I know
by experience, so far have I extended my dominion. Drudgery, calamity,
exasperation, want, are instructors in eloquence and wisdom. Action is
the raw material out of which the intellect moulds her splendid products;
experience is converted into thought, as a mulberry leaf is converted into
satin. The manufacture goes forward at all hours.

" If it were only for a vocabulary, the scholar would be covetous of
action. Life is our dictionary. Years are well spent in country labors;
in town; in the insight into trades and manufactures; in frank intercourse
with many men; in science; in art; to the one end of mastering in all their
facts a language by which to illustrate and embody our perceptions...
The perception of the worth of the vulgar is fruitful in discoveries. " [105]

Emerson set forth a new concept of American literature, a new choice
of subject matter, a change in approach and a new concept of writing,
truly national in character. This concept, voiced in 1837, antedates by
many years the call of Whitman in his later *Leaves of Grass*.

Developing his ideal of a national literature Emerson stated his belief
that the commonplace of everyday living and the truth of American life
formed proper subjects for poetry — replacing the idea of foreign subject
matter.

" I hear with joy what is beginning to be said of the dignity and necessity of labor to every citizen. There is virtue yet in the hoe and the spade, for learned as well as for unlearned hands... Instead of the sublime and beautiful, the near, the low, the common is explored and poetized. The literature of the poor, the feelings of the child, the philosophy of the street, the meaning of household life are the topics of the time. It is a great stride. I wish not for the great, the remote, the romantic. I embrace the common, I explore and sit at the feet of the familiar, the low. What would we really know the meaning of? The meal in the firkin; the milk in the pan; the ballad in the street; the news of the boat; the glance of the eye; the form and gait of the body; show me the ultimate reason for these matters; show me the sublime presence of the highest spiritual cause lurking, as always it does lurk, in these suburbs and extremities of Nature. " [106]

Thus, Emerson hailed the commonplace in poetry and the relationship of man to all Nature. Minister, college lecturer, poet, essayist, he established a new concept of literary values for the new nation of America in a new world. Rebellious against literary conformity and tradition, he became a seeker after truth and the eternal verities unfettered by formalities. He helped to direct the course of modern American poetry by turning away from traditional bases and conventions. These same facts, in addition to his love of man, sensitivity to Nature, beauty, and moral law, and his emphasis on the American mind and American idealism, made it possible for him to accept and recognize Whitman and *Leaves of Grass* in 1855. And these literary attributes of Emerson show reflections in the poetry of Carl Sandburg.

Among the Sandburg poems published in his latest volume entitled *Wind Song* (1960) is one which reads:

" There is only one man in all the world
And his name is All Men... " [107]

These lines represent a meeting of the Emerson and Sandburg minds, an approval of the Emersonian literary pioneering as outlined in the 1837 Harvard address. The Emersonian call for themes embracing the real life of the American citizen is carried out more voluminously in Sandburg poetry than in that of any other American poet, dead or living.

Emerson represented in mid-nineteenth century literature the American *Man Thinking*. His probing intellect sought to reconcile his deep religious faith with the theories of science then coming into prominence. The result was the projection of the mind outward to nature and the external aspects of the world — to a Beyond. A very elevated moral standard characterizes Emerson's poetry and prose. We shall, in the discussion of Sandburg's poetry, see the position of Sandburg in the realm of Man Thinking.

Excerpts from Emerson's essay, " The Poet " will further serve to illustrate the parallel concepts of poetry:

" The poet is representative. He stands among partial men for the complete man, and apprises us not of his wealth, but of the commonwealth...

"I know not how it is that we need an interpreter; but the great majority of men cannot report the conversation they had with nature... Their appulses have sufficient force to arrive at the senses, but not to reach the quick, and compel the reproduction of themselves in speech... The poet is the sayer, the namer, and represents beauty;... he is a beholder of ideas and an utterer of the necessary and the casual. We do not speak now of men of political talents, or of industry and skill in meter, but of the true poet... Our poets are men of talents who sing, and not the children of music." [108]

"The poet's habit of living should be set on a key so low and plain that the common influences should delight him... [109] We do not, with sufficient plainness or sufficient profoundness, address ourselves to life, nor do we yet chant our own times and social circumstance... We have yet had no genius in America which knew the value of our incomparable material, and saw in the barbarism and materialism of the times another carnival of the same gods whose picture he so much admires in Homer... Our log-rolling, our stumps and their politics, our fisheries, our negroes and Indians, our repudiations, the wrath of rogues and the pusillanimity of honest men, the northern trade, the southern planting, the western clearing, Oregon and Texas are yet unsung! Yet America is a poem in our eyes; its ample geography dazzles the imagination." [110]

How perfectly the Emersonian concept of poetry and poetic interpretation was adaptable to the early environment, the difficult growing years of Carl Sandburg! According to the Emersonian concept, Sandburg was by nature and circumstance endowed with the fundamental materials of poetry. The poetic tools came with young Sandburg's love of nature, his love of books, constant desire for reading, intimate contacts with poverty, work in varied forms, determination and struggle to secure an education — and finally Lombard College. Sandburg in his poetry describes his own time and social circumstances. He never hesitated to voice the commonplace, to seek out spiritual causes; he was among those poets in the early twentieth century who recognized the need for reform and whose early poetry reflected the inequities of that period — "another carnival of the same gods" as those of ancient times. In the tradition of Emerson, he profoundly "addressed himself to life."

Emerson, as one of the first great names in American literature, and, as the literary innovator of the nineteenth century, opened up the path for Whitman in the same century and for Sandburg and his role in the poetry renaissance of the twentieth century. Sandburg's adherence to the idea of a national literature, interpretation of the commonplace in American life, and his conception of the poet's vital role in a changing society stem directly from the New England literary movement at the head of which was Emerson.

* * *

We know that Sandburg read other New England poets who were contemporaries of Emerson and who reflected the Emerson influence. In this New England group was Emily Dickinson, who in turn influenced very directly the poetry of Sandburg. Sandburg himself once openly stated, during his early Chicago days, "that he owed more to Emily Dickinson than to Whitman. " [111]

There is little similarity in the social backgrounds of the two poets; for Emily Dickinson lived a quiet life in an austere Puritan family in Amherst, Massachusetts. Her manner of living was almost that of a recluse, of a retreat within four walls of her home, within her garden, as well as a retreat within her own self. Such a cloistered existence may have been due to the early death of a young lawyer whom she regarded highly, or possibly to her self-imposed rejection of a later love affair. Her literary production is, in part, the interpretation of a sensitive, frustrated being possessed of a high moral code, the interpretation of a lonely and anguished soul. In common with Emerson, she possessed a love of nature, and wrote nature poetry of great beauty and delicate symbolism. She shared the transcendentalist outlook fostered by Emerson in his struggle against the narrow confines of Puritanism; she pondered on the challenge of science to orthodox religion. But social issues, such as the Civil War, were, for the most part, outside her spiritual realm. Her love poetry is characterized by deep feeling, by a spirit of renunciation, by a certain mysticism, and by an intimate knowledge of death.

Emily Dickinson was a realist, in a restricted sense, in that she closely examined and analyzed her own mind. Much of her poetry was a fragmentary *journal intime*, somewhat comparable in its self-analysis to the *Journal Intime* of Frédéric Amiel of Geneva. She permitted only four of her seventeen hundred poems to be published during her lifetime. Most of them were collected and published by friends after her death. A brief glimpse at the posthumous publications will show that Sandburg is in a direct line of descent.

Emily Dickinson exercised an incalculable influence on modern poetry; for she, with Emerson, recognized the necessity of a break from the confines of contemporary verse, the need for the presentation of New England thought, and for a less restricted religious outlook. She experimented with new verse forms, used homespun words of common life rather than words of her intellectual Amherst neighborhood; she gave fleeting glimpses of ordinary living, with a distilled intensity and with beauty of color and sound; she dared to employ occasional irregularities of rhythm, speech peculiarities, and even dissonance to express the frustrations of life which she knew so well. There is an occasional calculated awkwardness, a deliberate change of meter. Yet her poetry possesses a richness of metaphor and exquisite imagery, and an inner symbolism that mirrors human experience.

The images in the poetry of Emily Dickinson are almost jewel-like in their brilliance and captivating beauty; their lustre is in pleasing contrast to the brief simplicity of the lines which form their background.

> " Lightly stepped a yellow star
> To its lofty place,
> Loosed the Moon her silver hat
> From her lustral face.

All of evening softly lit
As an astral hall —
' Father ', I observed to Heaven,
' You are punctual ! ' " [112]

The perception of emotional suffering, the elevated spiritual quality of
her verse and a penetrating self-analysis may be seen in the following
lines :

" After great pain a formal feeling comes—
The nerves sit ceremonious like tombs;
The stiff Heart questions—was it He that bore?
And yesterday—or centuries before?

The feet mechanical
Go round a wooden way,
Of ground or air of Ought, regardless grown;
A quartz contentment like a stone." [113]

Sandburg has written many poems of emotion, but perhaps his self-
analysis, in respect to emotional feeling, may best be seen in lines from
" At a Window " :

" Give me hunger,
Give me hunger, pain and want,
Shut me out with shame and failure,
From your doors of gold and flame,
Give me your shabbiest, weariest hunger !
. . . . .
But leave me a little love." [114]

In the study of Sandburg's poetry we see a wealth of imagery, at times
of delicate beauty, at times of vivid color; or it may mirror strength and
power; or it may assume spiritual significance. In his poem entitled
" Public Letter to Emily Dickinson " may be seen both the imagery and
symbolism that enhance the quality of his poetry :

" Flame and thorn were there
in and around five roses,
winding flame, speaking thorn.

Pour from the sea
one hand of salt.
Take from a star
one finger of mist.
Pick from a heart
one cry of silver.

Let be, give over
to the moving blue
of the chosen shadow.

. . . . .
Share with the flamewon,
choose from your thorns,
for God to be near you,
for God to be witness." [115]

Emily Dickinson has been acclaimed by most critics as a genius, a master of her art. Carl Sandburg acknowledges his debt to her imagery as follows:

"You gave us the bumblebee who has a soul,
The everlasting traveler among the hollyhocks,
And how God plays around a back-yard garden." [116]

* * *

We know that Sandburg became an admirer of Oliver Wendell Holmes while he was still a young boy delivering newspapers in Galesburg, for he speaks of Holmes in *Always the Young Strangers*. Holmes was a practicing physician of Cambridge and Boston, Massachusetts; but his greatest talent lay in the teaching of medicine, first at Dartmouth from 1838 to 1840 and then in the Harvard Medical School from 1847 to 1882. However, he was also learned in the fields of literature and theology; and he became a poet and a master of prose as well as professor of medical science. Although Dr. Holmes wrote some rhyming verse, his sudden rise to fame came by way of prose written by request for *The Atlantic Monthly*, edited at that time by his friend the poet, James Russell Lowell. This extended prose contribution, entitled *The Autocrat of the Breakfast-Table*, was followed by *The Professor at the Breakfast-Table*. One of Holmes' most famous poems was " Old Ironsides, " which saved the historic warship, " The Constitution, " from being discarded; his best poem was " The Chambered Nautilus "; and in his " Last Leaf" appear the tender sympathy and concern for suffering that may be found in many Sandburg poems. However, it is the form of his writing, rather than the content, which found favor with Sandburg, for it possessed the strength and ruggedness of men toughened by the struggle that has helped to shape American national character. Holmes' intellectual passion for science aroused in him an aversion to insincerity, to stupidity and to bigotry which he never hesitated to attack on the lecture platform or in his writings. The style of his prose is orderly and ardent, fearless yet possessed of a warmth, mingled with wit. There is a quality of elasticity in both his prose and poetry, suited to his subject matter. This elasticity or concordance of technique to subject matter is widely evident in the prose and poetry of Carl Sandburg; and there is a similar wide diversity of theme in the writings of both Holmes and Sandburg. Holmes' revolt against the technique of rhyming verse was of particular interest to Sandburg, who quotes this New England poet as follows: " Oliver Wendell Holmes, skilled rhymester, told a young poet: ' When you write in prose you say what you mean. When you write in verse you say what you must.' Having said this to the young man, Holmes bethought himself and then wrote: ' I was thinking especially of rhymed verse. Rhythm alone is a tether, and not a very long one. But rhymes are iron fetters; it is dragging a chain and ball to march under their encumbrance; it is a clog-dance you are figuring in when you execute your metrical *pas seul.*' " [117] Sandburg in his defense of free verse leans heavily on this poetic theory of Holmes.

* * *

Henry David Thoreau was in his youth a close friend and protégé of Emerson. To Thoreau every manifestation of nature contained a lesson, and was a subject worthy of a poem. The river, the woods, the ponds, the hills, the fields, swamps, meadows, the birds, trees, the seasons—all were of absorbing interest. After he had graduated from Harvard, he wished to follow a literary career, and Emerson provided his own Walden Pond and the woods and fields around it as a laboratory for Thoreau's ventures into writing of nature. Here, in a simple cabin in the woods, Thoreau found his greatest happiness, for he was at home with nature. The experiences and impressions of his Walden Pond years, combined with intensive reading (for he could read in six languages) became the material for his many books and poems. The language of his writing was frequently that of the common people of Concord and the surrounding neighborhood; the meter of his poems fitted his moods, sometimes abrupt and rough in form, but filled with imagery. A spirit of revolt against any kind of totalitarianism pervades his social writings. He was a critic of human institutions and he worked actively for the abolition of slavery. As a social critic he was one of the forerunners of the realism and aggressiveness of twentieth-century literature.

Because of similarities in taste, it is not difficult to see the reasons for Sandburg's relationship to Thoreau. The poem " Mountains " by Thoreau bears kinship not only of theme but of strength to the Sandburg " March of the Hungry Mountains. " Thoreau's beloved birds formed the subject of his " Respectable Folks, " a poem comparable in poetic treatment to Sandburg's " Bird Talk, " " Kansas Seasons, " " People of the Eaves, " " Brown Gold, " and " Spring Cries. " Characteristic of Thoreau's nature poetry are the following lines from " Haze " :

> " Bird of the sun, transparent-winged.
> Owlet of noon, soft-pinioned,
> From heath or stubble rising without song,—
> Establish thy serenity o'er the fields." [118]

In the delightful imagery of this poem, in its softness and grace, its fluidity of line, we see the intimate and personal influence of Emerson, and the style of poetry that was to influence later writers. Sandburg's " Fog " is a worthy companion piece to Thoreau's " Haze. "

> " The fog comes
> on little cat feet.
>
> It sits looking
> over harbor and city
> on silent haunches
> and then moves on." [119]

* * *

Another New England poet, John Greenleaf Whittier, also a contemporary of Emerson, believed with Emerson in poetizing the commonplace, and deplored the lack of pastoral poetry in American literature. As early as 1847 (but ten years later than Emerson's famous Harvard address), Whittier (as had Emerson) emphasized the poetry of human life and nature as a type deserving of special attention; and he became a pioneer in the field of New England pastoral poetry. His finest pastoral poem is " Snow-Bound, " rich in description, local color and genuine sentiment. In " Snow-Bound " we find a succession of clear but simple images, without the symbolism fostered by Emerson; yet it has the sincerity which is found in Sandburg poetry.

There are several parallels in the lives of Whittier and Sandburg which are interesting; and some parallel concepts of poetry which invite comparison. Whittier was of humble lineage, the son of pious Quaker parents. He became a newspaper editor and an ardent anti-slavery man; and in his editorial columns and in his poetry he carried on a crusade for human freedom. His anti-slavery prose writings and poetry first gained fame for him, and have been assembled to form an important portion of his collected works.

" The Farewell, " which is Whittier's poetic interpretation of a Virginia slave mother's grief for her daughters sold into slavery, cannot fail to arouse a deep emotional response in the reader. The reader of Sandburg prose will recall the description of the slaves on the way to the auction block in his biography of *Mary Lincoln—Wife and Widow*. In Whittier's " Proem " are lines expressive of the hatred of oppression felt both by him and by Sandburg :

> " Yet here at least an earnest sense
> Of human right and weal is shown;
> A hate of tyranny intense,
> And hearty in its vehemence,
> As if my brother's pain and sorrow were my own." *

Another common characteristic of the two poets is a feeling for the importance of the ballad in preserving local or national tradition and primitive history. In Whittier's poem, " Skipper Ireson's Ride, " his version has a foundation in oral tradition, yet there is historical background for a portion of it. As a boy, Whittier had heard from relatives and visitors many stories of the rigors of early New England, also stories of witchcraft, of adventure—tales of folklore; and these he retained in his memory to weave them later into poetry such as in " The Wreck of Rivermouth. " Thus Whittier helped to awaken an interest in New England's past as a subject for poetry. In his later years, because of his feeling for religion, he also contributed devotional lyrics and hymns that became beloved and las ing. Yet he is best known for his pioneer efforts in New England pastoral poetry, more recently brought into greater prominence by Robert Frost.

---

* John G. WHITTIER, in *Masterpieces of American Literature*, edited by Mark Van Doren, Harcourt, Brace and Co., New York, 1936, p. 159.

"Corn Hut Talk" and "Corn Prattlings" by Carl Sandburg may be compared to the "Corn Song" of Whittier in theme and spirit, though not in form or rhythm.

Whittier celebrated the sea beaches of New England as does Sandburg the lake shores of Illinois. The Massachusetts farm lands provided special inspiration for song to the early poet, as the mid-western prairie later provided Sandburg with the inspiration which made him a pioneer in prairie poetry. As in Sandburg's prairie poetry, there is a joyous exultation in Whittier's pastoral idylls, notably in his "Barefoot Boy," which contains a picture of country life drawn from his own childhood, a life which contributed

> "Knowledge never learned in schools,
> Of the wild bee's morning chase,
> Of the wild flowers time and place,
> Flight of fowl and habitude
> Of the tenants of the wood." [120]

Emerson and the New England writers exerted very strong influences on American literature as well as upon Sandburg. Volumes of Emerson are to be seen in many of the rooms of Sandburg's home so that they may be immediately available to him. Emerson, not Whitman, first set forth the literary creed by which the American scholar and writer would be directed. This runs counter to the impression held by some that the strongest influence upon Sandburg was Whitman. As we shall see, Sandburg's admiration for Whitman cannot be denied; but in Emerson and the New England group he found influences that existed prior to Whitman. In fact, Whitman's own debt to Emerson was not sufficiently admitted by the New York poet, for in his later years he disclaimed having read Emerson before writing *Leaves of Grass*, in spite of the fact that he had mailed to the Concord writer a copy of the first edition with a letter addressing him as "Master." (A portion of this letter will be presented). From the *Journals* of Emerson, from the speeches and *Essays* of Emerson, Whitman drew much of the material for his poetry. Whitman wove into the fabric of his poems Emerson's prior "stand for all humanity and the all-inclusive humanitarianism of his nature. In a very true sense Emerson was the spiritual father of *Leaves of Grass*." *

Sandburg draws upon Emerson for his belief in the sanctity of the individual mind; for the belief that "America is itself a poem"; that the commonplace, the common man are poetic material; that poetry of protest (when protest is called for) is the mark of Man Thinking. He draws also from Thoreau the spirit of protest when non-conformity to custom is not in the interest of the common welfare.

Carl Sandburg studied deeply the writings of the New England authors who opened the paths of American literature. It is only natural therefore, that for him these literary inheritances should contain lessons of value, particularly those of Emerson and Emily Dickinson. Her experimentation,

---

* Russell BLANKENSHIP. *American Literature*, Holt, Rinehart and Winston, New York, 1949, p. 300.

" in debt to Emerson, and in love with the image, the word, and learning, anticipates the metaphysical strain in the verse of today." Her originality, with that of Sidney Lanier, " heralded afar off new themes, new forms; their verse (and Whitman's) formed the pronaos of modern American poetry; as did the tales of Mark Twain the pronaos of modern American prose." [121]

C. WALT WHITMAN

When Emerson in 1855 saw fit to acknowledge literary worth in the *Leaves of Grass* of Whitman his recognition proved to be the turning point in Whitman's career. The younger poet was overjoyed by such recognition from an established intellectual and literary critic and wrote to Emerson, calling him dear Master and Leader as follows:

" Those shores [the ' ever satisfying ' shores of that newer America] you found. I say you have led The States there—have led Me there. I say that none has ever done, or ever can do, a greater deed for the States than your deed. Others may line out the lines, build cities, work mines, break up farms; it is yours to have been the original true Captain who put to sea, intuitive, positive, rendering the first report...

" Receive, dear Master, these statements and assurances through me, for all the young men and for an earnest that we know none before you... that we understand what you have indicated... and that we will stick to it and enlarge upon it through These States."

Walt Whitman [122]

Sandburg poetry is sometimes referred to as a continuation of the Whitman tradition. There are wide differences between the poetry of the two men, yet there is no doubt that the Whitman influence upon the living poet is recognizable and that Sandburg owes a debt to Whitman.

Sandburg gives us a realistic view of American life of the twentieth century. He exults in the achievements of America, as did Whitman before him; he glories in the great cities and in the ingenuity of the American people, as did Whitman; he writes of the steel mills of Gary and Pittsburgh and Birmingham and of the prairie country and American agriculture. Yet he maintains a carefully considered attitude toward society and toward government, a disciplined thought more reminiscent of Emerson than of Whitman. In Sandburg's " Four Preludes " may be seen his cautious conservatism which the lessons of history teach:

" It has happened before.
Strong men put up a city and got a nation together,
And paid singers to sing: ...
The only singers now are crows crying, ' Caw, caw, '
And the sheets of rain whine in the wind and doorways,
And the only listeners now are—the rats—and the lizards." [123]

Sandburg freely acknowledges the general indebtedness of American poetry to the culture of Europe and the Orient; as did Whitman in his later prose writings and in " Passage to India "; in Sandburg poetry we read of the moral and political lessons drawn from Spain, Greece, Rome, Persia, from the autocracy of Napoleon, or from the absolutism of the late Hohenzollerns; we read of the richness of culture and wisdom of Rabelais and Hugo. While both poets recognize that Europe, Asia and the Christian religion have been the forerunners and the physical and cultural antecedents of America, both share the ideal of New World democracy as the supreme song of their poetry; both hope to further the idea of a national literature, a literary expression characteristic of America.

Whitman realized, as had Emerson before him, that America in his day had as yet no truly national literature. He sadly proclaimed : " No land or people ever existed so needing a race of singers and poems differing from all others, and rigidly their own, as the land and the people of our United States need such singers and poems today, and for the future... As long as the States continue to be dominated by the poetry of the Old World, and remain unsupplied with autochthonous songs, to express, vitalize and give color to and define their material and political success, and minister to the people distinctively, so long will they stop short of first-class Nationality and remain defective." [124]

Whitman wished his poetry, particularly in " Song of Myself, " to celebrate the democratic scene, American occupations and events, the prairies and states, the violent contrasts and rapidity of street movement in the cities. He conceived of the United States as producing future breeds of tolerant, free, healthy citizens who would have no desire to become a conquering nation, but rather a leading nation of peace, though not incapable of becoming a nation of war, should the occasion demand it in the interest of physical survival or of the survival of democratic ideology. With civil and religious freedom as a firm basis, Whitman believed, a new edifice of literature could be built to express political and scientific truths through the medium of poetry. He regarded politics, science and poetic literature as an ideal trinity. To him the duty of the literary artist was the paving of the way for a new theology :

" The prophet and the bard
Shall yet maintain themselves, in higher stages yet,
Shall mediate to the Modern, to Democracy, interpret yet to them
God and eidólons." [125]

To Whitman, democracy, as a minister of Christian principles, must be an inseparable part of truly great poetry.

In Sandburg's writing, such poems as " Prayers of Steel, " " Our Prayer of Thanks, " " The Four Brothers " and " Fire Dreams " bear testimony to his feeling for religion and to the basic significance of religious freedom and faith as pillars of democracy.

Both poets believed that American artistic expression should be strong, and when necessary, rough and tough; it should inspire freedom, faith, courage, wisdom, the will to great decisions, the firmness to demand justice; yet it should express the idealism of liberty, equality, fraternity. Emerson had earlier set forth these requirements of the literary artist.

Whitman believed that poetry could arise " from labor gangs, boatmen, miners," [126] from all who toil with their hands, the poetry revealing the genius inherent in the people. The language of the working man is necessary to translate his native humor and indigenous expression; to be truly illustrative, such poetry must contain the slang and lingo of the workman. Poetry, in its far-reaching evolution, must not exclude grass-roots life and language. Sandburg believes in the power of homely speech, dialect, lingo, slang; by means of it, he lustily depicts the life and environment of those who know the fresh winds of the prairie or the crowded sidewalks of the city and of those whom industrial society has forced into the fold of the less-privileged. Both poets write of the American nation, but Sandburg amplifies and selects also the lot of the individual, and in so doing, gives to the individual appropriate or characteristic language. This is the authochtonous expression for which Whitman had called (and the common or the " vulgar " experience and vocabulary for which Emerson had previously called as early as 1837).

We have already noted Sandburg's advocacy of free verse, his staunch defense of unhampered expression. Free verse was the medium employed by Whitman in *Leaves of Grass*. For Whitman believed that by the middle of the nineteenth century the time had arrived to shatter the barriers of form dividing poetry from prose. He believed that poetry would henceforth " win and maintain its character, regardless of rhyme, and the measurement-rules of iambic, spondee, dactyl, etc.; and that, even if rhyme and those measurements continue to furnish the medium to inferior writers and themes, the truest and greatest *Poetry* (while subtly and necessarily always rhythmic, and distinguishable easily enough) could never again, in the language, be expressed in arbitrary and rhyming metre, any more than the greatest eloquence, or the truest power and passion." [127] He believed that conventional rhyme, as the medium of the highest practical and spiritual expression, must inevitably fail; that the size, the rapid growth, the emotions and pride of developing democracy, with the oncoming of steamships, railroads, factories, telegraphs, could best be expressed in prose poetry, in rhythmic but unrhymed verse; that the vastness of industry, the dignity of practical labor, could best find adequate expression in lines unfettered by rhyme. Sandburg has written in very free verse, but in verse of his own taste and not as an imitator of Whitman.

Sandburg was honored by being invited to write the foreword to the special 1921 edition of *Leaves of Grass* published to commemorate the hundredth anniversary of Whitman's birth. In this preface he writes :

" *Leaves of Grass* is the most wildly keyed solemn oath that America means something and is going somewhere that has ever been written : it is America's most classic advertisement of itself as having purpose, destiny, banners and beaconfires... Whitman's best single characteristic and authentic poem is ' The Song of the Open Road. ' Probably the most majestic threnody to death in the English language is Whitman's long poem, written just after the assassination of President Lincoln, entitled ' When Lilacs Last in the Dooryard Bloomed. ' Some readers consider ' Passage to India ' the poem of profoundest meanings and vision.

" Among lovers of Whitman, the one line that probably haunts most often is ' Out of the Cradle Endlessly Rocking. ' The epithet most frequently quoted in political controversy is ' the never-ending audacity of elected persons.... '

" Among the writings in *Leaves of Grass* there are poems which are masterpieces of the art of poetry... *Leaves of Grass* is a book to be owned, kept, loaned, fought over, and read till it is dog-eared and dirty all over.... The most highly praised and the most roundly excoriated book America has produced—that is Walt Whitman's *Leaves of Grass....* In stature, pride, stride and scope of personality he is a challenger." [128]

Sandburg responded to the challenge of Whitman in one respect more completely than has any other twentieth-century poet. Whitman in his " Democratic Vistas " issued this challenge : " The People !... Literature, strictly considered, has never recognized the People, and, whatever may be said, does not today. Speaking generally, the tendencies of literature, as hitherto pursued, have been to make mostly critical and querulous men. It seems as if, so far, there were some natural repugnance between a literary and professional life, and the rude rank spirit of the democracies... I know of nothing more rare, even in this country, than a fit scientific estimate and reverent appreciation of the People—of their measureless wealth of latent power and capacity, their vast, artistic contrasts of lights and shades—with, in America, their entire reliability in emergencies, and a certain breadth of historic grandeur, of peace or war, far surpassing all the vaunted samples of book-heroes or any *haut ton* coteries, in all the records of the world." [129]

Sandburg's response to this challenge of Whitman was *The People, Yes*.

Whitman's poetic theory had considerable influence upon Sandburg poetry—but some of the similarities between the two poets may also be coincidental to parallel concepts of the function of poetry in two great minds in modern American literature.

D. VICTOR HUGO

The influence of Victor Hugo on American thought during the mid-nineteenth century was strong. This influence was due not only to the prose and poetry of Hugo but also to his political and social pamphlets, letters and speeches. The *Almanac* of the Whig political party in America in 1854 carried the speech of Victor Hugo in April of that year while in exile from France because of his writings. The Hugo speech was delivered at the funeral of Jean Bosquet, also a political exile from France. I shall not quote the entire speech but only the portion dealing specifically with negro slavery in the southern plantation states of America. After speaking of the death of French revolutionaries by the sword, the scaffold and the gallows, Hugo looked for help from an enlightened future " for the deliverance of every nation, the enfranchisement of all mankind. " He concluded his influential speech as follows: " Friends, our sufferings give us a claim on Providence; God owes us a reward. Let us then cherish a manly faith and make our sacrifice with gladness. Oppressed of all nations, offer up your wounds. Poles, offer your misery; Hungarians, offer your gibbet; Italians, offer your cross; heroic transported brothers of Cayenne, of Africa, offer your chains; exiles, offer your proscription; and thou, O Martyr!, offer thy death to the liberty of the human race. Vive la République ! " [130] The New York *Tribune* reprinted and published the Hugo speech. This French writer's denouncement of all forms of oppression—including negro slavery —is given a prominent place in the opening pages of the second volume of the Sandburg biography, *Abraham Lincoln: The Prairie Years*.

There are evidences both in Sandburg prose and poetry of the influence of Hugo—an influence to which Sandburg readily agrees. *

Les Misérables was the particular work which exercised the deepest influence of Victor Hugo on Carl Sandburg; for young Sandburg (according to his own admission) read *Les Misérables* not once, but many times when he was a boy. Characteristics of *Les Misérables* appear in the works of Sandburg. Above all else, *Les Misérables* is humanitarian. Portrayed against the society of a complacent and self-centered *bourgeoisie* are the deceived and downtrodden lower classes. There is also the contrast of the vice and corruption of certain so-called " respectable " people and the innate goodness of many *misérables*, such as Jean Valjean. We find a wide variety of characters, scenes and emotions; we find the stark realism of the misery of the poor, of prison life; and even the pathos of scenes of underground Paris; and we find the exalted idealism of Marius, the son of a soldier of the upper classes, who becomes a leader of the revolutionary movement of the common people. Marius is a portrait of Victor Hugo himself.

We recall that during Sandburg's college years his sympathy was greatly aroused by the sad plight of the very young boys at work long, long hours in the darkness of a glass factory, heartlessly exploited at the expense of their education, their economic welfare, their health, even their eyesight. Here we sense the influence of Victor Hugo, whose emotional responses were so aroused by the plight of the little street gamins of Paris that he called public attention to those conditions in *Les Misérables*.

In both prose and poetry, young Carl Sandburg wrote of the pathos of the young boys in the Millville glass works; and both the prose and poetry resulting from this appeal to his emotions, were published in his college volume with the full approval of Professor Wright. At a later date, in the *Chicago Poems*, Sandburg wrote on behalf of those citizens of Chicago who suffered from the oppression of the industrial system, as Victor Hugo had written on behalf of *Les Misérables* under the social system of Paris. Sandburg's writings show his ability to express the same strong sense of compassion and humanitarianism which Hugo exhibited in his poetry, as in " Pour Les Pauvres " :

---

* When Carl Sandburg was asked by the writer of this study if he had been influenced by Victor Hugo the immediate response was : " Very definitely. "

" Donnez, riches ! L'aumône est sœur de la prière.

. . . . .

Donnez ! Il vient un jour où la terre nous laisse.
Vos aumônes là-haut vous font une richesse.
Donnez ! afin qu'on dise : Il a pitié de nous !

. . . . .

Donnez ! afin qu'un jour à votre heure dernière,
Contre tous vos péchés vous ayez la prière
D'un mendiant puissant au ciel ! " [131]

The evocation forming the concluding pages of young Sandburg's publication, *In Reckless Ecstasy* (which will be quoted at the end of this section of the thesis) resembles in spirit some of the poems of Hugo, such as " La Prière Pour Tous. "

Throughout all his poetry, Sandburg is an advocate of the spirit of brotherhood. He pleads for democracy and humanitarianism in life before meeting the final democratizing force of death. The poem " Cool Tombs " in its symbolism is an example of his plea for the spirit of brotherhood. Its moving lyricism makes it one of the best-remembered and significant of the shorter poems. In its gentle but emotional lines we find the names of famous personages who have suffered great tribulation in life before entering the democracy of the dead wherein all are leveled to equality :

" When Abraham Lincoln was shoveled into the tomb, he forgot the copperheads and the assassin... in the dust, in the cool tombs.
And Ulysses Grant lost all thought of con men and Wall Street cash and collateral turned to ashes... in the dust, in the cool tombs.

Pocahontas' body, lovely as a poplar, sweet as a red haw in November or a paw-paw in May, did she wonder ? Does she remember ? ... in the dust, in the cool tombs ?

Take any streetful of people, buying clothes and groceries, cheering a hero or throwing confetti and blowing tin horns... tell me if the lovers are losers... tell me if any get more than the lovers... in the dust... in the cool tombs." [132]

On the subject of death Victor Hugo wrote some of the most poignant and moving poetry in French literature. The death of loved ones (particularly of his daughter, Léopoldine in 1843) had brought deep anguish into his personal life. He many times chose to use death as the symbol of a mighty leveler :

" Passons, car c'est la loi; nul ne peut s'y soustraire;
Tout penche; et ce grand siècle, avec tous ses rayons
Entre en cette ombre immense où pâles nous fuyons." [133]

To this French poet death represented a great, yawning abyss into which all men enter on a basis of equality, regardless of previous station or status.

Thus both Sandburg and Hugo employ a concept of death as the ultimate metaphor of democracy. In the poetry of both men runs a spiritual essence, a religious undertone. Both poets are lyricists; yet both write on social and political questions. In both writers we see the advocacy of justice and of the rights of the common man. In 1845 Hugo was appointed a Peer of France by Louis-Philippe. He later began the publication of a democratic journal, *Le Peuple Souverain.* His *Les Châtiments* (1853) became famous as a fusion of poetry and political satire.

In the writings of Hugo there are grandiose ideas of republican government and a tremendous sweep of exultation such as we find in Whitman, who gave little profound thought to economic needs or to opposing views; whereas Sandburg better understands human relationships and the various economic and political principles animating democracy and is not addicted to verbose glorifications, but recognizes more fully the frailties of human nature, and is, therefore, less confident of perfection. His carefully considered ideas contain sincere evaluations and are expressed in measured terms. Sandburg does not strive to emulate Hugo's style of writing; but he is quite conscious of Hugo's conception of the vital role of a poet and prose writer in relation to society. He states that Hugo's portraiture of the street gamins of Paris, of the manners and customs of French society has remained strongly in his mind through the years. These impressions were intensified by many re-readings. Hugo's nonconformity to tradition, his journalistic endeavor, social criticism, political criticism, his love of the humble, his appeal to the rich to share with the poor and his hope for human progress —all these found favor with Sandburg. The " enfranchisement " of the human race envisioned in Hugo's writings and speeches is in accord with Sandburg's pleas for the Family of Man.

Further evidence of the Hugo influence is in the quiet, contemplative poem " Interior " which is an introspective self-portrait of Sandburg as he sits in his study at night, surrounded by his books.

> " One more day of bread and work....
> The man barefoot in moon silver
> Mutters ' you ' and ' you '
> To things hidden
> In the cool of the night time,
> In Rabelais, Whitman, Hugo,
> In an oblong of moon mist." [124]

Rabelais, underneath a vein of humor, was a satirist in his early writings and I believe whatever influence of this kind he may have had on Sandburg is evident in the *Chicago Poems* and in *The People, Yes.* I think we must admit some influence because of the fact that Sandburg mentions Rabelais in his poetry—not only as shown above, but in reference to Rabelaisian humor, and again in such passages as the following, referring to Immeasurable Men : " Of Rabelais, is it admissible that he threw an excellent laughter and his flagons and ovens made him a name ? " [135] The humor of Rabelais is directly quoted in Sandburg's novel.

Rabelais was a realist, though not in the more restricted sense of the nineteenth-century realists who insisted on meticulous detail. He portrayed the life of people in action, and was more interested in human energy than in beauty. He wrote with prodigious power; and because of the sixteenth-century religious struggles between Catholicism and Protestantism, he strove in his later works to give an impartial presentation of events and to include various levels of society. Rabelais was a scientist and possessed a great desire to learn. This desire for a large fund of knowledge, and for a broad view of humanity may also be seen in Hugo and in Sandburg.

E. FRANÇOIS VILLON

François Villon (1431-1485) was a master of mediaeval French poetry, whose work Carl Sandburg particularly admires. Sandburg in the introduction to his volume, *Complete Poems*, cites the viewpoint of John M. Synge concerning the varied audiences interested in the poetry of Villon : " Many of the older poets, such as Villon, used the whole of their personal life as their material, and the verse written in this way was read by strong men, and thieves, and deacons, not by little cliques only." [136]

Villon wrote in archaic French of the good and bad of Parisian society. Particularly in style and method of expression does the reader detect the influence of Villon upon Sandburg. French critics agree that Villon was an artist in poignancy of expression; and his poetic discipline was subordinated to his inspiration and deep feeling; expression of emotion was more important to him than restrained meter. " Il serre l'idée dans l'image, courte, franche, saisissante : c'est un maître de l'expression nerveuse et chaude. Mais l'ensemble va comme il peut : rien ne se tient." [137] Because of his excellent education at the University of Paris (where he received the B.A. degree in 1449 and the M.A. degree in 1452), and because of his wide acquaintanceship of that time, he possessed a large and varied vocabulary; and he chose to enrich his poetry by the introduction of colloquial or street language. Villon then, as Sandburg today, was able to " see beneath both beauty and ugliness; to see the boredom, and the horror and the glory "; [138] frequently he wrote in a spirit of wistful reverie or even brooding melancholy, as in " Regrets de la Belle Heaulmière, " for he knew that beauty is fleeting and evanescent. This observation is not uncommon in poetry. We find that this sense of the vanity of human life also pervades Sandburg's poetry, as in the poem " Autumn Movement."

The outstanding merit of Villon's verse is its intense subjectivity. It is a voice of experience, poignant in its portrayal; there is no pretense; it is stark naturalism. Villon expressed himself with complete frankness whether in complimentary or denunciatory fashion. He expressed honest estimates concerning himself and others. He held in cruel manner his poetic mirror up to human nature and portrayed all types of individuals whom he knew, even those at the lowest level of society.

Some of Villon's poems seem to modern readers coarse and indelicate for they portray truthfully the more sordid side of mediaeval Paris. Others, such as " Ballade des dames du temps jadis, " with its refrain " Où sont les neiges d'antan ? " are of a wistful delicacy; and the beautiful " Ballade que Villon faist à la requeste de sa mère pour prier Notre Dame " is one of the loveliest to come from his pen and reflects a tender and humble piety.

In his verse there is a great vitality; his lines contain not only the clamor and patter of the street, but also the Latin of the scholar and the piety of the prayer book;

> " Du Psalmiste je prends les dits :
> Delectasti me, Domine *
> In factura tua, si dis :
> Noble enfant, de bonne heure né,
> A toute douceur destiné,
> Manne du ciel, celeste don,
> De tous bienfaits le guerdonné **
> Et de nos maux le vrai pardon ! " [139]

As in Sandburg's *The People, Yes*, we find in the writing of Villon the contrast between poems on obscure people and poems on Jeanne d'Arc, on Queen Blanche the Lilial and on Charles, Duke of Orléans in whose court he was once a guest; we find the street ballad " Ouvrez votre huys, Guillemette " and we find the singing of worshipers in ancient churches. In " Ballade des Pendus " is the grim pathos of those condemned to death for misdeeds; in contrast, in " Le Dit de la Naissance de Marie d'Orléans " is the joy of the common people over the birth of a daughter to the Duke of Orléans.

These varied contrasts in French society as portrayed by Villon invite comparison to the Sandburg scope of portrayal; as do the transitions from crude, rough verse to stanzas of poetic grace and loveliness. There is in Villon's poetry that sharp perception that also characterizes *The People, Yes*. This French poet was fond of popular proverbs and folk-sayings. One rather long poem, " Ballade des Proverbes, " contains nothing but old French proverbs set to verse. A portion of it reads as follows :

> " Tant parle on qu'on se contredit,
> Tant vaut bon bruit que grace acquise,
> Tant promet on qu'on s'en dédit,
> Tant prie on que chose est acquise,
> Tant plus est chère et plus est quise ***
> Tant la quiert on qu'on y parvient,
> Tant plus commune et moins requise,
> Tant crie l'on Noel qu'il vient." [140]

We shall study Sandburg's extensive use of the proverbs, the homely gossip and the quiet convictions of the common people as interpreted in his longest poem *The People, Yes*.

The vernacular of the Paris streets that one reads in the *Jargon* and *Ballades* and various poems of Villon has its American counterpart in *The People, Yes*.

---

* Seigneur, vous m'avez comblé de joie en me montrant l'œuvre de vos mains.
** Comblé.
*** Cherchée.

F. The Bible

We have already noted that the Reverend George Washington Gale in 1837 led two hundred settlers from the Mohawk Valley of New York to the great prairie of Illinois to found a college which would teach Christian principles to those pioneers opening up the country.

It was but natural therefore, that the Bible proved a dominant influence in the lives of the early Galesburg settlers. A few decades later (1874) August Sandburg and his bride settled in the community of Galesburg. They too, were deeply imbued with the Christian principles instilled in them before leaving their native Sweden.

As a student at Lombard College (1898-1902) Sandburg stated his religious philosophy, which appeared at the end of his first volume of poems *In Reckless Ecstasy*. The spirit of this deep-rooted philosophy—in the form of an evocation—was a motivating guide throughout his life.

" O Forces and Potentialities that circumscribe the destinies of men, move me always to know the right thing to do. Let me always, in my decisions and actions lean rather toward equanimity than ardor... Give me a stout heart to face entrenched error, and a tender feeling for all the despised, rejected, and forsaken of mankind. Let me not be maudlin in my pity; let me feel my kinship with all men in such a manner that I may sympathize in just measure with those on the pinnacles of opulence and with those at the bottom of the pit.

" Make me a good mixer among people, one who always passes along the Good Word. Let me laugh in the right place; deliver me from mysticism; and lead me to think no man's opinion final...

" Free me from grim resolves; teach me gently to fasten my attention to the thing at hand and proceed at it with patience, faith and the inward gaiety that wears out opposition. Constrain me to common sense... Let me reach for unknown stars that are beyond my grasp rather than clutch at baubles of custom and superstitition.

" May the potencies of song and laughter abide with me ever. Assuage my toil with a lust of beauty, and forgetfulness of self that means a Higher Selfhood. And above all, Eternal Giver of all Good, if I don't accomplish what I plan, give me, I pray you, to smile at my losses, pick up the shattered ideal, and pass on to another try." [141]

Does this personal idealism and faith stated so early in life not forecast Sandburg's great sympathy with human suffering, his impulse to extend a helping hand to the oppressed, his confidence in mankind, his humanitarianism, his hope that men may become brothers through understanding?

In defense of the *vers libre* which Sandburg employs in his poetry, he cites the Bible as evidence of the power and strength of free verse. In the preface to his volume *Early Moon*, a book of selected poems for young people, the author declares:

" The Bible is one of the sublime sources of free verse. The creation of Moses, the Book of Proverbs, Ecclesiastes, the Sermon on the Mount, the

' Love Chapter ' of the Apostle Paul, these are in the free verse style of writing poetry." [142]

It is not difficult to detect the influence of Biblical style, particularly of the Psalms, on many of the Sandburg poems. Industrial metaphor and the style of the Psalms are combined in " Prayers of Steel " :

"Lay me on an anvil, O God.
Beat me and hammer me into a crowbar.
Let me pry loose old walls.
Let me lift and loosen old foundations.

Lay me on an anvil, O God.
Beat me and hammer me into a steel spike.
Drive me into the girders that hold a skyscraper together.
Take red-hot rivets and fasten me into the central girders.
Let me be the great nail holding a skyscraper through blue nights into
    white stars." [143]

In " Glass House Canticle ", also, is the reflection of Biblical style:

" Bless Thee, O Lord, for the living arc of the sky over me this morning.
Bless Thee, O Lord, for the miracle of light to my eyes and the mystery
    of it ever changing.
Bless Thee, O Lord, for the laws Thou hast ordained holding fast these
    tall oblongs of stone and steel, holding fast the planet Earth in its
    course and farther beyond the cycle of the Sun."[144]

The subject matter of the Bible is quite familiar to Carl Sandburg, as evidenced in many of his poems. There are many instances of Biblical references, many instances of a religious understructure of faith and hope supporting his poetry, of a fundamental spiritual essence. This underlying and gently pervading spiritual essence is no mighty cathedral concept, but rather a quiet infusion exemplified by one of the youth's prose writings at Lombard College called " Anthem in Stone " :

" It is only a little stone church with a little square tower. No cathedral this, with massive sides that throw out long shadows. Only Religion's Cottage in a country town. Green vines clamber over the gray stones from spring to winter and a few evergreens near give a contrasting gray and green all the year. How often it glides—tiptoe in my memory. When the jar and rack of the world are too discordant and jumbled, this little old church comes to my mind like a soothing poem set in sweet sounds.

" I call it my anthem in stone and I have wondered if those who built it ever thought that each small stone is as true and sweet and as holy and beautiful as any monolith of a mighty cathedral. St. Peter's and its dome, Milan and her hundred spires, may be oratorios, but as we sometimes prefer a twinkling star of the night to the great, glaring sun of the day, or a humble lyric to a grand and awful tragedy, so would I at times prefer to the world the little gray church, my anthem in stone." [145]

The spiritual values of Sandburg's writing may perhaps be characterized not as mighty carillons from magnificent cathedrals, but as the humble, quietly pervading tones from Religion's Cottage. These qualities have deservedly won him recognition among the churches of America. I personally know of sermons based upon Sandburg writings—even upon a single Sandburg poem.

In various phases of Sandburg poetry we perceive a synthesis of emotion and Biblical thought and a fused understructure of faith and hope :

" Shall there be now always
Believers and more believers ?...
Shall tumult, grandeur, fanfare, panoply, prepared loud noises
Stand equal to a quiet heart, thoughts, vast dreams
Of men conquering the earth by conquering themselves ? " [146]

The Reverend Norman Vincent Peale of Marble Collegiate Church of New York City has characterized Carl Sandburg as having " the quality of New Testament patience and Old Testament faith." [147]

The foregoing influences had their literary effect on Sandburg for varied reasons. Emerson first set forth and clarified the role of the poet in the evolution of America as a nation and in the formation of a national literature. He turned the poet's attention to the American theme, to the essential dignity of the American man and the common American tongue as a medium of literature. Whitman's message is partly a reproduction and also a furtherance of Emerson's creed; he set down in poetry many of the views of the New England transcendenialists. The New England poets experimented briefly with meter and verse form; Whitman experimented widely and set down in vigorous poetic statement and significance the teachings of the transcendentalis s. The sensitivity and immediacy of his verse helped to replace the intricate barriers of older diction and verse form, and it became an ardent voice of American democracy.

Sandburg's interest in the poets who share his own particular appreciation of these values is apparent not only in his readings in the literature of the American tradition but also in his avowed admiration for Villon and Hugo. Social questions, the democratic tradition, interest in the common man, lyricism and a flair for image-studded style were immediate points of contact between Sandburg and the earlier influential American poets. His deep faith in humanity and his religious background explain in part his adoption of a Biblical mood in certain poems. The social reformist fervor of Holy Writ and its strong moral protest find obvious echoes in his verse. These influences, along with the strong moral and political influence of Lincoln, led him to adopt his role as a poet of the American people, deliberately shouldering the task as outlined by Emerson and Whitman in a new and more universally comprehensible, or democratic, form.

Washington Post Portrait of Carl Sandburg by Ellsworth Davis.

PART II

CARL SANDBURG INTERPRETS AMERICA

I

ASPECTS OF AMERICA IN SANDBURG WRITING

The life of Carl Sandburg might be described as an evolutionary process, first of the assimilation of a young man of immigrant stock into a cosmopolitan society that itself was developing a national, American identity and consciousness; and then of a growing dedication to the national image, as conceived by a poet of varied gifts and distinctive cast of mind. The associations of his early life, his family, his economic difficulties, the association with Professor Philip Green Wright, the fellowship with political reformers, with journalists and with poets of similar mind and powers, all helped to mold a poetic endeavor regarded by many as uniquely American.

The image of America represented by Sandburg is therefore an expanding image; for as he grew older, some aspects were shed, others taken up, modified, colored. However he never lost contact with his early associates, never lost sight of the views of the labor groups as he became a journalist, lecturer, scholar and a national literary figure.

There is, in consequence, a marked evolution in his picture of America, but this is caused less by any changes in the man than by the fact that Sandburg lived in a changing America, which was evolving, feeling its growing pains, stumbling and groping to maturity. This pageant-like growth was shared by Sandburg and may be relived in his writings. He chronicles America's growth through one of the most formative periods in its history. Let us look at Sandburg's picture of America.

A. The Land

The setting for this national portrait is sketched both historically and geographically, with a fine sense of local color and Sandburg's characteristic picturesqueness of image.

" In the beginning was virgin land and America was promises." [148]

(a) *Topography*

As a poet with a talent for portraiture, the background of his native land naturally figured largely in his poems, a background that achieved a considerable degree of accuracy in detail of the large and varied topography of the United States.

> " The salt oceans press in
> And push on the coast lines....
> Rivers cut a path on flat lands.
> The mountains stand up." [149]

He paints the New England seacoast with " beaten seas, " and " gray winds which blew gray patterns of sleet on Plymouth Rock " [150] in Massachusetts at the time of the landing of the Pilgrims. In the poem " New Hampshire, " he paints New England's sleepy twilight hills, thin white birch trees, black winter waters and White Mountains.

In the lines of " North Atlantic " the poet gives us his impressions of the ocean after leaving the port of New York in 1918. One feels the fog, sea waves and sea winds; the sense of timelessness and immensity, and the great age of the body of water that forms the eastern boundary of the American continent. Another poem gives a dual perception of the "Sea Hold "—not only the fascination exerted on men's minds (including his own) but also the physical hold of the sea upon the coast lands; the locale of the poem is a narrow strip of coast land bordering Chesapeake Bay not far from Washington. The oyster boats, the clam boats and the white houses add the human touch to the otherwise impersonal atmosphere of the power of the ocean.

The Potomac River on which is situated the city of Washington is briefly portrayed in lines of imagery and symbolism in " Smoke Rose Gold. " Farther inland, the landscapes of Virginia, West Virginia and Maryland are pictured from Harper's Ferry in images which trace a moving, animate, visible sensation in the reader's mind.

> " The mountains stand up around the main street in Harper's Ferry.
> Shadows stand around the town, and mist creeps up the flanks of tall rocks.
> A terrible push of waters sometime made a cloven way for their flood here.
> There are the long curves of the meeting of the Potomac and the Shenandoah;
> There is the running water home of living fish and silver of the sun.
> The lazy flat rocks spread out browns for green and blue silver to run over...
> It is a meeting place of winds and waters, rocks and ranges." [151]

The Appalachian Mountains, " born a million years ago " [152] and the Pennsylvania coal mines enter the natural scene. Sandburg enjoys the use of language and he delights in painting such pictures as that of Niagara Falls:

" The tumblers of the rapids go white, go green
go changing over the gray, the brown, the rocks.
The fight of the water, the stones,
the fight makes a foam laughter
before the last look over the long slide
down the spread of a sheen in the straight fall.
    Then the growl, the chutter,
    down under the boom and the muffle —
              . . . . .
    this is Niagara." [153]

Ohio is pictured with " its fields of grape vines in the north," [154] its
Ohio River in the south, the river which the French found and named
La Belle Rivière. Ohio, Indiana, and a portion of Illinois were once a part
of the eastern forested region :

" Out of log houses and stumps—canoes stripped from the tree-sides—
flat boats coaxed with an ax from the timber claims—in the years
when the red and the white men met—the houses and streets rose." [155]

The Midwest, Sandburg's own background, may be found in numerous
poems. (A special section will be devoted to the prairie country.)

To the west of the Great Plains there stretches from north to south the
high range of the Rocky Mountains. Their geological origin is described
by Sandburg :

" Across Nevada and Utah
Look for the march of the hungry mountains.

They are cold and white,
They are taking a rest,
They washed their faces in awful fires,
They lifted their heads in heavy snows." [156]

In the Southwest lies " the gray Mojave desert level interrupted by the
Grand Canyon." [157] The origin of this awe-inspiring immensity of the
Grand Canyon Sandburg describes as :

" The power and lift of the sea
and the flame of the old earth fires under." [158]

Looking " down in its darkest depths, miles down, the Colorado River
grinds, toils, driving the channel deeper. Smooth as glass run the streaming
waters—then a break into rapids, into tumblers, into spray, into voices,
roars, growls, into commanding monotones that hunt for corners and
jumping-off places. And how should a beautiful, ignorant stream of water
know it heads for an early release—out across the desert, running below sea
level, to murmur its lullaby, and see the Imperial Valley rise out of burning
sand with cotton blossoms, wheat, watermelons, roses, how should it
know ? " [159]

The " tireless gray desert " [160] through which the river passes has been
set forth in " Santa Fé Sketches, " in " Slabs of the Sunburnt West "

and in " March of the Hungry Mountains." In the volume *Wind Song* is seen the physical environment of ocean and mountain of a city of the Pacific Coast :

> " San Francisco lay in silver tones
> and the Golden Gate swaddled
> in frames of blue mountains... " [161]

The topographical features of the American continent play a less important role in Sandburg writing than the life and occupations of the American people; but a considerable degree of portraiture is added to the total effect of the poetry by presentation of the physical aspects of the land. This portraiture is the backdrop against which he paints the human scene; it is the setting in which to place the characters of an evolving and changing America.

(b) *The Prairie Country*

The prairie has a special significance for Sandburg. To him it offers a vast poem symbolic of ethnographic origins, of the interrelationship of the many factors of democratic economy, and of the endowment of life; it is a poetry of wide diversifications, varying with the years and seasons, yet remaining the substantial voice of America. As the prairie is the heart-land of America, as it is the " mother of men, waiting," [162] so should its poetry be the mother of poetry, " before the cities come, " for in the long history of the prairie, born in the glacial age, " the stretch of a thousand years is short." [163]

With Sandburg's vivid images of prairie life, the song of its people, past and present, the eloquent evocation of its land and history, the prairie took form in verse; he invested it with a spiritual quality, and its people with a special significance in America. They became instinctive with the land—with the valley land watered by the Mississippi and its tributaries. This was a milestone in the Sandburg poetic career, for his prairie country had given him song which firmly established him as Poet of the Midwest. This hitherto unsung theme is recognized not only in the Midwest but across all America. In Boston, when in June 1955 Carl Sandburg was awarded the Poetry Prize at the Boston Art Festival for a new and unpublished poem, "Psalm of the Bloodbank," the award was made by the poet, Archibald MacLeish, Professor of Literature at Harvard University. In presenting the 500-dollar prize before an audience of 8,000 people, Professor MacLeish paid the following tribute which so well expresses American esteem :

" To Carl Sandburg, poet of the American affirmation, whose reply to doubt, to depression, to the failure of heart of those who dared no longer trust the people, was *The People, Yes.* Biographer of one war President, friend of another, Mr. Sandburg has been a participant in the history of his own troubled generation as well as the recorder of the great American trial. He has been the singer of the city where no one before him thought song could be found, and the voice of the prairie country which had been silent until he came, and all this continent is in his debt—a debt which Boston and New England, by this award, acknowledge." [164]

Galesburg is the county seat of Knox County, Illinois. The midwestern prairie stretches out beyond the city in every direction. One may drive great distances through this country and the topography remains the same. Long level stretches of country display their great riches of fertile, black soil, and in summer time, mile upon mile of tall green rows of growing corn. The Illinois sun, the rain and the soil, and the wisdom and industry of the Illinois landowner all combine to produce magnificent crops of grain, not only for human consumption, but for the livestock of the region. Nature has generously endowed this section of the midwestern prairie with the requisites for successful agriculture.

To Carl Sandburg the agricultural section of the Midwest was an inspiration. To him the quiet landscape was a challenge to lyricism. The long poem " Prairie " was his answer. This is acknowledged to be the finest evocation of the farm lands of the vast Midwest in all American literature. Some of the more conspicuous aspects of the prairie country dealt with in the poem may be noted in the following discussion.

In his celebration of the land, Sandburg has created an American epic poem. The poet speaks of the glacial age, the earth's eruptions into mountains and a broad prairie rising between the great mountain ranges of the East and the West; he recalls the " red deaths " [165] of war in the history of the prairie; the history of Indian tribes and wigwam smoke; the story of the tribes driven westward; he evokes the coming of the pioneers, the memory of log houses, of sod houses, of coonskin caps, of blizzards and "chinooks " let loose from Medicine Hat, of timber claims, of pioneer wagons; of deer, and cottontail and gopher; of wolf howls; of " lonely men on horses " [166]; of the rise of cities in the Midwest. He sings of the evolutionary tide of life from the primitive frontier to the modern age, from the "call of a wild duck of an earlier era, to the riveter's chatter, the song-whistle of the steamboat of today." [167]

" I am here before the cities come.

. . . . .

I am dust of men.

. . . . .

I am brother and mother
To the copper faces, the worker in flint and clay,
The singing women and their sons a thousand years ago
Marching single file the timber and the plain.

. . . . .

A thousand red men cried and went away to new places for corn and
    women : a million white men came and put up skyscrapers, threw out
    rails and wires, feelers to the salt sea : now the smoke stacks bite
    the skyline with stub teeth.

. . . . .

O prairie mother, I am one of your boys,
. . . . .
I am a brother of the cornhuskers who say at sundown :
Tomorrow is a day." [168]

Here is the inherent voice of song of Swedish forebears ! Just as proudly
as the poet Tegner celebrated the rivers and valleys and brooklets, the
forests and " high-horned reindeer," [169] the waving rye-fields, the Christian
spirit of the people of his beloved Sweden, so Sandburg celebrated the
prairie cornfields and the agricultural centers of the Midwest, the bravery
of the pioneer, the genius of the country's builders, the love of life in the
great open spaces.

Tegner, one of the greatest Swedish poets, and staunch lover of his land,
saw beauty and poetry in every manifestation and form of life on the land;
he saw poetry in its valleys, in its herds of cattle, in its meadows, its white-
fleeced flocks of sheep, in its strong and mettlesome horses stamping in their
stalls, tugging at the fodder, or charging like storm winds under the open
sky. Sandburg likewise sees a poetic theme in the prairie cattle waiting in
the dawn for the opening of the door of the milking barn; or as they grace
the landscape in the moonlight. Through his eyes we see the wagon loads
of "crimson purple balls of radishes," "the marching corn," [170] the
trumpet-vine blossoms, the potato hills, the mocking-bird's nest in summer;
the November sunset, the autumn leaves and the loosening of the cornhusks
by the sun, rain, wind and frost of fall. As a result of his sensitive perception
we hear the " O-be-joyful " [171] song of the mocking-bird; we inhale the
fragrance of fall-time apples and the smolder of autumn bonfires. Such
pictures are possible in Sandburg's verse, not only because he is gifted with
the talent of vivid interpretation, but also because he has studied these
images at their source. He has not only seen, through many years, the
inspirational themes of the Great Plains, but he has experienced them.
His long hours in Kansas wheat fields as a farm hand gave him insight into
the feel of handling a pitchfork in " the sunburn of the day "; [172] he knows
why " the pearl-gray haystacks in the gloaming are cool prayers to the
harvest hands "; [173] he knows from personal experience the " threshing
crews yelling in the chaff of the straw-pile and the running wheat of the
wagon boards "; [174] he has helped with the winter storage of fall apples and
vegetables. But Sandburg sees far more than beauty and poetry in the
blossom of the dandelion; in the delicate yellows of the buttercup; these
blossoms, together with the mushroom, the thistledown and the corn are
to him people of the fields, who rise to go silently away in the autumn; to
him the cawing of the crow, the drum of the woodpecker, the vermilion
streak of the redwing blackbird, have meaning; to him the chatter of the
birds in spring is the announcement of the new season of growth and
promise; the banners of growing corn and the marching army of the
crickets are songs of summer and the progress of the crops; there is a litany
in the running water of the streams; the smoothness of old stones speaks
remembrance of many rains and the long life of abundance of the prairie;
the march of the white mist across a valley speaks a friendly language; all

forms of prairie life delight him and call for translation or interpretation: even the anthills and the angleworms, the toad and the woodroaches hold memories; but he does not think merely of their color or form or beauty as his eye sees them; he studies their growth, their associations, and to him they come to have spirit and meaning and melody. It is this spirit, this meaning, and this melody which lift the Sandburg verse above the ordinary poem. In the words of Emerson : " The spirit which suffices quiet hearts, which seems to come forth to such from every dry knoll of sere grass, from every pine-stump, and half-imbedded stone, on which the dull March sun shines, comes forth to such as are of simple taste." [175]

The prairie country is for Sandburg the symbol of the pioneering spirit that built America; it represents also the visible signs of American origins and permanence and the creative power of human labor and enterprise in a democratic community. The imagery bespeaks movement and progress in a vivid natural setting.

The Sandburg gift for words and images in depicting the countryside compares with (perhaps even surpasses) the great talent of the Swedish Nobel Prize winner, Selma Lagerlöf. No one who has ever read her *Story of Gösta Berling* can forget her descriptions of her native Värmland—her portrayal of the beautiful blue lake Vänern, the rich plains and the blue mountains—" with these mountains, the plain which is peaceful and rich and loves work, wages a perpetual war, in a friendly spirit, however... The mountains send out long rows of hills and barren tablelands way down to the lake. They raise great look-out towers on every promontory and leave the shores of the lake so seldom that the plain can but rarely stretch itself out by the soft, broad sands. " [176]

Is there a special love of nature born in Swedish writers ? Harry Martinson has excelled in his prose painting of the Swedish countryside in *Vägen till Klockrike*. Gustav Fröding, one of Sweden's most famous lyric poets, wrote exquisite nature poetry. Albert Engström had the gift of writing excellent prose on nature. [Engström may have exerted the greatest Swedish literary influence on Sandburg who has studied and translated Engström writing.] Many other Swedish writers have shown special aptitudes in the portrayal of country life.

In Carl Sandburg, " nature is loved by what is best in him." [177] To him, as to Emerson, nature is a " differential thermometer, detecting the presence or absence of the divine sentiment in man." [178] " Every moment instructs, and every object : for wisdom is infused in every form." [179]

Importance of the Prairie in American Life

The fields of the Midwest arouse a response in the receptive, experienced mind of the poet; they speak to him of achievement; of the creative life of the soil; of love of the soil and love of the people who work with it; of pride in the freedom and peace of rural living; of joy in the creative power of country labor; of gratitude for its gifts. The production of corn and wheat is a translation of the spirit of American democracy for it speaks of the brotherhood and interdependence of the cities, the grain elevators and the prairie farms.

The people of the prairie have been essential to the economic life of America. They fed the boys who " went to France in great dark days." [180] Sandburg interpreted their vital importance in his celebration of the midwestern agriculturalists—his cornhuskers, his " harvest hands handling crops, singing dreams of women, woılds, horizons " his " farmboys driving steers to the railroad cattlepens " [181] and providing their contribution to the American food market. His " crowds of people at a Fourth of July basket picnic, listening to a lawyer read the Declaration of Independence "[182] are his interpretation of loyal prairie citizenry proud of democracy and determined upon its preservation.

Yet the prairie is far from being a mere gallery of events. Behind it is seen the basic matter of American life, the dignity of labor, the " virtue of the hoe and the spade for learned as well as unlearned hands." [183] Even the farm horses, the fences are images of the economic life of the district, the path of progress of prairie history:

" They are mine, the horses looking over a fence in the frost of late October saying good morning to the horses hauling wagons of rutabaga to market.
They are mine, the old zigzag rail fences, the new barbwire." [184]

Though pictorial in quality, these descriptions have rhythm, the persuasive spirit of exultation, and of optimism and faith in the future, as the poet speaks of new cities, new people, speaks of yesterday " as a wind gone down, a sun dropped in the west, " [185] and looks forward with confidence to " a sky of tomorrows.' "[186] The poem " Prairie " celebrates not only the land itself, but its people, their emotions, and feelings, and dreams of the future. Because of his emotional insight, Sandburg finds a sympathetic response in the reader. " To have great poets there must be great audiences too." [187] The poem " Prairie " has been commented on and appreciated by a wide cross section of society.

" Buffalo Dusk " interprets a section of past history of the frontier, of the relentless march of civilization into the realm of the Indian, of the buffalo, and the wild life of the wilderness and prairie, to build for present-day living:

" The buffaloes are gone.
And those who saw the buffaloes are gone.
Those who saw the buffaloes by thousands and how they pawed the prairie sod into dust with their hoofs, their great heads down pawing on a great pageant of dusk,
Those who saw the buffaloes are gone.
And the buffaloes are gone." [188]

Poems of the Poet's Personal Recollection of Prairie Life

There are other poems of nostalgic memories, such as " Hemlock and Cedar " in which the boy described in the poem is Carl Sandburg himself, while still a youth in Galesburg in Knox County on the prairie:

" Thin sheets of blue smoke among white slabs... near the shingle mill... winter morning.
Falling of a dry leaf might be heard... circular steel tears through a log.
Slope of woodland... brown... soft... tinge of blue such as pansy eyes.
Farther, field fires... funnel of yellow smoke... spellings of other yellow in corn stubble.
Bobsled on a down-hill road... February snow mud... horses steaming... Oscar the driver sings ragtime under a spot of red seen a mile... the red wool yarn of Oscar's stocking cap is seen from the shingle mill to the ridge of hemlock and cedar." [189]

The " two Swede boys " [190] in the poem " House " are young Carl and his brother Martin; the poem also pictures Swedish immigrants connected with the settlement of the Midwest; Sandburg repeats this theme and the conversation in the autobiography of his first twenty years, *Always the Young Strangers*. The Uncle Joe in the poem is the Civil War veteran, Joe Elser, who lived in an upstairs room of the Berrien Street home of the Sandburgs.

Passing beyond the early settlement of the prairie many poems interpret modern prairie life. Sandburg pictures the loam of the prairie earth, the woodland slopes, the spring grass, and fall crops. In the present picture he sees both birth and growth.

" The orchard here is near and home-like.
The oats in the valley run a mile.
Between are green and marching potato vines
... here romance stutters to the western stars." [191]

To the poet a quarter-mile field of grass, waving seeds ripening in the sun, speak a lesson of " luminous firefly lavender "; [192] a half mile of improved farm land in the Monon River corn belt could scarcely remember now that " once it had a great singing family of trees." [193] The man with his hunting dog in tall slough grass reflects the poet's love of the prairie in the line : " This is a proud place to come to." [194]

Thus in the prairie poetry we find far more than mere sense impressions. The poems convey messages and meanings of far greater depth than the visual impressions of beauty on the surface. Sandburg possesses the ability to present in these poems some of the attributes of American democracy. There are lessons to be read by those who look beneath.

Some of the clearest images in Sandburg prairie poetry are symbols of American democracy. In " Landscape " the current of public opinion is symbolized by the hills and soil " shaped to the water's way of learning "; the direction of voices governing the people is determined by the majority voice of the " biggest wind and the strongest water." [195]

Even in his interpretation of a field of ripening corn, this spirit of democracy appears :

" The wind and the corn talk things over together.
And the rain and the corn and the sun and the corn
Talk things over together." [196]

Short poems interpret the interdependence of social groups in the American economy. " Corn Prattlings " is a delightful four stanza poem of pleasing imagery descriptive of " the laugh of the yellow ears " [197] amid their dress of maroon silk and shades of green indicating the approach of the autumn. The wandering pumpkin stems, the fall winds, the rich earth lend color and atmosphere to the scene as " the ears laugh in the husks now," [198] for the big job of growing is completed. They have contributed their share to American life.

Partly because of his imagery, partly because of his symbolizing, personifying, animating approach to the subject, Sandburg's portrayal of the prairie scene becomes a picture of the human evolution, the material development, of America. It is a delineation of dedicated human activity in the growth of the nation.

(c) *Cities*

Origins and Growth

" Out of the prairie brown grass crossed with a streamer of wigwam
   smoke—out of a smoke pillar, a blue promise— ... here I saw a
   city rise." [199]

Carl Sandburg was born in that period of American development which brought the rise of great cities across the continent. In early American history the colonists had, for the most part, led agricultural lives. In the New England colonies the settlers made their living by using the natural resources of the section—the land and the forests; while some turned to shipbuilding and commerce because of proximity to the sea and because the forests supplied the required material. In the central and southern colonies the fertility of the soil made agriculture the most important occupation.

Most Americans of the early days lived on farms or in small villages. But in the days of the Industrial Revolution and the Lincoln era, the trend was toward industrial centers, and the large cities arose. New York had for some time been a large city, due to its location on the eastern seaboard to which most foreign commerce came and where the great waves of immigration arrived. In the decade of the birth of Carl Sandburg, New York had less than 1,500,000 inhabitants; but in the period 1870 to 1920 increased threefold — to 5,000,000.

In 1870, Chicago had but 300,000 inhabitants; in 1920 it had grown to nine times that number—2,700,000. This rapid rise of large centers of urban industry was a distinctive feature of nationwide American development, and these figures assist in our comprehension of the *Chicago Poems* of 1916.

"Omaha and Kansas City, Minneapolis and St. Paul, sisters...,
   growing up
Towns in the Ozarks, Dakota wheat towns, Wichita, Peoria, Buffalo,
   growing up." [200]

But as these cities fast became centers of dense population, civic problems
arose which had not faced the inhabitants of the farms and small villages
of earlier days. The housing problem became a very serious one, in some
places critical; for the surge of inflowing population forced people to live
in very crowded quarters, often in old buildings in bad repair. These tenement districts soon degenerated into squalid slums and became a menace
to public health and safety. Big business monopolies came into being as a
result of rapid industrialization; and they remained largely unconcerned with
the social problems they created. Organized labor was still in its infancy
and little was done to alleviate these conditions.

With the influx of workers leaving agriculture for industry and with
the arrival of thousands of immigrants from Europe seeking life in the
New World but unable to speak the English language, these problems
increased. Social settlements were established for the aid of non-English-
speaking immigrants.

Young children had not sufficient room in which to grow up normally in
such overcrowded conditions; and these situations constituted only a partial
list of the inadequacies of the swollen cities in the period of industrial expansion and disorientation. To remedy such defects, a movement arose among
workers themselves and among many liberal thinkers of the time, who pressed
for social and economic reform. Among these social critics was Sandburg.

Chicago

In that era of industrial maladjustments came Sandburg's famous
poem " Chicago. " A portion of the poem will show the substance :

" They tell me you are crooked and I answer : Yes, it is true I have
   seen the gunman kill and go free to kill again.
And they tell me you are brutal and my reply is : On the faces of women
   and children I have seen the marks of wanton hunger.
And having answered so I turn once more to those who sneer at this
   my city, and I give them back the sneer and say to them :
Come and show me another city with lifted head singing so proud to be
   alive and coarse and strong and cunning.
Flinging magnetic curses amid the toil of piling job on job, here is a
   tall bold slugger set vivid against the little soft cities;

   Bareheaded,
   Shoveling,
   Wrecking,
   Planning,
   Building, breaking, rebuilding.

Under the smoke, dust all over his mouth, laughing with white teeth,
Under the terrible burden of destiny laughing as a young man laughs,
Laughing even as an ignorant fighter laughs who has never lost a battle,
Bragging and laughing that under his wrist is the pulse, and under his
    ribs the heart of the people,
        Laughing !
Laughing the stormy, husky, brawling laughter of Youth, half-naked,
    sweating, proud to be Hog Butcher, Tool Maker, Stacker of Wheat,
    Player with Railroads and Freight Handler to the Nation." [201]

Thus does the poet brutally condemn Chicago; yet in this brutal portrayal
Sandburg sees that the sheer vigor that caused the squalor has as its reverse
side the sheer strength and vitality that can be effective in bringing about
the reforms needed. He is a realist in that he does not lose faith or sense
of proportion. Indeed, he exults at the thought of the city lifting itself out
of the mire by its own power.

    Again, in " Halsted Street Car " we note the tone of bitterness, of misery,
of irony, and at the same time of sympathy, as it voices a social protest
over factory conditions existing in Chicago in the early 1900's :

           " Come you, cartoonists,
           Hang on a strap with me here
           At seven o'clock in the morning
           On a Halsted Street Car.

           Take your pencils
           And draw these faces
              . . . . .
             Faces
           Tired of wishes
           Empty of dreams." [202]

    In " Subway " is a picture of industrial conditions :

           " Down between the walls of shadow
           Where the iron laws insist,
           The hunger voices mock.

           The worn wayfaring men
           With the hunched and humble shoulders,
           Throw their laughter into toil." [203]

    In " Clark Street Bridge " is portrayed the mass movement of a teeming
city. Sandburg dissects as with a delicate instrument the multitudinous
moods and sensibilities of the people passing over the bridge; we see the
weary and underprivileged painted with a brush of tenderness; we sense
also the note of vitality, prosperity, business and entertainment—a composite
of Chicago life in the " wagons and people going, all day wagons and
people." [204]

    Wide as is his sensitivity to the infinite varieties of human condition,
the main effect on the reader is not always a pleasing one. In fact, the

reverse can often be the case. The effect that overrides all others in the social poems is not a sense of artistic merit. It is an effect of *engagement* or enlistment in a cause. Sandburg paints a human situation and his poems of social comment leave the reader deeply conscious of the human repercussions and consequences of social maladjustments. In so doing he communicates his own sympathies. But along with all the pathos and deprivation of these neglected victims of society, he also communicates a resilient and challenging faith. This is Sandburg's achievement.

In these poems Sandburg achieved for Chicago what Whitman achieved for his beloved Manahatta (New York) and what Victor Hugo did for the *Misérables* of Paris. He transferred into poetic prominence a great metropolis, interpreting for us many facets of its society, but with particular emphasis on the underprivileged, the poor, the downtrodden, the underdog. From out of the great stormy maelstrom of its teeming masses, he drew for us the factory girl, the stockyard workers, the cabaret dancers, the weary toiler on his way to work, the shovelman in faded overalls spattered with clay, the teamster, the negro dancer with the " lazy love of the banjo thrum," [205] the sweating ditch-diggers, the railroad section hand, the stockyard worker's family, the expectant mother, Mrs. Gabrielle Giovannitti, the onion picker, who comes down Peoria Street with kindling wood on the top of her head; the crippled man ill with tuberculosis, Anna Imroth who lost her life in a factory fire, the green and gray streams of working girls moving in the early morning on the downtown streets; Mamie, who, tired of the small town, came to Chicago hoping to find romance and real dreams " that never go smash "; [206] the hoboes of cattle cars; the gipsy woman and others. These are symbols of a city overcrowded, symbols of industrial disorganization and frustrated humanity.

In contrast, in the poem " Skyscraper " we see Sandburg's lyric evocation of a great city of steel and iron, of great masses of men and women, a city of tall buildings which "loom in the smoke and sun " of day and the " smoke and stars of night," [207]—buildings that rise to carry on the city's business, and speak in terms of human personalities and ambitions, until they assume personality and spiritual " soul " :

> " Prairie and valley, streets of the city, pour people into it and they mingle among its twenty floors and are poured out again back to the streets, prairies and valleys.
> It is the men and women, boys and girls so poured in and out all day
> That give the building a soul of dreams and thoughts and memories." [208]

With imaginative power, the poet utilizes such a realistic theme as a high building and brings it to life : " Wires climb with secrets, carry light and carry words and tell terrors and profits and loves." [209] The skyscraper represents the conception of the architect and the labor of construction men and seems alive with meaning and purpose, alive with smiles and tears, secrets, business, and tons of letters that go bundled from the building to all parts of the world bearing messages from within its high walls. The poet voices pride in these towering structures and makes them a symbol of industrial progress.

He also takes pride in the importance of Chicago as an increasingly busy lake port :

" By the teeming docks
I watch the ships put out.
Black ships that heave and lunge
And move like mastodons
Arising from lethargic sleep.

They pass the pointed headland,
View the wide, far-lifting wilderness
And leap with cumulative speed
To test the challenge of the sea." [210]

Sandburg presents many pictures of Lake Michigan, the sand dunes of its shores, the harbor where " the shadows of the ships rock on the crest of the low blue lustre of the tardy and the soft inrolling tide," [211] the lake —" the blue burst of lake, long lake waves breaking under the sun on a spray-flung curve of shore," [212] the picnic boat with its " rhythmic oompa of the brasses playing a Polish folk-song," [213] the lake shore with the " lone gray bird, dim dipping, far flying, alone in the shadows and grandeurs and tumults of night and the sea and the stars and storms, and the mist, the impalpable mist." [214]

He gives us short lyrics of tenderness and perception such as " Lost " :

" Desolate and lone
All night long on the lake
Where fog trails and mist creeps,
The whistle of a boat
Calls and cries unendingly,
Like some lost child
In tears and trouble
Hunting the harbor's breast
And the harbor's eyes." [215]

Were it possible to discuss other poems here, we should see factories, slaughter houses, railroad trains, street cars, bridges, the harbor, the mill-doors—even the telephone wires—employed as symbols of human existence.

In the poems about Chicago Sandburg has also pictured for us such places as Lincoln Park in which are situated the bronze statues of General Grant and Abraham Lincoln; North Clark Street, Harrison Street Court, a lake-front stone residence, the flowers to be seen in parts of the city, and the bridges. He wished for his people more beauty and more of the better things of life, more of the joy of living. The sprawling, too swiftly growing metropolis is given us by the hand of a word artist who loved his Chicago, and was forced to paint its portrait with harsh and garish colors, at the same time mingling with them some of the softness and delicacy of pastels. He records not only the physical characteristics of the city but also the city's traffic, the silences of the city and the lake by night; he depicts the dreams and aspirations of men; the frustrations, disappointments, bitterness of failures; the apparent helplessness of the underprivileged; the squalor and drabness of tenement districts; the personalities and activities of business men and women; the business section in both its beauty and its ugliness; the secluded palace of the rich man; the pathos and poignancy of the old woman " far wandered waif of other days, " who " huddles for sleep in a doorway, homeless." [216] This far-reaching power of many-sided perception reminds the reader of François Villon. Especially in the *Chicago Poems* we detect the direct expression of the spirit of Villon, when Sandburg combines verse of social criticism with lyrics of the city and its people. The poet saw beauty in Chicago life and this he gives us in brief lyrics of tenderness and emotion; but he also saw injustices in the great seething industrial metropolis and this he gives us with brash and satirical roughness and protest, just as Villon did.

There is an element of the epic in this collective treatment of a city, with its industry, its bustle, its " mud and gold," [217] its evolution, its " human comedy, " as Balzac would term it. With the epic element there is combined an element of social humanitarian purposefulness, an acute sense of national need.

In contrast to the short poem " Chicago, " " Windy City " (published in his fourth volume) is a long historical pageant of Chicago, of the nature of an epic, revealing the story of the city and its spirit. Here Sandburg has achieved a fascinating portrait of the very inception of the city as a " hitching place for the pony express," [218] and as a mere spot on the river to which the Indians had given the name Shee-caw-go, or the river of the wild onion :

> " The lean hands of wagon men
> put out pointing fingers here
> picked this crossway, put it on a map,
> set up their sawbucks, fixed their shotguns,
> found a hitching place for the pony express
> made a hitching place for the iron horse,
> the one-eyed horse with the fire-spit head,
> found a homelike spot and said : ' make a home '
> saw this corner with a mesh of rails, shuttling
> people, shuttling cars, shaping the junk of
> the earth to a new city." [219]

The poet traces the history of Chicago from its obscure and primitive origins to its more recent situation of progress, of constant change, of industrial growth, of building, rebuilding, where

> " Now the roofs and smokestacks cover miles
> where the deerfoot left its writing
> and the foxpaw put its initials
> in the snow... for the early moccasins... to read." [220]

The emotions of the people, the expansion of the city, the rise of a great new library, the spirit of progress, the pride of the author are depicted as he writes elliptically and with typical thought association of " the pay-day songs of steam shovels ," " the wages of structural iron rivets, " of sky-scrapers as " parallelograms of night-gray watchmen." [221]

The enormity of size, the pathos of the monotony of scene, the pride of growth and achievement, the satisfaction of constant development are impressions given us by Sandburg as he writes :

" Tell it across miles of sea blue water, gray blue land :
I am Chicago. I am a name given out by the breaths of working men,
laughing men, a child, a belonging." [222]

Sandburg shows us two Chicago cities in this poem. One Chicago is that of " the respectable tax-payers who ride the street cars and read the papers, ... the respectable people with the right crimp in their napkins reading breakfast menu cards "; [223] the well-dressed customers of the haber-dashery shops, the stranger who comes to the city and sees only the tall skyscrapers, the parks, the monuments, the famous clock tower. It is a Chicago as seen by individuals insensible to anything except outward appearance.

The other Chicago is that of the short-change artist; and of that part of the city where " the children play the alley is Heaven... and there are no policemen in Heaven "; [224] where little children often are the victims of fast motor trucks; where young boys steal coal from a railroad yard; where strikes and strike-breakers battle with each other and the police must intervene; where monotonous houses go for miles on each side of mono-tonous streets until they reach the open prairie.

" Forgive the jazz timebeat
of clumsy mass shadows,
footsteps of the jungle,
the fang cry, the ripclaw hiss,
the slant of the slit eyes waiting.

Forgive us if we work so hard
And the muscles bunch clumsy on us
And we never know why we work so hard—
If the big houses with little families
And the little houses with big families
Sneer at each other's bars of misunderstanding." [225]

Thus there are two contrasting moods in the poem, a pattern that occurs in many other of his social commentaries : the somber mood of realism depicting " the clumsy mass shadows " and undertones, the mood of the symbolism of " dust and bitter winds "; [226] and the buoyant mood of exultation and joyous sensibility as the poet writes of the building progress providing employment—" the wheelbarrows grin, the wheelbarrows sing, the shovels and the mortar hoist an exploit, the stone shanks of the Monad-nock, Transportation, the People's Gas Building, stand up and scrape at the sky. " " The bevels and the blue prints talk it over," [227] great dreams are dreamed in the minds of the builders, great aspirations take shape, proud things arise; great bridges come, so designed as to permit the passage of ore boats and wheat barges; overland trains arrive from the far west, the far east, the south, from Canada, until Chicago becomes the largest railway center of the world; boulevards grace the city, more hotels are built, larger shops appear, and more and varied industries; more skyscrapers speak " their mountain language." [228]

The two contrasting moods—that of critical realism and that of joyous pride—are fused in a mood of hopeful anticipation for Chicago's future in the following lines:

" It is wisdom to think no city stood here at all until the working men,
    the laughing men came,
It is wisdom to think tomorrow new working men, new laughing men,
    may come and put up a new city—
Living lighted skyscrapers and a night lingo of lanterns testify tomorrow
    shall have its own say-so." [229]

The river panorama and the artist's conception of Chicago at night offer colorful portrayals as we read of " night gathering itself into a ball of dark yarn " and the yarn changing to " fog and blue strands, " of the streets becoming canyons swarming with the " red sand lights of sunset, " and of skyscrapers " gone to the gloaming." [230]

Chicago is a city of contrasts, and the poet, who truthfully portrays it, must paint the city on a wide canvas to interpret the chaos of contrast and change. The varied contrasts are symbolized in the conclusion. The poet having written of " the bitter winds in the undertones " of discontent, now summons in eloquent appeal — in behalf of the future of Chicago — young white spring winds " white as the arms of snowborn children, " the strength of " fighting winter winds " and the freshening, inspiriting " blue " * winds " off the blue miles of lake." [231]

" Carry your blue to our homes." [232]

Washington, A Symbol of American Democracy

If Chicago was a symbol of a specific social situation and of industrial and human dynamism, the poet's interpretation of the city of Washington conveys a very different impression, that of American history in the making, a conception of the people and the forces which have helped to mold the American nation and its form of government.

The poet's first glimpse of Washington was, as we have already noted, as a young soldier on a day's leave in 1898. For him, the points of chief interest were the Capitol building, the White House, Ford's Theatre and the Peterson House. As he walked past the White House he meditated, he later tells us, ** on the thoughts and responsibilities of President McKinley on whose shoulders rested the burden of the war with Spain. Already he

---

* In Sandburg writing, " blue " is symbolic of happy imagination.
** See *Always the Young Strangers*, pp. 410, 411.

had studied long and seriously the story of Abraham Lincoln as the President in the White House during the War of Secession (1861-1865), so that the White House and Capitol building were very familiar to him from within the covers of books. Now he saw them. He walked past the Peterson House to which Lincoln had been carried fatally wounded by an assassin's bullet fired in Ford's Theatre across the street. Ford's Theatre he looked at both from the outside and the inside. These two buildings were destined by their association with Lincoln to become Lincoln museums—shrines of American history. Young Sandburg was not yet a writer, but these were his formative years when he was laying up a vast storehouse of experiences, impressions and memories later to become literature. This was a portion of his preparation for writing, a part of the groundwork. History reflected in the city of Washington would later become poetry : the White House, the Capitol, Ford's Theatre and the Peterson House would later be incorporated in monumental biography.

In later years Sandburg did much Lincoln research in Washington, at the Library of Congress and elsewhere in that city; and he was even given presidential permission and encouragement to familiarize himself with the interior of the White House. Thus he wrote with first-hand authority and a deep sense of atmosphere when composing the four volumes of *Abraham Lincoln: The War Years*. The Lincoln desk, the Lincoln bed, the Lincoln office room, the dining room, all the great rooms of the White House became a part of his mind and writing. Even the portraits hanging in the main hall became fixtures in his memory. The exterior of the White House, its grounds and walks, its surroundings; the War Department, Post Office grounds, Treasury Department; the historic Willard Hotel, the Capitol grounds, the Senate and House wings of the Capitol; the New York Avenue Presbyterian Church (Lincoln's church), St. John's Church (church of the Presidents), and many other landmarks of official Washington became a part of his assimilative mind to be translated into both poetry and prose.

In poetry, Sandburg presents the city of Washington in quite a different manner from that of Chicago. He gives us an impressionist's view of Washington—its symbolism in the life of the nation—its significance and meaning in the history of America. Much could be said of its impressive beauty, its architectural charm, for it is one of the beautiful cities of the world; but Sandburg chooses to interpret the city in terms of what it represents as a capital; it is therefore a translation of spiritual values, of moral appreciation of Washington as a symbol of the American story.

In *The Prairie Years* Sandburg symbolically defines the city of Washington in terms of history and human progress as " built on something resembling an oath that the States, North and South, belonged together and should meet at a half-way point." [233] We are told briefly of the march of progress beyond the Allegheny Mountains, and of the gold rush to California and the settlement of the West; " until it was seen that the little city with the big white dome on the Potomac River would be the gathering place of men from states at distances staggeringly beyond anything in the dreams and plans of those who placed and laid out the city... in the mystic float of the Capitol dome rested some mystery of the Republic, something that people a thousand miles from the Potomac River believed in and were ready to make sacrifices for." [234]

The white dome of the Capitol was unfinished at the time of President Lincoln's inauguration but was finished and the statue of Freedom put in place atop the dome before his assassination; therefore the completion of the dome is associated with the history of the Civil War and with the preservation of the Union of the States and of America democracy. In " Tangibles " the poet poses the question:

" Can a dome of iron dream deeper than living men?
Can the float of a shape hovering among the tree-tops—can this speak
    an oratory, singing and red beyond the speech of the living men?
There is... something... here... men die for." [235]

The poem, " Washington Monument By Night " is devoted to General Washington, his part in the Revolutionary War in which American independence was achieved, and especially the terrible winter at Valley Forge when his indomitable will and perseverance kept the struggling Continental army together in the face of great suffering, intense cold and lack of food and clothing. The name of General Washington is not mentioned in the poem: however, the imagery and symbolism convey the name and its significance perfectly to every American. This is a very effective illustration of Sandburg's successful fusion of biography, history and poetry:

" The republic is a dream.
Nothing happens unless first a dream.

The wind bit hard at Valley Forge one Christmas.
Soldiers tied rags on their feet.
Red footprints wrote on the snow...
... and stone shoots into stars here.
... into half-moon mist tonight." [236]

The monument, figuratively depicted as a " lean swimmer diving into the night sky, " commemorates the aspiration of the Republic and is also a memorial to the " iron man " who fought as a general to found it and was honored by being elected its first president.

Springfield

The city of Springfield, Illinois, is also described in terms of its historical past and its importance as

" Abraham Lincoln's city,
Where they remember his lawyer's shingle,
The place where they brought him
Wrapped in battle flags,
Wrapped in the smoke of memories
The place now where the shaft of his tomb
Points white against the blue prairie dome." [237]

Much could be written of the importance of Springfield as the capital city of Illinois and the site of the executive mansion. (Sandburg himself was given a distinguished part in the inauguration of one of the governors). To the poet this city is preëminently identified as the home of Abraham Lincoln as lawyer, Illinois legislator and President-elect.

New York, The Metropolis of America

" In the evening there is a sunset sonata comes to the cities,
There is a march of little armies to the dwindling of drums.
The skyscrapers throw their tall lengths of walls into black bastions on the red west.
The skyscrapers fasten their perpendicular alphabets far across the changing silver triangles of stars and streets." [238]

Sandburg chose to put New York into verse—in much the same manner as he chose to write of Washington—impressionistically. In " Trinity Place " he writes of Trinity Churchyard as the burial place of Alexander Hamilton (Secretary of the Treasury under President Washington) and of Robert Fulton, inventor of the steamboat. The reader is impressed by the implication that too many of the rights and liberties of our government are today taken for granted. In the march of progress and civilization, modern America is prone to forget at what cost of individual effort, sacrifice and devotion to ideals the great men of an earlier era brought about the achievements of today.

" In this yard bundle boys, scrubwomen, sit on the tombstones and walk on the grass of graves, speaking of the war and weather, of babies, wages and love.

An iron picket fence... and streaming thousands along Broadway sidewalks... straw hats, faces, legs... a singing, talking, hustling river... down the great street that ends with a sea.
... easy is the sleep of Alexander Hamilton.
... easy is the sleep of Robert Fulton.
... easy are the great governments and the great steamboats." [239]

The poem on the New York Woolworth Building (written in the 1920's) has several meanings. First of all, the building is a symbol of human progress, a symbol of the creative genius in the mind of man. It represents a dream in the mind of Mr. Woolworth and an achievement by the designers, blueprint men, engineers and construction men :

" There it was; his dream; all true;
The biggest building in the world.
Babel, the Nineveh Hanging Gardens,
Karnak, all old, outclassed.
. . . . .
It's a dream; all true; going somewhere." [240]

Such a great building was made possible by the purchases of the common people, the millions who buy from the many Woolworth stores the multitude of comparatively inexpensive articles on sale in them. Another facet of meaning is that of the instability of things, for the Woolworth Building has now been surpassed by the Empire State Building. And lastly there is an undercurrent of social criticism of the accumulation of vast wealth as opposed to the frugality which must be observed by others.

Similarly, in "Three Slants at New York" the poet gives differing interpretations of the city. This poem was also written in the 1920's and the date is important, for since then great changes have been made in housing conditions, in industrial conditions, in social legislation in this city, which had grown too rapidly to allow improvements commensurate with the population increase. In the 1920 poem New York is briefly presented as seen from the viewpoint of the poor of the tenement districts; as seen by those who seek the night life and night clubs of New York; and as it symbolizes the accomplishment of human effort and promise :

> "There is a rose and gold New York of evening lights and sunsets; there is a mist New York seen from steamboats, a massed and spotted hovering ghost, a shape the fists of men have lifted out of dirt and work and daylight and early morning oaths after sleep nights. There is a rose and gold mist New York." [241]

In "Night Movement—New York" we are given various aspects of the busy life which does not stop with the end of the day :

> "In the night when the trains and wagons start from a long way off
> For the city where the people ask bread and want letters,
> In the night the city lives too—the day is not all." [242]

The overcrowded 1920 period of New York life is summarized by the line wherein Sandburg writes of the bronze statue of Christopher Columbus as "the center of a turmoil of traffic from world ends gathered on Manhattan Island." [243]

A later poem published in 1953, is "This Street Never Sleeps." Here is presented the spirit of Forty-Second and Broadway, New York, with its great throngs of hurrying humanity :

> "At the corner
> of Forty-Second and Broadway
> it is feet and wheels
> wheels and feet
> far in the morning." [244]

In these poems Sandburg employs a technique that is multi-dimensional. A city or a skyscraper is viewed from a variety of standpoints; it is viewed pictorially, lyrically, and also with human overtones as the object described acquires characteristics and nuances associated with the humans whose activity it represents. It is viewed with historical or evolutionary dimensions as the object is transferred from a static point in time to that of growth and change : from this viewpoint it is a promise of the future :

> " — one tall skyscraper is torn down
> To make room for a taller one to go up,
>
> . . . . .
> To speak a living ' hello ' to the open sky." [245]

American cities are thus set by Sandburg not merely in the present, nor even in his own lifetime, but in a shifting complex of time and evolution, in which human activity and resourcefulness transfuse them with significance and tradition.

Contributions of the Cities to American Life

The foregoing discussion of Chicago, Washington, New York and Springfield illustrates four of America's great cities as celebrated by Sandburg. But he has also placed in verse the names of other great cities across the continent—cities with tall buildings—

> " Steel and concrete witnesses gazing down in San Antonio on the little old Alamo,
> Blinking across old Quaker footpaths of the City of Brotherly Love; shooting crossed lights on the old Boston Common;. . .
> Rising in Duluth to flicker with windows over Lake Superior, standing up in Atlanta to face toward Kenesaw Mountain,
> Tall with steel automotive roots in Detroit, with transport, coal and oil roots in Toledo, Cleveland, Buffalo, flickering afar to the ore barges on Lake Erie,
> Wigwagging with air beacons on Los Angeles City Hall, telling the Mississippi traffic it's night time in St. Louis, New Orleans, Minneapolis, and St. Paul." [246]

The importance of Omaha to the American economy is brought out in a brief poem named for this city on the Missouri River, which is the center of a large food production area. Omaha " feeds armies, and works to get the world a breakfast." [247]

As he witnessed the phenomenal growth of great cities throughout America, Sandburg analyzed the various reasons for their development. Primarily, of course, the large cities arose with the upsurge of an industrial economy, special factors contributing in many instances to the development. The poet has designated various cities as the products of special technical and economic factors and also as the products of transport and communications facilities—Pittsburgh, Cleveland, Gary, Allegheny, Youngstown, Birmingham and other cities owing their importance to steel and iron. Many cities of the West and Far West are centers of cattle-raising districts. Kansas City and Chicago became shipping centers for the live stock of these districts. Detroit, because of its strategic location in a lake system of navigation and its proximity to the iron ore regions, became the center of the automobile industry; Duluth became an important lake port for the shipment of the iron ore of its region. New York, Boston and Philadelphia initially rose to prominence because they were strategic sea ports. In the

Sandburg poems on New York the emphasis is on the traffic crowds arriving by sea from all over the world and on the commercial shipping with boats arriving by ocean and by two rivers. Thus the poet successfully identified American cities with their industrial or economic importance. His identification of Chicago as " hog-butcher of the world " [248] is generally recognized and accepted, and it very often appears in print in quotation marks—even in analytical accounts of American cities or industries or American life. Max Lerner for example, used it (in quotation marks) in his comprehensive volume, *America As A Civilization*.

America's cities are a very vital component of national life. Sandburg has given them a correspondingly important place in his poetry. To him a city is not merely a name or a place on the map; it is an aspect of American civilization contributing not only to the industrial and economic development of the nation but also to its cultural development.

Smaller Cities

The smaller cities which are closer to nature have a great fascination for the poet. He grew up in the small city of Galesburg, and to this city he devoted an entire book—the autobiography of his first twenty years, bearing the title *Always the Young Strangers*. The little city which he chose for his home in 1946 is Flat Rock, North Carolina, a city of beautiful homes, of cultured and interesting people, kindly and upright citizens, and of magnificent mountain scenery.

Sandburg characterizes the smaller cities and towns of America as having a general similarity to one another. Their citizenry is composed of substantial people who live more simply than city dwellers; here are to be found greater freedom, more room; the streets are uncrowded, life goes on at a more moderate pace; there is a baseball park; there are churches with spires; there are schools, quite often colleges; there are offices of professional men; there are superintendents of streets; a post office, a city hall; there are factories and grocery stores; Main Street runs through the center of the city; life is lived more quietly, but more fully. At the same time the passenger trains stop here, hurrying from the East, hurrying on to Chicago or to the speedmakers of Detroit or on to the great spaces of the West. By means of these speeding trains and through the local newspapers carrying dispatches from all the corners of the world, the small city has its wider contacts. It is in these smaller cities that the poet believes he " hears America "; [249] they are closer to the soil, which is the essential substructure of any country; there are many more small cities than capital cities or metropolitan centers, and more average Americans dwell in them; they more nearly represent a *genus Americanum*. They are composed of full-fledged citizens and voters, with more time to analyze questions of politics and economics, to study the trends, to search for answers, to enjoy social contacts. To the youth of the smaller cities there may come an irresistible desire to see the rest of the world; yet upon their return, their opinion is frequently that the rest of the world bears a very great resemblance to the small city of their origin.

The small cities where ordinary life is lived in a more ordinary manner are typified in the poem " The Sins of Kalamazoo," where the sins are " neither scarlet nor crimson " [250] but are of a drab tone; where more social contacts and interchanges of opinions permit a more genial existence, where there is less political pressure, where substantial merits are to be found in substantial ordinary citizens close to the elements of earth, air and sky; and where the uncontrolled and undirected voice of America, thinking independently, speaks for itself.

This " Kalamazoo " poem was written before 1920 and represents the poet's opinion at that time. In the poem he predicts the decline of small cities. In the early part of the twentieth century the small city was generally considered representative of what was characteristically American. But as the large cities continued to develop the small towns began to diminish in importance; and in the second quarter of the century a decisive turn of the currents of American energy has been in the direction of larger cities. The power of big city business and industry, the glamor of big city life, the big social changes and transportation changes have brought about the decline of the small town. Today there is a reaction in the direction of suburban life—hence a tendency toward a fusion of aspects of the small town and the large city. Thanks to greatly improved communications, the various sections of the far-reaching American nation have become much more closely united in thought and spirit. Sandburg's " Chicago Dynamic " (1959) indicates this fusion, as we shall see later, and the larger cities are now representative of American progress.

Many Names of Ethnographical Origin

It is interesting to note the broad scope of Sandburg's knowledge of cities and towns. Even the most isolated communities are deserving of poetic acknowledgment. Much color is given by his mention of the unusual names of the more remote communities where the designations derive from the North American Indians. These names have been proudly retained even in the large cities where the land once belonged to Indian tribes. Among such names are Kalamazoo, Omaha, Shenandoah, Chickamauga, Pottawatomie, Oklahoma, Waukesha and Sioux City. Under the title " Localities," Sandburg lists some of the unusual names of remote places, some of which he had seen. Among them are Death Valley, Hasiampa Valley, White Pigeon, etc.

" Wagonwheel Gap is a place I never saw
And Red Horse Gulch and the chutes of Cripple Greek.

. . . . .

On the Pecatonica Rivers near Freeport
I have seen boys run barefoot in the leaves
Throwing clubs at the walnut trees
In the yellow and gold of the autumn,
And there was a brown mask dry on the inside of their hands." [251]

In " Windy City " Sandburg writes of the schoolboy listening to " how the Pottawatomies...

> and the Blackhawks... ran on moccasins...
> between Kaskaskia, Kankakee, and Chicago." [252]

At the conclusion of the same poem are lines of distinctive local color :

> " Winds of the Windy City, come out of the prairie,
>   all the way from Medicine Hat.
> Come out of the inland sea blue water, come where
>   they nickname a city for you." [253]

(d) *Industries*

Industry is one of the great forces which have contributed to the strength of America; and Sandburg has chosen to interpret that force in poetry, notably in the long poem " Smoke and Steel." Sandburg here pays tribute to the patriotism and devotion of the workers in the sheet-steel mills and rolling mills and to the great importance of this gigantic industry. This poem is a pageant of steel that takes the reader into the very shops and factories of war-time—into the innermost workings of the mills. The poet has hooked his arm in that of a worker, learned the idiom of the steel mill, observed its multiple processes and, figuratively, he takes us with him. In his vivid picture we witness the fire and dust of the furnaces, the red dome of the ovens and the cindery sleeves of the workmen who toil grimly as they face " the buckets of fire exploding or running wild out of the steady ovens " and we see " the sleeping slag foam from the mountains " [254] transformed into molten metal :

> " A bar of steel—it is only
> Smoke at the heart of it, smoke and the blood of a man,
> A runner of fire ran in it, ran out, ran somewhere else,
> And left—smoke and the blood of a man
> And the finished steel, chilled and blue.
> So fire runs in, runs out, runs somewhere else again,
> And the bar of steel is a gun, a wheel, a rail, a shovel,
> A rudder under the sea, a steering-gear in the sky;
> And always dark in the heart of it and through it,
>   Smoke and the blood of a man.
>   . . . . .
> In the blood of men and the ink of chimneys
> The smoke nights write their oaths." [255]

As Emerson counseled, Sandburg has " grasped the hand " of the steel worker and taken his place beside him to be taught and to become " vocal with speech "; and in so doing he has " extended his dominion " and has been instructed " in eloquence and wisdom." The steel mill has been a " dictionary," [256] has given him insight into its manufactures; has given him the viewpoint both of labor and management—with the result that he has expressed its atmosphere, its place in industry and the war effort more completely than has any other writer. At the same time, with his particular art, the part and the whole became fused and the significance of this economic giant which, in a very real sense, is the backbone of national industry can be sensed all the way down to the most basic of operations.

The poem " Smoke and Steel " partakes of the epic in its presentation of the far-reaching localities of the steel industry and its importance in the growth of the cities, the growth of the nation and its significance to the Allied Armies in World War I. From the united industrial effort in the steel mills came the railway box cars for the transportation of wheat, corn, cattle; fruit from the West and South; freight loads of automobiles from Detroit; freight loads of the materials of war going to Europe—jeeps, guns, tanks, food. From the steel mills came the girders for bridges, steam-shovels and many war-time necessities.

To a lesser degree, other industries are introduced into Sandburg poetry and serve as an illustration of the importance of urban industry in American life. Chicago leads the world in the meat-packing industry, and typifies as a " Player with Railroads and the Nation's Freight Handler " one of the world's greatest railroad centers. Sandburg had ample opportunity to study industry connected with railroads, for his father, throughout his life, was an employee of the Chicago, Burlington and Quincy Railroad shop in Galesburg; therefore the poet had first-hand knowledge of railroad industry conditions.

One of the most poignant poems of the Chicago days was " Child of the Romans," which portrays the railroad section-hand as he stopped at noon to eat his humble meal of bread and bologna and saw the train whirl by—a Pullman train in which men and women were dining on steaks and strawberries at tables on which stood beautiful bouquets of roses and jonquils. The poem further portrays the duty of the section-hand to keep the road-bed so smooth that the

> ... " roses and jonquils
> Shake hardly at all in the cut glass vases
> Standing slender on the tables in the dining cars." [257]

The lake shipping industry is depicted in many poems in which the docks, the workmen, the steamers and the lake itself are described. Those who work in the construction of the skyscrapers are described; as are also dynamiters, the truck-drivers, the shovel-man and the bricklayer.

Urban industry is dependent on the labor of the people of the cities, even though it is becoming more and more mechanized. The industrial life of a city, in the final analysis, is a reflection of the life of a section of its people, and this portion of the urban population reflects the nature of the city's industries. The two factors are indispensable to each other in the economic scheme of things :

> " It is wisdom to think the people are the city.
> It is wisdom to think the city would fall to pieces
> and die and be dust in the wind
> If the people of the city all move away and leave no people at all to watch
> and keep the city.

The city is a tool chest opened every day,
a time clock punched every morning,
a shop door, bunkers and overalls
counting every day.

The city is a balloon and a bubble plaything
shot to the sky every morning, whistled in
a ragtime jig down the sunsets.

Everyday the people get up and carry the city,
carry the bunkers and balloons of the city,
lift it and put it down." [258]

Poetry of Industrial Criticism

Gary, Indiana (not far from Chicago), is an industrial city identified
with the manufacture of steel. Sandburg's first poetry of protest against
the steel industry was the poem " Mayor of Gary " written in 1915 on the
subject of the exploitation of the workmen in the mills. In the poem we
find irony, a spirit of criticism, and the challenge to human conscience which
characterized so many of the early Sandburg poems:

" ' Go into the plants and you will see the men doing nothing—machinery
does everything', said the Mayor of Gary when I asked him about
the 12-hour day and the 7-day week.

. . . . .

And I said good-bye to the Mayor of Gary and I went out from the
city hall and turned the corner into Broadway.
And I saw workmen wearing leather shoes scruffed with fire and cinders,
and pitted with little holes from running molten steel,
And some had bunches of specialized muscles around their shoulder
blades hard as pig-iron, muscles of their forearms were sheet steel
and they looked to me like men who had been somewhere." [259]

When we consider the much improved present-day industrial conditions
in American mills and factories it is difficult to imagine the conditions which
existed at the beginning of the century. Yet records prove that a seventy-
two-hour work-week existed in the steel industry until 1923. Exploitation
of workers was rife with the arrival of thousands of men and women from
the farms seeking work in the mills and with the arrival of millions of
immigrants who provided an abundant labor force accustomed to lower
living standards. In addition to the requirement of long work hours, the
industry included physical hazards; fatal accidents were not unknown. In
" Psalm of Those Who Go Forth Before Daylight " the poet describes the
steel workers returning home after the long day, as " brothers of cinders." [260]
Since adequate labor laws were not yet in force there were shop gate battles
of strikers and strike breakers and occasional deaths from these battles.
Sandburg exposed to his generation the fatigue, exploitation and degrada-
tion of the workers as well as the dangers existing in the steel works during
this transitional phase of growth.

Among industrial conditions attacked by Sandburg was insufficient protection against fire hazards. There is a fusion of poignancy and protest in the poem, " Anna Imroth, " named after the girl whose death in a factory fire was the result of lack of fire escapes.

In railroad industry there was ample cause for criticism. We recall that the poet's father, August Sandburg, in the previous century had worked all his life ten hours a day for fourteen cents an hour. He had worked cheerfully and steadily; and without any complaint as to the industrial situation, he had managed, with the help of his son, to support the family and to become a home owner. Living costs rose in the twentieth century, but labor and management were still far apart in the industrial and economic structure of American social history when Carl Sandburg in 1918, published the poem " Southern Pacific " :

" Huntington sleeps in a house six feet long.
Huntington dreams of railroads he built and owned.
Huntington dreams of ten thousand men saying : Yes, sir.

Blithery sleeps in a house six feet long.
Blithery dreams of rails and ties he laid.
Blithery dreams of saying to Huntington : Yes, sir.

Huntington,
Blithery, sleep in houses six feet long." [261]

Perhaps in no other poem has Sandburg so successfully combined industrial and social satire with the image of Death as the ultimate leveler of democracy. The poem portrays the early days of the rise of great industry when the business Titan occupied a position of materialistic superiority, and was treated with servility by his " ten thousand " employees.

The foregoing instances serve to show some of the tone of Sandburg's protest against industrial conditions of the early part of the century and how the people of industry spoke through him.

Since then the labor scene and working conditions have been transformed out of all recognition. There have come minimum wage laws, the National Labor Relations Act, the Taft-Hartley Act and other national acts pertaining to the relations of labor and management in industry. American government has always permitted open criticism by the members of its social structure. America is a society adhering to a policy of self-criticism. Carl Sandburg's position as a poet has been partially due to his protest against social and industrial conditions in need of correction. Emerson once said : " What the poetic youth dreams, prays, and paints today, shall presently be the resolutions of public bodies, then shall be carried as grievance and bill of rights through conflict and war, and then shall be triumphant law and establishment for a hundred years, until it gives place, in turn, to new prayers and pictures." [262] In allying his poetry with public issues, Sandburg has played an important role in espousing these public issues and forcing men to think and to realize what they were doing in accepting or imposing such conditions.

B. The People

However devoted Sandburg may be to the beauties and wonders of nature, to objective nature, it is nevertheless human nature which is the greater challenge to his literary energies. People and the affairs of human life constitute his greatest interest.

He delineates the many types of human personality which compose "the grand canyon of humanity" [263] that is American democracy. Because America is vast, and because its form of government is far-reaching in its implications, the concept of American democracy is not easy to define. It certainly cannot be defined in a short or simple sentence. One of the most successful of recent attempts at definition, that by Max Lerner, sets out the field which has preoccupied Sandburg. Lerner writes:

"American democracy may be defined as the institutions through which, and the social and moral context in which, the collective will can best be organized for the life purposes inherent in all human striving. It is the image that moved Whitman to his glimpses of democratic vistas, and Sandburg to set down the tall tales and the affirmation of *The People, Yes...* There are two major meanings—or better, a double aspect of meaning—of the idea of democracy. In one aspect it is free or constitutional government, a going system for assuring the safeguards within which the will of the people can express itself. In this phase—set off the more sharply because of the rise of the new totalitarianisms—the emphasis is on the natural rights of the individual and the limited powers of government, on the separation of powers, on civil liberties, on the rule of law, and the protection of freedom and property against the arbitrary encroachments of the state.

"In the second aspect the democratic idea is egalitarian. It emphasizes the rule of the majority. It presents the spectacle of a demos unbound, a whole people striving however imperfectly to make social equality a premise of government. It stresses the conditions for putting within the reach of the ordinary man the opportunities of education and the making of a living, regardless of his confessional faith, his ethnic group, and his social level...

"To round out the meaning of American democracy, a third factor must be added to that of individual freedom and of mass participation in the democratic process. It is the element of a moral sensitivity to the tragic human experience. America has the potential for this in the fact that one of the great sources of its democratic thinking is the Biblical tradition of Puritanism, including both the Old Testament passion for justice and the Christian allegory of love." [264]

Respect for the individual human spirit has been a part of the Sandburg personality since the college days of his Galesburg youth. It has intensified with the years.

In this particular respect, the Sandburg viewpoint is in accord with that of Whitman—but the former generally surpasses Whitman in treating the subject of the human mind and the human personality: just as before

Whitman, Emerson had exalted the individual—both in poetry and prose. In his sage and temperate essay on "Politics," Emerson declared:

"To educate the wise man the State exists... Truly the only interest for the consideration of the State is persons. The highest end of government is the culture of men; and if men can be educated, the institutions will share their improvement and the moral sentiment will write the law of the land.

"Under the dominion of an idea, which possesses the mind of multitudes, as civil freedom, or the religious sentiment, the powers of persons are no longer subjects of calculation. A nation of men unanimously bent on freedom, or conquest, can easily... achieve extravagant actions, out of all proportions to their means; as the Greeks, the Saracens, the Swiss, the Americans and the French have done." [265]

In 1855 came the more verbose statements of Whitman:

"Democracy feeds the highest mind, the soul. Man, so diminutive, dilates beyond the sensible universe, competes with, outcopes space and time, meditating even one great idea. Thus, and thus only, does a human being, his spirit, ascend above, and justify, objective Nature, which is incredibly and divinely serviceable... The shows and forms presented by Nature, the beautiful in living men and women, the actual play of passion in history and life—and from those developments, either in Nature or human personality, in which power transacts itself—out of these, the poet projects their analogies in literature." [266]

In 1953 came these words of Sandburg:

"The hammers of man from stone to steel,
the fire of man from pine flare to blowtorch,
the lights of man from burnt wood to flash bulb,
clew readings of man from hill fire to radar shadings,
the fights of man from club and sling
     to the pink mushroom of Hiroshima,
the words of men from spoken syllables
     to rushing rivers of books begetting books,
     to speech and image transmissions
     crowding the day and the night air
     for the looking and listening Family of Man—
the tools of man ever foretelling tools of new faces
     to be given new names—
     . . . . .
and man goes on a moon shooter." [267]

Sandburg shares with Emerson and Whitman a belief in the high potentialities of American democracy, and he shares with Emerson an awareness of possible pitfalls, whereas Whitman's early democratic views were those of an idealist. He wrote in a letter to Emerson to whom he sent a copy of his first thirty-two poems (the initial edition of *Leaves of Grass*): "The instincts of the American people are all perfect, and tend to make heroes." [268]

But shortly before the Civil War he became somewhat disillusioned. He realized that his ideal democracy based on perfect instincts did not yet exist. In 1856 he published his angry, bitter " Respondez ! "—a poem so ironic that he later sought to expurgate it from his *Leaves of Grass*.

Emerson's probing intellect sought to inquire, to challenge, even to protest. He saw the rising tide of industrialism which might envelop the individual; and against this threat of industrialism to the human dignity of the individual his voice was the clearest in his generation. His theory of democracy was not that of an uncritical idealist. Sandburg saw the individual oppressed by industry and the machine age; and in the tradition of Emerson and Thoreau he rose to the defense of the individual against the early injustices of an industrialized age. He voiced his faith in human advancement. He painted society as he found it. He traced its sociological, political and moral core with insight—but with a sense of evolution. Cities, the country, institutions, as we have seen, were for him primarily, reflections of their human content, a study of American man as seen by the poet.

Through the pages of *The People, Yes*, the people are metaphorically presented in many forms, as a polychrome; a console organ of changing themes; a mammoth resting between his cyclonic dramas; a sleeper, a waker; as fog, as a vast huddle with many units, as the grand canyon of humanity; as Pandora's box, as an avalanche; as a mountain slope holding a volcano of retribution, slow to gather wrath, slow but persistent in its onward heave and progress; as a builder, a wrecker, a builder again, a juggler, as a reservoir of the human reserves that shape history, as a monolith, a mover and a desperate hoper. Some of the finest Sandburg imagery and symbolism portray the American community, extol the idealistic concept of equality, but more particularly present the broad panorama of American civilization. While Sandburg in his verse may be the poet of the city and of the prairie, and of nature, he is undeniably a sympathetic poet of the people. Images of American people and places pass before the reader, and they extensively mirror the American scene.

(a) *Ethnological Origins of America*

To read Sandburg is to follow much of the moral, economic and human history from American foundations to the present day, with the period of his own life sharply defined.

The Spanish colonization period in the American Continent is evoked in " Santa Fé Sketches ". Sandburg endows the valley of Santa Fé with personality, giving it speech, thought, and memories of four hundred years :

> " Have I not seen the guns of Spain, Mexico
> and America go up and down the valley? " [269]

The valley witnessed Navajo Indians riding " with spears and arrows ", and Spaniards riding " with blunderbusses." [270] In " Santa Fé Sketches " there have entered references to the historical and cultural influence of the Spanish on the history of the Southwest, by the " pearl swords of conquest," [271] by the mixture of Spanish blood with that of the resident Navajo

Indian tribes, by the establishment of Christianity in the form of the Catholic religion, by the establishment of missions and churches, by the introduction of the cattle industry, new farming practices, new fruits and grains, and by the introduction of Spanish forms of architecture. These memories are centuries old but they are indelible in the history of southwestern United States, and the poet has vivified them in his evocation of Santa Fé and its valley. The Spanish influence is still to be seen in portions of the Southwest.

The English settlers in Virginia are referred to in the poem " Cool Tombs," and to a greater extent in prose. The English in the Massachusetts settlements Sandburg has described at length as the most influential colonists in the beginnings of America. These colonists will be discussed separately.

The French explorations in the New World also played an important part in American history. In 1673 Louis Joliet and Father Marquette reached the Mississippi River; and in 1682 Lasalle sailed down the Mississippi, claiming all its valley for France. In the poem " Joliet " Sandburg has celebrated the city named for the French explorer, and the geological origin of the river valley where the city is situated:

> " Talons of an iceberg
> Scraped out this valley.
> Claws of an avalanche loosed here." [272]

Nor has Sandburg neglected the original inhabitants—the Indians. The Spanish, the French and the English, each of them, invaded the lands of the Indians. The poet perceives the pathos and sadness of the plight of the red man, the victim of advancing civilization of the white man. This is one of the least publicized, one of the less lustrous chapters in American history; its poignancy, its tragedy, its record of reluctant abandonment of homeland and hunting ground by the Indian as he was pushed slowly farther inland—all these are compressed in the beautiful, wistful imagery of the poem " Early Moon." Here appears the sense of fantasy inherited by Carl Sandburg from his Swedish forebears. Just as the Norsemen called the rainbow *The Bridge of the Gods*, so Sandburg names the early moon a " silver papoose canoe of the Indian West." The poem is symbolic of the primitive history of America.

" Early Moon "

" The baby moon, a canoe, a silver papoose canoe, sails and sails in the Indian West.
A ring of silver foxes, a mist of silver foxes, sit and sit around the Indian moon.
One yellow star for a runner, and rows of blue stars for more runners, keep a line of watchers.
O foxes, baby moon, runners, you are the panel of memory, fire-white writing tonight of the Red Man's dreams.
Who squats legs crossed and arms folded, matching its look against the moon-face, the star-face, of the West?

Who are the Mississippi Valley ghosts, of copper foreheads, riding wiry
ponies in the night? — no bridles, love-arms on the pony necks,
riding in the night a long old trail?
Why do they always come back when the silver foxes sit around the
early moon, a silver papoose canoe, in the Indian West? " [273]

No Scandinavian saga could have presented more beautiful imagery
of nature, given more meaningful glimpses of the early history of the
" copper foreheads," or symbolized with more delicate pathos their story
before Indian Land Reservations for permanent homes were set apart by
national legislation.

(b) *America in 1620*

The Pilgrims

The Plymouth colonists of New England have been accorded recognition
in poetry by Sandburg in a moving tribute which could well serve as a
Thanksgiving reading at a celebration of that national holiday. The tribute
is in commemoration of the " Pilgrims in tall hats, the Pilgrims of iron
jaws " who, after drifting for months on beaten seas, " were glad and sang
to God " [274] for such food as nature in a new land could give them. An
evocation and prayer of thanks conclude the tribute.

The life of the Plymouth colonists is set forth in considerable detail in
Sandburg's prose volume, *Remembrance Rock*. Sandburg has attempted
the portrayal in saga form, relating the lives, emotions and deeds of the
courageous Englishmen who came to the New World to secure freedom
of worship. Although human experience is the central theme, Sandburg
singles out several aspects of that experience to delineate the beginnings of
the social, religious, economic and political evolution of America—the faint
beginnings of a working democratic system. While still aboard the
Mayflower these Englishmen had drawn up and signed a document which
forecast mutual protection by a " civill body politick " :

" We whose names are under-written, . . . having undertaken for yᵉ glorie
of God and advancement of yᵉ Christian faith,—. . . a voyage to plant yᵉ
first colonie in yᵉ Northerne parts of Virginia, do covenant and combine
ourselves together into a civill body politick. . . and by vertue hereof to
enacte. . . such just and equall lawes, ordinances, acts, constitutions, and
offices from time to time, as shall be thought most mete for yᵉ general good
of yᵉ Colonie, unto which we promise all due submission and obe-
dience." [275]

Sandburg has reproduced the entire document, including the names of
the signers—" this group of home-seekers hunting a foothold in the earth
to prove their faith and try their hope." [276] And he lays emphasis on the
sturdy character of the early Plymouth settlers who were for the most part,
" farmers and country folk, neither seafearing nor city-wise. Some were
middle-class, fairly well-to-do." [277] They were idealists determined to come
to terms with a new environment; men of purpose and integrity, who

accepted menial, strenuous work as a means of creating a Christian settlement in accordance with their religious idealism.

At the same time, Sandburg traces the dim elements of a nascent democratic experiment, allied not with European institutions and class structures but with a vital, dynamic society that could only survive through its own vigorous efforts and industry. He describes the threats to their survival—famine, disease, fire, drought, anxiety and the presence of neighboring Indians. Some of these threats necessitated an elementary type of military organization in the form of a stockade with cannon mounted for defense. In portraying the Plymouth settlement Sandburg also traces the early tendencies of the American economy. From the journals of Governor Bradford in 1623 he quotes:

" ' They begane to thinke how they might raise as much corne as they could, and obtaine a better crope than they had done, that they might not still thus languish in misery.' All concerned threshed it out in long talks, deciding in the end ' that they should set corne every man for his own particular.' To each person was given in fee an acre of land, his own. ' It made all hands very industrious ', noted the Governor, with much more corn planted and ' farr better contents.' " [278]

Thus the Plymouth settlers carried into the planting and harvesting of crops the same theory of private ownership as in their earlier housing plans. From Governor Bradford's Register of January 9, 1621, Sandburg quotes:

" ' We labor in building our town in two rows of houses, for greater safety : divided by lot the ground we build on : agree that every man shall build his own house, that they may make more haste than when they work in common.' " [279]

The more pious church members were chosen as the foremost law makers. Troubles which arose over a preacher sent from England necessitated the calling of a court and the establishment of a trial system. The minister and others with him were charged with trying to ruin the church and wreck the institutions of the colony. They were found guilty and sent back to England. Public whippings and confinement in the stocks were punishments meted out for lesser offences.

The religious element is strongly stressed. There remained complete belief in the goodness of the Creator, but at the same time a firm belief in Satan, as a Dark Power, an Evil Shadow who was always at work corrupting men's minds. The Plymouth colonists lived within the mental framework of fear, an invisible, malignant, pervasive Force; and prejudice and intolerance arose.

Sandburg does not describe in correspondingly great detail the Puritan society of the Massachusetts Bay Colony. Yet several pages illustrate the austerity of their religion and the political implication of their belief—namely a theocratic form of government in which only the ' elect ' or those chosen by divine grace to be saved could be the leaders of that colony. The magistrates were the church and the church was the magistrate. The great majority of the people could not become Freemen or voters, therefore these traits of theocracy were in opposition to the idea of democracy. While the laws of the Massachusetts Bay Colony did not apply to Plymouth, nevertheless their influence was felt. The people of Plymouth are delineated as " less cruel than those in Salem and Boston; less bigoted and less vainglorious and tyrannical than the others." [280]

Nor does Sandburg give a detailed account of the Jamestown settlement in Virginia. To do so would require a much longer book than the 1067 pages of *Remembrance Rock*. Nevertheless he differentiates between the Plymouth and Jamestown colonies by means of fictional characters coming by ship from Virginia to the harbor of Plymouth :

" They told of things seen and heard in the royal colony farther south, its leaders staunch for the Established Church of England, one of their purposes being to get land, trade and riches to lay the groundwork for an aristocracy, as in England. They would have manorial houses... In August of 1620, a Dutch ship had landed twenty Negroes brought from Africa... to be bought, sold, the same as oxen, cattle, sheep and other property." The Virginia colonists " favored a different way of life." [281]

For the greater part, Sandburg confines his presentation of early America to Plymouth. Detailed as is his portrayal of the high character of the three foremost leaders of the Plymouth settlement—Brewster, Bradford and Winslow—Sandburg depicts Roger Williams as a symbol of early New England's contribution to the American way of life.

Roger Williams was a graduate of Cambridge University, England. He had prepared for the ministry but had also studied law in the office of the English jurist, Sir Edward Coke. He was among the hundreds joining the migration to America in 1631. Williams was invited to preach in the Salem community. His religious tenets as a Separatist however were much broader in scope than those of the Puritan Salem church and he was banished from the colony because of his " new and dangerous opinions against the auchthoritie of magistrates." [282] Williams went to the Wampanoag tribe of Indians at Sowams. Later he founded a settlement nearby which he named Providence. By a grant from the Narragansett Indians he owned the land on which he settled, but the town of Providence took over, by arrangements soon made, the land he had acquired and allotments were made to private owners in town meetings.

Sandburg outlines the new and distinctive features which characterized this Providence government; the twelve original settlers signed with Williams the plan or constitution of these town meetings. In Providence, as elsewhere, one had to be a man of property to sit in the meeting and to vote; but in Providence one need not be a church member to vote; and only civil questions came before the town meeting, nothing religious. Williams established in his settlement the separation of church and state, toleration of varying religious beliefs, and voting privileges for all men of property. Williams was also important because he was the one white man who could converse with the Indians in their own dialect about their land rights; his knowledge of English law and government was an invaluable asset to him. Sandburg says of him :

" His book, *Key to the Indian Languages,* stood as the first written on the language, manners and beliefs of the American red men... Learning and books, the fellowship of educated men, these Roger Williams prized... Salutations and prayers of hope for the future, Williams gave to the newly rooted institution given the name of Harvard College. His prayers ran that Harvard College as it grew and flourished might become a great fortress and a watchtower for the cause of freedom of conscience.

" A poet and politician, a statesman and businessman, a farmer and an athlete, a preacher and a teacher, a man of many challenging words— Roger Williams stood as a high portentous figure in New England, perhaps the most original and daring political adventurer in the New World. He spoke welcome to the banished, the persecuted, the outcasts of conscience and belief. He could say with mingled wrath and patience, ' In these flames about religion... there is no prudent, Christian way of preserving peace in the world but by permission of differing consciences '... He had planted seeds in the minds of men... He hoped there would come from the seeds planted at Providence a republic of free men doing their best in the practice of a disciplined democracy." [283]

The Craftsmen of New England

The origins of native, home-based industry are to be found in this early settlement period. In the early days of colonization, men made most of their own utensils and furniture by hand. As time went on, a class of crafts-men appeared—a group whose special skills lay in the designing and construction of household articles. Men whose lives were dedicated to agriculture or to commerce and trade sold their products to the craftsmen who, in turn, began the sale of the furniture fashioned by them. This interchange of products might be termed the origin of specialized trades or occupations in America; the skills and trades of England were transplanted to a new soil and by men of no mean stock, who set themselves to achieve security and a firmly built society on the basis of industry.

The expertly made products of these New England craftsmen were of such beautiful and substantial design that they became highly prized; the furniture makers became famous and their original products are now valued antiques; the designs lived on in traditional American furniture.

" In oak and walnut
Those old New England carpenters hoisted and wrought.
Sunup till sundown they hoisted and wrought in oak and walnut.
Wood had a meaning and wood spoke to the feel of the fingers.
The hammer handles and handwrought nails somehow had blessings.

And they are gone now? Their blood is no longer alive and speaking?
They no longer come through telling of the hands of men having craft?
Let their beds and staircases, chairs and tables now lingering testify:
' The strong workman whose blood goes into his work no more dies than
the people die.' " [284]

The above lines are symbolic of the debt modern America owes to early New England—a heritage couched in the symbolism of these antique products so valuable today, and originating in early immigrant craftsmanship. This visible link, this continuation of past in present is, again, the multi-dimensional feature frequently employed by Sandburg, who goes to great lengths to show America as a country forged by the care and industry of those who molded her and bequeathed her to their descendants, with a certain infusion of the original spirit to be passed on. " The will and vision that motivated people in Plymouth did not fade but moved on alive... Their ideas won. Their visions came through... In a rather real sense these settlers, First Comers as some called themselves—they go on, their lessons worth our seeing." [285]

(c) *America in 1775*

We move now from the first establishment of American colonies to the formation of the sovereign State freed from all subservience to an outside power. In prose, Sandburg has written at length of the forces leading up to the American Revolution, the Declaration of Independence and the establishment of the American Constitution. He details the more liberal tendencies replacing the rigid religious life of the Pilgrims. The ideas of Roger Williams and the ideas of equality and political liberty gained headway.

The distinctive feature of Sandburg's portrayal of the American Revolution is not the discussion of military battles but the portrayal of the conflicts in men's minds between loyalty to England and the desire for political freedom. Sandburg has portrayed the two schools of political thought in America and two schools of political thought in England on the subject of American independence. " There were two Englands. The England of William Pitt and the people he speaks for; and the England of the King and his arrogant and selfish ministers " who had imposed on the colonies the Stamp Act, the tea tax, the closing of the port of Boston with warships. " Edmund Burke in the British House of Commons and William Pitt, the Earl of Chatham, in the British House of Lords... spoke of explosions to come and gave their solemn warnings that the American people must have the full rights of British subjects or there would be endless revolts." [286]

Likewise Sandburg has delineated with careful analysis the division of opinions in the colonies. He has depicted thoughtful persons seeing good and bad in both camps of political thought. There were " virtuous and candid men in all sects; all such are to be esteemed. There are vicious men and bigots in all sects; and all such ought to be despised." [287] No one put the situation more clearly, in Sandburg's opinion, than the patriot, Benjamin Franklin, who wrote in a letter to a friend in England:

" I am persuaded that the body of the English people are our friends... It is a million of pities that so fair a plan as we have hitherto been engaged in, for increasing strength and empire with public felicity, would be destroyed by the mangling hands of a few blundering ministers... We hear that more ships and troops are coming out... But, if you flatter yourselves with beating us into submission, you know neither the people nor the country." [288]

Thus the latter part of the eighteenth century in America is portrayed as a political battlefield where divided loyalties fought in a long-continued struggle. Sandburg has chronicled opposing doubts and loyalties, groping and resolution, narrow-mindedness and breadth of vision, bigotry and sincerity, staunch patriotism and staunch Tory loyalty, fear and courage, cruelty and generosity—all of these in America. Psychological analysis and philosophical implications are among the distinctive features of this picture of the Revolutionary period. The mental conflicts in the minds of men are given precedence over the military conflicts on the battlefield. However, Lexington is rightly portrayed as the initial military onset of the war.

Sandburg has, of course, chosen General Washington as the symbol of American liberty. Again, however, it is the character of the man together with his deeply persuasive influence that Sandburg stresses rather than his conduct of battle. Washington's relations with his men, rather than his character as Commander-in-Chief are stressed. He is shown at his headquarters in Cambridge in the summer of 1778 in his uniform faded and drab from years of wear; his army is described as quartered " some with their firelocks and blankets sleeping in Harvard College buildings, in the Episcopal Church and private homes of Cambridge, but the most of them dotting the fields and hidden in woods in shelters their own hands made; only the Rhode Island volunteers were in tents." [289] The soldier's attitude toward Washington was that of respect for a " divine zeal on his face, his unconquerable will, his absolute resolves." The soldiers " warmed to him and did things that looked impossible because he told them to." [290] By impressive personality and ability he led to victory an army of volunteers who had had no previous military training.

Human relationships, human conduct, human struggle, the inner conflicts of American man groping toward political liberty characterize Sandburg's prose story of the American Revolution. Along with this analysis the author portrays the evolution of American printing and newspapers, the evolution of colleges and educational systems, public libraries, arts and crafts.

We have earlier noted Sandburg's poems on the subject of General Washington as a symbol of American political liberty; in still another manner, he has thrown additional light on Washington as a national hero, as a statesman of responsibility and far-reaching vision. Sandburg wrote and published (1943) a syndicated newspaper article based on two letters of Washington in the Oliver Barrett collection of valuable manuscripts. One letter was written by Washington at Mount Vernon, September 5, 1785, to his friend, the Marquis de Chastellux in France:

" Dear Sir : My first wish is to see the blessings of peace diffused through all the countries, and among all ranks in every country, and that we should consider ourselves as the children of a common parent, and be disposed to acts of brotherly kindness toward one another. In that case, all restrictions of trade would vanish; we should take your wines, your fruits, and surplusage of other articles, and give you, in return, our oils, our fish, tobacco, naval stores etc.; and, in like manner, we should exchange produce with other countries, to our reciprocal advantage. The globe is large enough. Why, then, need we wrangle for a small spot of it? If one country cannot contain us, another should open its arms to us. " [291]

The second letter was written on the same day and addressed to " his Excellency Chevalier de la Luzerne." A portion of it carries much the same sentiment as the first letter :

" My wish is to see the sons and daughters of the world mixing as one family, enjoying the sweets of social intercourse and reciprocal advantages. The earth certainly is sufficient to contain us all, and affords everything necessary to our wants, if we would be friendly and endeavor to accommodate one another. " [292]

Sandburg cites the letters to show Washington not only as the distinguished leader of a new nation and a symbol of freedom, but also as an advanced thinker and a sincere humanitarian. These factors were among the many that originally gave rise to the Washington legend.

Sandburg has likewise emphasized the importance of Thomas Jefferson, another American who gave the best efforts and years of his life to his country before, during and after the War for Independence. Washington had begun the shaping of the national character by his leadership, his example and his personality. Jefferson helped to establish an intellectualized ideal of social order by defining American ideology more completely than any of his contemporaries. Jefferson is well known as the author of the Declaration of Independence; and this document is not merely the statement of the reasons for political separation, it also sets forth the general political philosophy of the new nation :

" We hold these truths to be self evident, that all men are created equal, that they are endowed by their Creator with certain inalienable rights; that among these are life, liberty and the pursuit of happiness; that to secure these rights, governments are instituted among men, deriving their just powers from the consent of the governed ; that whenever any form of government becomes destructive to these ends, it is the right of the people to alter or abolish it, and to institute new government, laying its foundations on such principles and organizing its powers in such form as to them shall seem most likely to effect their safety and happiness." [293]

These aspects of political philosophy Sandburg singles out in Jefferson as his greatest contribution to the evolution of American government. To Jefferson the welfare of the citizen represented the goal of political and social theory.

" He loved life and people and music
and books and writing and quiet thoughts—
a lover of peace, decency, good order,
summer corn ripening for the bins of winter,
apple trees waiting to laugh with pippins—
Jefferson loved peace like a good farmer.
And yet—for eight years he fought in a war—
writing with his own hand the war announcement
named the Declaration of Independence
making the Fourth of July a sacred calendar date." [294]

Jefferson would have preferred the quiet life among his books—the
life on his handsome country estate, from which he could see the University
of Virginia which he had personally founded. He

" ... would rather have had the horses of instruction
those eight years he gave to the tigers of wrath." [295]

But Jefferson was a dreamer of freedom and independence; he preferred
to match the " speech of steel and cunning " [296] of George III with his own
relentless speech of steel and idealism. Jefferson is a name dear to Carl
Sandburg. When the Jefferson Memorial was dedicated in Washington
in 1943 (not far from the Lincoln Memorial) Sandburg wrote for a nation-
wide syndicate of newspapers an article on the Memorial and the importance
of Jefferson as a political leader and guide, particularly as the author of
the Declaration of Independence.

" In the field of free speech and a free press, perhaps no other American,
whether in the realms of politics, journalism, law or philosophy, has
equaled him in statement and analysis so sure and basic that it holds good
for one crisis after another... So wide-ranging is Jefferson that good men
of both political parties claim him and cite chapter and verse. Some parts
of Jefferson's thoughts Lincoln absorbed so completely that they became
part of him and he didn't care whether his listeners found Jefferson or
Lincoln in what he was saying. " Jefferson wrote in one of his letters:
" The general spread of the light of science has already laid open to every
view the palpable truth, that the mass of mankind has not been born with
saddles on their backs, nor a favored few booted and spurred, ready to
ride them legitimately, by the grace of God." [297] In the continuation of
this article, Sandburg pays tribute to Jefferson and voices the belief that
the great statesman's writing, particularly the Declaration of Independence,
will be Jefferson's surest memorial, far outlasting any beautiful monument
dedicated to him in Washington.

Sandburg in his delineation of the evolution of American democracy
has chosen the portrayal of the foregoing major national figures as shapers
of the democratic ideal after the time of the Pilgrim Fathers, real founders
of this tradition.

(d) *The Pioneers*

Following the establishment of independence and of a firmly-based
constitution came the development of the hinterland of the nation. Toward

the end of the eighteenth century, the Northwest Territory, comprising the land between the Appalachian Mountains and the Mississippi River north of the Ohio River, came under the government of the new United States of America. In 1787, a plan for territorial government, for sale of the land and for the establishment of public schools was drawn up, and settlement of the new territory began immediately.

As the American pioneers began the intensive westward movement, they found life in the forested regions beyond the Appalachian Mountains difficult. In " Good Morning, America " Sandburg has paid tribute to the stout-heartedness of the intrepid pioneers, but in terms that show the conditions that faced them in reality :

" First came the pioneers, lean, hungry, fierce, dirty.
They wrangle and battle with the elements.
They gamble on crops, chills, ague, rheumatism.
They fight wars and put a nation on the map.
They battle with blizzards, lice, wolves.
They go on a fighting trail
To break sod for unnumbered millions to come." [298]

In the prose of *Always the Young Strangers*, Sandburg re-creates for us the pioneer days in Galesburg and its surrounding territory in Illinois. In the chapter " Pioneers and Old-Timers " he writes, partially from personal narration by settlers and old residents, partially from legend and record. Concerning the pioneers he writes :

" They had broken the prairie, laid the first roads and streets, built the first schools and churches, colored the traditions of the town and country where I was born and raised.
" They knew wagons, the pioneers and first settlers. They had eaten and slept in wagons and under wagons. They had studied every cubic inch of certain wagons, where to put their skillets and blankets, their plows, axes, hoes, seed corn, their six, eight, or ten children. Some had made part of their trip on flat-boats or paddle-wheel steamboats, the generation who arrived before the railroad came to Knox County in 1854. They had the color and distinction of those who could say they had left Ohio, New York, Tennessee or Kentucky in a wagon, driving their horses over wilderness trails, when often the feet of horses, the reins and spokes of wheels, tangled in underbrush. They camped where night found them and took up their journey again at daylight." [299]

Sandburg successfully captured the spirit of the period. He reproduced the agricultural economy by descriptions of plows drawn by four yoke of oxen; of great fields of Indian corn; of handmills for grinding the corn into meal; of humble cabins in which greased paper filled the window frames, in place of window glass.

Added interest is given the narrative by the introduction of people and places having some connection with Lincoln. The author shows us the home of Isaac Guliher, who had served as a private under Captain Abraham Lincoln in the Black Hawk War; we read of Abraham Lincoln, at a later date, in Galesburg, leaving his buggy in front of the Isaac Guliher home, to drink a dipper of cold water with old Sangamon County friends; we read of Daniel Green Burner who traded at a grocery in New Salem where Lincoln served customers. This same Mr. Burner had seen Lincoln march off to the Black Hawk War and had many memories of him and of New Salem. We read of Newton Bateman, whose office as Superintendent of Public Instruction of the State of Illinois was next to the office used by Lincoln in Springfield, where the two became great friends.

Picturing the cultural and religious origins of Galesburg, Sandburg writes of the Reverend Hasselquist who earned his passage from Sweden across the Atlantic by serving as a pastor for sixty Swedish emigrants. He rode hundreds of miles in stage-coaches over the prairie, traveled on horseback and afoot to organize congregations and schools; he believed in printing and founded the first Swedish-language newspaper in America, *Hemlandet*.

Thus in interpreting the pioneers and frontier life Sandburg pictures a society of resolute people of various origins, who represent the common man.

The American Economy Prior to the Civil War

Sandburg has written in *The Prairie Years* of the economic situation in the United States in the second quarter of the nineteenth century as follows:

" The South, in the early thirties, was an empire of cotton blossoms, and cotton bales, held in the loose leashes of cotton planters who lived on horseback accustomed to command. ...

" In the early thirties was weaving the fabric of an empire, a pastoral and agricultural nation, with its foundations resting on three chief conditions: (1) The special fertility of a certain strip of land for cotton crops; (2) the raising of the vast cotton crop by negro slave labor; (3) The sale of the crop to northern American and English cotton mills that sold their finished products in a constantly widening world market. The planters who had control of its destiny, were men of pride, valor and cunning...

" The North was a section of country groping toward control of water power, iron, steel, canals, railways, ocean-going boats. ... The shipping, fisheries, and farming interests of New England slipped back to make room for manufacturing interests. ... Cotton mills were the industrial phenomenon in New England. Each year they called for increasing tens of millions of pounds of cotton from the South. ... It was a process that shook up culture, religion, and politics in New England.... The spinning wheels of homes had become old-fashioned; spinning was to be done in cotton and woolen mills and clothes were to be cheap.

" From thousands of farms the people moved into industrial cities to go to work, men, women and children, in the mills. Other thousands of

New England farmers were selling out and moving via the Erie Canal into New York or Ohio, Indiana, Michigan and Illinois." [300]

These are brief excerpts from Sandburg's treatment of the opposing economies of North and South; and they show the historian's fair-minded approach to the subject. He clearly outlines the demarcations which were to test the strength of the American experiment in democracy.

(e) *Lincoln and the Great Trial of American Democracy: 1861-1865*

Sandburg in *The Prairie Years* set forth Lincoln's political principles, which exerted great influence on the popular mind. All of these principles cannot be enumerated here but one of the finest Sandburg characterizations of Abraham Lincoln in *The Prairie Years* is as follows: " He had been the Stubborn Man who had erected what was in his phrase ' a stumbling-block to tyrants'... If there had been any stubborn grandeur in the life of Lincoln, it was in his explanation of the Declaration of Independence, and his taking the words, ' All men are created equal' not only seriously and solemnly, but passionately. The simplest words, the shortest statements, the most blunt and direct thoughts he spoke, came from him connected with the shibboleths and passwords of the Revolutionary War.

" Lincoln understood that all men are not equal in faculties, dimensions, capacities. The accent and stress were to be on opportunity, on 'equal chance, equal access to the resources of life, liberty and the pursuit of happiness'... And this standard, this measure, would be ' a stumbling block to tyrants for all time to come '. In that phrase was an approach to the bottom philosophy of politics that shaped the watchword and actions of Lincoln." [301]

In this political theory we see the influence of Jefferson, together with the evolution of American opinion that would establish Lincoln as the representative of the popular will in the November election of 1860:

> " A Kentucky-born Illinoisan found himself
> By journey through shadows and prayer
> The Chief Magistrate of the American people
> Pleading in words close to low whispers :
> ' Fellow citizens... we cannot escape history.
> The fiery trial through which we pass
> Will lead us down in honor or dishonor
> To the latest generation...
> We shall nobly save or meanly lose
> The last best hope of earth.' " [302]

The last lines of the above stanza are, of course, Lincoln's words, which have been quoted throughout the world on many occasions.

> " Death was in the air
> So was birth.
> What was dying few could say.
> What was being born none could know." [303]

In the above lines Sandburg symbolizes the Civil War by death, the disappearance, of human slavery, which insured the birth of a new and greatly strengthened concept of freedom and by preventing the South from seceding to develop separately, maintained the Union of states.

In *The War Years* Sandburg has written of Lincoln as a guiding genius in the chaos of popular discord and differences in the early 1860's; a genius of patience and faith; a genius of wisdom who has been vindicated and proven of increasingly deeper significance with the passing of the years. Nothing could deter him from undertaking what he and his people believed to be honest and honorable procedures; at times there appeared a lack of exterior polish, but always, underneath the plain exterior, a devotion to freedom and justice for all. Lincoln inspired love and trust. There were times when he was slow in making decisions—perhaps even vacillating on minor issues—for the burden of hundreds of decisions every day rested on his shoulders, and most of these decisions were difficult, because they dealt with discontent and misery. His opponents hurled slander, half truths, insinuations, insults; freedom of the press permitted caricatures and abuse of him, and began " an insidious debauching of the public mind, a drugging of the public mind "; [304] freedom of speech permitted misinterpretation and charges of despotism; yet Lincoln insisted that democratic freedom of speech and press continue; he himself took great care in expression of his written or spoken thoughts : " In times like the present, men should utter nothing for which they would not willingly be responsible through time and in eternity." [305] His words of careful wisdom have lighted him " in honor down to the latest generation." [306] He was a

> " . . . tall tree in the possession of phantoms
> carrying a scheme of haze
> inevitably past changing sunsets
> and beyond into a baffling moonset
> on a mist horizon." [307]

He was a guide " to man as a struggler amid illusions." [308] He it was who looked into the struggle of his people and wrote in the midst of the chaos of abuse and admiration, hate and love, fear and trust : " If both factions, or neither, shall abuse you, you will probably be about right. Beware of being assailed by one and praised by the other." [309]

Lincoln, deeply believing in the democratic principle of individual thought and opinion, and respecting each individual human mind, expressed the sacred right to differing opinions in the minds of honest men when he said : " Actual war coming, blood grows hot and blood is spilled. Thought is forced from all channels into confusion. Deception breeds and thrives. Confidence dies and universal suspicion reigns. Each man feels an impulse to kill his neighbor, lest he be first killed by him. Revenge and retaliation follow. All this, as before said, may be among honest men only; but this is not all. Every foul bird comes abroad and every dirty reptile rises up. These add crime and confusion." [310] Yet Lincoln bore up under the terrific strain with humility of spirit, with faith in eventual justice.

Lincoln, as the Preserver of Union and Democracy, Becomes its Symbol

" Lincoln? Did he gather
the feel of the American dream
and see its kindred over the earth? " [311]

It is, of course, impossible for Sandburg to give us in brief poetry the comprehensive picture of President Lincoln which he has given us in the massive volumes of *The War Years*. Perhaps one or two brief excerpts from *The War Years* will explain better the import of the Lincoln poetry.

Sandburg, ever searching for cause and result in the analysis of public issues, sets forth the human causes operating in America at that period as " many and varied and moving, requiring the brush of chaos to do a mural of the crossed interests of climate and geography, of native and foreign blood streams, of bread-and-butter necessity, of cultural environment, of mystic hopes. " [312]

The Sandburg portrait of Lincoln in 1862 is that of a Lincoln excoriated, reviled, rebuked, harassed, discouraged, disappointed, yet a Lincoln possessed of the patience of Job; a Lincoln superbly humanitarian by instinct yet built of human flesh and blood attended by weaknesses; a Lincoln forced to reason at various periods that the best policy was to have no policy; a Lincoln appealing to his dissatisfied fellow-countrymen of the South for understanding; a Lincoln trying to do what seemed best as the occasion arrived.

The Sandburg estimate of Lincoln in 1863 is that of a natural leader in this chaos. As a lawyer, Lincoln had always had to consider two sides of the question. He had made a lifelong study of the curious balance of human affairs. Through the eyes of the poet, James Russell Lowell, then a professor at Harvard, Sandburg gives us the picture of Abraham Lincoln :

" The cautious, but steady, advance of his policy during the war was like that of a Roman army. He left behind him a firm road on which public confidence could follow; he took America with him where he went." [313]

Sandburg has characterized Lincoln as free from temper and prejudice —even with his assailants. He has skilfully delineated the slowly changing attitude of the people in the progress of a colossal war, their slow change from antagonism, criticism and ridicule to confidence, to a dim belief in the President's loyalty to great ends; to principles of duty and action; to a hazy realization that he was a true exponent of democracy, a distinctive executive of the popular will; so eminently representative of the people that he could qualify as their spokesman.

To Sandburg, Lincoln was the incarnation of two results of victory, Emancipation and Union. Sandburg portrayed him as an all-American type of leader who carried to further limits the social philosophy and political theories of Washington and Jefferson by teaching that human personality should be sacred and inviolable and by showing the essential trustworthiness, dignity, integrity and compassion of the common man, once he was given a lead by an enlightened government. Lincoln vindicated and redeemed the common man as the collective agent of his own destiny.

Robert E. Lee, Symbol of the Confederacy

In fairness to Sandburg's breadth of vision, one must also take note of the fact that he has given a prominent place in *The War Years* to General Robert E. Lee as a leader of the Confederate Army in Civil War history. This may be in some measure an effort to obtain balance by portraying a southern hero alongside the leader of the Union cause; but even more fundamentally it shows the influence of Lincoln and the inner conflicts of allegiance in the mind of Lee. In *The War Years* Sandburg tells us that President Lincoln in March, 1861 appointed Robert E. Lee a colonel in the United States Army and that General Scott felt that eventually Lee would have the high command of the Union Army. Lee was an admirer of the principles of Abraham Lincoln; he had never advised secession; had never been a slaveholder except by inheritance, and upon inherited ownership of slaves had sold them immediately. Sandburg further delineates Lee as follows : " He was neither a revolutionist, nor a secessionist, nor a Union-hater nor temperamentally joined to the men who had created the Confederacy and then asked him to fight for it. Lee was a conservative whose instincts favored a strong government... In a letter home in January of 1861, Lee wrote : ' Secession is nothing but revolution. Our Constitution was intended... for perpetual union '... On the question of slavery Lee's uncle, Richard Henry Lee, who was a member of the Virginia House of Burgesses from 1761 to 1788, had spoken deep hatred and had sought passage of a motion to lay so heavy a duty on the importation of slaves as effectually to put an end to that iniquitous traffic with the colony of Virginia. Robert E. Lee knew that George Washington held the institution to be an involved menace that must be dealt with delicately... ' But how can I draw my sword against Virginia ? ' The very asking of the question included its answer... Enfolded in the churchman and the Christian gentleman, Robert E. Lee, was the warrior," [314] for Lee had been educated as a soldier.

Knowing that as a colonel in the United States Army he might be required to march against his own state of Virginia, to raise his hand against his home and his relatives, Lee resigned his commission. The conflicting loyalties in his mind are sympathetically drawn—the conflict between his devotion to the Union, and his love of the Virginia of his home and family. Mrs. Lee is quoted as saying : " My husband has wept tears of blood over this terrible war." [315] Lee, after making his difficult decision, left his stately home in Arlington across the Potomac from the city of Washington and accepted the command of the Army of Virginia of the secession group of states.

The long and carefully studied delineation of the character of Lee in *The War Years* depicts the deep influence of George Washington upon Lee : " The reserve, the tenacity, the scruples, the exactitude, the piety, the patience and forbearance, the balances of justice and fair dealing, the bearing of distinction touched with aristocratic look—these ways of Washington he pondered. They haunted him." [316] Sandburg, as the biographer of Lincoln, has utilized the " balances of justice and fair dealing " himself, in his portrayal of the man whose armies opposed the armies of

Lincoln. The power of psychological insight has served him well; and scrupulous honesty has prevented him from presenting a biased opinion. Lee is portrayed as a man of noble character. In a memorial address on Lincoln, Carl Sandburg referred to Lee as " that sainted figure out of the South." *

Sandburg in his historical novel *Remembrance Rock*, has depicted the humaneness and magnanimity of General Lee at the time of his surrender to General Grant at Appomattox : " The commander of the Army of Northern Virginia, an idolized figure and a man of few words " had asked that his men who owned their horses be permitted to keep them for spring plowing on their farms and this request was generously granted, whereupon Lee voiced his belief : " Our returning soldiers must all set to work, and if they cannot do what they prefer, do what they can... There is much to be done which they only can do." [317] General Lee himself, was pardoned and restored to his full rights as a citizen of the United States.

In his portrayal of Lee, Sandburg has shown him to be kind-hearted and sympathetic; at the end of the war Lee surrendered with more concern for his men than for himself : " I have, indeed, nothing for my own men "; [318] whereupon Grant immediately directed that 25,000 rations be sent to the Confederate soldiers. Thus these aspects of Lee's character have been selected by Sandburg to show influences on the foundations of the America of today and on the transformation of institutions which confronted the North and South and on the final blending of forces in the evolution of the government of the United States.

These portraits of the past Sandburg has presented in his chosen role as interpreter of the American scene, in the context of its history. The theme running through this history he distinguishes as an evolving, practical concept of democracy, never completely defined in spite of the Constitution and its definitions, but a continuous concept being worked out in the lives and ideals and dealings of the men who have shaped America from the early days of the Plymouth Colony to the present day. It is also a concept inspired by the author's personal vision of Lincoln, who voiced unqualified faith in the justice of American man as the arbiter of national affairs, in spite of the faults in American society that Sandburg himself is first to point out.

(f) *America in the Late Nineteenth Century*

Sandburg coming to his own times in *Always the Young Strangers*, has drawn for us a portrait of a late nineteenth century prairie city. In what is, in effect, a social history of the period, he presents myriads of specific facts which constituted American daily life, as seen first by a very young boy, then by a young man and lastly by an American soldier.

---

* In Cooper Union, New York City, Feb. 13, 1956. Carl Sandburg as the speaker of the occasion, was given the use of the lectern which had been used by Lincoln in the same hall, Feb. 27, 1860.

He has given us a picture of the social background in which he grew up. Between his home and the railroad yards, two and a half blocks distant, the population was composed mostly of Swedes, yet there were also two English families, two or three New Englanders, a few Irish and Germans, and, in the early 1890's, a host of Italians—in one instance thirty of them in two houses next to the railroad. To him they were European history which had come alive. They gave him the feel of Europe, just as he himself so surely gives us the feel of Galesburg. He gives us a word-picture of the Little Dutch Band as it came to Berrien Street playing *Die Wacht am Rhein* and other stirring and sweet music for the people.

Further atmosphere is given by the picture of the scissorsgrinder swinging his hand bell and carrying on his back a grindstone which made a stream of firesparks as he put new and sharp edges on Berrien Street scissor blades; by the picture of the man with the bear which stood up on his hind legs and waltzed, or even climbed a telephone pole if sufficient money were offered his owner; by sketches of the handbill peddlers—" Us kids often were the bill peddlers if we were lucky enough to get the work." [319]

Among the recreational opportunities and amusements for the young boys of the period were games of baseball with a broomstick for a bat. Sandburg pictures the Galesburg-organized baseball games played on the Knox Campus grounds, knot holes in the surrounding fence providing the means by which the Berrien Street boys watched the play. We are also given a picture of the Knox County Fairs, of horse races, of the first appearance of the Edison talking phonograph, and of the circuses that came to town.

Industrial aspects included are the work and life of railroad men, the hazards of railroading in the 1890's and the eventual development of the Westinghouse automatic safety coupler.

The series of national economic crises, especially the financial Panic of 1893, and their profound effects upon midwestern community life are presented in a deeply moving picture in which stoic determination and courage stand revealed; there is pathos in the story of the food shortage.

The gradual changes involved in the social and economic story of the late nineteenth century are notable features of the account. Sandburg tells us of the lamp-lighter who came along at dusk, carrying a small ladder upon which he climbed to light the gas burners in the street lights; of the change to the electric arc lamp for Berrien Street, and the passing of the era of the familiar lamp-lighter whom the boys loved and missed; of the fences and gates around all the yards, and then of their gradual disappearance as roving or straying livestock became less and less characteristic of this agricultural community.

A brief glimpse of the culture of early Galesburg is given in accounts of the educational opportunities which the little city afforded, and in accounts of some of the famous personages who appeared on the stage of the old auditorium. Since Galesburg was an important railroad junction, it was a convenient rail stop and attracted many traveling stage players, entertainers and lecturers, such as William Jennings Bryan and Robert Ingersoll.

In writing of his early years in Galesburg, Sandburg has not merely set forth his own life, he has chronicled a phase of American history by his story of the assimilation of European immigrants. At the same time, the accounts of his family life, his social surroundings and primary schooling reveal the development of his impulse for learning and literature. There is disclosed his liking for poetry and for history; and in his very early reading of *The History of Napoleon Bonaparte*, of *Napoleon and His Marshals*, of Hugo's *Les Misérables* is shown his desire for knowledge of European subjects. As well as characterizing an epoch, *Always the Young Strangers* represents actual life-influences on the author as a later poet-historian. It also forecasts (perhaps unconsciously on the part of Sandburg) how America, in its incorporation of European cultures along with its own strong traditions, would become a vital part of his mind and writings.

The Spanish-American War

The chapter entitled " Soldier " from *Always the Young Strangers* gives us America from the viewpoint of an enlisted man in 1898. Here Sandburg gives us his impressions of military life in the Spanish-American War.

" On the fairgrounds at Springfield we were quartered in an immense brick building used for livestock exhibits... While still in civilian clothes I was handed a Springfield rifle and put through the manual of arms and company drill... In about ten days I slid into a uniform, a heavy blue-wool shirt, a coat of dark blue with brass buttons that went to the throat, pants of light-blue wool cloth double as thick as the coat cloth. This was the same uniform that the privates under Grant and Sherman had worn thirty-five years before, intended for wear in those border states where snow fell and zero weather might come as at Fort Donelson the night Grant attacked. The little cap wouldn't shed rain from your ears, and above the stiff black visor it ran flat as though your head should be flat there. I felt honored to wear the uniform of the famous Union armies and yet I had mistrust of it." [320]

Of a portion of his military life in Puerto Rico, Sandburg writes as follows:

" Soon after daylight on July 25 we sighted a harbor and moved into it. Ahead we saw gunfire from a ship and landing boats filled with blue-jackets moving toward shore. We were ordered to put on our cartridge belts, and with rifles get into full marching outfits. We heard shooting, glanced toward shore and saw white puffs of smoke while we stood waiting our turns to climb down rope ladders into long boats called lighters. We were rowed to a shallow beach where we dropped into water above our hips. Holding rifles over our heads, we waded ashore...
" We began a march up mountain roads. The August tropic heat was on. We carried cartridge belt, rifle, bayonet, blanket-roll, half a canvas pup tent, haversack with rations, a coat. We still wore the heavy blue-wool pants of the army of the Potomac in '65, and thick canvas leggings laced from ankles to knees... I tore a third of my blanket away, so as to lessen the weight to carry. Some let the whole blanket go. It was an eight-mile march upgrade. Men fell out, worn-out, and there were sunstroke cases." [321]

His account continues by relating that after several months of military service, his " one hundred and fifty-two pounds in April had gone down to one hundred and thirty pounds in August. Many were gaunt and thin, with a slight yellow tint on the skin of hands and faces. " [322]

In the accounts of the Spanish-American War, we note an element in Sandburg that enjoys the chronicling of scenes from the American pageant for their own sake, regardless of social comment and regardless of whether or not they throw light on American democracy. This account represents a total involvement by Sandburg in a war on the part of the United States, with no attitude of detached criticism of the war itself, or of war as a means of policy.

From the standpoint of Sandburg's later critical writings on war as a policy, it is important to remember that in this account he reports personal war service—in soiled uniform and from the viewpoint of the exhausting battle-front. He is proud to have served his country, and to have taken part in the conflict.

The mustering-out papers of Carl Sandburg at the close of the war bore the inscription: "A good soldier, service honest and faithful." [323] With pride he still wears in the lapel of his coat the military service button awarded him by the government after the war.

The Turn of the Century

" Then the fat years arrive when the fat drips.
Then come the rich men baffled by their riches,
Bewildered by the silence of their tall possessions." [324]

The phenomenal growth of large cities which could not readily absorb the millions of immigrants, the rapid expansion of industries which became so big as to be unwieldy and beyond proper management, the rise of great fortunes among isolated captains of industry who scarcely knew what to do with their sudden wealth, were marked characteristics of the social changes in the United States in the late nineteenth century and early twentieth century.

Woodrow Wilson set forth the situation as follows :

" With great riches has come inexcusable waste... We have been proud of our industrial achievements, but we have not hitherto stopped thoughtfully enough to count the human cost, the cost of lives snuffed out, of energies overtaxed and broken, the fearful physical and spiritual cost... With the great government went many deep secret things which we too long delayed to scrutinize with candid, fearless eyes." *

Tensions in social thought troubled Americans of that period. They gradually came to realize that self-sufficient individualism must reach a

---

* Allan NEVINS and Henry Steele COMMAGER *America ; the story of a free people*, Oxford, Clarendon Press, 1943, pp. 359, 360.

compromise with American society as a whole. The needs of the complete society must be considered, or else individualism would result in glaring inequalities. Some of the very rich realized the social disparity; and many multi-millionaires voluntarily began the founding of hospitals, libraries, museums, and the endowment of colleges and universities. Andrew Carnegie was among those pioneering in the foundation of libraries. Yet such measures were not sufficient to remedy the situation; the need for Federal measures, for more equitable control of wealth in the rising industrial economy, became apparent.

In this context of the release of industrial potential and energy which developed modern, industrialized, capitalist America, Sandburg's early poems of the Chicago period take on the value of social documents. While great fortunes had been amassed by a few individuals large sections of the working classes existed in intolerable personal conditions, for which the cities had no immediate answer, until social conscience and working class pressure of an increasingly organized nature gradually combined to provide more suitable conditions.

Thus the Chicago poems of Sandburg are of particular interest in that he who was able to paint the feelings and conditions of the ordinary people, and who felt the vocation to do so, laid bare these stresses and unsatisfactory conditions. At the same time, however, he was sufficiently broad-minded and inquiring to be able to set this presentation in its national context, and to see, in this period of growing pains, the origins and material of which prosperity, social-mindeness, the vital expanding economy and the modern nation were being formed. Sandburg's accomplishment is therefore the placing of this period of Chicago life in its historical setting, showing whence it had come, and at the same time, showing the roots of future development. He speaks not in terms of production norms and investment patterns, but in terms of human endeavor and responsibility. Man, and in particular, American man, has been the force that has molded American life. It is men's vitality that exists alongside the squalor, the sense of justice that exists alongside abuse and vice which eventually are adjusted and something better results. In the Emersonian tradition, Sandburg urges looking from Better ahead to Best. This is the basis of Sandburg's concept of American development and of American democracy—a critical analysis and the taking of steps toward improvement. It is an evolutionary conception of man closely analyzed, and in its poetic presentation closely and sympathetically painted. He communicates and infuses his faith.

Sandburg's protest is in accord with long American tradition. It was a protesting religious spirit following the Reformation that brought the English Pilgrims and Puritans to the New World. Roger Williams objected to the theocracy and intolerance of the Puritans. Samuel Adams, Thomas Jefferson, Benjamin Franklin and many others protested against the political oppression of George III and some of his ministers and against the incipient force of a native aristocratic element which in the person of Hamilton gave voice to the sentiment: " Your people, sir, is a great beast." [325] Emerson in the nineteenth century was the prominent voice of protest in literature and on the lecture platform; but there were other contemporary dissenters such as Thoreau and Whittier who wrote appeals for political equality. Wendell Phillips gave voice to the forces of abolition. The spirit of inquiry and protest is inherent in the character of the American nation.

(g) *Social Pictures of the Midwest in the Early Twentieth Century*

" Il n'est pas de meilleure fortune ni de plus grand honneur pour la littérature que lorsqu'elle trouve l'occasion de se coordonner avec un grand mouvement social, avec un courant politique important, et sans s'y enchaîner, de le servir." [326]

— Sainte-Beuve.

Urban Life

In the discussion of Chicago as a growing, overcrowded city, we have already seen many social pictures of its struggling people in a shifting economy. These portrayals are not left in abstract terms, but are brought home to the reader by the pictures of hungry women and children; of under-paid workers; of striving immigrants; of tenement dwellers; and by brief glimpses of child labor and the exploitation of the young;

" Of my city the worst that men will ever say is this :
You took little children away from the sun and the dew,
And the glimmers that played in the grass under the great sky,
And the reckless rain; you put them between walls
To work, broken and smothered, for bread and wages,
. . . . . .
For a little handful of pay on a few Saturday nights." [327]

This social theme is repeated in " Mill Doors " in protest against the human cost in the greatly expanded industrialism. The tragic situation is fearlessly held up for public examination as the poet dramatically evokes the plight of those who are " old before they are young." [328]

The overcrowded social structure of the city was also clouded by the disproportionately great number of incoming job hunters, surpassing the amount of employment available.

" Last week she got eight cents a box, Mrs. Pietro Giovannitti, picking onions for Jasper,
But this week Jasper dropped the pay to six cents a box because so many women and girls had answered the ads in the *Daily News*." [329]

There is the noonday portrait of the woman who made cigars with " fingers wage-anxious "; on the arrival of the noon hour for food and relaxation, she is silhouetted within a window-frame of the walls of the cigar factory overlooking the river. Sandburg has pictured her, feeling at her throat, seeking the cool moving air of the outdoors over the river :

" At her throat and eyes and nostrils
The touch and the blowing cool
Of great free ways beyond the walls." [330]

The picture of the pawnshop man is symbolic of the industrial and social distortion of the period; for he " knows hunger, and how far hunger has eaten the heart of one who comes with an old keepsake. " [331] The wedding rings and baby bracelets, the watches of gold and silver and other deeply personal treasures brought to him for money, tell their stories.

The social structure of this period included many types in addition to the afore-mentioned; the policeman, the dynamiter, the ice-handler, the teamster, the ditchdigger, the undertaker, the gravedigger, the newsboy, the house painter and others. Among the immigrant variations pictured are Greeks, Italians, Hungarians, Poles, Germans, Russians, Slavs and Swedes.

In contrast to this poverty, the poem " A Fence " is Sandburg's ironical glimpse into the life of the millionaire in his great stone house at the lake front. Around it are high iron palings with steel points :

" As a fence, it is a masterpiece, and will shut off the rabble and all vagabonds and hungry men and all wandering children looking for a place to play.
Passing through the bars and over the steel points will go nothing except Death and the Rain and Tomorrow." [332]

The social contrasts and maladjustments toward which Sandburg directed much of the caustic realism of his earliest *Chicago Poems* were gradually remedied, and it is not easy now to picture conditions as they then existed. Harry Hansen, the literary editor of the Chicago *Daily News*, knew both Sandburg and his poems quite well. His overall assessment of " Chicago " and " Windy City " shows how close to the scene Sandburg was : " These two long poems identify him particularly with the sidewalks of Chicago. They may well picture, for a later age, the industrial hegemony. " [333]

People in Outdoor Life

Outside this industrial hegemony, however, there existed other modes of life without these depressing aspects. Lake shipping from the port of Chicago offered an opportunity for work out of doors, and the poet pictures the freedom of the boatman's life as he lounges placidly on his ship on Lake Michigan the day before its scheduled departure, watching clouds and winds, knowing that tomorrow the throbbing of the ship's engines and the play of the ship's pistons will be its call to life and the boatman's call to the vocation of his choice :

" Tomorrow we move in the gaps and heights
On changing floors of unlevel seas
And no man shall stop us and no man follow
For ours is the quest of an unknown shore
And we are husky and lusty and shouting-gay." [334]

Many Sandburg poems portray people in rural districts. An illustration of the happy life of the great outdoors is that of the " Plowboy " plowing in the dusk the last furrow. " [335] The gleam of the brown turf and the smell of the soil in the cool moist haze of an April evening are portions of the poetic descriptions in which Sandburg conveys the joy of prairie living, and the contentment of the people who turn to the soil for their vocation; the same lines convey the poet's love of the life-giving earth, the functional beauty and the good that he sees in the farmer in the fields.

Prairie life and prairie production are so closely identified in the poet's mind with the fundamental supporting structure of American economy that in " Corn Hut Talk " he has personified the prairie autumn harvest in terms of man's needs and wants and dreams. The " handshake of the pumpkins " is the gift of food for human consumption. " There is hope for every corn shock " as a gift of " shoes for rough weather in November," [336] as a gift of shirts for early May. Even the five o'clock prairie sunset is personified as " a strong man going to sleep after a long day in a cornfield." [337]

Naturally, it is possible to touch on but a few of the aspects of American life that Sandburg has crystallized in his verses; but these excerpts convey the hardship, the poverty, the brilliance, the sheer activity whether in factory or on the farm. Work and life are shown, however, not merely as a set of conditions, but as a frame of mind, a human reaction, a personal identification—and in cases a dedication. In other cases, work has become soulless. In portraying these opposing aspects of work, Sandburg has shown human feelings and not abstracts.

Professional People

It may be said of the early poems (particularly of *Chicago Poems*) that they do not reflect enough contacts with the professional groups of society. They do, however, reflect contacts with musicians and artists of the concert stage, and with people of the poet's own profession in the field of journalism, poetry and prose writing. As a newpaper reporter, one of his earliest assignments had been coverage and criticism of cinema productions; even in boyhood days, as a stage-hand at the Galesburg Auditorium (where nearly all New York stage productions stopped if they had achieved sufficient success to warrant a western tour through Chicago, Omaha, Denver and the West) he had seen such productions as *Hamlet* and he had seen *Monte Cristo* with James O'Neill. Contacts with musicians are reflected even in the early poetry. A study in contrasts in the workings of the human mind in one individual is set forth in poetry describing the power of the music of Mischa Elman. An individual who in deep despair could see only gloom and uselessness ahead in life went to an Elman concert. The concert given by the great musician rebuilt and reshaped his outlook on life from despair to happy anticipation. " He was the same man in the same world as before. Only there was a surging fire and a climb of roses everlastingly over the world he looked on." [338]

We note the happy and exalted mood of the music of Jan Kubelik, the famous violinist whose " bow ran fast over all the high strings fluttering and wild," [339] his brilliant playing likened to the laughter of young girls in

Bohemia in the company of their lovers on a Sunday afternoon; or again the poet describes the music of the versatile violinist as interpreting in low, quivering notes the depth of joy of a mother over a new child.

Reflecting the poet's kinship to those of his own profession are brief poems to Emily Dickinson and Stephen Crane. Another is dedicated to R.F. who may be Robert Frost, for Frost and Sandburg were warm friends in the Chicago days. Sandburg was later to dedicate a book *(Home Front Memo)* to Stephen Vincent Benét and poems to Archibald MacLeish. In the early days of *Poetry* magazine, and while with the Chicago *Daily News*, he came into close contact with many poets and prose writers and journalists.

But it is not until a later date, when Sandburg essayed poems of broader vision and greater literary attainment, that more of the professional types of society came within his poetic horizon. If we were to accept his judgment of the legal profession by his concept of lawyers in the *Chicago Poems*, it would be an unflattering picture. One can only conclude that he had not come in contact with good lawyers, or that his early judgment may have been colored or warped by the experience of his father in Galesburg when a mortgage on property he had bought from another Galesburg citizen came to light in the safe deposit papers of the deceased mortgage holder; in this manner August Sandburg was compelled by law to pay the mortgage after he thought the property had been paid for. Such an unfortunate situation was not the fault of the lawyers (for none were employed); the condition may have arisen from negligence in an unwise business transaction, or from lack of information on the part of both persons. A lawyer at the time of purchase could have been August Sandburg's best friend, for he would immediately have investigated the title to the property to discover whether it was clear and unencumbered. We cannot consider the poet's earliest judgment of lawyers as a complete portrayal of the legal profession. The Cook County of that Chicago period cannot be held representative of American life of today—or indeed of many other sections of America in that unhappy period of 1910-1920. I am reminded of President Wilson's words concerning the need for reform in these years:

" The nation has been deeply stirred by a solemn passion, stirred by the knowledge of wrong, of government too often debauched and made an instrument of evil. The feelings with which we face this new age of right and opportunity sweep across our heartstrings like some air out of God's own presence, where justice and mercy are reconciled and the judge and the brother are one." *

Sandburg has written with deepest respect since then of the law practice of Abraham Lincoln in Springfield, Illinois, and his interpretation of the spirit of Constitutional Law as President. In carefully considered prose, he has written at length of the development of Constitutional Law, and of

---

* Allan NEVINS and Henry Steele COMMAGER, *America; the story of a free people*, Oxford, Clarendon Press, 1943, p. 382.

many famous lawyers of the nineteenth century. He came, at a later date, to know intimately members of the legal profession. He collaborated (1949) as we have previously noted with Oliver R. Barrett, a Chicago lawyer, in a volume of prose entitled *Lincoln Collector*.

More particularly in his later prose works has Sandburg dealt with the evolution of the liberal professions in the history of America. In the early twentieth century a new class of professions emerged and he has given them appropriate recognition in poetry by his portrayal of engineers, architects, technical experts, scientists and men of specialized skills. This recognition began as early as the writing of " Windy City " when he " mentions proud things " [340] and catalogues them; he emphasizes the importance of bevels and blueprints for this was a period when rapid industrialization brought forth many new skills.

In " Good Morning, America," the poet pays sincere tribute to the country's professional engineers who designed and constructed America's great cathedrals, her bridges, her railroads, her skyscrapers, her ships, for it was in the trained minds of these men that the plans were conceived and it was by their specialized techniques that the plans were executed. They represent " the endless yearnings of man for the beyond, for lights beyond." [341]

Poems on American Family Life

" I asked professors who teach the meaning of life to tell me what is happiness.

. . . . .

And then one Sunday afternoon I wandered out along the Desplaines River
And I saw a crowd of Hungarians under the trees with their women and children... and an accordion." [342]

I believe that Sandburg's concept of greatest happiness is that derived from family affection. One could not complete a discussion of people who are subjects of Sandburg poetry without making mention of those individuals who are dearest to Carl Sandburg's heart—his family. Nor would a discussion of his poetry be complete without making mention of poetry based on family life and affection.

Young Carl Sandburg was reared in a family in which love and mutual devotion were paramount. This is clearly demonstrated in the autobiography of his first twenty years, *Always the Young Strangers*. The volume was dedicated to " Mary, Mart and Esther," his two sisters and brother. The strength of affection is noteworthy. In his *Early Moon* poetry, under the heading " Children," we find the following delightful expression of nostalgic memories of childhood; and because it is to be hoped that something of the play spirit exists in all of us, this recollection of the poet's childhood memories and associations may perhaps have an even greater appeal to us as adults; it means something to an adult beyond the comprehension of the child, and has an appeal to each, but in a different way.

"Upstairs"

"I too have a garret of old playthings.
I have tin soldiers with broken arms upstairs.
I have a wagon and the wheels gone upstairs.
I have guns and a drum, a jumping-jack and a magic lantern.
And dust is on them and I never look at them upstairs.
I too have a garret of old playthings." [343]

We have previously noted that the first volume of poetry was dedicated to Mrs. Sandburg, the second to his two daughters, Janet and Margaret, the third to Col. Steichen (Mrs. Sandburg's brother) and the fourth to Helga, the youngest daughter. Further proof of the family devotion comes from many sources. One of the best sources is Professor Bruce Weirick, a longtime intimate friend of the poet, and now Professor Emeritus at the University of Illinois and author of an excellent book, *From Whitman to Sandburg in American Poetry*. From an article written in 1952 by Professor Weirick on Carl Sandburg, I wish to quote:

"How does Carl keep it up, at seventy-four? Going endlessly up and down America, reading his poems, gathering his folklore, taking a flyer on his first novel—of a thousand pages—at seventy, and with ten or a dozen books in mind right now, some of them half finished, keeping a sharp eye on the latest Lincoln discoveries; where does he get the immortal fire that makes him still delight like a young man to run a race? Well, I have been spying on him, and I have a theory. The episode of his sister and the portfolios is very revealing.* And the night he sold his Chicago home he happened to be at my house in Urbana while Mrs. Sandburg was in Elmhurst signing the papers, and I could not help but hear their telephone conversation. I hope Carl will forgive me, but it was gentle and excited, tipped with love's fires; as though they had just discovered each other. I think his women 'look after him.' Every day he is God in this Scandinavian Valhalla, free to come and to go; free to work and to be fed when he is ready; free to love and be loved." [344]

Concerning the poet's understanding of people, Mrs. Sandburg ** displays her own remarkable understanding of human nature when she says:

---

* His sister had presented Sandburg with a large scrap-book of published clippings which she had saved over many years—clippings about her famous brother.

** Mrs. Sandburg is a highly intelligent woman in her own right, but as the wife of Mr. Sandburg she prefers to work quietly in the background of his literary life, helping him with his career. She proofreads for him and discusses and helps evaluate poems before publication. She helped compile the representative selection for the unique publication, *The Sandburg Range*. Sandburg is proud of her intellect; and to reporters interviewing him he points out the literary and intellectual ability of his wife, remarking that in many areas of knowledge she is the better equipped of the two—such as in mathematics and science. Following her distinguished college career, Lilian Paula Steichen was a Latin teacher before she married Carl Sandburg.

" I have never felt left out. And I never felt that I had a right to interfere with Mr. Sandburg. I would have been selfish. The two most understanding men I have ever known are my husband and my brother, and both have attained some degree of greatness in their field. So I think understanding and greatness go together. I have known of artists having their heads turned by fame—but I don't believe they were great in the first place." [345]

The foregoing evidences of family affection explain the presence of deeply personal family portraits among the poems. A word picture of Mrs. Sandburg in her Chicago flower garden is set forth in the poem " Paula." Among several poems written for Mrs. Sandburg, we find " The Wind Sings Welcome in Early Spring " which characterizes the devotion of the couple. In lines of beautiful imagery of spring " wind-pushed, singing, silver and purple, " he bids her " come along now, come along always." [346]

While on his European trip as a war correspondent in 1918, he wrote the poem "Home Thoughts," clearly reflecting love for his family, the long, slow hours without them, the " drag on the heart, the iron drag of the long days. " [347]

Many poems are fond portraits of the Sandburg daughters. Particularly filled with imagery of the Scandinavian heritage is the poem " Helga " :

> " The wishes on this child's mouth
> Came like snow on marsh cranberries;
> The tamarack kept something for her;
> The wind is ready to help her shoes.
> The north has loved her; she will be
> A grandmother feeding geese on frosty
> Mornings *; she will understand
> Early snow on the cranberries
> Better and better then." [348]

Even in picturing his young daughter, Margaret, when learning to write numbers, the poet resorts to imagery. Some of the numbers are " straightforward, military, filled with lunge and attack, erect in shoulderstraps " while others may be " saluting each other as dancing sisters " or " swinging to handclaps like a trapeze actor." [349] His daughter Janet is " young light blue calling to young light gold of morning." [350] In his poetry of family life Sandburg has emphasized its basic importance in the American tradition.

In the social portraits of these Chicago days, i.e. in the context of his own time, Sandburg observes the nation with a non-partisan, non-political eye; with the eye of a prophet who distills the wisdom of the past and with a moral imperative attempts to arouse his readers from the errors and economic inequalities of the machine age. He detaches himself from

---

* The reference to a grandmother in the poem is a reference to Sandburg's maternal grandmother who kept geese and ducks in Apuna, Sweden, where Sandburg's mother helped her feed them at the two ponds on their Swedish farm. The imagery of the Swedish landscape has been partly derived from his immigrant parents and partly from Carl Sandburg's year in Sweden as a war correspondent in 1918.

politics more by instinct than by deliberation, and redefines the guiding light of justice and idealism that has been the directive force of American tradition. Because his humanitarianism made him susceptible to the social and economic distortions of industrialism as it existed in that period he became the best known poetic interpreter of the rise of the industrialized and rapidly expanding cities of America—a period that ushered in a new system of transportation, finance and an economy which would bring a greatly changed national picture.

(h) *The American People and World War I*

The first war poems of Carl Sandburg are not his greatest. But there is implicit in them a fundamental shift of opinion when compared with his earlier discussion of the Spanish-American War. Then war, as a campaign, was faced unquestioningly. Now in the more mature Sandburg the main reaction is horror at the thought that fine young men, selected for strength and vigor, must become targets for guns, "fixed in the drag of the world's heartbreak, on a long job of killing, sixteen million men." [351] In the poem "Iron" he pictures "broad, iron shovels scooping out oblong vaults" in the battlefields—and symbolizes the horrible futility of war by the line: "The shovel is brother to the gun." [352] These poems are a reflection of his own personal aversion to war in principle, and of his opinion of war as a moral wrong. The United States had not yet become involved in World War I when these earliest war poems were written, and the poet was not yet as deeply stirred by war as in later days. He writes of the unavailing waste and destruction, together with the general hideousness of human sacrifice; even in the poem " Wars " there is an impersonal expression rather than kindled indignation.

The American Spirit in 1917

But the war touched the poet more deeply by 1917; in a memoir on General Joffre, who visited America in the interests of the war effort, Sandburg described him as having the dynamic voice " of the long firing line that runs from the salt sea dunes of Flanders to the white spear crags of the Swiss mountains," " the man on whose yes and no has hung the death of battalions and brigades "; the man who " speaks the tricolor of his country, now melted in a great resolve with the starred bunting of Lincoln and Washington." The response of America to the appeal of General Joffre was that of " American hands and voices equal to sea breakers." [353]

In November 1917 came the long poem " The Four Brothers " in angry condemnation of the Kaiser. It is a voice of indignation that thirty million men must offer themselves to stem the tide of war brought on by " the last of the gibbering Hohenzollerns "; [354] and it reflects his opinion that the time had come for America to enter the war to aid in the preservation of democratic principles as opposed to military might and despotism. This shift of opinion from a horror of war's brutalities to a firm decision that

America must enter the conflict is taken by a man conscious of the meaning of war for the soldier, and it was a step that symbolized the change in American national opinion over these years.

The American spirit in 1917 is forcefully interpreted in the lines:

" At first I said it in anger as one who clenches his fist in wrath to fling his knuckles into the face of someone taunting;
Now I say it calmly as one who had thought it over and over again at night, among mountains, by the sea-combers in storm.
I say now... only fighters today will save the world, nothing but fighters will keep alive the names of those who left red prints of bleeding feet at Valley Forge in Christmas snow." [355]

Moreover, the poet voices personal regret that he (because of his thirty-nine years) must stand on the sidewalk as an onlooker, as he sees regiments of young men march past " with drums and guns and bugles—and the flag." [356]

America felt deeply the bravery and courageous self-sacrifice of those youths who were willing to " throw away their lives by hunger, deprivation, desperate clinging to a single purpose imperturbable and undaunted."[357]

The tragedy that such a war could come again to America, who had fought a war of her own in defense of the national liberty, was in the mind of the poet. His " heart tightened, a fist of something felt his throat," as he watched young Americans marching to join the greatest " man-hunt of men " ever remembered; leaving " homes empty, wives wishing, mothers wishing." [358]

In the war and post-war poetry, the young men who fought were always in the poet's mind—their personal sacrifices and contributions deserving of honor and deepest respect and gratitude. Only they could fully comprehend the horror of " getting shattered in shambles of reek and fire "; only they could fully comprehend the supreme acts of sacrifice and devotion in line of service; yet both productive and fighting forces were necessary to victory, and Sandburg pays tribute to both as he portrays a people and a country with " strengths, lights and faiths to wrestle with any dark destinies ahead." [359] These lines reflect the patriotism and the hopes of America in 1917.

In the later war poetry there is a fusion of humanitarian instinct and devotion to democratic idealism. The poet expressed American hopes that the war would prove to be a cleansing of the world from power-mad tyrants; that peace and the freedom of the democratic way of life might become the voice of the people in many lands. " Out of it all a God who sees and pierces through, is breaking and cleaning out an old thousand years, is making ready for a new thousand years." [360]

The War as Seen by Carl Sandburg in Europe

By 1918 Carl Sandburg was in Europe as a war correspondent. In this official capacity of staff foreign correspondent for the Newspaper Enterprise Association, Sandburg wrote of conditions in Europe toward the close of World War I. He listened to the conversations of soldiers, and he talked with soldiers; and, as a representative of American journalism, he was granted interviews with important personalities such as Constantine Greaves, former chamberlain of the court of Russia and campanion of Czar Nicholas; reports of such talks and interviews thus gave first-hand information; at other times he volunteered his own views for publication. In one instance he reports from Christiania, Norway, the views of a Copenhagen newspaper editor who had published his own impression of a trip to the Danish-German border when the first " big break in the German revolution came " and the Kaiser fled to Holland. Prussian officers with their epaulettes torn off were described, as were also the common soldiers who were running affairs for themselves.

" ' What do you think about the armistice terms ? ' we ask a young infantryman, who answers : ' They are only the terms of the big ones, the few. Now we are going to see if the people themselves will handle it better... It was not the people who wished the war. We have all the time wished peace and it is the time now for us to fix the terms of peace.'

' Will the peace in Germany come the same way as in Russia, with the whole overclass disfranchised ? '

' Those who willed the war and expected to gain from it must pay for it... The people have taken the power.' " [361] Thus ran the story of the confidence of a youthful German soldier.

On December 28, 1918, there was published in America a report sent from Norway by Sandburg with information given by a man who had just returned from five months in Kiev, Moscow and Petrograd. This information dealt with the size and character of the Bolshevik Army.

" They said in some places [in Russia] there are now a million Red Guards in the army. Many young men are going in who don't care about Bolshevism. They want to see fighting, and they get better to eat.

" So many thieves have been shot down in the streets that a good healthy thief prefers army life to the risk of street robbery. It is a common saying that all the old professional crooks have either gone into the army or into other countries... The Bolshevik Government is trying to establish a monopoly on robbery. The motto is : If there is going to be any stealing let the Soviets do it... There is a new militarism in Russia. Six hours work a day and two hours a day military drill was the rule in all the shops and factories I heard spoken of." [362]

In January, 1919, Sandburg wrote of the presence in Stockholm of General Trepoff, former Russian premier under the Romanoff regime, and of his effort to organize Russian forces for a counter-attack against the Bolsheviks, a military campaign which would " use Finland as a base, and which would enter Russia from the north, having the capture of Petrograd as its first objective." [363]

Sandburg also wrote of conditions in Finland, based on information in Stockholm. Stockholm estimates placed the number of starving people in Finland at 1,500,000 or one-half of Finland's population; 27,000 were in prison camps; and a Finnish Socialist committee at Stockholm claimed that more than 10,000 of the imprisoned Socialists had died from lack of food.

In the same month of January, 1919, Sandburg wrote of the Czar's abdication, and mailed to the United States the translations of the last personal entries in the Czar's Diary, showing that Nicholas Romanoff had renounced his crown hoping thereby to strengthen his armies. " My abdication is necessary... The cause is one such that it is necessary to take a conclusive step to save Russia and uphold the armies at the front." [364]

Again in January, 1919, Sandburg wrote of the " ravaged lands and decimated populations... A former Russian nobleman pleads with me as an American citizen to gain him an interview with President Wilson so that he may present evidence which he swears will bring the American Chief Executive to throw 200,000 American troops into Russia. He urges that it would be the height of American idealism for boys from New York, San Francisco and Chicago to push on to Moscow and save civilization from the clutch of the Bolsheviks... And from Finnish circles... they have told me, with sober and zealous face, that thousands of Finns, massacred by the white terror, were forced to dig their own graves and then were shot down and thrown into the trenches their own hands had dug... The light in the eyes of the Finns who told me the story in Stockholm was a weird light of eyes that had seen unearthly things." [365]

On January 6, 1919, the content of Sandburg's syndicated column is almost prophetic of the future, in one of the paragraphs quoting Constantine Greaves, former chamberlain of the court of Russia. After a two hour interview with the former Russian nobleman in Stockholm, Sandburg sent a long report to the United States which was spread across the front page and given large headlines covering seven columns in a Cleveland newspaper. The key paragraph emphasizes the anarchist aspect of the Russian Revolution and is interesting particularly in comparison with the later Russia of the mid-century. It reads as follows:

" The Bolsheviks say: ' Let us turn the world upside down and see how it will run that way.' ' They must eventually fail, even if the civilized world permits them to do what they please. But there is great danger that they may spread their doctrines from Russia and threaten all other nations,' says Greaves."

The Sandburg column described Mr. Greaves as belonging " to the centrum, which is not Bolshevik and not monarchist—but constitutional democracy. At this interview, the Russian presented the need for intervention by the Allies and America with 200,000 soldiers to help overthrow the Red Army and establish order in Russia. ' I know the Russian people. The masses of them would stand by and look on at the war between the Reds and the intervening Army... They would willingly accept the new government which would be established... The Russian peasant cannot understand how he himself should be the government. He is not like the French peasant, nor the English or American workingman. His religion and schools have never taught democracy to him.' " [366]

It is interesting to compare the above with the present-day story of the Russian Revolution written by Boris Pasternak, who in *Dr. Zhivago* speaks with intellectual honesty and with consideration for the people and for individual rights, and respect for the human mind; his book is in sympathy with the Russian Revolution against the Czar; but it laments the deterioration of freedom which replaced royalist repression. His Russian people are ever in his mind. He writes :

" When the revolution came and woke him up [the Russian peasant] he decided that this was the fulfilment of his dream, his ancient dream of living on his own land by the work of his hands, in complete independence and without owing anything to anyone. Instead of that he found he had only exchanged the old oppression of the Tzarist state for the new, much harsher yoke of the revolutionary super-state." [367]

Concerning Russia today, we read in Pasternak's book :

" Everything established, settled, everything to do with home and order and the common round, had crumbled into dust and been swept away in the general upheaval and reorganization of the whole of society. The whole human way of life has been destroyed and ruined. All that's left is the bare, shivering human soul, stripped to the last shred, the naked force of the human psyche for which nothing has changed because it was always cold and shivering and reaching out to its nearest neighbor as cold and lonely as itself... The immeasurable greatness which has been created in the world in all the thousands of years... It is in memory of all that vanished splendor that we live and love and weep and cling to one another." [368]

The journalistic career of Carl Sandburg thus shows him not only as an interpreter of America, but also as a reporter of war-time and post-war conditions in Europe for the benefit of American readers. In direct contrast to the freedom of critical expression permitted Sandburg in America was the suppression of critical expression imposed on Pasternak in Communist Russia. Banished from the Writers' Union, threatened with exile, his book refused publication within Russia, he had to submit to that silence enforced where there is a deterioration of freedom. In many ways he seems to me a Russian Sandburg. He loved his people. He felt " bound to Russia by birth, life and work" and could not "imagine his fate apart from Russia." * Pasternak was *of* and *for* his people, but not privileged to speak *to* his people. Sandburg is privileged to speak loudly on behalf of any inequalities and has done so on many occasions, winning the respect of his government and the love of all who know him for his appeals are on behalf of moral justice, on behalf of humanitarianism.

Sandburg's journalistic experience abroad, his interviews with military leaders, common soldiers, political leaders and refugees combined to make of him one of the better-informed Americans concerning the European situation after the first World War.

---

* Paris Edition of the New York *Herald Tribune*, Nov. 3, 1958.

(i)   *Post-War Chicago*

After his duties as a war-correspondent in Europe had been completed Sandburg returned to Chicago. He found changes in the social conditions because of the rapid war-mobilization of industry. Some of the conditions of post-war Chicago may be gathered from his articles appearing in the *Daily News* after his return from Stockholm. Since his literary talents had become nationally and internationally recognized, he preferred to write columns of a literary nature; of interviews with important people living in, or visiting Chicago; and columns on problems of general civic interest. Seeing dark clouds of discontent and trouble in the " Black Belt " of Chicago, he wrote a series of articles urging intelligent civic planning to prevent serious outbreaks. He urged the City Council to do something for the young soldiers returning from the battlefields of Europe and asking for their old jobs in the stockyards, only to be apprised that the meat packers had given these jobs to negroes willing to work for less pay.

Had the Sandburg pleas been heeded, the Chicago Race Riots that ensued (1919) might possibly have been averted. Because of his knowledge of conditions, Sandburg was delegated by the *Daily News* to investigate the situation following the riots. The articles that he wrote on his findings attracted the attention not only of Chicago but of the entire nation. These articles immediately were recognized as being of considerable sociological importance and were collected and published in treatise form for use in groups studying social conditions, and for collateral reading in college sociology classes.* They are regarded as a classic treatment of the question even today, and are still in wide circulation for study purposes. The seventy-one pages of the treatise contain Sandburg's careful analysis of living conditions in the " Black Belt " (the biggest overcrowding problem ever to have existed in Chicago). He connects these findings on one hand with " blind lawless government failing to function through policemen ignorant of Lincoln, the Civil War, the Emancipation Proclamation, and a theory sanctioned in a storm of red blood; and on the other hand, with a gaunt, involuntary poverty from which issues the hoodlum. "

Among his recommendations at the close of the treatise, was the following: " The race question is national and federal. No city or state can solve it alone... A commission consisting of men and women from both races should be appointed to investigate and make recommendations. Such a commission, if it has the right people on it, takes the thought of people away from violence. That was our experience in the Atlanta riots." *

This recommendation of Sandburg is prophetic, for decades later race riots were to require federal intervention.

---

* *The Chicago Race Riots* by Carl SANDBURG: published by Harcourt, Brace and Howe, 1919, 71 pages. Introduction by Walter Lippman.

(j) *The Lost Generation*

One of the strongest war poems to come as an aftermath of World War I is entitled " And So Today," which is the Sandburg interpretation of the burial of the Unknown Soldier in Arlington Cemetery near Washington. The poem has been widely quoted in America. Here the poet states ironically that the lesson of the soldier's supreme sacrifice cannot be fully known by the orators at the formal ceremony, who " file this human document away in granite and steel—with music and roses, salutes, proclamations of the honorable orators." [369]

Sandburg has the deeply rooted conviction that such sacrifice of life has not even yet been fully comprehended; and he evokes the memory of earlier battles in American history involving great loss of life; he evokes the " skeleton riders on skeleton horses, the ghosts of the bony battalions " [370] of the Potomac, the Rio Grande, the Ohio and the Rappahannock. He expresses both hope and a tinge of ironic doubt in this poem to the Unknown Soldier. The helpless, hopeless spirit of disillusionment after President Wilson was unable to secure ratification by the United States Senate of the Covenant of the League of Nations in 1919, following the holocaust of World War I, is reflected throughout the long poem which concludes with the saddening burial of the Unknown Soldier " under a sky of promises." [371]

The poem is indicative also of the despondency and feeling of futility felt by *the Lost Generation*, those writers who had returned from the armed services following World War I, to the despair of the 1920's; and it is illustrative—painfully so—of the despair felt in America after President Wilson failed to obtain the ratification of the disputed Covenant when he returned from Paris. Further interpretation of the period of disillusionment is contained in the poem " Crimson Changes People " in which Sandburg employs the symbol of the " useless gesture " of the hand of the returned soldier " trying to say with a code of five fingers something the tongue only stutters." [372] In the Sandburg " Prayer After World War " is a searching plea for some faint ray of hope :

> " Wandering oversea singer,
> Singing of ashes and blood,
> Child of the scars of fire,
> Make us a new dream, us who forget.
> Out of the storm let us have one star." [373]

The poet is seen here as a social conscience and a voice of national awareness, for people in all walks of life felt this despair, horror at the waste of human life, frustration and lack of direction; for the one positive feature, the emergence of the League of Nations, had failed. Through the medium of his verse and journalism Sandburg communicated and made articulate much that was merely sensed by others.

Sandburg, in later years, tried to analyse this period of despair since he felt strongly that the Unknown Soldier and all those who fought with him had been betrayed.

" A great war has its hundreds of heroes whose names stand out, blazed high on the public records. But they are only a handful and often what they did would not have been possible except for the hundreds of thousands, even the millions, who hammered out weapons, raised and transported food, wrote letters sending messages of faith, love and hope—those anonymous ones too vast for the record, these and the loyal soldier who does his plain, humdrum duty—they and the Unknown Soldier belong to each other.

" What if the sleeping one there at Arlington tonight should wake and speak to these anonymous ones? He might have any one of a thousand questions to ask, and perhaps not least would be ' Wasn't the war we fought supposed to be a war to end war?' And perhaps someone with a solemn face and a voice not free from grief and guilt would answer : ' Yes, but when peace came we didn't know how to keep the peace. We made mistakes.' " [374]

Sandburg voiced the fact that there were many people " praying, thinking, hoping " that never again would there be a " betrayal of the Unknown Soldier who fights and gives his all—even his life. Perhaps we have found the will and vision. Time will tell—time and our will and vision." [375]

(k) *Economic and Industrial Problems of the People (1930-1940)*

Both Europe and America suffered long years of serious depression as the century moved out of the 1920's. Therefore literature, if true to life, could not, in the period of the 1930's, be gay or nonchalant. *The People, Yes* is the product of an analytical approach to the challenge of the decade :

> " The unemployed
> without a stake in the country
> without jobs or nest eggs
> marching they don't know where
> marching north south west—
> and the deserts
> marching east with dust
> deserts out of howling dust-bowls
> deserts with winds moving them
> marching toward Omaha toward Tulsa—
> these lead to no easy pleasant conversation
> they fall into a dusty disordered poetry." [376]

Sandburg communicates to the reader a spirit of compassion for those whom the depression forced into the ranks of dislocation and economic want. The man " idle amid plants also idle " [377] was human tragedy.

> " Who can make a poem of the depths of weariness
> bringing meaning to those never in the depths?
>
> . . . . .
>
> How can a poem deal with production cost
> and leave out definite misery paying
> a permanent price in shattered health and early old age?" [378]

To Sandburg human relations and human fellowship in this stream of economic unrest were an integral part of the story of the dislocation of the period, and deserving of the most serious study. These strains were common to the entire industrialized world at this time. Russia was sealed off by self-chosen seclusion. On the continent of Europe, some countries swung to Fascism in an attempt to solve their economic, political and financial problems. The problems facing America were universal problems associated with the depression and general social bankruptcy. As totalitarianism increased its challenge to the free democracies of the world, so eminent a writer as Ernest Hemingway, in his *Green Hills of Africa,* wrote that he had finished " serving time for society, democracy, and the other things." [379] Carl Sandburg on the other hand remained one of the strong voices of democracy. He shared the life of the average American citizen.

He bitterly lamented the toll in human suffering; the sight of jobhunters handed refusals until they despaired of ever finding work again; yet he recognized that there were also loafers " misled with the idea that the idle poor should imitate the idle rich." [380] He had deep compassion for those with " savings gone, furniture and keep-sakes pawned and the pawntickets blown away in cold winds "; [381] and for those who had " crossed over from the employables into the unemployables." [382] The migratory harvest hands, the loan shark victims, the victims of the installment house wolves, the wandering berry pickers, were objects of the author's pity.

He pointed to many imperfections in our government in the 1930's :

" Stocks are property, yes.
Bonds are property, yes.
Machines, land, buildings are property, yes.
. . . . .
The rights of property are guarded
by ten thousand laws and fortresses.
The right of a man to live by his work—
what is this right?
and why does it clamor? " [383]

Such imperfections were not confined to the 1930's. Neither are they confined to the United States nor the New World; such pictures were not unknown in English history or in French history. We turn the pages of the poetry of François Villon to find in mediaeval France, Villon's " Question au clerc du Guichet " ou " Ballade de l'appel."

" Se fusse des hoirs Hue Capel
Qui fut extrait de boucherie,
On ne m'eut, parmi ce drapel,*   * linge
Fait boire en cette écorcherie.**   ** lieu de torture
Vous entendez bien joncherie? ***   *** tromperie
Mais quand cette peine arbitraire
On me jugea par tricherie,
Étoit il lors temps de moi taire? " †

† François VILLON, *Œuvres.* Edition Garnier, Paris; p. 156.

In Sandburg's belief, the people of today are not entirely products of present civilization but of past civilization as well : " They are what they are because they have come out of what was." [384]

In further criticism : " ' The poor of the earth hide themselves together,' wrote Job meaning in those days too, they had a shantytown." [385]

As Sandburg pictures the poorer sections of the large cities, he writes not only with realistic criticism, but also with faith in gradual improvement :

> " In the slums overshadowed by smokestacks
> In the tomato cans in the window-sills
> The geraniums have a low weeping song,
> ' Not yet have we known the sun,'
> Modulated with a hoping song
> ' Some day we shall meet the sun
>
> . . . . .
> And be no longer stunted.' " [386]

He senses the reality of the class hatreds and wars that arise from such conditions, and he believes their greatest effect has been to retard the advance of popular governments, and to encourage " gang wars, civil tumults, industrial strife, international mass murders."

> " And the war lasts till the hate dies down...
> And after the strife of war begins the strife of peace.
>
> . . . . .
> Though the hate of the people dies slow and hard.
> Hate is a lingering heavy swamp mist." [387]

In this manner Sandburg, in his painstaking and illuminating story of the evolution of the common people over the earth, traces their efforts and failures, and their slow gains in various regions. Symbolically he writes :

> " In a hothouse room where sunlight never came
> Hundreds of monster plants winding and twisting
>
> . . . . .
> Crept and reeled in processions
> Of obedient giant clowns and dwarfs, grotesques,
> Symbols of an underworld not yet organized by man,
> Tokens of plenty and hunger in the controls of man
> And the master of these dumb clumsy growths,
> A drawf and a hunchback, a deep believer
> In the spirit of man mastering material environment,
> Out of Schenectady a wizard loving mankind in peak and abyss,
> Saying science and invention are the enemies of human want
> And the world is organized to abolish poverty
> Whenever the people of the world so will." [388]

In the above lines Sandburg writes of Steinmetz, the famous mathematician and electrical engineer, as a symbol of men with free imaginations and special skills " bringing changes into a world resenting change "; [389] such men, as wise leaders and counselors, are the best hope of the people.

Sandburg does not abandon his faith in democracy, when he urges the need for such wise leaders or guides at the head of national affairs. He affirms the American presidential government pattern, and maintains the belief that, despite all imperfections, the American people must be trusted with the care of electing their governors. And he champions the cause of collective man as the shaper and maker of human destiny. He well knows that there are men who can't be bought—that present-day society is a paradox " wherein man is brother to mud and gold, to behemoths and constellations "; [390] that " the strong man, the priceless one who wants nothing for himself and has his roots among his people, comes often enough for the people to know him and to win through into gains beyond later losing." [391] He builds his case on firm foundations of popular strength through long-continued, concerted effort. He portrays the people as a builder, learning by experience; as a builder of democratic government in which authority is eventually vested in themselves:

> " In so few eyeblinks
> In transition lightning streaks,
> The people project midgets into giants,
> The people shrink titans into dwarfs." [392]

The people constitute the " one and only source of armies, navies, work gangs, the living flowing breath of the history of nations "; [393] the people are the only supreme word, the source of political strength; but this is achieved only through solidarity of aim and the light of vision.

The author presents Lincoln to the reader as a symbol of faith in democracy even when his country knew mass chaos and internecine strife, as one who never lost sight of the American dream of freedom and unity. As " humble dust of a wheel-worn road, slashed sod under iron-shining plow," [394] Lincoln experienced the sternest of personal trials and vicissitudes and could fully comprehend the struggle of the common man, for he too, had been a struggler.

" It is the many he knows, the gaunt strong hunger of the many." [395]

It is, therefore, as a follower of Lincoln and all that he came to stand for that Sandburg voices his own belief that the common people are the hope of humanity and the most reliable basis of government:

> " The people is a lighted believer and hoper—
>
> . . . . .
> The panderers and cheaters are to have their way in trading on these
>   lights of the people?
> Not always, no, not always, for the people
>   is a knower too...
> Knowing what it knows today with a deeper
>   knowing than ever...
> The people, a knower whose knowing
>   grows by what it feeds on
> The people wanting to know more, wanting." [396]

" Time is a great teacher " [397] and the ability of the people to think things over, to select, to decide—to reach " for lights beyond the prism of the five senses, " [398] to act with concerted effort—all these are important factors in popular sovereignty. The people of a democracy have the strength and ability to survive failure, disappointments and depressions, to achieve success, to envision the Family of Man :

> " In the drive of faiths on the wind today the people know :
> ' We have come far and we are going farther yet.' " [399]

In *The People, Yes*, Sandburg becomes more than ever a fighting spirit for the democratic principles of his country.

I am reminded of a parallel in the literature of France :

" Mais que Hugo aussi était dans tout ce peuple ! . . . Non pas vers qui chantent dans la mémoire, mais vers qui dans la mémoire sonnent et retentissent comme une fanfare, vibrants, trépidants, sonnant comme une fanfare, sonnant comme une charge, tambour éternel, et qui battra dans les mémoires françaises après que les réglementaires tambours auront cessé de battre au front des régiments." [400]

Sandburg has always been " in this people "; but never in a more defensive mood. His word power, though not *chantant*, becomes a vibrant, surging charge. In this array of force lie his evocation of democracy with a " dignity of deepening roots," [401] his flag of hope " which ties itself yonder-yonder." [402] As portraiture of the common people, *The People, Yes* is a book " so passionate and alive that, like the spirit of a plant or an animal, it has an architecture of its own, and gives to nature a new thing." [403]

(1) *The American People and World War II*

Carl Sandburg is not a believer in war. The spirit of America, hoping for peace and still bearing deep marks of the aftermath of World War I —the war to end wars—is characterized as follows :

> " The steel mill sky is alive,
> The fire breaks white and zigzag
> Shot on a gun-metal gloaming.
> Man is a long time coming.
> Man will yet win.
> Brother may yet line up with brother." [404]

Both pathos and tragic symbolism are contained in the war poem " A.E.F." :

> " There will be a rusty gun on the wall,
> The rifle grooves curling with flakes of rust.
> A spider will make a silver string nest in the
>   darkest, warmest corner of it.

" The trigger and the range-finder, they too, will be rusty.
And no hands will polish the gun, and it will hang on the wall.
Forefingers and thumbs will point absently and casually toward it.
It will be spoken among half-forgotten, wished-to-be-forgotten things.
They will tell the spider : Go on, you're doing good work." [405]

Nevertheless, this poet made radio broadcasts and public speeches on behalf of the Roosevelt policy during the early course of World War II. In November 1940, on election eve, the last five minutes of a two-hour nation-wide broadcast, ending at midnight before the opening of the polls, were given over to Carl Sandburg, who spoke to a radio audience estimated at eighty million listeners; his broadcast was the only one by a political independent during the nation-wide hook-ups.

On June 7, 1941, in the cause of national unity, at a time when the momentous decision of American entry into the war alongside Great Britain hung in the balance, Sandburg addressed a mass meeting of 24,000 people in the Chicago Stadium. The closing lines of his speech demonstrate his loyalty to President Roosevelt's war policy :

" The future is beyond any man's reading. We are moving into an adventure beyond the horizon and I am taking my chances with those who say : ' God bless the President of the United States.' " [406]

In Sandburg, the journalist, is that spirit of Americanism which includes freedom of speech, freedom of the press and freedom of religion. These freedoms he dramatically dealt with in a syndicated article published May 11, 1941, entitled " Murderers of Books." In it he forcefully deplored the public banning and burning of certain books by the Hitler regime in Germany—valuable books which would be lost to posterity unless measures were taken outside Germany to save them. A memorial service, honoring these particular books, was held in the Library of Congress, Washington, D. C., and an organization formed to preserve, by reprinting, all such books deemed valuable to posterity. Sandburg's article on the Hitler ban and the book memorial service at the Library of Congress made such a profound impression on the public mind that a portion of it is herewith reproduced :

" In a Library of Congress hall a little memorial program was given. And why not ? Why shouldn't a living library, representing a nation and a people building an arsenal of democracy, memorialize certain books ?

" Over Nazified Europe these books have been put to death. With grimaces, jeers, maledictions, these books have been burnt, banned, published as dead, and the epitaphs chosen. Einstein, the German Jew, the mathematician with a hair-trigger imagination—his works are *verboten.* The little song of the " Lorelei " by Heinrich Heine, the wit, the lyric writer, can't be read or sung except behind closed doors with an eye and an ear ready for the Gestapo, who might have heard about this personal taste in literature and music. And Thomas Mann was once read in the original German as published in what was then his country; if now in Berlin, Bremen, Breslau, Munich, they read Mann—they do it in secret and hide the forbidden book where they hope no informer might find it. Many more authors and books could be named. The theory of the [Nazi] authorities is that these books are destroyed for all time."

Other writers and other books are mentioned by Sandburg; among them are the writings of Karel Capek, the Czech, who died " in part from sheer heartbreak " because he no longer cherished life after Czechoslovakia had died its political death, with other deaths to come. In general, the books burned by the Nazi regime were those which advocated freedom of conscience and freedom of religion. Sandburg concludes :

" Maybe this is partly what the shooting is about. At least in the United States of America an organization has well under way the reprinting and restoration of every book of permanent value officially destroyed, purged, assassinated in Europe. These books have crossed the Atlantic Ocean for a rebirth and resurrection, available in the original languages for anyone the wide earth over who wishes to read them." [407]

Thus does Sandburg condemn the Nazi regime and its policy requiring death for outspoken believers in freedom and religious toleration, and for the books of such believers.

The Japanese attack on Pearl Harbor on December 7, 1941, stunned America with the impact of its shock, and the vast implications of its horror; but reaction came swiftly—and unanimously. On December 21, Sandburg wrote in his newspaper column that the approaching season could be darker; because a world that came near crashing still remained to struggle though by very narrow margins of circumstance.

" There was a free world, very imperfect, heavy with many wrongs, yet a world having definite political and personal freedom. Much of this free world is wrecked, humanly torn, bleeding, starving. Yet an immense section of it stands, sees, resists, fights, refuses to accept the Nazi anti-Christmas idea, prays for those in bondage and their eventual release. The phrase ' anti-Christmas ' goes well enough for the Nazis. Free-world readers of *Mein Kampf* find it a howling wilderness stony and bare of Christmas feeling... Faith, hope, kindly words and deeds, except as of direct arithmetical, bookkeeping benefit to Germans, are a snare and a delusion. *Mein Kampf* might be entitled Me ! Me ! Me ! or I ! I ! I ! and mislead no one... " It is " vast reeking ego, gone raving. With almost a touch of miracle came the national unity of the United States... The Japanese deed at Pearl Harbor... smote home to every American-hearted listener of the news and the tolling bells of doom... Now the pure Aryans of Berlin yoke themselves with the pure Mongols of Tokyo. Now it is four-fifths of the Family of Man signed up for a finish fight against the New Order in Europe and the Pacific. The ' New Order ' will be outfought and outthought. The war ending when ? " [408]

Sandburg threw all his support to President Roosevelt in his conduct of American participation in World War II.

In his newspaper columns during World War II, Sandburg had high praise for the " intellectually restless." To him the " intellectually restless " in American history contain some of America's greatest names. Benjamin Franklin, Thomas Jefferson, Abraham Lincoln, Thomas Edison and the Wright brothers had restless minds. " Any new military secrets that help us win this war, any new machines, processes, methods, will come from men who couldn't sleep nights because of ideas that fired their restless brains. " [409]

During World War II Sandburg was a visitor in many camps of the Armed Forces. Thousands of young soldiers came to know him and loved him. Still younger boys throughout America like to get his autograph.

He wrote with understanding sympathy of young boys in the war zones of Africa and Sicily, in the islands of the Pacific; he voiced deep concern for the young soldiers returning from the war, for young men hospitalized as victims of the war, of their slow gains mentally and physically; of a psychiatric division in a Naval Hospital; of mental readjustments; of physical rebuildings and of plastic surgery; of the dark inner strengths beyond casual fathoming in wounded veterans in hospitals; of the tragic toll of war even among many of those left alive; of shattered nerves and battered bodies; of battle experience that can never be fully communicated.

After writing in his novel of the horror and the nightmare, the courage and the vision at Anzio, at Saipan, at Okinawa, Sandburg presents a poem, " The Young Dead Soldiers " by Archibald MacLeish. This poem is a moving tribute to those who paid the supreme sacrifice in World War II; and it is a plea for lasting peace as the deepest expression of reverent gratitude.

" The young dead soldiers do not speak.
Nevertheless, they are heard in the still houses: who has not heard them?
They have a silence that speaks for them at night and when the clock counts.
They say: We were young. We have died. Remember us.
They say: We have done what we could but until it is finished it is not done.
They say: We have given our lives but until it is finished no one can know what our lives gave.
They say: Our deaths are not ours; they are yours; they will mean what you make them.
They say: Whether our lives and our deaths were for peace and a new hope or for nothing we cannot say; it is you who must say this.
They say: We leave you our deaths. Give them meaning. Give them an end to the war and a true peace. Give them victory that ends the war and a peace afterwards. Give them their meaning.
We were young, they say. We have died. Remember us." *

---

* This poem was included in *Remembrance Rock* (p. 1003), with the permission of its author, Archibald MacLeish, a close friend of Carl Sandburg.

President Franklin Delano Roosevelt

Sandburg, although a political independent, was, as we have already noted, a friend of President Roosevelt. The President himself conducted the poet through the White House in order that he might be thoroughly familiarized with it while writing of the White House years of President Lincoln. The furnishings associated with Lincoln were carefully designated. (President Hoover had also extended presidential courtesies to him at the White House.)

Thus, knowing of the friendship with President Roosevelt, we perceive and respect the depth of personal emotion and sense of loss in the poem " When Death Came April Twelve 1945." It is the Sandburg requiem at the death of the President, who, war-worn and fatigued by heavy responsibility, died suddenly. The poem is intensely moving in every line, infused with some of the profound emotional power and feeling with which the poet endowed the memorable closing of *The War Years:*

" And the whitening bones of men at sea bottoms
  or huddled and mouldering men at Aachen,
  They may be murmuring,
  ' Now he is one of us ',
  one answering muffled drums
  in the realm and sphere of the shadow battalions.

. . . . .

  Dreamer, sleep deep,
  Toiler, sleep long,
  Fighter, be rested now,
  Commander, sweet good night." [410]

In characterizing President Roosevelt as a " dreamer," Sandburg saw the President as symbolizing the Four Freedoms which he hoped humanity would accept as a future goal.

" Freedom of speech, freedom of worship, freedom from want and freedom from fear " [411] expressed the aims of Roosevelt's social pioneering.

Although these aims are far from realization, they are deeply humanitarian and in accord with Sandburg's vision of the Family of Man :

" . . . ' You are going too far when you talk about one
  world flag for the great Family of Nations,'
  they say that now.
  And man, the stumbler and finder, goes on,
  man the dreamer of deep dreams,
  man the shaper and maker,
  man the answerer. " [412]

To Sandburg, victory in World War II meant not merely winning a war over enemies in both the Pacific and the European theatres outside the United States of America; it meant the conquest of ourselves by learning the lesson from World War I of how to keep the peace when rewon. "What through war we have learned of human solidarity and national unity, what lessons we have gained, while making war, of the value of co-operation and humility, these we can hope to carry into peacetime for victory in the fields of wider personal freedom and of advances in national discipline and domestic welfare." [413]

On July 9, 1944, a Sandburg column was published in a syndicate of American newspapers—a column which in later years demonstrated the accuracy of his appraisal of international events during World War II. Excerpts from this column read as follows:

" The pitiless and inevitable consequences to follow this great war are harder to read beforehand than any previous war known to mankind, because never before has a war involved such a variety of motives, peoples, causes, such vast armed forces of populations, such immense and diversified areas of conflict.

" Whatever forms of control against future wars arise after the present slaughter ends will depend on the will, the vision and human lights of those who run the controls.

" Any scheme of international order that looks good on paper will depend for its working well on the character and personality of the men entrusted to operate the scheme." [414]

In the summer of 1950 the North Koreans marched into South Korea. During the Korean crisis the consulting-editor of the Chicago *Sun-Times* reprinted in the *Journal of the Illinois State Historical Society* the above paragraphs from the Sandburg column, which had been prophetic in their import.

In writing of the first atomic bomb Sandburg speaks of it as a joint international accomplishment; he describes the scientists who perfected the bomb as " pilgrims who had toiled to a far height to find themselves on a path skirting a precipice and only the strong could look with calm into the unfathomable pits of gray mist and rolling black clouds below the steep edge where their feet had clung "... But the author has faith in the ability of man to be the master of a brighter destiny : " Man goes on... Man is a changer. It is within possibility that you, my dear ones, may become the witnesses of the finest and brightest era known to mankind. You shall have music, the nations over the globe shall have music, music instead of murder. It is possible. That is my hope and prayer—for you and for the nations." [415]

In such vein Sandburg speaks his belief that peace is conceivable to men of good will; and that it is each citizen's duty to keep peace alive and freedom vital. In spite of the shortcomings of democracy he voices his faith in a finer America than we have yet seen.

(m) *Americans Today*

Chicago Today

" Today something else is wanted than the most perfect work composed by recognized rules. For us the greatest poet is he who in his work most stimulates the reader's imagination and reflection. The greatest poet is not he who has done the best; it is he who suggests the most; he not all of whose meaning is at first obvious, and who leaves you much to desire, to explain, to study, much to complete in your turn." [416]

—Sainte-Beuve

A " Poetic Reprise for Chicago's Laureate " was the title of the *Life* magazine article which described the signal honor conferred upon Carl Sandburg in the late summer of 1957 when through the special efforts of a group of industrialists and city planning officials, he was invited back to the midwestern metropolis from his present home in the kindlier climate of North Carolina. The committee had been appointed to honor and pay tribute to the city's present imposing architectural heritage. It invited Carl Sandburg to re-examine Chicago, to inspect the new buildings along with the historied and venerated old ones, to re-examine the mills and great industrial plants, to revisit the scenes of his former journalism and early poetry days. The committee invited him to write about Chicago in a new Chicago poem to be delivered as guest of honor at the Chicago Dynamic banquet.

Sandburg's tribute was delivered as an address; its lines fall rhythmically and impressively upon the listener's or the reader's mind. To illustrate the poet's opinion of the effective tide of progress and improvement in industrial and social conditions, not only in Chicago but in the nation, I shall present a portion of the Sandburg " poetic reprise " :

" Chicago Dynamic "

" We live in the time of the colossal upright oblong.
We are meeting in the city where the skyscraper was born.
But the first ones are overtowered by the far taller ones who laugh at how far they can gaze and what they see in the daytime across Lake Michigan and the Illinois prairie.
. . . . .
Speaking across the cool blue of the night mist :
What are we saying on the skyline?
. . . . .
Today's Chicago Dynamic has cut loose from old traditions and begun to make new ones." [417]

" I have seen an awareness and an anxiety about how Chicago builds today and tomorrow... far surpassing anything I have known in past generations. I have listened to what Chicago is saying on its skyline, writing proud with new tools and materials, slender shafts of stainless steel rising many floors with ease and grace, steel structures in gay porcelain robes gathering the colors of the rainbow into the skyline to flash with silver, bronze, copper and gold already there." *

Thus Sandburg symbolizes in the " writing " on the skyline the city's progress in terms of the human mind, the human will, the horizons of human

---

* Carl SANDBURG : "Chicago Dynamic" in the Library of Congress, Washington, D.C.

vision. These lines are very different from those which in an earlier day proclaimed the pathos of tired faces coming as though from a twisted " gargoyle spout." [418] His 1957 tribute to Chicago is proof of how a poet with a sense of social responsibility can serve as a force for moral and economic improvement in his community. At the same time, his treatment of the theme shows a consciousness of the advances that had been made. The social historian brings his picture up to date.

Thus, in celebrating the heritage of a newer and greater Chicago, the early Sandburg poems had been indisputably proven to be poems not only of harsh realism but also of social challenge. They represented a process of thought that moved beyond simple lyric poetry—an art which embodied the emotional climate of the metropolis in the early decades of the twentieth century. Somewhat in the manner of a trial lawyer, Sandburg presented his case to a Court of Appeals, for a revision of the existing social, moral and industrial codes of ethics. The case which he presented aroused debate, discussion, introspection, contemplation, action. Such stimulation of thought and emotion is one of the tests of poetry. Sandburg, as a poet of argument and protest, challenged the public conscience.

On his 1957 visit to Chicago, Sandburg was also taken to Gary, Indiana, to re-examine conditions among steel-workers of that city. In 1915 he had written the ironic pcem " Mayor of Gary." In that poem he had criticized working conditions in the steel industry.

By contrast, on the summer inspection tour among the steel-workers of Gary in 1957, it was a cheerful and contented poet who joked and talked with the Gary steel plant employees. In a portion of his 1957 "Chicago Dynamic " speech, Sandburg said : " If I had not seen the passing of the twelve-hour work day... I would not be here tonight. I like it and give it praise that the 21,000 men in the Gary Steel Works have an eight-hour day, a five-day week, time and half for Saturday. I give it praise that the workers have shower baths and lockers, and they can leave their eight-hour shift clean of body and in a change of clothes, if they so wish.

" If I had not written many poems, good, not so good, or rather bad, about Chicago, if I had not written about Chicago as a great world city, proud and strong for all the ugly and brutal, if I had not loved Chicago as Vic'or Hugo loved his Paris, as Charles Lamb loved his London, I would not be here tonight saying: ' Cheers ! and more cheers ! to the Chicago Dynamic Committee and their works and aims.

" If I had not written many poems, good, not so good, or rather bad about the steel mills and the men who make steel... If I had not tried desperately to capture the wild, flaming, violent grandeur of the process of making steel, if it were not for my hopes and attempts at writing an epic of steel and its makers, I would not be here tonight." *

Thus we have, in Carl Sandburg's own words, proof of his intentions in the earlier poems. His poetry may not have been " the most perfect work composed by recognized rules," but he had become the greatest poet of

* Library of Congress, Washington, D.C.

Chicago, for he had "suggested the most" and he had given Chicago "much to desire, to explain, to study, much to complete in its turn"; [419] and Chicago had completed much, leaving a present heritage for posterity to enjoy, emulate and continue.

In Sandburg's opinion Chicago had at last begun to think of itself in terms of the welfare of its people, in humanitarian terms, in terms of the future of its citizens. The city planning program and building program had carried their architectural plans and blueprints "*beyond economics and into the realm of people.*" "I see a degree of vision and good will that I believe cannot fail of good results." *

In one of his early Chicago poems, Sandburg had, as always, warned against mediocrity, in his line:

"Keep away from the little deaths." [420]

In 1957 he had praise for those who had "made no little plans", but had aimed "high in hope and works" * for the lasting benefit of the people of his beloved Chicago. Suggesting, as always, that improvement and human progress cannot admit complacency, but must prescribe a constant inventory, and vigilance, a self-examination, he poses three questions:

"Where did we come from?
Where are we now? Where are we going?
Chicago Dynamic faces these unafraid and strong." *

The Nation Today

In speaking of the American nation of today in the 1957 Chicago speech, Sandburg describes the social, economic and industrial progress of the country as follows:

"Chain supermarkets from coast to coast,
Concrete highways spanning the continent for a motorized America,
Millions of horses vanished into horizons of thin air to be replaced by
    millions of steel tractors, skyways and airport time-tables,
The candles of the early Lincoln generation replaced by Edison's light
    bulbs,
The sweated trades and slum needle workers amalgamated and moving
    into middle class comforts."

There is a touch of light irony as he describes the comforts enjoyed by the modern generation:

"And now the people, the vast millions by printer's ink and billboards,
    by neon signs and show windows, by radio and TV mandates over
    the airways night and day, the vast millions told to live better, to
    want more, to live more easy, to have more fun and comfort and
    even luxury." *

---

* Library of Congress, Washington, D.C.

But he pays sincere tribute to his America people who, in the face of two great World Wars, forged paths of industrial progress and of social and economic improvement. As evidence of American growth and development rise great buildings:

" Tall oblongs in orchestral confusion from the Battery to the Bronx, Along Market Street to the Ferry flashing the Golden Gate sunset.

. . . . .

Who are these tall witnesses? Who these high phantoms? " *

They are symbols of human progress, of human ingenuity. In the mind of the poet they speak of the march of American civilization in terms of the American people.

" They have made these steel skeletons like themselves— Lean, tumultuous, restless." [421]

But Carl Sandburg would recall to his people the lessons of past history, the sacrifice, the cost in human lives through pioneering in a new and untried world, the cost in human lives through the War of Independence, through the war to preserve the American democratic ideals of equal rights, the World Wars in defense of democracy.

" And now there is a material prosperity, a fat-dripping prosperity, surpassing any previously known.
And now there is complacency and conformity among the young people—to such an extent that educators on Commencement Day feel called to tell these young people:
' Beware of being satisfied with things as they are!
Beware of conformity in ideas!
This time of nuclear weapons and cold war is a crisis, the latest one.
There have been many others in the making of this nation.
The call to hardship, toil and combat runs like a blood-scarlet thread over and through the story of our American people.
It has cost to build this nation.' " *

In the above lines Sandburg's light irony is more clearly perceptible. Here he attacks, as he holds forth in admiration. Balancing, and to a certain extent outweighing opulence, have come a " complacency and conformity," a mixture of self-indulgence and self-interest. Here is a tendency toward a spiritual poverty instead of the material poverty of earlier times. But he notes these conditions with only a mild remonstrance, with little of the earlier crusading spirit. As later passages show, he has lost none of his confidence in the American people to direct their own affairs:

" Always the path of American destiny has been into the Unknown And never was it more true than now—the path of America leads into the Unknown." *

* Carl SANDBURG : " Chicago Dynamic," Library of Congress, Washington, D.C.

Sandburg has faith in the ability of his people to meet the challenges that come; the American people have always had the courage of their convictions; nor have they ever been afraid of the Unknown.

" In the Dark Ages many there and then
had fun and took love and made visions
and listened...
Then as now were the Unafraid

. . . . .

In either Dark Ages or Renaissance have there
been ever the Immeasurable Men, the Incalculable
Women, their outlooks timeless? " [422]

On February 12, 1959, Sandburg paid further tribute to the courage and vision of the Americans in facing the challenge of the new and untried— the Unknown—when, as a guest speaker before a joint session of Congress in Washington, he gave praise to " the mind and will of the men who created and navigated the marvel of the sea, the Nautilus, and her voyage from Pearl Harbor and under the North Pole icecap." [423]

The poet was a guest aboard an American Airline's 707 passenger jet plane on its first flight from New York to Los Angeles, and was asked to write his impressions for publication. Sandburg interprets by vivid flashes this first passenger jet flight across America at a speed of nearly 600 miles an hour, and four miles above the earth. He feels that this narrowing of the distances between states and rivers will cement the country still further.[424] To him the flight was an image of man's irrepressible search for knowledge and advancement and an achievement that further unifies the people of a wide continent.

The " lean, tumultuous, restless " people, symbolic of a young nation, face the Unknown Future " unafraid and strong." In his commentary accompanying Edward Steichen's " Road to Victory " photographic exhibit he has written:

" America, thy seeds of fate have borne a fruit of many breeds, many pages of hard work, sorrow and suffering—tough strugglers of oaken men— they live on—the fathers and mothers of soldiers, sailors, fliers, farmers, builders, workers—their sons and daughters take over—tomorrow belongs to the children." [425]

Even in his declining years Sandburg has retained an interest in young people and is obviously liked by them; but there is a distinction between the spirit of the young people of the generations he has known and whose spirit he shared, and the particular problems of the youth of this present day, 1962. There are fresh sociological departures in the present young generation which he does not attempt to portray in detail. However he has not altogether neglected the problems of youth and present-day questions. In the face of the seriousness of public school integration problems today, Sandburg's plea is for moderation in efforts to integrate the races. Concerning present-day poets, he states: " Age is all relative. I have a younger heart than most of the poets. Three-fourths of the poets we have nowadays were born old." [426] Before the General Federation of Women's Clubs, he expressed himself so strongly on the subject of some of the modern television commercials and their influence on young people that Miss Arlene Francis was sent to the Sandburg home to interview him on television for further clarification on his views. The filmed interview gave the public a warming insight of a man not afraid to speak his mind on any subject concerning people. Said the poet : " I can name items on TV that for me are priceless. The personalities I have come to know. The travel that I've had— scenes that I'll never have time to visit... I could name hundred of scenes of that kind." But not a word did he retract of his concern over a certain portion of TV advertising which " is filled with inanities, asininities, silliness and cheap tricks." " But," continued Sandburg, " the part that's priceless pays for the faults—except there's no estimating what's being done to the health and morals over the country among the young people by such commercials." [427]

Carl Sandburg, in his autobiography, speaks his deep interest and faith in the young generation of Americans :

" One thing I know deep out of my time : Youth when lighted and live and given a sporting chance is strong for struggle and not afraid of any toils or punishments or dangers or deaths. What shall be the course of society and civilization across the next hundred years ? For the answers read if you can the strange and baffling eyes of youth." [428]

Thus Sandburg in his portrayal of the American people has given us a comprehensive, evolutionary study of shifting social patterns, and he has traced the development of American society as a product of the people who compose it. His concept of American democracy is that of a moving or evolutionary process, given meaning only in the context of the time in which the term is used. In poetry he has traced the national growth from a cosmopolitan, immigrant society grafted upon a basically English colonial society, and growing up until it became an assimilated association with its own traditions; a society that has developed far from the chaos of the great industrialized cities of the latter part of the nineteenth century and the early part of the twentieth century by its own capacity for self-redemption and improvement; a society evolving complex social, poli.ical and economic structures through the development of scientific techniques and educational systems.

His primary interest is, however, in the role of the human being or individual man, viewed collectively in the shaping of his country, and in the formation of a political philosophy that is an assertion of the responsibility of the individual. He believes, as Emerson believed, that each human personality is deserving of respect. Sandburg has set forth this belief as follows :

" Some sacred seed lurks deep in each human personality, no matter how lowly its arrival on earth. To give any such seed the deepest possible roots and the highest possible flowering is the vision and hope of those ideas of freedom and discipline that constitute the American Dream." [429]

This poet-historian who has devoted his life to writing in both poetry and prose of the American people was invited by President Kennedy to contribute the foreword to the Chief Executive's recent book, *To Turn the Tide*. A portion of the Sandburg foreword reads as follows :

" From day to day and midnight to midnight the President looks out at the multiple mirrors of the changing chaos of global history... Never between world wars have public report and private rumor dealt with so many factors overbalanced by the unknown...

" The President is the Head Watchman of ' government of the people, by the people, for the people.' His every sentence, every spoken or written word goes to the eyes, ears, minds of millions of people reading or listening... Here we have in a book of speeches and messages of our President, a colossal survey of America and its people, their human conditions, their problems that must be faced, the terrific complications overseas and around the globe.

" The Inaugural Address of President Kennedy is a manner of summons to citizens by the new head of our great Republic. Around nearly every sentence of it could be written a thesis, so packed is it with implications. Later came his message to Congress on the State of the Union. Here we have history in a panorama of fact... in our time of terrific storm, unprecedented change, humanity at a crossroads amid endless forked lighting... on pages sometimes having bursts of light and hope and always the composure that goes with true courage.

" Plainly he has had humility, scruples, care and anxiety about what he thinks, writes and says, hoping to mislead no one, hoping his words will stand up and make sense and perhaps wisdom for his own time and later times. When our generation has passed away, when the tongues of praise and comment now speaking have turned to a cold dumb dust, it will be written that John F. Kennedy walked with the American people in their vast diversity and gave them all he had toward their moving on into new phases of their great human adventure." *

Sandburg in his appraisal of the President as the leader of the American people voices his faith in the continuation of this " great human adventure." He believes that America has the will and vision to desire and to achieve not only material progress but new spiritual goals, improved cultural accomplishments and educational advances; that the future is a challenge to the potential of the scholar and the aspirations of the human spirit. He believes with Thomas Edison that the realm of science and invention as well as the areas of politics and human relationships are still in the evolutionary stage; and that they will continue to challenge the mind of the scholar, the scientist, the inventor—the mind of Man Thinking.

---

* President John F. KENNEDY. *To Turn The Tide*, Harper and Brothers, New York, 1962, Foreword by Carl Sandburg.

C. THE LANGUAGE

Relation of Sandburg Vocabulary to American Life

Poetry is something more than the mere translation of the beautiful and aesthetic; it is a translation of life; and as we have analyzed Sandburg's choice of words in his poems, we have discovered that his chosen vocabulary followed a very definite pattern. He has carefully selected words or vernacular appropriate to the situation or milieu. In the Emersonian tradition, he " expresses the experience of a new age " [430] and the multiform American people have become his dictionary, his source of multiform language. Even the American Indian of the early history of America has become for him a source of word-power.

" The red and white men traded plants and words back and forth.
The Shawnee haw and the Choctaw root, the paw paw, the potato, the cohosh and your choice of the yellow puccoon or white,
A cork elm, or a western buckthorn or a burning bush, each a wahoo and all of the wahoo family
These from the tongues of name givers, from a restless name changer, the people." [431]

The names of former Indian tribes dot his writing throughout the several volumes of poetry—Apache, Cherokee, Shawnee, Sioux; as do names of rivers, cities and lakes derived from the Indian, such as Chattahoochee, Ohio, Okoboji, Saugutuck. He has composed one brief poem on the understanding of snow by the Pottawatomie Indians, who sang their understanding as they dug holes in the ice to let down fishhooks and who "chattered it in the wigwams when blizzards shook the wigwams." [432]

The wild flowers of forest and field speak a language through him. The wild aster in the fence corner speaks to white people a farewell to summer; the red man called the aster, " It-brings-the-frost "; [433] the scarlet pimpernel speaks a storm sign if its petals close in the sun, and is the " poor-man's weather-glass." [434]

The Sandburg vocabulary adapts a variety of terms characteristic of the worlds of law, religion, the Army, Navy, music and the arts; the sea, politics, journalism, the Bible, and the sciences; factories and mills, the farm and the city, trees and the varied faces of nature. He gives us samples of the dialect of the southern negro, the Santa Fé engineer, the Texas ranger, the Arkansas traveler, the Mississippi River pilot, the New Mexico horseman, the Ozark mountain driver, words of a Republican Governor of Illinois, a Pennsylvania Quaker poet, President Lincoln—and many more.

The following lines accentuate in symbolic vein the diversity of the American people and their susceptibilities and the need of a poetry of transitional moods and forms :

" The clods of the earth hold place
close to the whir of yellow hummingbird wings
and they divide into those hard of hearing
and those whose ears pick off

a smooth hush with a little wind whimper across it
and then again only the smooth hush." [435]

Sandburg, in his desire to write of a diversified people, has heeded the
admonition of Whitman to future poets : " Great poets will be proved by
their unconstraint. Of the traits of first-class writers, nothing is finer than
the silent defiance advancing from new free forms... The American bard
shall delineate no class of persons, not one or two out of the strata of
interests—and not be for the eastern states more than the western, or the
northern states more than the southern... Language impermeates all, and
has its bases close to the ground." [436]

There are instances in which Sandburg's deliberately chosen primitive
form of expression has become crude, as in " To a Contemporary Bunkshooter," with its overabundance of slang and vituperative phrase. This
unrestrained imitation of the speaker expresses scorn and indignation and
is a satire on bigotry and attracted a mixed reception. Some have defended
it on the grounds that the poet consciously and successfully reproduced
the language of the speaker—just as Sandburg often attempts to reproduce
the vernacular of the subject; while others, with good reason, criticized it
on the grounds of its sub-standard English, its vehement and vulgar phrases.

Among the literary critics who felt the language was justified was
Professor Llewellyn Jones who defended the poem as follows :

" When Sandburg satirizes persons it is always in their official capacities... His Billy Sunday poem offended many religious people
who did not know when they first read it that a woman Ph. D. was
then planning to include it in an anthology of the world's great
religious poetry. It turns Billy Sunday's own kind of language back
at him, and it puts Mr. Sandburg's interpretation of Jesus into
words which make it actual. This is necessary, for most people have
obtained their idea of the expiatory death of Jesus from stained glass
windows in churches..." [437]

Nevertheless, the excessive amount of slang and rough language employed
in the poem is to be deplored. The vituperation and disrespect cannot be
condoned even though tempered with lines of a reverent nature, such as :

" Jesus had a way of talking soft—
and he helped the sick and gave the people hope.

. . . . .

I've been to this suburb of Jerusalem they call Golgotha, and I know
it was real blood spurted in red drops where the spear of the Roman
soldier rammed in between the ribs of this Jesus of Nazareth." [438]

Aside from slang, Carl Sandburg has given individual identity to the people
in his poetry by language intended to be vehicular, and a conveyer of station
and status; by " singing what belongs to him or her and to no one else." [439]

Whitman, both in his poetry and in his prose articles, proclaimed the
need for strictly American speech, yet in this respect he was a contradictory
example. He declared himself as no *dolce affettuoso*; and throughout his
poems borrowed liberally from other languages; words of distinctly foreign

origin dot his verse, such as *camerado, libertad, me imperturbe, trottoirs, feuillage, éclaircize, allons, respondez, ma femme, cantabile;* even the word " Americans " he preferred at times to replace with *Americanos.* In spite of the fact that he admonished other poets to " study out the land, its idioms and men," [440] he himself frequently employed phraseology obviously not in the American idiom.

Of Whitman's language, Emerson once said that the Oriental *Bhagavad-Gita* and the New York *Herald* both seemed to be components of the language structure of the early editions of *Leaves of Grass.*

Robert Burns faithfully portrayed the colloquial speech characteristic of the Scottish Highlander. His diction was not that of Edinburgh. Carl Sandburg frequently uses in similar vein American colloquial expression —as the speech of many groups.

If the reader searches for Shakespearean measure and control, he need not expect to find it in Sandburg verse. If he seeks the aesthetic purity and poetic grace of Keats, he will not find it in Sandburg verse (although Keats was one of the poet's models in his Lombard College days). The " Grecian Urn " of Keats offers its beauty; Sandburg's verse offers its strength, the vitality of human affairs, the human interest variations, and the volume of the American scene.

Thus a variable verse discipline is part of Sandburg's poetic theory. Strong sentiment is conducive to this form of expression, but this looseness of form does not prevent his poetry from being a forceful medium of human interpretation, of social function; a realistic poetry of moral purpose.

One of the best professional appraisals of Sandburg's poetic style and form is that of Harriet Monroe, who wrote :

" The free-verse rhythms which this poet prefers are as personal as his slow speech or his massive gait; always a reverent beating-out of his subject. In some of the war poems his rhythms sound like guns booming. Or again, under softer inspiration, his touch becomes exquisitely delicate. Indeed, there is orchestral richness in his music; he plays divers instruments. Such lyrics as ' The Great Hunt,' or ' At a Window,' have a primal fundamental beauty, a sound and swing as of tides, or bending grain. The spirit of this book is heroic, both in its joy and its sorrow.

" What Sandburg does is not, as some students seem to infer, the complete sweeping-away of metrical pattern. There is an underlying three-time or four-time beat in each poem, his preference leaning oftener than with most poets, to four-time which admits the generous use of spondees —sometimes four long syllables in succession—from which he gets most of his telling effects. But in his underlying pattern, Sandburg permits himself more variety than the prosodic laws have allowed for, especially in the number of syllables to a bar, and in the free verse rests. In four-time especially he uses this freedom quite wonderfully to get rhythms as different as in the quick-stepping ' Gone ' and in the slow-moving ' Our Prayer of Thanks '; while in ' The Great Hunt,' which begins in a creeping four-time, he tries with magical effect the old but rarely used trick of changing the beat to three-time for the final stanza. And in two poems as different in movement as 'Bringers' and 'Four Preludes on Playthings of the Wind' the underlying pattern is three-time and almost straight iambic. On these patterns Sandburg, like all poets but more skillfully than most of them swings the larger tides of his cadences." [441]

Sandburg has a sensitive ear for rhythm. When we hear him read his poems, or listen to the recordings of them, we realize that they contain more rhythm than appears on the printed page. He controls the pace of his poetry by proper duration of pauses for emphasis and by giving each syllable its proper length. (The poet E. E. Cummings employs a visual method to suggest this control by his very unorthodox punctuation, such as the placing of a period *before* a word, or by placing a semi-colon or colon after words which they should not properly follow).

There are several literary devices employed by Sandburg to aid in achieving a total impression and rhythmic effect in his poetry. They include the Sandburg ability to portray artistic but meaningful contrasts, such as in " Joliet " where the railroad tracks divide the gray walls of the penitentiary from the smokestacks of the steel works, and where the sun on two canals and one river divides that part of the valley which is " God's " and that part which is " man's " and makes " Three stripes of copper or gold or shattered sunflower leaves." [442]

Likewise the poetic power of parallel phrasing and repetition serves Sandburg well, as in the six lines of " Kreisler," each of which begins with the same words " Sell me a violin "; or as in the lines :

> " There are freedom shouters
> There are freedom whisperers.
> Have I, have you, been too silent ?
> Is there an easy crime of silence ?
> Is there any easy road to freedom ? " [443]

In the couplet below is an example of combined parallel phrasing, repetition and assonance which produce a forceful expression :

> " Hate is a vapor fixed and mixed.
> Hate is a vapor blown and thrown." [444]

Sandburg's capability of achieving rhythm by a cumulation of effect may be particularly noted in " The Long Shadow of Lincoln : A Litany," in " Man The Moon Shooter " and in many portions of *The People, Yes.*

A balancing of sentence units is frequently employed to produce a rhythmical similarity together with graphic portrayal such as we find in the lines :

> " Acquaintance with death, sir,
> comes by ice and is slow, sir,
> comes by fire and is fast, sir,
> comes by the creep of clock-hands,
> comes by the crash of split-seconds." [445]

The device of onomatopoeia is employed, on occasion, for realistic effect, as in the stanza on " Niagara " or in lines such as " the grinding of the earth on its gnarled axis." [446]

In many places alliteration produces a striking effect such as the " cataract of coloratura " [447] of the Italian children of Chicago; here it serves to make memorable the complex of peoples in the metropolis and the multiform nature of a vast society transformed by industrialism, and helps to vivify the variegated urban pageant and to remind the reader of the many and diverse culture waves of immigration from across the Atlantic.

In the foreword to the volume *Early Moon*, Sandburg defines the function of the poetic imagination in recording human experience by giving a short talk on poetry to a junior audience, with various explanations for young people as to what poetry is made of and how long men have been making it :

> " ... What is poetry ? This is a question no man has ever answered in such a way that all men have said : 'yes, now we know what poetry is.' When Walt Whitman says : ' The poet is the answerer ' we are interested. If we could know just what he means by ' the answerer ' we would know what he means by ' the poet.' Another poet has said poetry is ' emotion remembered in tranquility.' Now, poetry is supposed to be the aesthetic art which gathers the beautiful into words. Beauty depends on personal tastes. What is beauty for one person is not for another. It has been said that, as no two leaves in a forest are the same, no two human characters are precisely alike. The personality that each of us has is strangely woven of millions of little facts, events, impressions out of the past and present." [448]

Sandburg then proceeds to discuss how our viewpoints change as the years go by, and how a poem which once held nothing in it to challenge our interest may later take on a glint or shade of meaning we had not noticed before. As years go by, " experience writes out new records in our mind life, and we go back to some works of art that we rejected in the early days and find values we had missed." [449] The events of our lives such as childhood, laughter, work, friendship, love, success, failure, pain, illness and death of loved ones, all leave marked impressions on us; and as time advances, these experiences create in each of us the power to see in poetry or in prose values not hitherto within our selective grasp.

This approach to the language and technique of poetry bears a resemblance to that of Wordsworth as stated in the Preface to *Lyrical Ballads:*

> " The principal object proposed in these Poems was to choose incidents and situations from common life, and to relate or describe them, throughout, as far as was possible in a selection of language really used by men, and, at the same time, to throw over them a certain coloring of imagination, whereby ordinary things should be presented to the mind in an unusual aspect; and further, and above all, to make these incidents and situations interesting by tracing in them the primary laws of our nature." [450]

Sandburg regards poetry as a means of communicating distilled human experience. He has combined varying language forms and free verse rhythms with native subject matter to record collective American life. In word, style, metaphor, image and symbol he has attempted to portray an American society which is founded both upon immigrant cultures and upon three and a half centuries of life in a New World which is very different from the Old. He has made an effort to present the assimilation of European cultures; to reflect the psychology and mental mood of the machine age; to present the American spirit in two World Wars and in the Great Depression period; to present an America now inextricably involved in world politics. To do so has required a mobile and vivid language.

Washington Post Portrait of Carl Sandburg by Charles Delvecchio.

PART III

AMERICA AND CARL SANDBURG

I

CARL SANDBURG'S PLACE IN AMERICAN LITERATURE

A. CARL SANDBURG'S POSITION AS AN AMERICAN POET

Perhaps the most revealing way of estimating the value of Sandburg's interpretation of twentieth-century America is to compare him with other modern poets and their achievements. Such comparisons necessarily include poets whose work dates from the early part of the century, since in this period occurred a marked stylistic break between past and present traditions in poetry—a change from conscious formality to a more amplified structure and to themes of modern life.

(a) *Edwin Arlington Robinson and Carl Sandburg*

In the early 1900's the names of three poets—Masters, Lindsay and Sandburg—were commonly spoken of together as contemporaries belonging to the " Chicago School " of the " New Poetry " of the period.

However, by some literary critics Edwin Arlington Robinson (1869-1935), has been designated as the Dean of the New Poetry, because his writing in the 1890's bore some of the characteristics of the new poetic theory. Robinson grew up in Gardiner, Maine (the Tilbury Town of his poetry). He entered Harvard in 1891, seven years before Sandburg entered Lombard College. One of his most important volumes, *The Man Against the Sky*, appeared in 1916, the same year in which Sandburg's volume of *Chicago Poems* was published. Robinson was not an experimenter in free verse; but his firm lines veer away from the rhetorical devices, the aestheticism, the restricted subject matter, the imitative qualities and standardization of the older poetry. His poem " The Man Against the Sky " reveals the tensions existing between the intellectual and aristocratic traditions of nineteenth-century New England and the questioning spirit of the modern twentieth century. However there is very little empathy in this poem; it is intro-spective; the inner processes of the mind of " The Man Against the Sky " are not delineated. The man represents the struggle in Robinson's own mind—the divisiveness of present day thought as he saw it himself.

Robinson was a New England Puritan with a Puritan's austere and conventional viewpoint; his poetry reveals a mere glimmer of the transcendentalism of Emerson whom he admired, and it lacks Emerson's inner calm, courage and assurance; it lacks the attunement to nature that is a powerful asset in Emerson and Sandburg. The poetry of Robinson is not national in scope; it is, for the most part, localized in New England. However his one visit to England supplied him with material for his interpretation of the Arthurian legends. Though the material for these legends is mediaeval in origin, Robinson injected them with the spirit and thought of modern times so that they aid in interpreting contemporary life as well.

Briefly etched personality sketches permeate Robinson's writing. Both his poetry and that of Sandburg possess an uncommon gift of character analysis, of psychological interpretation. Some of the best poetry of both men is poetry of protest; both are masters of poetic imagery; both present a religious aspect within their poetry. Robinson's faith is perhaps less sure, a more questioning faith, a darker view of life, yet a viewpoint not without hope that life must mean something more than mere existence. His " Calvary " is numbered among the finer poems of the century :

> " Friendless and faint, with martyred steps and slow
> Faint for the flesh, but for the spirit free,
> Stung by the mob that came to see the show,
> The Master toiled along to Calvary;
>
> . . . . .
>
> But after nineteen hundred years the shame
> Still clings, and we have not made good the loss
> That outraged faith has entered in his name.
> Oh, when shall come love's courage to be strong !
> Tell me O Lord — tell me, O Lord, how long
> Are we to keep Christ writhing on the cross ! " [451]

These lines serve also to illustrate some of the distinctive differences between the two poets. Technically, Robinson is a finer poetic artist. His poems are smooth and nicely cadenced; they belong, for the greater part, to the traditional style in existence prior to the poetry renaissance (though his trilogy, *Merlin, Lancelot*, and *Tristram*, is written in blank verse).

A probing intellectuality, a critical analysis of human nature and individual circumstance reinforce Robinson's talent as a personality painter. In " Gift of God " (which some critics consider autobiographical) he depicts the selfless love of a mother whose son's renown is " far from flags and shouts "; but

> " She crowns him with her gratefulness,
> And says again that life is good;
> And should the gift of God be less
> In him than in her motherhood,
> His fame, though vague, will not be small,
> As upward through her dream he fares,
> Half clouded with a crimson fall
> Of roses thrown on marble stairs." [452]

Robinson has created many lasting character portraits which linger in the mind of his readers. " The Master " provides an excellent picture of Lincoln facing both abuse and praise in his conduct of the Civil War and presents also a criticism of society of the period. Brief, sharp imagery and trenchant word power give us " Miniver Cheevy," the dreamer; " Richard Cory," the gentleman; " Reuben Bright," the butcher grieving over the death of his wife; " Bewick Finzer " living with his regrets over lost wealth. Robinson could draw these pictures of tragedy and frustration because he himself had known frustration in his early life. He could paint human suffering because he had endured tribulation. Chronic mastoiditis had impaired his hearing. The death of his father and the subsequent loss of the family fortune mismanaged by a brother forced his withdrawal from Harvard before graduation. He suffered deeply from thwarted ambition, poverty and misunderstanding. Therefore moral and social problems became subjects of his poetry and they carried with them a spirit of disillusionment. In " The Man Against the Sky " the man is seen but briefly in the light of sunset at the top of the hill.

> " Where was he going, this man against the sky ?
> You know not, nor do I." [453]

This " darkening hill " faces many of Robinson's characters. The above lines indicate Robinson's questioning spirit. He himself has stated that the poem " meant merely through an ironic medium to carry materialism to its logical end and to indicate its futility as an explanation or justification of existence." [454] Sandburg in 1942 referred to Robinson as " the somber American poet who saw many seekers in his country as his ' bewildered children in kindergarten, all trying to spell God with the same blocks.' " [455]

The America which Robinson portrays is the eastern section, chiefly Maine, New York, Massachusetts and New Hampshire. Yet he is not typical of New England. He was a type of New England aristocrat in a tragic or dramatic role; and he portrayed people confronted with the difficulties and hardships of commercial success. At the same time his Puritan conscience sternly reproved him for his shortcomings to the point of producing morbidity. He interpreted his own personal background, his ancestry and viewpoint in the poem " New England " :

> " Passion is here a soilure of the wits,
> We're told, and Love a cross for them to bear;
> Joy shivers in the corner where she knits
> And Conscience always has the rocking-chair,
> Cheerful as when she tortured into fits
> The first cat that was ever killed by Care." *

In these lines are revealed the wry humor and the tinge of pathos and tragedy with which he endowed many of his Tilbury Town characters. Even the unselfish mother in " Gift of God " must endure " a cross."

---

* *Modern American Poetry*, edited by Louis Untermeyer, p. 161.

Robinson's analysis of frustrated human beings and of the social environment which produced their individual disillusionment carries with it a tinge of humor which at the same time is colored or distorted by a sense of failure or inadequacy. Even his affluent " Richard Cory " who " glittered when he walked " [456] was haunted with a sense of having failed to derive any real worth or happiness from life; he was a paradox of glitter and despair.

Robinson's humor is not of the variety which eventually came to find a place in Sandburg's writings. Since a sense of humor is an indispensable ingredient of every-day living, Sandburg, after the early Chicago days, began to introduce a minimal amount of it in his writing. In his nature poetry there is " a high majestic fooling " [457] in the laughter of the corn, of the wind and the sun; the " jack-o'-lantern " with terrible teeth, and stern, reproving features speaks to the children and " the children know I am fooling." [458] There is a sly humor (such as one finds in the poetry of Robert Frost) in Sandburg's " Prairie " picture of the horses at rest, looking over the fence to say " good morning" to the horses hauling wagon loads of produce to market; there is humor in the description of the little wrens in the wren house as Sandburg compares their housekeeping problems to those of humans; in the recent poem " Auctioneer " (1960) are lines depicting some amusing aspects of an auction sale. There are many witty quotations in the folk-sayings of *The People, Yes*. Many laughable incidents in young Sandburg's life in Galesburg are related in *Always the Young Strangers*. The portions of Sandburg's novel which portray the eighteenth and nineteenth centuries contain witty sayings and excerpts from humorous readings. In the readings Sandburg's fondness for the humor of Rabelais is set forth by quotation; but in the section dealing with the Puritans there is no humor, for their life was grimly serious and fraught with danger. Robinson's Puritan ancestry (Anne Bradstreet was one of his forebears), may account, in part, for his grim sense of the comic. His depressed attitude toward life and people as opposed to Sandburg's whole-hearted faith in people is a distinguishing difference between the two poets. Sandburg says : " I doubt whether any man can have health or even a little fun out of his democracy unless he has some deep-rooted faith in the people. In one passage of *The People, Yes*, I put a lot of proverbs made by the people. One way or another these proverbs have the breath of the people." [459] Many of these proverbs reveal situations of wholesome comedy.

In spite of Robinson's expressed admiration for courage and fortitude, there is in his poetry a pervasive melancholy, as opposed to the optimism of Sandburg. Dr. Raymond Tschumi, in his book *Thought in Twentieth Century English Poetry* has analyzed this trait of Robinson as follows :

" Because many characters in his poems are human failures, and because sadness and disgust are the dominant notes in Robinson's poetry, it should not be inferred that he is a pessimist. He is rather an idealist whose ideal beauty is intimately linked with the darkest aspects of living." *

---

* Raymond Tschumi, *Thought in Twentieth-Century English Poetry*, Routledge and Kegan Paul Ltd., London, 1951, p. 270.

Robinson wrote 1400 pages of poems and upon his death left behind some of the finest poetry of the twentieth century. *Children of the Night* contains poetry of quiet, straightforward word power that will remain expressive of his professional genius and his talent for revealing human experience. He incorporated in his work some of the best of the older poetic tradition, and by his sharpness of epithet and directness of speech anticipated the new poetic theory of Masters, Lindsay, Sandburg, Frost and others.

(b) *Edgar Lee Masters and Carl Sandburg*

Edgar Lee Masters, born in Kansas, came of Puritan ancestry. When he was still quite young the family moved to Lewiston, Illinois. Here he grew up, studied law and in 1891 went to Chicago where he became very successful in his profession. Those who knew Masters tell us that his mental powers covered a wide range—history, literature, law and science; that his thoughts were continually grappling with the major problems of man's existence—with the place of religion, with historical perspective, with social adjustments; and that he had " a tremendous hunger to know all about people." * A lawyer by vocation, he turned to the writing of poetry and prose as an avocation. Early in the century he published several small volumes of poems, most of which were imitative in nature and received scant attention. By 1914 he resolved to begin writing of some of the inequities which he saw around him through his profession. From these records of human life he began to draw his subjects. He determined to expose the social injustices which he perceived and to place the scene along the Spoon River which he had known in his boyhood, the scene to include a cemetery where indictments could be made without restriction. Out of these plans came his famous *Spoon River Anthology*. Masters in this volume utilized a system of epitaphs and epigrams which had captured his interest in *The Greek Anthology*; and through these epitaphs he permitted the dead of his fictional Spoon River village cemetery to speak the truth about themselves; to defend themselves against misjudgments, to reveal their secrets and the injustices heaped upon them by slander and intrigue while living; or, by contrast, to speak a few simple lines on a plain and well-regulated life or to speak from the graves of ancestral pioneers in meditation on the old and the new. These soliloquies are short but significant. They present an interlace of materialism and idealism, of thwarted ambition and spiritual victory. They portray a lawyer's hatred of sham and deceit. Masters has placed the names of many people in these epitaphs of his *Spoon River Antho- logy* to illustrate the frustrations and monotonies of existence, the difficulty of attaining ideals, and the constant struggle toward brighter and finer horizons.

" Life all around me here in the village :
Tragedy, comedy, valor and truth,
Courage, constancy, heroism, failure—
All in the loom, and, oh, what patterns ! " [460]

---

* Eunice Tietjens, *The World at my Shoulder*, Macmillan Co., New York, 1938, p. 46.

Free verse is the poetic device used to convey the mental vitality of Masters. Colloquialisms contrasted with majestic speech depict his wide acquaintance with people and social problems. *Spoon River Anthology* is a milestone in the evolution of American poetry, and is considered by some critics to be one of the most important books since Whitman's *Leaves of Grass.* It contains a synthesis of the traits of the towns and small cities. Nevertheless it pictures humanity in general; in its many starkly condensed character sketches it bears a resemblance to the earlier brief portraits by Edwin Arlington Robinson. It is a forerunner of *Main Street* by Sinclair Lewis, but with less of the novelist's defeatism. Masters even achieves a kind of exaltation, a greater universality; for he includes the idealism of some who have attained success through long struggle, and he gives a place to the wisdom of age, to those " who have lived the great range of life." [461]

Master's viewpoint is that of a lawyer, a skilled and trained analyst of human motive and human achievement; thus he is able to appraise with judicial impartiality when he examines people, places and things. His analyses are more trenchant than those of Sandburg in poetry (but not as meticulous and complete as Sandburg's prose portraits). Both poets are concerned with social, moral and political problems in the American scene, but the scope of Sandburg's portrayal is wider. There is a pervasive cynicism in Master's writing. In his *Spoon River Anthology* the mordant commentaries convey a dominant note of frustration, a lament for the waste of human vitality. Both Sandburg and Masters write satirically of hypocrisy, bigotry and cruelty; although there is more pessimism in Masters' picture as he delineates the vices and bigotry as well as the spiritual aspirations of the village, whereas Sandburg reveals a greater faith in human nature. The creator of the Spoon River fictional village could not have written " Good Morning, America " or " Prairie." In Masters there is a love of nature, but to a lesser extent than in Sandburg. His Lucinda Matlock is pictured as she

> " Rambled over the fields where sang the larks,
> And by Spoon River gathering many a shell,
> And many a flower and medicinal weed—
> Shouting to the wooded hills, singing to the green valleys. " [462]

But this is not the buoyant song of Sandburg's " Prairie " in its expression of vital significance in the American scene. In spite of Masters' assertion that " It takes life to love life " [463] and of his expression of admiration for the fullness of life, he reveals a disillusionment and a bitterness; whereas Sandburg reveals a dynamism. Masters' effective appeal to social conscience, his exposure of injustice and bigotry, his reach for the universal by multiple portraiture constitute some of the distinguishing features of his work. These traits the two poets possess in common. They were intimate friends in their early Chicago days. Edgar Lee Masters wrote the warmly sympathetic tribute to Sandburg that appeared on the jacket cover of the original edition of *Chicago Poems.*

Spoon River Anthology was at first received with hostile criticism and aroused nationwide discussion of its author's attack on hypocrisy, intolerance, deceit and narrow provincialism. However, the book finally received wide acclaim. Masters' search for truth and justice is set forth in diction and technique superior to that of Sandburg; but in his later works he never attained the vividness of his *Spoon River Anthology*, which was his only great success. Masters wrote voluminously, and in fairness to him his biographies of Stephen A. Douglas, of Lincoln and of Whitman deserve greater recognition than they received. Among his ten later books of poems, *Domesday Book* and *New Spoon River* deserve mention. While there is something of the fearlessness of François Villon in the frank revelation of both good and bad, Masters' work lacks the vitality and scope of Sandburg.

(c) *Vachel Lindsay and Carl Sandburg*

Vachel Lindsay was born in Springfield, Illinois. Unfortunately, he could not adapt himself to his surroundings or his times. A visionary and an optimist, Lindsay lacked a sense of practical values. He never understood the world about him and felt lost in it. He was a worshiper of Lincoln and a worshiper of beauty; and he possessed the instincts of an artist. He walked alone, in 1906, through the South; in 1908, through the Central Plains states; and in 1912, through the West. But even with this intimate knowledge of the country, he was unable to transfer the impression successfully to the printed page. Lindsay was possessed of a high idealism, of a love of culture, of art, but he failed to balance them with the fundamentals of human judgment and human values. His poetry was therefore a blend of fantasy, of beauty, of idealism; he himself was a blend of poet, Utopian dreamer and missionary, preaching a combined gospel of beauty and religious regeneration. In the end he learned the need of human emotion in poetry and published his volume *Candle in the Cabin*; but death in 1931 cut short what seemed to appear a promising career.

His approach to poetry was humanitarian and religious and contains a note of protest against oppression and social discrimination. While both Lindsay and Sandburg were inspired by the traditions of the pioneer Midwest, Sandburg had a more mature understanding of them and interpreted them with greater restraint and validity.

In poetic texture, Lindsay's " Chinese Nightingale " is perhaps his finest poem. Others likely to live are " Abraham Lincoln Walks at Midnight " and " The Apple-Barrel of Johnny Appleseed," together with " The Congo," which he termed a study of the negro race, pointing out that the Christian religion is the best hope of those who inhabit the forest along the African river. Having witnessed in his travels through the South the colorful and superstitious characteristics of the southern negro of that period, Lindsay was interested in the syncopational quality of their ballads and folk tunes, and his sense of fantasy provided the medium for combining these elements in " The Congo." This unusual and boisterous fusion provides a definite contribution to folk poetry, but it also carries with it a vaudeville touch which offers entertainment rather than sincere and deep emotion. Lindsay's poetry lacks the strength, the massiveness, the vitality and courage, the human touch of Sandburg's poetry, and is gradually receding from its earlier hold on the American public.

With the passing of time Sandburg emerged alone from this group of Chicago poets in a field of his own because of the power and originality of his poetry, and because of his success in historical and biographical prose.

(d) Robert Frost and Carl Sandburg

Both Robert Frost and Carl Sandburg have given many long years to literature. Robert Frost was born in 1875 in San Francisco, California; after the death of his father in 1885, his mother brought her children to New England where many generations of Frosts had lived. In 1892 Robert Frost entered Dartmouth College, but soon left to earn his living in one of the Massachusetts mills; in 1897 he entered Harvard University. In later years he sailed with his family to England where he wrote poems about his own New England and rose to instant fame. After his return to the United States in 1915, many honorary degrees were awarded him from American universities; the Pulitzer Prize for poetry was awarded for his volume *New Hampshire* and he became a professor in residence at Amherst College. Another volume, *West Running Brook*, appeared in 1928; *A Further Range* in 1936, *A Masque of Reason* in 1945.

The poetry of Robert Frost establishes him as a great pastoral poet and particularly as a poet of New England life and soil, nature and temperament. Frost's lines contain a gentle delicacy of expression; and they reproduce the environmental vocabulary of the New England countryside. Frost, too, loves nature—the New England trees so delightfully pictured in his poem " Birches," the farms as evidenced by " The Pasture " or " Mending Wall "; and he likes people. He has observed them as a scholar from his professor's chair at Amherst College; he has observed them as a farmer from his New England farm. He observed them as a traveler both at home and in Europe. His theory of poetry is similar to that of Sandburg in that he chooses to use words of common speech. Unlike Sandburg, however, he does not feel impelled to employ slang. His poetry is more regional, more abstract, has a more cadenced quality, a greater grace; but it is more restricted in scope, has not the national sweep and vision of Sandburg poetry. The poetry of both writers is filled with emotional appeal and with symbolism, in spite of the variance of individualistic diction. The poetry of both men looks beyond mere appearances, to spiritual meanings and relevancies; both men have a talent for pictorial quality—a talent for vivifying. As Carl Sandburg endowed his Chicago " Skyscraper " with living attributes, with soul and individuality, so does Robert Frost endow his " Mending Wall " with personality:

" Something there is that doesn't love a wall,
That sends the frozen-ground-swell under it.
And spills the upper boulders in the sun;
And makes gaps even two can pass abreast." [464]

The poet bids the newly balanced stones used in repair of the wall:
" Stay where you are until our backs are turned." [465]

A gently phrased but convincing meditation pervades his lines, particularly those dealing with earth and nature. Robert Frost declares:

> " Nature's first green is gold,
> Her hardest hue to hold.
> Her early leaf's a flower;
> But only so an hour.
> Then leaf subsides to leaf.
> So Eden sank to grief,
> So dawn goes down to day,
> Nothing gold can stay." [466]

In similar vein Carl Sandburg in " Autumn Movement " laments the short life span of beauty: " The northwest wind comes and the yellow is torn full of holes, new beautiful things come in the first spit of snow on the northwest wind, and the old things go, not one lasts." [467]

One of the best-known Frost poems, " Birches," is partially autobiographical. A few of its lines will illustrate this:

> " when I see birches bend to left and right
> Across the line of straighter darker trees,
> I like to think some boy's been swinging them.
>   . . . . .
> I'd like to go by climbing a birch tree,
> And climb black branches up a snow-white trunk
> *Toward* heaven, till the tree could bear no more,
> But dipped its top and set me down again." [468]

Much of Frost's poetry provides great reading pleasure; it is poetry of provincial charm and neighborliness, which, however, often assumes a universal aspect. A specific instance of this may be noted in " Tuft of Flowers ":

> " ' Men work together ', I told him from the heart,
> ' Whether they work together or apart.' " [469]

A current analogy to " Mending Wall," with its universal applicability, can be drawn with reference to the Communist wall constructed in Berlin:

> " Before I built a wall I'd ask to know
> What I was walling in or walling out,
> And to whom I was like to give offense." [470]

In similar vein other poems by Frost, though describing the rural New England scene, have universal as well as local significance. In " Stopping by Woods on a Snowy Evening " (one of his many unforgettable poems), there are overtones other than the beauty of snow-covered woods contained in the lines; rather does one sense the struggle between duty and love of beauty:

> " But I have promises to keep
> And miles to go before I sleep." [471]

There is a somber mood—but also a mood of serenity in much of his writing. Herein lies one of the greatest differences between Frost and Sandburg. There is in Frost's poetry a timid retrospection, a negative approach, a refusal to recognize the immigrant problem and the problems brought about by the Industrial Revolution. In " The Death of the Hired Man " he laments the weariness and exhaustion of the old agricultural order by portraying facts of a vanishing way of life; thus he frequently takes a backward look, an attitude of impracticality. This makes for nostalgic poetry that has a quieting and pleasing effect upon the reader but it takes little account of the tensions of modern life. Seldom does the poet face the hard facts of the anguish of struggle in a rapidly moving industrialized society; economic and political problems do not concern him. In contra-distinction, no American poet has so successfully presented impressions of city life in the machine age as Sandburg, who resents the dislocation and social problems resulting from industrialization—but he does not reject the machine age; instead he accepts it and seeks solutions as part of the story of progress. He firmly captures the dynamic and vital spirit of his country. His social poetry leads us to an awareness of the poignancy of the historical moment which he both shares and feels. The French critic Jean Catel, in comparing the two poets, made the observation : " Robert Frost, c'est le poète des pionniers qui se reposent; Sandburg des pionniers qui poursuivent leur tâche." [472] Frost stayed aloof from national problems during the 1930's and for this was reproved by other poets of the time; similarly in World War II he took a disapproving view of President Roosevelt's war policies. Some writers have believed that there may be a note of self-reproach in Frost's lines :

> " The blows that a life of self-control
> Spares to strike for the common good
> That day, giving a loose to my soul,
> I spent on the unimportant wood." [473]

A serene reserve, a quiet control served both his life and his poetry. He has attempted to put unassuming " truth of feeling " into his verse and asserts that the philosophy contained in the following stanza is " all that he is answerable to." [474]

> " If you should rise from Nowhere up to Somewhere,
> From being no one up to being Someone,
> Be sure to keep repeating to yourself
> You owe it to an arbitrary god
> Whose mercy to you rather than to others
> Won't bear too critical examination.
> Stay unassuming. If for lack of licence
> To wear the uniform of who you are,
> You should be tempted to make up for it
> In a subordinating look or tone
> Beware of coming too much to the surface,
> And using for apparel what was meant
> To be the curtain of the inmost soul." [475]

Robert Frost adheres to the great tradition of pastoral poetry and is considered by some literary critics the best nature poet since Wordsworth. He occupies without question a foremost position among American men of letters. His meditative verse, his poetic dialogues and descriptive sketches are much enjoyed and widely admired. He was honored by being invited to recite his poem " The Gift Outright " at the inauguration of President Kennedy, January 20, 1961.

America cherishes these venerated poets; she needs the pastoral beauty, the quiet grace and the academic dignity combined in Robert Frost; she needs the prairie singing, the fighting struggle of urban experience and the wide humanitarianism of Carl Sandburg.

* * *

Poetic Technique and Social Role in Sandburg

In summation, the problems with regard to the poetry of Sandburg, after comparison with his contemporaries, are the following:

How far can his own peculiar freedom of verse, style, vocabulary and technique, which sometimes degenerate into unartistic adornment, be classed as poetry?

How far can his deep concern for the welfare of the individual in combination with his lack of a deep psychological penetration of the individual in the lines of his poetry be reconciled with the need for a life-like, convincing portrait of the American scene?

How far can his apparent inconsistencies in treatment, swinging from sharp criticism of abuse to expression of confidence in the general system, be viewed as part of a cohesive view of the American scene?

These criticisms have been made of Sandburg in discussion of his separate verse collections; and in this context, comparisons of his verse with that of the poets we have just reviewed have not always been to Sandburg's advantage. These problems find a central place in his work and furthermore, are part of a consideration of his poetic role which is the basis of this present study. Technique and poetic mission are basic to the discussion of all poets, and none more so than Sandburg, the writer who has set himself the task of representing and portraying America, a project as vast, in its own way, as was that of Balzac when he undertook to paint the *comédie humaine* of the France in which he lived.

In appraising Sandburg's poetry we find it noteworthy for breadth and volume. However, there are limitations and gaps in Sandburg's interpretation of America as he has seen it and experienced it. There is little of the South in his poetry, although in the six volumes of the Lincoln biography the South receives its full share of history, and the South is not altogether omitted in his poetry, for we have the poems on the Shenandoah Valley, on Harpers Ferry, on the Potomac River. The New England section of America is far more completely interpreted by Robert Frost. Carl Sandburg has not, however, omitted New England altogether.

In the Chicago poems he has not shown many of the political cross-tensions which agitated that urban society. He has, however, shown to a certain extent the power of machine politics of that period, the power of money in elections at that time. Theodore Roosevelt and Woodrow Wilson, as we have already seen, also laid bare these political evils of the age of rapidly expanding cities. In his poetry Sandburg's moral and political protest is his own personal and particular protest viewed with a sympathy for the down-trodden. In his historical biography however, the political tensions of nineteenth-century America are painstakingly and minutely detailed. Like the Lincoln he portrayed, his mind was indexed and cross-indexed with human and political causes. In no other American biography can be found comparable sympathy for human causes.

One may say that Sandburg in his poetry views America from within the American image; he has not the detachment to see the American image as the foreigner does in the context of world affairs. His is an American's portrayal of the nation, though the portrayal derives from an awakened and aroused social consciousness. As late as the 1930's this aroused social consciousness reacted and scourged with the lash of a prophet those who sought to warp and control men's minds; and into *The People, Yes* went the failure and the strength, the chaos and the achievement, the mediocrity and the ambition, the good and the bad that make up America. Sandburg has been among the men of character whom Emerson would designate as the conscience of the society to which they belong; as such, he understands why America is what she is and at the same time, as the prophets of old, he reminds her of her true role in the context of her past history. As a realist, he portrays the nation as his conscience sees it; as an idealist, he portrays what he believes to be the true or idealized America of tradition; for this reason he has vigorously criticized departures from the justice and freedom of that tradition; and he still reacts against some of the social and international problems which have been glossed over by others. Because of his conscientious portrayal, his view cannot be an entirely detached one. Nor can the picture be termed complete although it is the most comprehensive portrayal of America in poetry to date.

From a technical viewpoint, Sandburg's poetry is a mixture of faults and genius, since it is experimental in method of construction, frequently uses colloquial idiom as a medium of expression and has capacity for image making found in few poets to such an extent. His early efforts at free verse sometimes led to clumsiness of structure and loss of the desired effect, because he was unable to employ the new methods to the fullest advantage. The technique employed in his lines does not always reach the full extent of Sandburg's capability; and in such instances the desired effect fails to materialize, because of a lack of sharpness. Thus the experimental verse forms which Sandburg, with deliberation, elected to employ as a vehicle expressive of status, in his social poetry do not always attain the standard which the humanitarian content deserves.

However, in many of the shorter poems, such as " Cool Tombs," " Village in Late Summer " and " Street Window," the form adequately assists the image and aids in conveying the tenderness, the sympathy or the irony.

Sandburg deliberately set himself the task of reproducing colloquial idiom, the vernacular of the men portrayed, and also, which is equally significant, a vocabulary immediately comprehensible to a broader cross section of the American public. Avoidance of "poetic diction" he regards as an effort at poetic realism, in that communication is opened between the poet and the public at large.

Urbanite singer of cities though he is, Sandburg expresses a provincial flavor. In some of the early poems of social purpose in which he set for himself the task of employing sub-standard slang, we find a forced effect. In "To a Contemporary Bunkshooter" he felt impelled to use certain phrases and the result is an impression of the piling-up of harsh, rude words, an effect that is unnatural. Few more savage poems existed in American literature prior to World War I. Such lines bring to mind the venomous poem "Respondez!" of Whitman. In this poem (which he later rejected, and which was not printed in European editions) Whitman in violent invective and bitter irony satirized post-Civil War society:

"Let murderers, bigots, fools, unclean persons, offer new propositions!
. . . . .
Let churches accomodate serpents, vermin, and the corpses of those who have died of the most filthy diseases!
. . . . .
Let him who is without my poems be assassinated!
. . . . .
Let the reformers descend from the stands where they are forever bawling!" [476]

The difference between Whitman and Sandburg in the two instances lies in the fact that Whitman was satirizing American society through three pages of fury; whereas an angered Sandburg was attacking an individual who seemed to have little conception of the plight of those in his audience who were suffering from the industrial and social maladjustments of metropolitan Chicago.

A forced effect is obtained in other Sandburg poems such as "The Old Flagman," in which the introduction of crude phraseology distracts attention from the simple, underlying thought of the lines; the picture becomes blurred and incomplete in the reader's mind.

Thus in his search for the proper colloquial idiom Sandburg has at times over-extended this method of expression. Though one can understand his point of view, and appreciate his reasons for the choice of slang and of irregularities of speech, nevertheless, the effect is lost, in some instances, in the displeasure which such words arouse in the reader.

In contrast, the imagery of the nature poems and short lyrics is more successfully communicated because the poet is free to speak his own thoughts in richer and finer language harmonizing with his response to the beauties of nature, and with lyrical emotion.

In the social poetry Sandburg does not always carry the picture beyond description and immediate impression; and he is not apparently concerned with a probing psychological penetration in his individual portraits. He stays nearer the surface than many, and therefore is more readily comprehensible. In this respect he forms a marked contrast with poets like T. S. Eliot, who are particularly intent on plumbing the individuality of their subjects and whose impressionism is augmented by a complexity of psychological associations. Sandburg does not often essay such complicated situations; although in *The People, Yes* we find such situations. In his " Four Preludes " he more nearly approaches Eliot's method :

> " The doors were cedar
> and the panels strips of gold
> and the girls were golden girls
> and the panels read and the girls chanted :
> > We are the greatest city,
> > the greatest nation.
>
> . . . . .
>
> The doors are twisted on broken hinges.
>
> . . . . .
>
> The feet of the rats
> scribble on the doorsills;
> the hieroglyphs of the rat footprints
>
> . . . . .
>
> tell us nothing, nothing at all
> about the greatest city, the greatest nation." [477]

In contrast to Eliot and other poets of a similar cast of mind, Sandburg for the most part prefers a direct technique; he chooses to keep his poetry straightforward in expression and easily communicable. Eliot's technique is superior; but he, too, uses free rhythms when they suit his purpose. However, a sense of human frustration and failure pervades his interpretation of modern society; while Sandburg, though with less polished expression, moves forward from frustration and negation toward affirmation, constructive criticism and active participation in human affairs.

The reader of Sandburg poetry occasionally meets with vagueness of meaning—though rarely—for Sandburg is not intentionally obscure. But one cannot be sure of the correct interpretation of a poem such as " New Song for Indiana Ophelias "; and the author, himself, admits that he has forgotten the meaning of certain of his poems written forty years ago. Among the hundreds of poems it is inevitable that some appear dull and flat, such as " Whiffletree " or " Very, Very Important." It cannot, however, be said that such obscurity has been deliberately cultivated, or that it is the result of highly complex analysis.

Sandburg's verse represents a venture into the democratizing of poetry. He wished to create poetry understandable by a wide range of readers and to include audiences beyond the reach of the traditional poetic craftsmen. This at times leads to a paradox of sensitivity and toughness; there would almost seem to be two Sandburgs in his poetry—the solitary, and the social-minded; the poet " of the quiet corner, of green fields and the earth serene in its changes, and the poet of streets and struggles, of dust and combat, of violence wanton or justified, of plain folk living close to a hard earth..." [478]

The venture, when judged from a traditional viewpoint, contains too great a sacrifice of artistry by the preponderance of hard-hitting vernacular, roughness of form, lack of taste and discipline in the social poetry. Sandburg came to realize this; and improved his word selection in each of the first five books, for " every attempt was a new start, each venture was a new beginning." [479] He also progressively improved his poetic discipline until in 1928 he achieved his most successful form and diction in the volume *Good Morning, America*. In the title-poem of this volume vernacular and proverbs are confined largely to the eleventh section; and more than one critic has stated that the proverbs as included in " Good Morning, America " " became art." [480]

Sandburg's objective was that of creating a verse of common words, a poetry comprehensible by common people, a poetry with varied levels of audience appeal. He shaped his product to reach each audience on its own terms, within an overall effort to express American experience with emotional honesty. Such freedom must not therefore be judged as the antithesis of art, but as its extension and as a widening of its range of communicability.

Professor Lionel Elvin, of Oxford University in his volume of literary criticism based on his University lectures expresses the desire that poetry should become more widely available in a democratic society. He asks whether " some of the difficulty of modern poets is not overcultivated... What Wordsworth gained by describing a poet as ' a man speaking to men ' would be a good thing for poetry now... Has not the time come when the poet can seek moral and critical support less from coteries and more from his people ? " [481]

Robert Frost also consciously aimed at the democratization of poetry but approached the problem from a less-inclusive viewpoint. His methods were more orthodox, his psychology more subtle. He preferred " Hamiltonian aloofness to Jeffersonian sociology," [482] and in this preference he differs from Sandburg.

The editors of *The American Scholar* have attempted to assemble a wider audience for poetry—not merely among critics and writers but among general readers. Joseph Wood Krutch, one of the contributing editors, voices an opinion similar to that of Professor Elvin concerning the possibility that many modern poets may make their own task more difficult by preferring to be ambiguous, by " avoiding metaphors of ' significant resemblance ' in order to achieve ' organicism,' as though the excellence of a poem were to be measured by the number of opportunities it offers the critic " [483] to try to explain it. He condemns poets who write only for other poets; he believes that poetry is much less effective when it strives to be pure poetry and nothing else. This is a reaction against ' ivory tower ' groups and against exclusiveness. Professor MacLeish of Harvard, expresses the desire for a closer relationship between educational institutions and the creative arts. He believes that poetry can transfer events of the world to the human imagination " where they can come alive with feeling..." As opposed to journalism which is concerned " with the look of the world, poetry is concerned with the feel of the world." [484] In this sense poetry is important as a transmitter of value judgments.

America now has an official consultant in poetry in the Library of Congress. Louis Untermeyer was one of the poets to occupy the post. Mr. Untermeyer stresses the importance of "the commonplace and a common form of communication" * in present-day writing. He conceived as the most important function of his office the widening of poetry audiences. He wishes to make poetry a part of the American household as well as a part of the American literary heritage. As editor of the Library's Archive of Recorded Poetry he sought to include recordings of verse as a portion of his intensive program to reach a larger audience.

Sandburg's aim has not been art for art's sake. His poetry illustrates " the code and creed of those writers who seek to widen the areas of freedom for all men." [485] He felt that the creative writer had a social responsibility to express himself and that silence on living issues could be negative propaganda leading to the deterioration of freedom. He frequently risked writing a bad poem for the sake of voicing an opinion or criticism when occasion warranted public expression. However, this ' vulgarization ' (in the original and true sense of the word) was never free from some of the risk suggested in the ambiguity the term has come to possess.

This social responsibility of the poet was the subject of a syndicated newspaper article published by Sandburg during World War II, following the death of Stephen Vincent Benét: " Like Archibald MacLeish, Edna Millay, Ben Hecht and other American poets, Benét and those of like viewpoint let their writing go forth for the moment, hoping a little good might come of it, and keenly aware that it will not do to wait, revise, wait longer, revise some more... There is sheer loveliness of timing in that Chinese proverb ' The dawn does not come twice to wake a man.' But two or three major American poets have held themselves in foxholes of safety and silence. They have the safety that goes with taking no risk of utterance that later might not look good... In this time of terrific storm, unprecedented change, they have answered questions... by keeping the silence that has the ease of saying nothing... while the world hurricane rages." [486]

Sandburg has never failed to accept his full share of social responsibility in times of local or national emergency, although he well knows that " to be of the moment and speak out of it is to sacrifice a certain goal of perfection of art." [487] He prefers a work of courageous struggle to an achievement of technical skill.

The essential function of Sandburg's poetry in dealing with critical contemporary issues is moral; his aim is not didactic but thought-provoking; if his verse is at times rough-hewn, it nevertheless possesses a fundamental stability. It offers richness of thought and native wisdom; and in the tradition of Emerson and Whitman it elevates ordinary humanity.

The ideas and content of Sandburg's poetry reveal, for the greater part, the expression of a balanced judgment and careful forethought. As a young man, Sandburg stated in his volume *Reckless Ecstasy*, the need for balanced

---

* Washington *Sunday Star*, April 15, 1962, p. B3.

judgment: " No cause can be hurt by discussion. Let an idea be brought out into the light of day where the sun and the rain of thought and speech can play on it, and if it is good, it will grow, and if it is not good, it will perish." [488] One sees a change of Sandburg's viewpoints in the war poems published in 1916. The first war poems showed only his hatred of war; those written later, but published in the same volume, showed him entirely in favor of aid to the Allies. When the Second World War broke out in 1939, he favored strict neutrality; but by 1941 his view had shifted, and both in the press and on the lecture platform he again favored aid to France and Britain: " We saw that this was the fight of a people who had certain freedoms; rather than live under the Hitler ' New Order,' they would prefer to die fighting and have ever afterward the sweet forgetfulness of death. What the British have been able to take and stand up under shows that there is something in their claim that there are things worse than death." [489] This inconsistency or change of opinion in Sandburg is understandable; it is not a fault, but rather the result of long and careful consideration, and the mark of a broad mind.

Sandburg in true American tradition, believes that democracy is a welding of opinions and holds to this theory that " no cause can be hurt by discussion." He believes that the people of a democracy have the right of self-determination after proper consideration of a wide variety of opinions dealing with the issues in question—both minority opinions and majority opinions. All sides of a question should be heard sympathetically. In *The People, Yes* he defends the principle of open discussion as one of the fundamental tenets of democracy. " The contact of ideas goes on... let the argument go on." [490] His own view is usually one which favors a middle-of-the-road policy, namely, one of moderation, whether on the question of racial integration, labor disputes or other important public problems. On such questions his breadth of vision is similar to that of Lincoln, and shows his faith in the collective judgment and wisdom of the people in the final analysis. The abuses and drawbacks of this popular form of self-determination he regards as infinitely preferable to a totalitarian alternative.

It is interesting to compare these ideas of popular government with those of Jean-Jacques Rousseau whose theories helped to influence the French people in their revolt against the social order of the time of Louis XVI. Rousseau wrote that man is born pure and that false organizations of society corrupt him; that progress in the arts and sciences has not advanced man's morals and habits.* Since his ideas of republican government were based, in part, on his trust in the fundamental goodness of man, on his belief in human liberty and political rights for the people, he set forth in the *Contrat Social* the theory that a legitimately organized society should exist by the agreement of the people, by the consent of the governed, by the *volonté générale:* that this *volonté générale* can exist as a governing force because it involves " the total alienation of each associate, together with all his rights, to the whole community; for ... as each gives himself absolutely the conditions are the same for all; and, this being so, no one has any

---

* Jean-Jacques ROUSSEAU. *Discours sur les sciences et les arts*, Part II.

interest in making them burdensome to others." * Rousseau considered this theory as a practical application of human freedom to political institutions and contended that the general will is right and always for the common good : absolute, inalienable and indivisible. He further defined the relationship of the individual to the Sovereign people as follows : " Each of us puts his power in common under the supreme direction of the general will, and in our corporate capacity, we receive each member as an indivisible part of the whole." * The omnipotence of the Sovereign people he defined significantly : " Each man alienates, I admit, by the social compact, only such part of his powers, goods and liberty as it is important for the community to control; but it must be granted that the Sovereign is sole judge of what is important." ** In this manner should individual liberty be secured.

Rousseau's theories were among those marking a transition from mediaeval political tradition to a democratic idealism. Although he was emotional and sentimental, he was very influential in initiating an enthusiasm for political freedom and for individual participation in public affairs. His ideas of popular sovereignty were stimulating and far-reaching in their effect. They lacked, however, some of the more logical and practical aspects of modern representative democracy.

Sandburg is indeed, conscious of the fallibility of collective democratic judgment and decision. On labor disputes, for instance, he writes : " The lower orders are slowly moving up. Sometimes they want more than is good for them. Their leaders sometimes go too far... My convictions were confirmed and deepened in a recent talk with a public-opinion analyst who said all the groups—high and low, intellectual and illiterate—know more than any one group." [491] As a poet he has never hesitated to express criticism in public group or private decision whenever he believed criticism was called for. This ability to entertain criticism within the democratic system, and the hope of improvement thereby, he regards as one of the most valuable advantages of the American form of government.

However, in The People, Yes the reader might conceivably wonder if the poet's criticism did not go too far. Does America really have all these faults ? Not all politicians are lying politicans, not all business executives are " racketeers of business," nor are all labor leaders " lying labor skates." [492] Not all powder and munitions manufacturers are scheming and profit-mad. Sandburg refers to " balances of pride and shame," [493] to the profiteering of those " ' respectable scoundrels ' who reaped their profits from the government's necessity in money, blankets, guns, contracts " [494] during the Civil War of Lincoln's time. His criticism of judges and bankers is often too severe. Sandburg is pointing out isolated instances, of course, and follows his criticism with the picture of the Pittsburgh Scotsman who gave away his quarter billion dollars before he died, and of the Chicago man who gave millions of dollars to Negro schools of the South. He points out that between the two extremes of those who

---

* J.-J. ROUSSEAU. Du Contrat Social, Paris: Classiques Larousse, p. 25.
** Du Contrat Social, Paris: Classiques Larousse, p. 37.

" live in mansions overly swept and garnished, or in shambles overly foul " [495] are the great masses of average people who have the ability to recognize perversions of justice, and who, in spite of such perversions, continue in the path of human progress.

> " This old anvil laughs at many broken hammers.
> There are men who can't be bought.
> The fireborn are at home in fire.
> The stars make no noise.
> You can't hinder the wind from blowing." [496]

The People, Yes may seem to some readers almost paradoxical in its content. While it is Sandburg's evocation of democracy, it is at the same time a criticism of American society; and the reader pauses to try to reconcile the poet's advocacy of democracy and his severe criticism of the maladjustments, the waste, greed and corruption that are at times able to creep into government. Sandburg stated his case much more clearly in his World War II speech of August 19, 1941—a speech later broadcast by radio, September 9. His statement is :

" Because we have looked over all the other systems and found that they too have waste, corruption, demagoguery and other evils, and we take our chances on the democratic system because of what it has that the other systems don't have. Who knows better than we who are believers in the democratic system the many precise points where it needs study and devotion, patience and prayer ? Yet we fasten our faith deeper and deeper in it.
" Why ? Because we have not yet seen a system that works better, because by the very nature of its working in the long run it gives more people more chances to think, change their way of life if they want to, than any other system. It has more give and take, more resilience, ductility and malleability, more grand wisdom, than any other system. It represents man the seeker, man the restless experimenter and adventurer...
" The dream that holds us will never come true to a perfect finish. The Man of Galilee once told his fellow fishermen ' Be ye perfect ' knowing well that they could never be perfect but knowing that they would go farther if they dreamed and tried to reach a perfect finish." [497]

A foreign reader coming to American shores could gain an erroneous impression of the country from *The People, Yes* unless he proceeds to a careful analysis of the poem. This is what the literary critic, Willard Thorp, means when he characterizes significantly the didactic quality of *The People, Yes* and names it "one of the great American books.... Whatever may be the name you put to it, a foreigner will find more of America in *The People, Yes* than in any other book we can give him. But he will have to spell it out slowly." [498]

Sandburg is not always able to present a cohesive solution to a social problem. He approaches questions and conditions as they arise, with an attitude of mind that has remained consistently inquiring, though evolving with his generation—with the evolution of America. Any attempt to form judgment of his pronouncement must therefore, be made cautiously, with a consideration for time and circumstance. Literary judgment of him must be relative.

One of the most serious faults to be found with Sandburg's criticism of America in *The People, Yes* is that he is often unable to offer immediate practical suggestions as to remedial measures. Yet in some instances he does set forth suggestions, as in the concluding pages of the volume :

> " After allowing for items to protect future operation
> every cut in production cost should be shared
> with the consumers in lower prices
> with the workers in higher wages
> thus stabilizing buying power
> and guarding against recurrent collapses." [499]

His view of capitalism has changed with the system itself throughout his lifetime. In the early Chicago poems he criticized the inequity existing between the extremes of wealth and poverty and he challenged misuse of wealth. But he was not a foe of private enterprise; nor was he a foe of the capitalistic system except wherein it needed improvement. Professor Philip Green Wright taught him that capitalism had sufficient resiliency to permit improvement and therefore to survive as a system of government and at the same time to increase the welfare of the people. Sandburg writes of Lincoln's view of capitalism as " the fruit of labor." * He now believes capitalism to be a " dynamic evolving structure " [500] which can (as has been proven) evolve through unity of purpose, and by means of sincere efforts on the part of men of all political faiths. Reforms in the structure and functioning of American capitalism have brought wide changes since the early days of powerful trusts, big business and the business Titan or Tycoon existing at the turn of the century. Ownership in large industrial organizations is now ordinarily diffused among stockholders. In many instances, corporations have taken the place of the magnate; and a single personality as head of a large business firm has usually been displaced by a board of technologists, with experts in the various fields of the corporation's business—such as advertising, engineering, production, personnel relations and financing. Thus a corporate mind consisting of many skilled minds has become management; in cases where an individual has remained at the head of a large firm, that firm in order to survive has had to meet the sharp demands of competition; and all businesses have had to meet the power of labor unions and of the demands imposed by national government regulations.

More and more frequently, ordinary people—or the common man—have come to be participants in capitalism as stockholders in large corporations. In fact, there has been a recent tendency to depict the American economy as a " people's capitalism." **

Thus some of the ills of American society which Sandburg has criticized have been gradually ameliorated : a more even distribution of wealth has

---

* *The War Years*, Vol. 1, pp. 380, 381.

** Max LERNER, *America as a Civilization*, Simon and Schuster, New York, 1957, p. 289.

been effected by taxes on the income of corporations and individuals; trade unions have been organized and have achieved constitutional means of having a voice in industry by the bargaining power with management, and they have helped to balance the economy of the American capitalist system. Sandburg sees imperfection in both management and labor organization; he sees human weaknesses in an open society; but in an open democratic society each individual has equal opportunity under law to rise to political and economic achievement. Sandburg has placed words in the mouth of Roger Williams which clearly state his own views:

" The ambitions, greeds and corruptions that ever menace a democracy Williams knew first hand. Yet he would take his chances with the people."[501]

Solutions to such problems are not simple. Sandburg knows this—and he prefers in most instances simply to present the question for public consideration. He has been in an excellent position to do so for he has lived closer to reality than many poets and as a journalist he has been in immediate contact with public affairs. He has written " thousands of news stories about politics, has witnessed scores of conventions and reported meetings of legislative bodies, including the Congress of the United States." [502] In one of his newspaper articles Sandburg writes:

" A provocative editorial writer likes to say : ' Today I shall ask questions and be Socratic and write on a clean new page what I find out. And if I end with merely asking questions and not answering them that will be all right. Socrates did it. And Henrik Ibsen (than whom which playwright is greater ?) once said his dramas mainly were intended to ask momentous questions.' "[503]

In such manner the question is placed in the public mind and stimulates public interest. The solution then lies where Sandburg wishes it—in the hands of the people.

The Sandburg social poetry aims at perfect candor; at the same time, in the search for justice it also aims at projecting the ideal :

" I should like to be in the same moment
an earthworm (which I am) and
a rider to the moon (which I am).

. . . . .

I believe more than I can ever prove
of the future of the human race
and the importance of illusions,
the value of great expectations." [504]

The value of " great expectations " and hope are expressed throughout his poetry by the symbolism of great doors, of windows, series of hills, of far horizons, sunlight, rainbows, winds and stars; and by an infinity of tomorrows. Dreaming scholars and scientists are " Man on a Quest." [505] " Man will never arrive, man will always be on the way." [506] Sandburg has attained a place of importance among modern American poets; but one wishes that the humane, democratic content and the moral tone of his poems were supported by that more mature linguistic discipline and technical skill which they merit. Some French critics have compared Sandburg poetry to that of Verhaeren in French literature; and indeed the critical estimate of Verhaeren could be applied in similar vein to Sandburg: " On sent tant de frémissement, de chaleur et de générosité que l'on voudrait oublier tout ce que son art comporte de rocailleux et de relâché. Il a voulu, pour magnifier son temps, créer l'ample forme qui lui convînt, et l'on ne peut méconnaître le souffle qui l'anime, soit dans ses longues complaintes, soit surtout dans ses hymnes aux grandes forces de la vie moderne." [507] Sandburg's poetry in spite of its regional dress " speaks to the world in its compassion for the plight of man and in its attempt to feel the heart behind the world of the machine." [508]

In this present evaluation of Sandburg verse the admonition of T. S. Eliot in reference to modern poetry, comes to mind:

" We are all apt to be somewhat on the defensive about our epoch. We like to feel that our own epoch can produce great art—all the more so because we may have a lurking suspicion that it can't: and we feel somehow that if we could believe we had a great poet, that would in some way reassure us and give us self-confidence. This is a wish but it disturbs critical judgment, for we may jump to the conclusion that somebody is a great poet who is not; or we may quite unfairly depreciate a good poet because he isn't a great one. And with our contemporaries, we oughtn't to be so busy enquiring whether they are great or not; but we ought to stick to the question: ' Are they *genuine*?' and leave the question whether they are great to the only tribunal which can decide: *time*." [509]

In the case of Sandburg we can answer: he is *genuine*.

Sandburg's verse is not poetry written for approval and praise by a few selected coteries. It is neither formal nor rhetorical. Just as he has pictured the American people as " a polychrome, a spectrum and a prism," [510] so has he constructed his poetry to reflect a synthesis of American people and occupations. The values of his verse rest on authority that is experiential rather than traditional. Many of the lyrics and nocturnes qualify as poetry of a high order; there is nobility of mood in such poems as " Four Preludes," " Prayers of Steel " and " The Long Shadow of Lincoln " which integrate image and meaning, visual clarity and intellectual aspiration. They are many evocations of human possibility. But between the two extremes of the orchestral richness of " fugitive airs in the classic manner " [511] and the raw vitality of undisciplined street clamor, there are varying degrees of quality. Nevertheless, in his attempt at democratizing poetry, Sandburg has had considerable success. Professor Margaret Schlauch of the University of Warsaw, has acknowledged the worth of Sandburg's efforts in experimental techniques of poetic communication, and his attempts to reach a large and varied audience. She has praise for Whitman's straightforward language and the rhythms of unstudied speech, and declares that " among the representatives of the humanist school, none recently writing English poetry shows the effect of Whitman's example more clearly than Carl Sandburg " [512] but the solution of the best means of democratizing poetry has not yet been reached, for " the problem of language still challenges those who are schooling themselves towards a mastery of their medium in the service o a broad and humane art, able to appeal simultaneously to a wide public and to specially equipped critics and colleagues." [513]

Sandburg's work has had an emancipating influence in that it has helped to widen both the range of suitable subject material and the rhythmic range of American poetry; and it has increased the number of poetry readers. He has popularized the development of American themes and directed attention to the fundamental forces of American life by his emphasis on the importance of the soil, of great industries and of the intellectual achievements of the scholar, particularly in the field of science.

" But Sandburg does more than describe his time and place. He proves that the machine age, even in the city environment, cannot quench that mystic spark that has long guided the way to individual decency and high social ideals. He proves that with the coming of the mechanized life Americans have not allowed the divine gift of righteous indignation to be displaced by a mental gesture of passive acquiescence. He proves that men can look through the smoke of factories and still glimpse beauty untarnished by the smudge and that some few still dream of a better day that may be achieved through the exercise in an alien world of a few old-fashioned virtues." [514]

A wide humanitarianism, a moral earnestness, a broad insight into features of American life that are significant in the evolution of the nation and an abiding faith in democracy are distinguishing features of his work. In interpreting the feelings and aims of the people the social poetry in its varied fusions of voice and mood, in its less disciplined form, does not comply with conventional literary standards, but it nevertheless achieves an important pragmatic significance by its appeal to the common consciousness. With its sympathetic analysis of human relationships and its identification with the currents of national life it is addressed to the American conscience and to the potential existent in the American people.

B. CARL SANDBURG AS A PROSE WRITER

(a) Biographer and Historian

The place of Carl Sandburg in American literature cannot be fairly or adequately assessed without consideration of his position as a prose writer. He has made his greatest contribution to American literature in the six volumes of *Abraham Lincoln: The Prairie Years* and *The War Years*.

The first widely read biography of Lincoln (1866) was published by Josiah Holland. Being the first, it helped to establish a certain tone for many Lincoln books to follow, with emphasis on the rugged virtues of the President. The next notable biography by Ward Lamon (1872) refuted some of the information contained in the Holland account. Lamon had been a legal associate of Lincoln in the Illinois days and had ridden the Eighth Judicial Circuit with him as a lawyer. In 1888 appeared the biography by William Herndon, the law partner of Abraham Lincoln in Springfield.

While this offered much personal information on the Springfield period in the way of recollections, it could not attain the stature of later biographies, for Herndon was not possessed of the stability of Lincoln, and his accounts were colored by his dislike of Mrs. Lincoln, who regarded him with even greater disfavor.

In 1890 appeared the massive biography *Abraham Lincoln: A History* by John G. Nicolay and John Hay, who had served together as Lincoln's secretaries during his presidency. This is an invaluable account and served as a standard reference work for decades. Yet compendious as are these volumes, they are conventional, and they do not present the moving human picture of Lincoln given in *The Prairie Years* and *The War Years*.

Another important contribution to early Lincoln biographies was that of Ida Tarbell (1896), whose personal research brought added color and freshness to the Lincoln portrayal; but her account is brief and extends only to the period of Lincoln's early interest in law.

A combined portraiture of Lincoln and his times had not yet appeared. Following the outbreak of World War I and the rising threat of totalitarianism, a renewed interest in the basic principles of American democracy brought a renewed interest in Lincoln. A one-volume biography by Lord Charnwood appeared in 1917, a volume distinguished by its discerning conception of the place of Lincoln in the American political story.

In 1926 came the Sandburg *Prairie Years*, distinctive in the field of biographical literature. The two volumes comprising it represented the first adequate treatment of Lincoln as growing into manhood concurrently with the rapidly developing industrial, economic, social and political changes in the Midwest and in the United States, some of the changes being interrelated with world events and commerce. " Into America came men, women and children who saw the dark year of 1848 in Europe, when the barricades and battalions of revolution arose from London to Moscow, from Prussia to Sicily." [515] The French February Revolution which spread throughout Europe, sent hundreds of thousands of homeless peasants and city laborers toward America.

Sandburg brought to *The Prairie Years* an unusual combination of talents in the pursuit of historical study—his artistry as a poet and his skill as a journalist. The unique fusion of history, biography, poetry and journalism carries *The Prairie Years* to nearly 1000 pages. In tracing the rise of the prairie lawyer, Sandburg secured information from many sources, particularly from Lincoln's letters and papers, speeches and writings. The author also spent much time in the regions of Kentucky, Indiana and Illinois where Lincoln had grown from childhood to manhood, and he received considerable assistance from personal interviews in these localities.

Drawing from his many sources of information, Sandburg sets forth a wealth of history and tradition. On his early pages moves the slow, difficult pageantry of the pioneers crossing the Appalachian Mountains through Cumberland Gap into Kentucky; we see the stark backbone of Muldraugh's Hill as it becomes a landmark in the early life of Abraham Lincoln; Rock Spring farm and the Knob Creek Farm; the primeval forests of Kentucky of the early nineteenth century, the humble one-room log cabins which sheltered Abraham Lincoln; the simple but difficult life of the pioneers striving to eke out of the soil enough to eat: all these pictures and many more pass in vivid imagery on the Kentucky pages of *The Prairie Years.*

The Salt River, the Ohio River, and the early boats on these rivers are pictured for us as the Lincolns move from Kentucky one hundred miles deeper into the wilderness, to settle in Indiana near Little Pigeon Creek; here " it was the wilderness loneliness he became acquainted with; solved, filtered through body, eye, and brain, held communion with in his ears, in the temples of his forehead, in the works of his beating heart... his bare feet were intimate with the clay dust of the hot dog-days, with the clay and mud of spring and fall rains; he was at home in clay.... In the cornfields his bare feet spoke with the clay of the earth. The color of clay was one of his own colors.... He lived with trees, with the bush wet with shining rain-drops, with the lone wild duck riding a north wind and crying down a line north to south, with the faces of open sky and weather, with the ax which is an individual one-man instrument, these he had for companions, books, friends, talkers, chums of his endless changing soliloquies." [516]

Books were young Lincoln's greatest companions. " Books lighted lamps in the dark rooms of his gloomy hours." [517] His best friend was the man who would lend him a book; by his own resourcefulness he taught himself logic, history, mathematics, even the foundation of his later profession of law.

We read of the illnesses and suffering of the early Indiana settlers, of the work of the woodsmen and farmers, of the rise of little communities such as Gentryville, with its grocery and blacksmith shop, of the little church in the wilderness which the Lincolns helped to build, of early ballads sung by the settlers, of waterfront life in the Anderson Creek region; and we read of the coming of lawyers with books in their saddlebags on the ferry-boat crossing the Ohio.

The pageant broadens to include the coming of steamboats down the Ohio, and ox wagons and pack horses passing through Gentryville toward the Wabash River.

In 1831 the pageant went farther westward to include Illinois and the settlement of New Salem. The author depicts young Lincoln as keenly sensitive to the ways and words of the people of New Salem; he pictures for us the homes, occupations, elections, politics, the church and school, the debating and literary societies; he introduces the proverbs and folk-sayings of the people; their tradesmen and teachers; Mentor Graham, with whom Lincoln studied mathematics and surveying; Bowling Green, with whom he studied law; the Black Hawk Indian War in which Abraham Lincoln was a captain of the Illinois volunteers. Sandburg traces the story of Lincoln as postmaster, as grocer and general store helper; as an Illinois legislator and as an independent lawyer with an office in Springfield. In Springfield, the story branches in many directions to include scenes in the Illinois legislature, court room trials, court cases, a shirt-sleeve court in a cornfield, Springfield society, and the marriage of Abraham Lincoln and Mary Todd.

The hundredth chapter of *The Prairie Years* is one of the most interesting from the point of view of nineteenth-century progress, for it describes the building of railroads across the Mississippi River. Lincoln's law practice included many transportation cases; and Sandburg delineates Lincoln's life as inextricably fused with the development of the West.

The later part of the biography portrays the life of Lincoln as a member of the United States House of Representatives; the growing turmoil as North and South seethed with speeches, epithets, dissensions and anger over the ever-widening slavery question; the invitation to Lincoln to address a New York audience at Cooper Union in New York City; the speech and audience in detailed description; the nomination of Lincoln for the Presidency, his election, the secession of seven southern states from the Union; and the prairie years of Abraham Lincoln end as he leaves Illinois to be inaugurated as the sixteenth President of the United States.

When he left Springfield for Washington to assume the Presidency, his memory was already " indexed and cross-indexed with tangled human causes." [518]

No other Lincoln biographer has been so successful in portraying the various facets of character of the Illinoisan who became America's greatest personal tradition. Sandburg's methods are those of an impressionist— vast accretions of facts, speeches, stories, individual accounts and actually recorded incidents which gradually build up the picture until it becomes the most intimately revealing interpretation of Lincoln yet produced. As often as possible, the characters are permitted to speak for themselves, such methods being adapted to the story of Lincoln, because of the breadth of his personality and the wide diversity of his experiences.

In many places the prose of *The Prairie Years* is almost poetry. In a critical estimate of *The Prairie Years*, William Allen White wrote in the New York *World:*

" No one but a poet with a poet's patience and a poet's understanding could have written this book. It will stand as one of the great portraits of Lincoln before he went to the White House." [519]

The Lincoln biography was taken up again and brought to a conclusion in *The War Years* (1939) : four massive volumes, totalling over 2400 pages and well over one million words. The twenty years required for the entire six volumes of biography proved to be such a task that Sandburg stated there were many times he feared he might not live to see them finished. The twenty-six chapters of *The War Years* contain 426 half-tones of photographs, 244 cuts of cartoons, plus letters and documents which aid greatly in recapturing the evaluation of Lincoln both in America and abroad.

The method of Sandburg's interpretation is unusual but highly successful. In every possible manner he reflects the personality of Lincoln and the national problems confronting him during his tenure of office as President. He gives us documented opinions, newspaper portraits and quotations from all sections of the country, North, South, East, West; he gives us articles from leading periodicals and books, portions of Congressional records, telegrams, documented conversations; miniature biographies of important men and women in all parts of the nation; military records, diaries, war accounts—until in the course of the 2400 pages the volumes become a great panorama racked with social conflicts, economic strife, political feuds and military campaigns. Yet all of these accounts are unified by Sandburg's portraiture of Lincoln as the central figure with various expressions of public opinion focused upon him.

This method of portrayal becomes a vast assemblage of human interpretation, both subjective and objective in character. The volumes do not represent mere quotation, for they are correlated by the author's searching spirit of analysis and by his literary artistry in depicting a people in chaos, when acts and deeds were " often beyond fathoming because they happened in a time of great storm." [520]

In volume I of *The War Years* Sandburg presents the complexities and difficulties of the situation confronting President Lincoln at the very inception of his term of office; he portrays for us in miniature biographies the members of the Lincoln Cabinet, the generals and statesmen surrounding him, the members of Congress, the chaotic condition of the country, the initial steps toward emancipation; the political, economic, social and military aspects of the years 1861 and 1862; and the struggle of Lincoln in his search for competent generals.

In volume II, the author presents the year 1863 as a storm center in all its varying aspects; the Emancipation Proclamation; the causes and effects of military campaigns, the significance of battles lost or won rather than the detailed account of battles and campaigns themselves; the dedication of Gettysburg as a National Soldiers' Cemetery; the significance of Gettysburg in the course of the war; and the importance of the Vicksburg campaign.

Sandburg gave us the widely diversified American opinions of Lincoln in 1861 and 1862; but these opinions slowly modified until in 1863 " at home and abroad judgments came oftener that America had at last a President who was all-American. Lincoln embodied his country in that he had no precedents to guide his footsteps; he was not one more individual of a continuing tradition, with the dominant lines of the mold already cast for him by Chief Magistrates who had gone before.

" The inventive Yankee, the Western frontiersman and pioneer, the Kentuckian of laughter and dreams, had found blend in one man who was the national head. . . . To be alive for the work, he must carry in his breast Cape Cod, the Shenandoah, the Mississippi, the Gulf, the Rocky Mountains, the Sacramento, the Great Plains, the Great Lakes, their dialects, and shibboleths. He must be instinct with the regions of corn, textile mills, cotton, tobacco, gold, coal, zinc, iron. He would be written as a Father of his People if his record ran well, one whose heart beat with understanding of the many who came to the Executive Mansion." [521]

Volume III deals with events of the year 1864. Sandburg describes August 1864 as the most difficult and darkest period of the entire four years of Civil War; and he painstakingly depicts the political conflict between Lincoln and McClellan, the general who had for so long been the ungrateful recipient of Lincoln's patience. Sandburg lifts volume III above a record of complete political chaos, military failures and social discord by his ingenious insertion of a long chapter on the personality of Lincoln, including his sense of humor. Lincoln's reëlection is clearly set forth as a vindication of his policies, even in the face of great opposition.

Volume IV deals with the events of 1865 from January through a portion of April. Sandburg portrays the condition of North and South, the political, economic, agricultural and industrial situation at the beginning of 1865, the second inauguration in March, the close of the War in April, the assassination of the President and the grief of a nation over the loss of the President.

In the final volume of *The War Years* Sandburg portrays reactions to the coming of peace—but none more warmly expressed than by President Lincoln on April 12, 1865 in reply to a Confederate asking the Chief Executive about a proclamation of amnesty. " I love the Southern people more than they love me. My desire is to restore the Union. I do not intend to hurt the hair of the head of a single man in the South if it can possibly be avoided... All that I ask is that they shall annul their ordinance of secession and send their delegates to fill the seats in Congress which are now vacant awaiting their occupation." [522]

From the standpoint of literary artistry, the two final chapters of *The War Years* constitute one of the most deeply moving pieces of prose in American literature. With all the power of his talent for word and phrase, Sandburg delineates the shock of the entire nation as " a stricken people came to their altars..." [523]

He also interprets the impact of the Lincoln story as felt in distant parts of the earth. Even men in the far Caucasus asked Tolstoy to tell them more of Lincoln. Though Tolstoy believed Lincoln to be not as great a general as Napoleon or as skilled a statesman as Frederick the Great, he stated that Lincoln overshadowed other national heroes through " peculiar moral powers and greatness of character." Hardships and experience taught Lincoln that "the greatest human achievement is love.... The greatness of Napoleon, Caesar or Washington is moonlight by the sun of Lincoln. Washington was a typical American, Napoleon a typical Frenchman, but Lincoln was a humanitarian as broad as the world." [524]

In the words of the author himself: " Out of the smoke and stench, out of the music and violet dreams of the war, Lincoln stood perhaps taller than any other of the many great heroes. This was in the minds of many... And to him the great hero was The People. He could not say too often that he was merely their instrument." [525]

The final chapter is based entirely on documented facts—yet written in moving cadences. It is Sandburg's deeply-felt tribute as he leads his readers along the thousand mile funeral procession from Washington to Springfield, which was attended by more than seven millions of people who saw it and were part of it. The people, the masses " shaped it into a drama awful in the sense of having naïve awe and tears without shame. They gave it the color and heave of the sea which is the mother of all tears... such a final pilgrimage had never before moved with such somber human outpouring on so vast a national landscape." [526]

The deep emotion and sympathy with which Sandburg wrote the concluding chapters of *The War Years* are made known to us by Evald Benjamin Lawson, President of Upsala College (New Jersey) where Sandburg was given an honorary degree of Doctor of Literature following publication of the volumes. President Lawson, in whose home the biographer was a guest, writes of the occasion as follows: " The celebrated author was giving us something of the background of *The War Years*. ' I never knew,' he said with a dark, mystic inflection in the voice, and pauses that were profound, ' I never knew that one pair of eyes could shed as many tears as fell from mine when I was writing the chapters ' Blood on the Moon ' and ' Vast Pageant,' Then Great Quiet.' " [527]

In *The War Years* Sandburg assembled the largest cast of characters ever brought together in American literature; yet not one single character or event is fictitious. Monumental as is the biography, there is no part of it that is uninteresting reading, for it represents the Lincoln life and surroundings and in them everthing is pertinent. Since in its vastness it is national in scope and includes the national heroes as well as the great masses of people, their aims—their lives and traditions—it assumes the nature of an epic or a saga.

The War Years immediately achieved enormous success among literary critics. The work received recognition for its scholarship, its thorough documentation and also for its distinctive literary method.

Clifton Fadiman said: " *The War Years* displaces the hitherto standard Nicolay and Hay. Anyone who wishes to know what Lincoln was thinking, doing and feeling from the day of his first election to the day of his assassination, will in the future have to refer to Sandburg." [528]

The reader of *The War Years* is inspired with a deeper faith in the stability of democracy, a deeper understanding of the American way of life. He emerges with heightened respect and reverence for Lincoln, whom Sandburg portrays with substantiated candor, but with infinite devotion, " not as a demi-god, " [529] but as a great and valiant personality. The author has " given him no noisy place in the hall of heroes—but a dear and still one in the chamber of the heart." [530]

Professor Allan Nevins of Columbia University, summarizes from the historian's viewpoint the importance of *The War Years:* " Everyone who knew of Sandburg's rich, if unconventional, equipment for his task— his poetic insights, his mastery of human nature, his power of selecting the vital human details from a mass of arid facts, his command of phrase and imagery, and above all, his feeling for the mingled humor, pathos, shoddiness and grandeur of democracy—expected a remarkable work. To history he brought just the faculty that the London *Spectator* had detected in Lincoln himself, ' a mind singularly representative and singularly personal.' No one, however, was prepared for the particular kind of masterwork that he laid before the country." [531]

The Prairie Years and *The War Years* have already become a part of world scholarship and literature, both by direct adaptation and by translation.

Other biographies of Lincoln were written following World War I. An excellent one-volume biography by Emil Ludwig (1930), is to be found in most libraries. A splendid one-volume Lincoln biography is that of Benjamin P. Thomas (1952), an ably qualified student of Lincoln's life, a trustee of the Illinois State Historical Library. Mr. Thomas' chapter, " Profile of a President," is an excellent resumé of the status of Lincoln in the hearts of the American people.

The most recent extensive biography of Lincoln is that of J. G. Randall, formerly Professor of History at the University of Illinois. The four Randall volumes are entitled *Lincoln The President*. Professor Randall did not live to complete more than half of the fourth volume (subtitled *Last Full Measure*) which was carried on to conclusion in 1955 by Richard N. Current, a colleague of Professor Randall at Illinois (presently at the University of Wisconsin). Professor Randall's first two volumes appeared in 1945. He is at his best when treating of Constitutional problems and questions of policy and politics.

Randall and Sandburg have each their distinctive merits as Lincoln biographers. The one employs the philosophy of war and political history as a basis; the other achieved one of the greatest human interpretations of a single period ever composed, written by a literary genius skilled in the interpretation of history and human rights. The two writers were exceedingly good friends; and Professor Randall, in the Preface to his Lincoln volumes, writes : " For the stimulus of a great personality, for comparison of notes, and for access to his ample stores of material, the author acknowledges with gratitude and affection his indebtedness to Carl Sandburg." [532]

In the biography, *Mary Lincoln: Wife and Widow*, Sandburg (with a documentary appendix supplied by Carl M. Angle) wrote of Mary Todd Lincoln in her early years in Lexington, her Springfield years, and the society of official and diplomatic Washington of the 1860's.

After long and painstaking research in his study of Abraham Lincoln, Sandburg felt that the early biographers had not done justice to Mrs. Lincoln. The early biographies written while Mrs. Lincoln was still living were very unfavorable to her, not only because of adverse newspaper reports during her declining years, but also because she had openly criticized some of the contemporary writers. Therefore, after a serious consideration of old letters, old newspapers, government records, manuscripts of members of the official White House family of the Lincoln administration; after contacts with the Lincoln, Hanks and Todd families, and after detailed study of court house records and physicians' statements, Sandburg wrote a separate story of the President's wife. In it he presents a much more charitable perception of the subject than that of a century earlier.

Among the early accounts of Mrs. Lincoln were those written by W. L. Herndon, and Ward H. Lamon. Mary Clemmer Ames, a contemporary of Mrs. Lincoln, wrote (in 1875) in her volume, *Ten Years in Washington:* " As a President's wife, she [Mrs. Lincoln] never even approached the bound of her opportunity." [533] While the account by Mrs. Ames is, in part, hostile and critical, she was among the first biographers to recognize that the contemporary picture of the President's wife might have been overdrawn.

Mrs. Katherine Helm, niece of Mary Todd Lincoln, in 1928 wrote a much kindlier account, in which she refuted some of the information contained in the Herndon biography; and within the present decade two very sympathetic biographies of Mary Lincoln have been published, one by

Irving Stone, *Love is Eternal*, and another very excellent one by Ruth Painter Randall, entitled *Mary Lincoln*, published in 1953. In her acknowledgements Mrs. Randall says : " Finally I wish to record the cherished words of a great and beloved personality. In moments of doubt and groping for expression I have remembered with affection and gratitude Carl Sandburg's advice to me about this book : ' Write it in your own way and write it as a woman.' " [534] And her biography is written from an understanding feminine viewpoint.

Sandburg has, with substantiation, portrayed Mary Todd as a woman of culture in her genteel Kentucky background, as a devoted wife and mother, as a First Lady of social success during her early residence in the White House; but then failing health began to take its toll; and tragedy was to wreck what diminishing strengths remained to her from the pressure of a brain malady. " She lived, suffered, wept, sat in candlelight and shadows, and passed out from the light of the living sun." [535]

The Sandburg biography was influential in helping to secure for Mrs. Lincoln the impartial judgment and compassion of which she, now proven an infirm and tragically stricken woman, is deserving.

Other biographical works by Sandburg include *Steichen The Photographer*, *The Photographs of Abraham Lincoln* (written in collaboration with Frederick Hill Meserve), *A Lincoln Preface*, *A Lincoln and Whitman Miscellany* and *Lincoln Collector: The Story of the Oliver R. Barrett Collection*. This last volume is not only profusely illustrated but is also a large and valuable source book of information. It represents the collaboration of a renowned collector and a distinguished biographer recognized as a foremost authority on Lincoln; and it has deservedly won a high position in the esteem of historians and the general public.

Sandburg has also written one autobiographical volume, the story of his first twenty years, *Always The Young Strangers*, from which most of the accounts of his childhood and young manhood have been drawn in the preparation of this thesis.

Always the Young Strangers has importance as a study of the cosmopolitan America that resulted from the great waves of immigration in the last century; it embodies the story of American struggle and change as they affected the lives of the immigrants, August and Clara Sandburg, and of their children born as American citizens. In addition to being an autobiography, the book portrays the economic upheavals which took place in the last two decades of the nineteenth century. The title is taken from a line of Sandburg's poem " Broken-Face Gargoyles " and symbolizes his hope and belief that the new generations will be the means of continued social and political progress. The mobility of style allows progressively maturing expression as the narrative proceeds with accounts of Galesburg life, and of the author's outlook as a youth :

" Often in the 1890's I would get to thinking about what a young prairie town Galesburg was—nearly twenty thousand people, and they had all come in fifty years. Before that it was empty rolling prairie. And I would ask : ' Why did they come ? Why couldn't they get along where they had started from? Did I know America, the United States, because of what I knew about Galesburg? In Sweden all the people in a town were Swedes, in England they were all English, and in Ireland all Irish. But here in Galesburg we had a few from everywhere... What is this America I am a part of and where I will soon be a full citizen and a voter? And what is freedom?

"I said I would listen and read and ask and maybe I would learn. By guessing and hoping and reaching out I might get some of the answers."[536]

(b) *Novelist*

Remembrance Rock, (1948) Sandburg's one historical novel, might be entitled The American Pilgrims' Progress, for it portrays the evolution of American democracy. It is therefore, of considerable significance in a study of the social, economic and political development of the nation.

"The idea for this book", says Sandburg, "has fascinated me for a long time; an epic, weaving the mystery of the American Dream with the costly toil and bloody struggles that have gone to keep alive and carry further that Dream. At the time I decided to undertake the work, the war was on... The book slowly grew into proportions beyond what any of us had expected, leading into four and one-half years of writing. The war has now come to its end, but a portrait of America, getting the lights and shadows of the American Dream, past and present, is perhaps more wanted now than at any previous hour." [537]

The book is composed of a prologue, three long sequences and an epilogue. In the prologue the theme of the American heritage is presented by the fictional Justice Windom, a retired Supreme Court Associate Justice, when he speaks in a radio address in Washington to the people of the United States: "Living men in struggle and risk, in self-denial and pain, in familiarity with sacrifice, wounds and death—those living men of the past paid the cost... Long before this time of ours America saw the faces of her men and women torn and shaken in turmoil, chaos and storm... yet there always arose enough of reserves of strength, balances of sanity, portions of wisdom, to carry the nation through to a fresh start with an ever renewing vitality... Men and women who gave all they had and wished they had more to give—how can we say they are sunk and buried? They live in the sense that their dream is on the faces of living men and women today... They ought not to be forgotten—those dead who held in their clenched hands that which became the heritage of us, the living." [538]

In the rich and varied 1067 pages, Sandburg presents the three sequences of a long struggle in behalf of freedom, conceived during the religious conflicts in England and Holland and pursued across the Atlantic to Massachusetts and down to the present day. The determined effort to keep alive the new concepts of freedom is vigorously portrayed as scene after scene of the American story is unfolded. The analysis of the Pilgrim mind is excellent; and the pictures of the turbulent division of loyalties in the

Revolutionary period are the best interpretations of those troubled loyalties yet to appear in American literature.

American democracy was founded primarily upon the moral, religious and ethical standards of the early settlers; it was molded by an ideal based upon the sovereignty of the people and the rights of the individual; it was further shaped by a philosophy of growth and change. The third sequence of the novel portrays this growth and change in the evolution of nineteenth-century life in America, and it includes the story of the Erie Canal; the story of water travel and land travel to the Midwest; the settlement of the Midwest; the Industrial Revolution; and the Civil War period.

The last part of the volume is devoted to World War II days; and to the ideas and viewpoints of the returning soldiers.

" The soldier knows the real story of the war; he feels it sharply. This war has a thousand faces... and a fantastic variety of means for testing a boy's brain, for stretching his nerves, for exposing his heart or burying his heart... The war must be lived to be understood. We can tell you only events, of what men do. We can see and tell you that this war is brutalizing some among your sons, and yet ennobling others. War happens inside a man. It happens to one man alone. It can never be communicated. That is the tragedy—and perhaps the blessing." [539]

This book is Sandburg's most complete evocation of the American heritage, and presents his faith in the future of America " through the storms to come and the stars coming after the storm." [540]

Sandburg has placed his own thoughts in the closing words of Justice Windom : " My dear ones... you whose faces I cherish... you will please me for the love I bear you—by reading this manuscript in the sequences as I have carefully arranged them—book by book—and may it be that as you live with these repeating faces that weave a blood-scarlet thread over and through the story of our country—may it be that you find tokens and values worth your time in living with them and my time in the many years I have given them—so be it—my blessings go with you always." [541] Thus, this historical novel is Sandburg's personal legacy to the American people.

The spirit of American democracy has received one of the fullest expressions thus far accorded it in our national literature in the biographical and historical writings of Carl Sandburg. While his poetry conveys an extensive approach to American life and history it must be said that in his prose writings Sandburg gives some of the most important clues to his thinking on America.

Sandburg's prose presents a wider, a more detached viewpoint than his poetry. Particularly in the historical biography does he set forth foreign opinions of Lincoln, of the Civil War and of the nineteenth-century American economy. Many foreign newspaper accounts—particularly the London *Times*, the London *Spectator*, and the Manchester *Guardian*—are introduced; many foreign observers are quoted; many foreign visitors to the White House are portrayed and their opinions set forth; foreign magazine views of the United States are presented; foreign editorial judgments given. Editorial, newspaper and magazine and personally pronounced opinions within the United States, are, of course, set forth on a much wider scale; scathing criticism and warm adulation are both given; the views of cabinet members, senators, diplomats, lawyers, preachers, poets, prose writers, lecturers, Northerners, Southerners, farmers, business men, slaves and abolitionists—all these and many more give to the pages of the historical biography its authenticity; as do letters, documents, state and Federal records. Sandburg has followed the same method of presentation in his novel, but in a much less detailed manner. His aim has been the same, namely, to present the picture from many angles and viewpoints.

Prose as an instrument of communication does not subject an author's views to the same reshaping, concentration and magnification as does verse. If poetry has a more telling effect on the reader or hearer by arousing sympathy or feeling in him, by appealing to his aesthetic sense, prose tells more of the original feeling of the author, in purer and more direct form. It bespeaks the intention and conviction of the author in greater detail. Thus the fact that, to a considerable extent in his Lincoln biography and even more obviously in his novel, Sandburg deliberately took up the subject of the American nation shows that his desire to portray his country had become a ruling principle. His writing represents a form of literary nationalism in its comprehensive conception of the American story.

C. Emergence of Sandburg Writings Abroad

Malcolm Cowley in writing of " American Books Abroad " has stated that when works of American authors have reached Europe they have, generally speaking, followed one of two paths. One path has led directly to England, thence northeastward through the Germanic countries to Scandinavia; the other path has led from America to France, then through the Slavic countries and down to the Mediterranean. The northern route through England is the path usually followed by American books distinguished for historical scope and for realism and for human warmth as opposed to intensity of emotion; while those reaching Europe by the southern route are frequently characterized as technically inventive, or lyric, or as possessed of depth cf logic. Whitman's *Leaves of Grass* followed the northern route through England before reaching literary recognition in the Latin countries; while Poe was first welcomed by the Symbolist poets in Paris.

Sandburg's literary heritage from England is a wide heritage, as is that of most American writers. We are told that Shakespeare " he loves and calls his own "; [542] and we recall the brief Sandburg poem " They All Want To Play Hamlet." References are made in other poems to Milton and to Cromwell; and in his prose are references to Ruskin, Carlyle, Macaulay, Scott, Keats, Browning, William Butler Yeats and others. We know that Gray's " Elegy " meant much to him; that he considered " Piers Plowman " " a great though neglected poem," [543] and it is not difficult to detect a literary inheritance from these two poems.

In England certain literary critics had begun to discover the early twentieth-century American poets, Robinson, Frost, Masters, Lindsay and Sandburg, sometimes before their recognition in the United States. Robert Frost's earliest volumes of poetry were first published in London. The British writer, Rebecca West, was among the first Europeans to bring Carl Sandburg to international attention. In 1926 Miss West edited a volume entitled *Selected Poems of Carl Sandburg*, which was published in London. In the pages of her introduction she stated that " no writer of Anglo-Saxon descent, no representative of the New England tradition has described the break between Lincoln's America and modern industrial America as poignantly as Carl Sandburg." She also stated that most English literary critics in 1926 believed that poetry should be lyric, and were inclined to demand that the poet should write " brief and perfect verse " and that therefore the individualized talent of Sandburg was not too easily accepted. Yet she praised the breadth of vision in his art which " is dominated by an image so vast that it requires as house-room not one but a thousand poems." [544]

There is no language barrier between British and American literature; therefore any American publication is always readily available to readers in England by direct order from the United States. Direct London publications of Sandburg's works include the following: *Smoke and Steel* in 1922; *Rootabaga Stories*, 1924; *The Prairie Years*, 1940; and *Storm Over the Land* (a modification of *The War Years*) in 1943. Canadian publications include *The People, Yes*, 1936; *The American Songbag*, 1936; *Rootabaga Stories*, 1936; *Smoke and Steel*, 1938; and *Storm Over the Land* in 1942.

In 1925 G. Ruben Berg, a Swedish literary critic, visited the United States and after his return to Sweden published his impressions of American literature in his volume *Moderne Amerikaner* in which he devoted his attention to the American writers who had appeared after 1910. Berg designated Sandburg as one of the important and influential contemporary poets. Within a few years many of the American writers mentioned in *Moderne Amerikaner* appeared in Swedish translation, for Berg's publication inspired Swedish interest in American literature.

In the Royal Library of Stockholm are Swedish translations of Sandburg poetry, the translation of *Always The Young Strangers* and of the Lincoln biography. The foreword to the Lincoln biography translation was written by Ebba Dalin, eminent author and lecturer. In the Nobel Library of Stockholm are all the major volumes of Sandburg in the original English.

As early as the 1920's Mrs. Anna Lenah Elgström, of Stockholm, became interested in the poetry of Carl Sandburg. The writings of Mrs. Elgström are prominent in literary periodicals; she is also a novelist, and is well known for her political and social writings in the newspaper *Sydsvenska Dagbladet*. Independent in her political convictions, the ideals of the disciplined democracy of which Carl Sandburg has written in American prose and poetry, and the strength of his literary production, have long appealed to her. She introduced his poetry into Sweden by editing and publishing in 1934 a collection of his poems, translated into Swedish by three leading poets, Elmer Diktonius, Artur Lundkvist and Erik Blomberg.

Where Sweden is concerned, there is naturally a certain pride in the achievement of a man of Swedish ancestry. Mrs. Elgström expresses a view not uncommon among Swedish admirers of the poet when she says : " Very definitely he was influenced by Swedish culture—perhaps more unconsciously than consciously. His religious feeling and his feeling for people who work with the soil are influences from Sweden." * She also believes that Sandburg has influenced modern Swedish poetry. His influence is particularly felt in the school of the " young poets." [545] She feels that Sandburg poetry embodies great freedom of expression and wide choice of subject matter—and this " spirit of freedom is particularly appealing to young writers." *

In a world where the problems which Sandburg reflected and protested against were universal problems and increasing in scale, sensitive minds of poets and writers, thinkers and humanists were also protesting. Against this background, the emergence of Sandburg on the international scene led to his translation by other poets of a like mind, who in turn were encouraged by him and sharpened by his hard, unmuted protests; therefore it should not be surprising that the three poets who translated Sandburg poetry into Swedish feel a sympathetic understanding after the lông task of transfer of thought and spirit from one language to another. Diktonius demonstrates courage in his own poetry—" I would flame like northern lights "; [546] and he demonstrates a feeling for nature in his desire to " be green forest." [547] Erik Blomberg is among the Swedish poets who reflect glimpses of the chaos of war, and a war-torn mankind :

" My heart is imprisoned, my heart has been thrown
In shackles that bind the whole world." [548]

We recall the forlorn spirit of the Sandburg poem published in 1920, " Crimson Changes People " :

" Did I see a crucifix in your eyes
And nails and Roman soldiers
And a dusk Golgotha?

. . . . .

Did I see moths in your eyes, lost moths
With a flutter of wings that meant :
We can never come again." [549] **

In the poetry of Artur Lundkvist we see a strength of expression which may represent an influence of Sandburg. We note his love of cities in the poem " Bring Me Young Noisy Cities " and in another poem in which

" You hear the roar of factories, roar of the heavy
Loaded trains, the rattle of riveters, the clang
Of steel on steel." [550]

---

* In an interview granted to the writer of this study in 1958.

** Sandburg's World War II poem *The Man With the Broken Fingers* was translated into Swedish within four weeks of its publication in America in 1942; it was also translated into Norwegian, Danish and Russian at about the same time.

In Lundkvist's poem " The Stone Cutter " it is interesting to compare the architecture of the poem in its forcefulness and strength to the architecture of the " Chicago " poem :

" I am a stone-cutter
I work in stone with hammer and chisel.
I hew.
I shape the stone.
Blocks. Pillars.
What shall become of it ?
Temples standing through the centuries ?
Poems — dreams — visions in stone living to the evening of life ? " [551]

But it is in another of the " young poets," Harry Martinson, that there is a more nearly kindred spirit to that of Carl Sandburg. Martinson upon his publication of *Vägen till Klockricke*, was elected to membership in the Swedish Academy. A considerable portion of his prose and poetry has been translated into English, and seems to me to show a Sandburg influence. His *Vägen till Klockricke* has been translated into English as *The Road*, and is well and favorably known.* A collection of his poems is included in *Twentieth Century Scandinavian Poetry*, printed in Denmark and available in the United States through arrangements by the Scandinavian Book Club of Franklin Park, New Jersey.

Harry Martinson (1904-) as a very young boy was deprived of both parents; his father died in 1910; and his mother emigrated to America in 1911, leaving him behind to be brought up by the parish of Jämshög in Blekinge; his greatest interest was in schooling; in 1920 he went to sea, visiting many European countries; he worked for his passage to the United States; spent some time in the West Indies and South America; and on a British ship sailed to South Africa, India, China and Vladivostok; returned to Sweden to comply with his military service requirement; again sailed to West Africa, returning to Stockholm only in 1928, after having seen much of the world by ship and by long walking excursions inland. As had Carl Sandburg, Harry Martinson in his youth worked at many jobs to earn a living. The experiences with many people in many stations of life endowed both these writers with factual observation, keen and varied interests, an analytical discernment and a respect for the individual human spirit. Martinson in his efforts to create a new medium of poetic expression and to renew the language of poetry shows the influence of Sandburg, and of Edith Södergran of Finland, who rejected the traditional form of poetry and abandoned rigid patterns, seeking a form permitting free expression of inspiration.

Martinson's *Vägen till Klockricke*, or *Road to Bell Country*—compares with Sandburg's *Always The Young Strangers*. *Vägen till Klockricke* is an autobiographical account which portrays the wanderings of literate, educated rovers in Sweden, in search of peace and contentment—perfection. In its allegory and symbolism, its lyric prose, its reverence for human

---

* Published 1955 by Reynal and Company under the auspices of the Anglo-Swedish Library Foundation.

nature and its love of the nature of earth and air and sky, in its passages of deep wisdom, in its reflection of mankind, the volume displays both talent and temperament which invite comparison with Sandburg.

The superb imagery of Martinson's poetry is exemplified in " Visual Memory " in which " thin birches stood on Stockholm's nesses " reflected with " brittle lines swaying in the water, broken, rocking, white like optic water-lilies," yet, when an oil barge approaches the shore,

" The rainbow shimmer of the oozing oil
— a spectrum saga —
Began to fight with the swaying white rods of the optic lilies.
They fought, they fought like China's exotic dragons ! " [552]

To anyone who has admired the majestic beauty of Stockholm, " the city that floats on the water," [553] this is a characteristic description.

Martinson's " Cable Ship," reminiscent of his experiences in the West Indies, portrays the seamen after repairing an Atlantic cable :

" It's millionaires in Montreal and St. John discussing
The price of Cuban sugar and the lowering
Of our wages...
We patient cable fishermen
Then lowered the mended cable
To its place in the sea." [554]

These lines reflect the influence of Sandburg's social criticism. The sardonic comment is of a gentler nature than that of Sandburg, but the lines show a similar regard for human values in the minds of the two poets.

Each time I look at my copy of *Vägen till Klockricke* *—The Road*, as it is translated in English—I am reminded of the poem of Sandburg "The Road and The End." This poem could have been written by either poet— and could appropriately accompany the picture of Martinson's literate rover of the Swedish countryside.

Sven Linner, literary critic of the Upsala *Nya Tidning*, has drawn an analogy which further supports my comparisons of the two writers : " Sandburg has, as has Harry Martinson with us, kept the childhood ability to be fascinated by a world which every day manifests new wonders." [555]

There are interesting variations of Swedish opinion on the writings of Sandburg. Some of the Swedish people believe he has attained distinction chiefly for his poetry, others prefer his prose. Following official disclosure of the names of individuals upon whom honorary Doctor of Philosophy degrees were to be conferred by the University of Uppsala, the Upsala *Nya Tidning* on April 20, 1950, published an article on Sandburg which began as follows : " It is naturally for his extraordinary contribution as a lyricist that the author, Carl Sandburg, is being honored by the Faculty of Philosophy "; [556] yet the official University citation in June stated : " Author

---

* Klockricke is a real location in Sweden—meaning *The Realm of Bells* or *The Kingdom of Clocks*, but cannot be accurately translated. Martinson employs it symbolically as the search for perfect happiness.

Carl Sandburg's poetry and prose works have been read and known all over the world and he is one of the greatest names of those of Swedish descent in the United States..."* In 1953 the poet-historian was awarded the Medal of the Royal Order of the North Star in recognition of his contribution to literature.

The Sandburg book which has reached the widest reading public in Sweden is *Always the Young Strangers*, for the Swedish people feel that Sandburg received strong influences from the homeland of his parents who are affectionately portrayed throughout the volume. While Carl Sandburg is not "a Swede who became an American author," [557] but an American born of Swedish parents, the fact remains that Sweden has a right to emphasize the importance of his lineage. Aage Heinberg says: "The Americans regard him as one of their own. Perhaps not all are going to know it, but in certain circles, it will be remembered that the humanity so beautifully portrayed was that of the old immigrant who toiled with American earth but had his roots in Sweden." [558] Sven Linner wrote in similar vein concerning the picture of the immigrant parents: " Hard work, Lutheran faith, scrupulous honor—one would like to think these qualities were Swedish traits produced in their homeland." [559]

In studying the Linner review which was published in 1953 in the Upsala *Nya Tidning*, I note the difference in perspective in which Europeans and Americans view the Illinois background of *Always the Young Strangers*.** John K. Hutchens in the Book Review section of the New York *Herald Tribune* characterizes the volume as "a memorable American autobiography that superbly recaptures the boyhood of Carl Sandburg, that fondly but truly paints the portrait of a prairie in a time long gone." [560] While Linner says: " Sandburg saw some of the men who had actually set their plows in the ground where later his childhood town grew up... A European reader is struck by the shortness of historical perspective... by the fact that all this could happen just a short century or half-century ago!... Back of the pioneers there is absolutely nothing. Under a thick layer of historic mould one stumbles upon the rocks of timelessness..." [561]

From such information as is available it would seem that " Smoke and Steel " and " Chicago " may have been the first Sandburg poems to be translated into Russian (1930). In 1935 " Work Gangs," " Early Moon," " Buffaloes " and " Night Movement—New York " were translated by G. Petnikov for his book entitled *Petnikov East and West*. In 1939 Ivan Kashkin and M. Senkevich translated " Psalm of Those Who Go Forth Before Daylight," " Halstead Street Car," " Skyscraper," " Grass " and "Prayers of Steel" for the volume entitled *Twentieth Century American Poets*.

We have already noted the American Exhibition in Moscow in 1959. This Exhibition attracted wide attention in Russia; and in 1960 a small anthology of American poetry was published by the Foreign Literature State Publishing House in Moscow. The collection was edited and translated by Ivan Kashkin

* From the official citation on file in the Carolina Rediviva Library of the University of Uppsala.

** This Sandburg autobiography was also translated into Portuguese in 1954; and into Chinese for readers in Nationalist China on the island of Formosa.

and was entitled *I Hear You, Poets of America*. Among the poems of Sandburg selected for translation and inclusion in the anthology were " Choices," " Chicago," " Potomac Town in February," " Illinois Farmer," " To Certain Journeymen," " Threes," " Prairie " and " Mr. Attila."

An analysis of the poems translated into Russian would lead to the belief that many of those selected might be turned to propaganda. " Prairie " and " Illinois Farmer " may have been chosen for the encouragement of agriculture. " Threes " mentions the Russian Revolution for Bread, Peace, Land. " Mr. Attila " (written during World War II) is a satire on war; but to the Russians it would recall the European military campaign of Attila the Hun. " Chicago," " Choices," " Halstead Street Car " and " Psalm of Those Who Go Forth Before Daylight " are poems of social protest and may have been selected to serve propaganda purposes of the Communists who, since the leadership of Lenin, have declared their intention of abolishing the capitalistic system in non-Communist nations. It is significant that the poems of social protest have reappeared in various Russian publications from time to time.

In 1961 an abridgment of Sandburg's biography of Lincoln was translated by Gribanova and Shaeffer. No comment on the translation has reached the writer of this thesis other than the mention of translation. Nor can it be stated with certainty that this volume is available to the general reading public in Russia, although apparently a copy of the edition is in the Lenin Library in Moscow. As is well known, neither the Russian writer nor the Russian reader enjoys intellectual freedom. Literature, before being given to the public, is rigidly scrutinized for compliance with the post-war " Zhdanov decree " adjuring all writers as " engineers of the soul " to adhere strictly to the dogma of " socialist realism "; and if the literature is deemed incompatible with Communist purposes it is withheld from circulation. Freedom of speech, freedom of the press, freedom of religion and government " of the people, by the people, and for the people " as set forth in the six volumes of Sandburg's biography of Lincoln do not fit in any totalitarian system of government.

While Sandburg was in Russia at the time of the American Exhibition he met with a group of magazine editors in Moscow. He has given us a portion of this interview as follows :

" I asked them what was the general opinion and feeling about Lincoln and they answered in effect, ' He gave freedom to three million slaves and did not hesitate to make war and shed blood to make sure the slaves stayed free.' " * Thus it would seem that Boris Pasternak had taught the lesson of guarded language—or even the lesson of silence—on varying concepts of freedom behind the East Berlin wall.

This is in marked contrast to the open admiration of Lincoln expressed by Tolstoy in the last century. Concerning the national heroes and statesmen of history, Tolstoy stated : " Lincoln was a man of whom a nation has

---

* Carl SANDBURG, "Civil War Centennial Address", in Coolidge Auditorium of the Library of Congress, October 25, 1961.

a right to be proud. He was a Christ in miniature, a saint of humanity whose name will live thousands of years in the legends of future generations. We are still too near his greatness, and so can hardly appreciate his divine power; but after a few centuries more our posterity will find him considerably bigger than we do. His genius is still too strong and powerful for the common understanding, just as the sun is too hot when its light beams directly cn us." In further describing Lincoln's greatness of character Tclstoy continued: " He was what Beethoven was in music, Dante in poetry, Raphael in painting and Christ in the philosophy of life." *

Spanish translations of Sandburg's works include *Tormenta sobre la Tierra: Lincoln y la guerra civil estadounidense* (1945) from the author's *Storm Over the Land* which is taken mainly from the Lincoln biography; also *Maria Lincoln, esposa y viuda*, which was first printed in Chile (1945), and is available to all Spanish-speaking countries. While Sandburg's prose is better known among Spanish readers, his poetry has also attracted attention, as may be seen from a literary criticism written in Buenos Aires by J. Z. Uriburo in 1945. This Argentine critic writes of Sandburg as a courageous poet of American democracy and also as a prose writer who has prcduced such exhaustive works on the United States Civil War and President Lincoln that he has become an acknowledged authority on these subjects.**

In Paris, as early as 1920, Jean Catel wrote in *La Revue de la Quinzaine* an article lamenting the many difficulties attendant upon translation of American poetry into French. He expressed regret that Emily Dickinson had not yet been translated into French, " et plus près de nous Carl Sandburg, Lindsay, Masters, Marianne Moore." 562

In 1925 Sandburg's prose work *Rootabaga Stories* for children was translated into French under the title of *Au Pays de Routabaga* by Léon Bazalgette.

In 1956 *The People, Yes* became available to readers in France in the translation *Le Peuple, Oui*.

In Paris an anthology of poetry entitled *Les Meilleurs Poèmes Anglais et Américains d'aujourd'hui* was published in 1958 by the Société d'Édition d'Enseignement Supérieur. The volume is the work of Paul Ginestier, *Maître de Conférences* at the University of Hull, and contains a *lettre-préface* by Jean Cocteau of the French Academy.

In his tribute to the translator for introducing the best modern poets of England and America to French poetry readers, Jean Cocteau writes:

" La poésie est un organisme et tous les vrais poètes du monde se comprennent même, disait Rilke, si les idiomes qu'ils emploient diffèrent. Car la poésie est une langue à part, commune à n'importe quel poète. Elle est aussi une sorte d'exhibitionnisme suprême, lequel, par chance, s'exerce chez les aveugles.

" Votre ensemble est, à mes yeux, un album de famille, où chaque visage ressemble à l'autre sans rien perdre de sa singularité." 563

---

* Tolstoy quoted by SANDBURG, *The War Years*, Vol. IV, pp. 377, 378.
** J. Z. URIBURO, 131, *Editorial Futuro*, Buenos Aires, 1945.

The selections for translation from Sandburg poetry are not the finest poems from an artistic or aesthetic point of view; the longest selection is from the Sandburg " literature of power "—from *The People, Yes*. The other selections are from the volumes of the *Chicago Poems*, and *Smoke and Steel*; and they appear appropriately under the headings "La Vie Moderne" and "La Guerre et la Mort".

Paul Ginestier pronounces Sandburg a kind of " American Verhaeren," [564] in his love of life and in certain aspects of his poetry. If we compare the writings of the Flemish poet with those of Sandburg we note, indeed, that the style of both poets is varied, at times cadenced and highly lyrical, at times rough and strident. Both poets excel in forceful imagery and subtle symbolism. While Sandburg abjures rhyme in favor of free verse, Verhaeren chooses rhyming lines but does not insist upon rhyme, preferring above all else pictorial expression and strength of affirmation. His *Flamandes*, because of its boldness of expression, was at first greeted with protest. Yet Verhaeren became the national poet of Belgium.

To the reader who compares the subject matter of Verhaeren and Sandburg, there appear resemblances not only in social criticism, but also in delight in natural beauty. As Sandburg depicts the industrial ascendency of the city of Chicago in the early twentieth century, so does Verhaeren portray a similar viewpoint in his *Campagnes Hallucinées* (1893) and *Les Villes Tentaculaires*, (1895) both of which deal with the pervasion of industrialism in Europe. From " La Ville " a brief excerpt will serve to illustrate the spirit of the poetry, as well as the power of imagery and social symbolism :

" Ses murs se dessinent pareils à une armée
Et ce qui vient d'elle encore de brume et de fumée
Arrive en appels clairs vers les campagnes.

C'est la ville tentaculaire,
La pieuvre ardente et l'ossuaire
Et la carcasse solennelle.

Et les chemins d'ici s'en vont à l'infini
Vers elle." [565]

When one reads Sandburg poetry translated into French, the comparison we have noted may be seen more clearly (and at the same time the reader may take notice of the skill of the translator in transferring both thought and form of line). The following lines, descriptive of the unbalanced economy during the depression of the 1930's, are taken from *The People, Yes:*

" Ça et là dans la rue un homme
jeune, dur comme de l'acier
qui pose de façon glaciale les questions
venant de ses entrailles brûlantes.
Élevé dans un monde motorisé d'essais et d'erreurs
Il mesure au millionième de pouce,

. . . . .

> Il a manié des outils électriques munis de crosses,
> Pistolets à gâchette-interrupteur, et cependant
> Il ne peut pas comprendre et peut en nommer des milliers
> Oisifs comme lui dans des usines également oisives.
> Il étudie ce qu'est l'objet de la justice
> Et révise ses idées sur l'argent, le confort, la renommée." [566]

The following lines, also translated from *The People, Yes* illustrate the use of symbolism to express tragedies that are beyond the power of man to control; and they show further reason for comparison with Verhaeren :

> " Nous demandâmes au cyclone
> de se détourner de notre grange
> mais il ne nous entendit pas." [567]

The poetry of both Sandburg and Verhaeren exhibits force, warmth of feeling and compassion. Both writers share a genuine optimism based on the greatness of human life and progress and the promise and hope of future achievements. The Flemish poet symbolizes this hope in his lines :

> " L'esprit de l'homme avance et le soleil couchant
> N'est plus l'hostie en or divin qui fertilise.
> . . . . .
> En attendant, la vie ample se satisfait
> D'être une joie humaine, effrénée et féconde;
> Les droits et les devoirs? Rêves divers que fait
> Devant chaque espoir neuf, la jeunesse du monde ! " [568]

In 1916 Carl Sandburg published his poem " Drumnotes " in commemoration of great world figures who had died during that year. Among those commemorated was Émile Verhaeren.

In 1958 *Abraham Lincoln: The Prairie Years and The War Years* was translated into German and published by the firm of Paul Zsolnay of Vienna and Hamburg. The German title is *Abraham Lincoln, Das Leben Eines Unsterblichen.* The book is a complete translation of Carl Sandburg's one-volume edition, is 874 pages in length, and contains forty illustrations. The publishers announced it as having been designated " the greatest historical biography of our generation." [569]

The release of the German edition was timed to coincide with the 100th anniversary of Lincoln's famous " House-Divided " speech, which even after a century is considered of value to the whole world, according to the statement in the introduction :

" Im Jahre 1858 hat Lincoln in seiner Heimatstadt Springfield in seiner berühmten ' House-Divided '-Rede aufgezeigt, dass eine Regierung nicht bestehen kann, die halb der Freiheit und halb der Sklaverei anhängt. Heute, nach hundert Jahren, gilt dieses Wort der ganzen Welt." [570]

The introduction to the volume, written by the Federal Minister of Education of Austria, Dr. Heinrich Drimmel, refers to Sandburg's biography as " already having become a classic in its field." Dr. Drimmel pronounces it something more than a classic and standard work among Lincoln biographies. ... " Because it is not only the work of a scholar for other scholars; it gives an account of the statesman and politician to the statesman and politician; to others with less important affairs, an account of a man with ordinary problems, of his mistakes and his blunders, of his sorrows and his consolation, of his despair and his joy. This courage may prove of comfort to many, because of the very courage which life demands." [571] This particular character study of Lincoln in the difficult tensions of great chaos has been of value to individual Americans in time of personal distress, as has been amply proven. President Roosevelt is said to have turned to *The War Years* for counsel and sustaining faith during World War II. The Presiding Bishop of the Protestant Episcopal Church of the United States, Henry K. Sherrill, has written : " Carl Sandburg has placed all lovers of the American scene greatly in his debt and has been a source of inspiration to many people. Particularly am I grateful to him for his work on Abraham Lincoln. These are books which I read and re-read; whenever I need new insight into the problems of the individual, I read again the story of Lincoln's dealing with people in great distress during the Civil War." [572]

No finer tribute could be paid to Lincoln or to his biographer than that paid by the Austrian Minister of Education in stating his conviction that this portrayal of the idealism of the Great Emancipator should be placed in the hands of men living today—especially in the hands of youth—for each age needs heroes.

" Jede Zeit braucht Helden. Dem heute lebenden Menschen, vor allem der Jugend, deren Idealismus der Nützlichkeit gerühmt wird, sollte darum dieses Buch in die Hand gegeben werden." [573]

Of all the writings of Sandburg, *The Prairie Years* and *The War Years* are the volumes most likely to continue in influence abroad.

II

CARL SANDBURG AND HIS CRITICS : IN THE UNITED STATES AND ABROAD

According to statistics from *The Publishers' Weekly* at least four thousand American poets published volumes of poetry in the United States during the twenty years covering the literary " renaissance "—1912 to 1932. Since Carl Sandburg is one of the major American poets who came into prominence during this period, it was inevitable that he should become the object of considerable literary criticism both at home and abroad. The range of criticism has been wide, for this poet brought not only a revolutionary style to poetry but new life and new subjects, and he emphasized the importance and gravity of the many problems confronting the rapidly growing American nation, being particularly disturbed by the tensions and the ominously stratifying class lines developing in a republic which had prided itself on being classless. A less thoughtful writer might have been inclined to bleak pessimism; but relying on his own essential nature Sandburg proceeded with independent thought, with originality and with what Marianne Moore terms in a poet "the courage of his peculiarities." [574] The French critic, Sainte-Beuve, had in the previous century stressed the importance of originality in literature in a period of transition:

"Le don critique... devient même du génie lorsque au milieu des révolutions de goût, entre les ruines d'un vieux genre qui s'écroule et les innovations qui se tentent, il s'agit de discerner avec netteté, avec certitude, sans aucune mollesse, ce qui est bon et ce qui vivra; si, dans une œuvre nouvelle, l'originalité suffit à racheter les défauts." [575]

Twentieth-century critics often condemn this nature in a poet, for originality usually seems in the beginning a peculiarity. When the poem "Chicago" first appeared in *Poetry* magazine (March, 1914) it was widely discussed. It was followed by eight other Sandburg poems, "Jan Kubelik," "The Harbor," "The Hammer," "At the Window," "Lost," "Who am I?," "Momus," "The Road and the End"; but it was "Chicago" that readers talked about most, and eventually they talked about it more than anything *Poetry* would ever print." [576] Two years later, when Henry Holt and Company published the volume entitled *Chicago Poems*, came the varied reactions of the nation.

Among examples of the most severe criticisms were the following: "Ill-regulated speech that has neither verse nor prose rhythms"; [577] "dull and shapeless"; [578] "grinding, crashing, angular words"; [579] "uncouthness"; [580] "vulgarity"; [581] "a failure to distinguish prose matter from poetic material;" [582] and "assaults on the English language." [583]

Some of these harsh criticisms are quite justifiable; others are not, for they represent critical opinions not yet readjusted to the changing needs of the times. The "ill-regulated speech" which the Boston *Transcript* deplored exists in many instances. The *Transcript* also rightly referred to Sandburg as "having a strong, unpleasant imagination." [584] But the situations of which he wrote were not fancied or imagined, they were unpleasantly real. The *Dial*, of which Emerson had been at one time a publisher, proclaimed Sandburg as "rather gross and sentimental." [585] "Gross" was a justifiable characterization of some of the early poems such as "Who am I?," in which Sandburg writes of Truth in terms which offend some readers; yet in more elevated phrasing in the same poem he portrays Truth as saying: "I am the most elusive captive in the Universe." [586] Sandburg preferred, as did the Imagists, to employ the exact word rather than the traditional word of poetry. Therefore, if "grinding, crashing, angular words" were called for to portray a situation exactly, they were his medium of expression. But it is unjust to characterize all of the *Chicago Poems* as being composed of such words, for there are many lines in this early poetry that could well be placed in the more orderly verses of writers adhering to traditional conventions.

As opposed to such severe criticism, Harriet Monroe stated in *Poetry* magazine (May, 1916) that in the *Chicago Poems* Sandburg gave " the city in a masterpiece of portraiture "; [587] *The Review of Reviews* referred to the volume as containing " poetry shaped like a statue of Rodin "; [588] while Amy Lowell called it " one of the most original books the age has produced " [589] and praised the cadence of the poems " Chicago," " Fog," " Nocturne in a Deserted Brickyard " and others; and in further contrast to the severe criticism of the Boston *Transcript* she saw in the touches of Scandinavian mysticism an element of beauty in the Sandburg imagination and characterized his use of refrains in *Chicago Poems* as highly poetic. Amy Lowell also made an observation which other critics had overlooked, namely that there appeared in these early Sandburg poems a new viewpoint in modern American poetry which introduced a foreign strain to mingle with the predominantly Anglo-Saxon American strain, thus producing new ideas.

From the foregoing may be gathered the diversity of criticism. Carl Sandburg was not alone in reaping this harvest of traditionalist censure. All the " new poets " met with rebuffs. Joseph Wood Krutch, contributing editor of *The American Scholar*, recently published in his column a comment made by Mark Van Doren forty years ago when the two were discussing some of the earliest work of the " new poets " : " So far as I can see they don't even hope to write good poetry : they are just determined not to write bad poetry." [590]

The early part of the twentieth century was a difficult time for all Americans—not merely for poets and critics. Poetry could survive only by serving the needs of the nation and by having a practical application to life. Therefore the reader must take into consideration the national background before he can attain a true perspective of any poetry of that period. " Even the best poetry needs the penumbra of its own time and place and circumstances to make it full and whole." [591]

In spite of the rough-hewn quality, looseness of form and intrusion of slang and crude language, the *Chicago Poems* survived.

By 1922 criticism had become much less severe, and Sandburg's poetry, which by that time included four volumes, had taken on importance. The influence of changing times and changing standards was being felt and accepted. Some critics still used the word " crudity " to characterize his style : others considered the poetry as showing a marked advance in delicacy of form and refinement. Sandburg's refusal to choose decorative words for his poetry still brought some censure; but his use of the non-literary language of the man in the street was received with less vituperation than that which had been heaped on *Chicago Poems*. Sandburg was not only using less of it in his poems but selecting with greater care the words from the vernacular. H. L. Mencken in his criticism of these first four books of poetry declared : " Nobody in American literature has ever panned in the pebbles of common speech and come up with more nuggets." [592] Some critics saw in " Prayers of Steel " a response to Whitman's plea for poetry that would both express democracy and employ distinctively American speech.

The social value and vitality of the poet's subject matter became more generally acknowledged and by 1924 Sandburg was a much sought-after guest lecturer in Chicago. Schools, societies, poetry circles, and the University of Chicago welcomed him. He became established in the American literary world, along with other pioneers who produced new forms of poetry, new novels, new drama as well as new literary criticism. H. L. Mencken, the leader of this new literary criticism, in his editorship of the *American Mercury* defended the new writers of acceptable literary stature, including Pound, Anderson, Sandburg, T. S. Eliot, Dreiser and Lewis.

It is interesting to compare these American criticisms with those of the British author and critic, Rebecca West, who in 1926 published a book of selected Sandburg poems. Her estimate of the first four Sandburg volumes contains both praise and censure. Miss West writes: " He is characteristically Middle-Western in that his poems have no great sense of melody but a strong sense of rhythm. Carl Sandburg is an accomplished musician who is famous both for singing and for his researches into American folk-song, and the music of his poetry is based on the technique of the banjo.[593] ... He shares with the Imagists some of their important principles, such as the use of fresh, racy words, and of suggestion. He uses everything he sees that looks to him like a good subject; Mrs. Pietro Giovannitti, the Hungarians with their kegs of beer on the picnic green, the workmen who spill Peloponnesian syllables as they sit in a Chicago lunchroom." [594] She considers the power of his native idiom to deal with man's problems as one of the chief determinants of his art; yet laments that " his poetry is often marred by a coarsely intruding line that turns it from poetry to propaganda." She also makes an observation which helps explain the difficulties of rhythm in Sandburg verse: " His lines will not reveal their music unless they are read with a Middle Western accent which is very much slower than English speech." [595]

Professor Llewellyn Jones in his analysis of the Sandburg verse of these early volumes makes a similar observation concerning the quantitative syllable rhythm:

" Most English poets have echoed the old opinions of the grammarians that there is no syllable quantity in English, that with us accent takes the place of the Greek and Latin quantities, so that accented and unaccented syllables correspond to their long and short. And it is true that our heavy speech does override our quantity—but the quantity is there nevertheless.

" Whoever reads Sandburg poetry... finds that the rhythm will remain because it does not depend on accent but the rhythm is inherent in the syllable lengths. So true is this that it is only by giving each syllable its proper length, that the logical reading of the poem is revealed. In 'Pocahontas...

Did she / wonder
Does she / remember'

the whole paragraph really reads in metrical lines of two feet each, except the second: ' Sweet as a red haw in November,' which has four.

"Mr. Sandburg achieves his extraordinarily slow pace here, the pace indeed of a funeral march, by his conjunctions of long syllables, not two in one foot, making a spondee, but letting them cut across feet, making the pace even slower." [596] The first analyses of Sandburg's philosophy to appear in a British journal was written for *Poetry Review* in 1930 by Gordden Link who affirmed the poet's "sympathy with human suffering" and "confidence in humankind." [597]

In the 1930's American criticism proclaimed *The People, Yes* as one of the great books of the decade. Because of its vitality and daring, *The People, Yes* was classified as "literature of power." [598] This term was applied to the great works appearing between 1922 and 1939 — that period which, in the United States, was characterized as providing an equilibrium of polarized violence in literature as well as in politics. To this "literature of power" of the 1930's belong Wolfe's *Of Time and The River*, Faulkner's *Absalom! Absalom!*, Eliot's *Murder in The Cathedral*, Hart Crane's *The Bridge* and Anderson's *Winterset*.

Willard Thorp, one of the four editors of the *Literary History of the United States*, has made a thorough analysis of *The People, Yes*. In its form he sees both art and artlessness, poetry and prose, rhythmic verse and short paragraphs presenting only a cluster of images. In its content Mr. Thorp sees collected wisdom—the wisdom of Lincoln, and the wisdom of lesser American figures whose words sustain the people. Lincoln's affirmations are employed to present the ideals of the American Dream. There is much symbolism in *The People, Yes* which must be studied carefully before the reader is aware of its fullest meaning. Mr. Thorp considers the volume one of the strongest voices raised on behalf of democracy to appear in the discordant, distressed decade of the 1930's.

The period 1941-1945 was a relatively unproductive period in American poetry, because of World War II, while the period 1945-1953 was a time of international tension and of anxiety as to the durability of the peace. In poetry no new strong voice appeared and literary critics tell us that "the commercial publishers almost ceased issuing poetry because they could obtain almost none with the appeal of Frost, Sandburg, or Benét. One by one the elder poets collected their verse—MacLeish, Williams, Aiken, Sandburg, Frost, Stevens, Pound, Eliot—in monumental, volumes." [599]

The absence of criticism of poetry during this period does not mean that Sandburg was lost to the public. Quite the reverse was true.

In considering European criticism of Sandburg poetry we find that Ruben Berg of Sweden states that Sandburg influenced modern Swedish poetry. Mrs. Anna Elgström says that her favorite Sandburg poem is *The People, Yes* "although this does not conform to the school of the classicists to which many Swedes feel poets must belong." * In her foreword to the volume of Sandburg poetry edited by her, Mrs. Elgström refers to the American author as follows: "Carl Sandburg is one of the fireborn who understands the shadow we call life." [600]

---

* In an interview granted the writer of this study in 1958.

Artur Lundkvist of Stockholm pronounces Sandburg "the most typically American of the new poets... a humanist of spontaneous pity and compassion who developed rapidly toward musicality and artistic consciousness." [601] In common with most critics, Lundkvist sees in Sandburg's poetry a violent hatred of injustice, along with a warmth and gentleness. This Swedish poet and critic also believes that Sandburg is the first important voice in poetry of the masses of immigrants in the New World; and he feels that he has given them a new place in American consciousness.

In the Carolina Rediviva Library in Uppsala are many references to the writings of Carl Sandburg by various critics who seem in agreement on the Sandburg personality displayed in all the writings as possessed of a " deep spirit of democracy." [602] They believe that he is generous and tolerant toward individual differences of opinion; that his religious feeling is vital but not dogmatic and that today he is still able to look at life with a youthful spirit. They consider his love of the earth a characteristic shared with the Swedish people—for now and then he likes to put aside his writing and commune with " the greatest and most original source of everything—the soil of the earth." [603]

In France an *Histoire Littéraire des États-Unis* was published in 1953 by Professor Cyrille Arnavon of the Faculté des Lettres at Lyon. This volume is of interest to an American for it gives the history of American literature as seen through the eyes of a specialist in French literature. Professor Arnavon characterizes the writings of Carl Sandburg as " certainly the most American " [604] of those emerging from the sponsorship of Harriet Monroe in her magazine *Poetry*. He characterizes the Chicago poetry as " stridente, chaotique, mais puissamment idéaliste néanmoins," [605]. His statement that the subject matter consists of " scènes de la rue, des instantanés de la métropole, des vignettes de la moisson," could apply especially to the earliest poems; but beginning with the war poems of the first volume the scope of subject matter progressively widens. The range of emotions covered in the criticism has been generously dealt with; " que ce soit pitié, terreur, souffrance et aussi bien joie de vivre, tendresse, humour." [606] The critic declares that neither arrogance nor a consideration for taste restrains the poet. But perhaps the arrogance is not wholly to be condemned, for it stems from the poet's human sympathy. A more kindly evaluation is that by Louis Untermeyer: " It cannot be said too often that Sandburg is brutal only when dealing with brutal things, that his ' vulgarity ' springs from love of life as a whole, not from affection for a drab or decorative part of it... The strength of his hatred is exceeded by the challenge of his love." [607]

Professor Arnavon, while praising the poet's great love of humanity, speaks disparagingly of the subject matter as representing " le manœuvre, l'immigrant, la prostituée, le criminel, bref toute une population fluide et anarchique." [608] He judges the poetry disproportionately in terms of the *Chicago Poems* only and fails to characterize the subject matter of the poetry appearing after 1916. It is unfortunate that the reader is left with the above characterization. Arnavon does not mention men in Sandburg poetry of such stature as President Lincoln, President Franklin Roosevelt, General

Joffre in the Chicago stadium, the soldier heroes of the two World Wars, or the tributes to the men of science for which Sandburg received from the hands of scientists the Albert Einstein Award. A widely diversified array of humanity is portrayed in Sandburg poetry. Wherever Sandburg sees people he finds a challenge to poetic expression—in the cities, in the steel mills, in the concert halls, in the prairie fields, on ships, in the camps of the Armed Forces and among the strugglers during global depression. In brief character studies and in longer poems of amplitude he has attempted to create a total impression of American democracy at work; and in the manner of Emerson, he finds no condition " inopportune or ignoble." [609] The American critic, Willard Thorp, says of Sandburg's diversified subjects : " One is reminded, as one reads his poems, from which pour all the occupations, classes, regions, types, races of America, of Lincoln shaking hands with the crowd which flowed ceaselessly through the White House, learning from each face some new thing about the people." [610]

Professor Arnavon's most severe criticism of Sandburg poetry is that it exhibits an insufficient control of form, that the lines are " à mi-chemin entre prose et vers." [611] It is indeed doubtful whether some of the early vignettes may be regarded as poetry; some of them, such as " Choose " and " In a Breath " more nearly approach prose. Sandburg likes the long free line established by Whitman although he loosens the line even more than Whitman. Nevertheless in the better poems one finds a distinct cadence and rhythmic beat. Mark Van Doren, in writing of Sandburg verse recently (1960), feels that the long, looping lines help to express his broad view, " even a huge view that takes in everything visible and many things that are invisible." [612] Professor Arnavon, too, though severely critical, refers to Sandburg's work as a noble talent which has produced some " trouvailles ravissantes " [613] and he predicts that some of the poems will endure.

The criticism of Sandburg poetry by Paul Ginestier, the French anthologist, in his volume entitled *Les Meilleurs Poèmes Anglais et Américains d'aujourd'hui*, is less severe than that of Professor Arnavon published six years earlier. Inclusion in the anthology may be considered an honor, for M. Ginestier has translated into French all the English and American poems chosen for presentation to French readers and he writes in his introduction :

" Si j'ai eu beaucoup de mal à choisir — des milliers d'œuvres me plaisant plus les unes que les autres — je souhaite à mon lecteur autant de plaisir à lire ces poèmes que j'en ai eu à les traduire." The translator appraises Sandburg's work as follows : " Ses *Chicago Poems*, dans leur élémentaire brutalité, reflètent bien l'influence de Whitman sur un homme qui a vécu l'épopée des *Leaves of Grass*." [614] M. Ginestier affirms that their strength and strange music truly reflect the formidable rise to industrial power of the city of Chicago and the rapid ascendency of the Middle West. He has analyzed this relationship, as is shown by his statement that these poems seem to be less appreciated now than twenty years ago because they bring unpleasant memories and show a deficiency in artistry. Many critics agree that some of the early social poems reflect little credit from the viewpoint of artistry. If they survive in future years, it will be because they characterize the social history of the time. Sandburg himself says: " If some of them seem not to be for this hour, they can be passed by as annals, chronicles or punctuation points of a vanished period." [615]

M. Ginestier summarizes his appraisal of Sandburg poetry in this comparison: " Il y a enfin chez lui un amour élémentaire de la vie qui en fait une sorte de Verhaeren américain," and he forecasts " un côté Saga qui va se développer avec le temps." [616] This " côté Saga " did develop not only to a certain extent in poetry—such as in " Prairie," " Early Moon," " Good Morning, America," or " Slabs of the Sunburnt West " —but it also found larger expression in *The Prairie Years, The War Years* and in the long novel.

Another recent criticism of Sandburg poetry is that by Margaret Schlauch, who holds the chair of English Philology at the University of Warsaw. Professor Schlauch in her book *Modern English and American Poetry* (1956), voices the questions which she hears so often: " Is there no justified use of experimental techniques today? And are there no poets worthily using language and technique, as the social function of poetic communication demands that they should be used? " [617] She answers both questions affirmatively, citing the tradition of Whitman as beneficially affecting the English-speaking world by his direct language and long, irregular lines and by the rhythms of speech derived from the people about him. She characterizes the Whitman school as " the humane school of poetry, in contrast to the anti-humanism of Pound and those who lower humanity through a verse medium." [618]

Professor Schlauch regards Sandburg as the foremost English-speaking representative of the Whitman school. She sees in *The People, Yes* a " treasury of popular speech woven into a tissue of democratic poetic statement, of uneven merit but great imaginative appeal. It contains humor and satire, suffering and despair and sharp warning to oppressors, all lit up by the vast anonymous wisdom of the people that is expressed in proverb and anecdote, wise-crack and cliché and the sudden flash of insight." [619] She acknowledges the importance of Sandburg's democratic poetry but levels criticism at a " flatness of effect "—using as an example the concluding lines of *The People, Yes*, and terming them an " unhelpful query ":

" In the darkness with a great bundle of grief the people march. In the night, and overhead a shovel of stars for keeps, the people march:

Where to? What next? " [620]

There are critics who disagree with Professor Schlauch's interpretation of these lines. Alan Jenkins of Galesburg, Illinois, who has maintained a long personal and professional friendship with Carl Sandburg, comments on the words " what next " as always having been words of " the challenge of events " to Sandburg. He characterizes Sandburg as having " the unfailing child-like appetite for ' what-next ' and the joy of the game of living. Many of us as we age, lose our capacity for wonder, our childlike appetite for ' what-next.' Not so Sandburg." [621] In his characterization

Mr. Jenkins proceeds with illustrations of this personal trait in the poet. Louis Untermeyer in his edition of *The Poetry and Prose of Walt Whitman* designates *The People, Yes* as a " title and a promise which would have pleased Whitman. Whitman's prophetic vistas are renewed in Sandburg's apostrophe to the family of man "; and Untermeyer quotes the concluding stanza including the above lines as expressive of Sandburg's optimism " looking forward to a community of comrades in universal brotherhood."[622]

To me the symbolism of the " stars " is the most important part of the concluding lines of *The People, Yes*. These lines resemble in spirit (though in more restrained expression) the lines of Whitman :

" Forever alive, forever forward,
Stately, solemn, sad, withdrawn, baffled, mad, turbulent, feeble, dissatisfied,

. . . . .
They go ! they go ! I know that they go, but I know not where they go.
But I know that they go toward the best — toward something great." [623]

Sandburg expressed the same idea in his 1959 magazine article on the first jet flight across the United States. " Man has been called ' the improbable animal.' You never know what he's going to do next. He has performed so many wonders of valor, discovery, invention, that he has forgotten who first dreamed that man could fly. You think of this strange and blessed device [the jet plane] man has wrought, and you know that it is only a beginning and a promise." [624]

Carl Sandburg himself, in a nation-wide broadcast, January 25, 1941, from the Metropolitan Opera House in New York, quoted two stanzas from *The People, Yes* concluding with the aforementioned passage and his own personal comment : " To me these lines have some of the deep vitality of the people—forces and motives operating in our way of living today. And they will be going on tomorrow, too." [625]

Professor Schlauch has praise for the ideological content of Sandburg poetry, but feels that " human survival today clamours for something more definite." She speaks of Pablo Neruda of Chile as " especially close to North America because of his themes, his debt to Whitman and to Abraham Lincoln and his broad and deep understanding of the people : their needs, sufferings and great traditions." [626] She believes that Neruda's poem " Let the Rail-Splitter Awake " shows superior skill in combining ideological intention and technique. Her selections of Sandburg's poetry (*The People, Yes, Slabs of the Sunburnt West* and *Smoke and Steel*) do not include his later poems. She believes that Neruda gives a " sense of culmination which is generally lacking in Sandburg and Whitman "—and cites the " satisfactorily climactic endings of his poems, using " Song for Bolivar " as an example :

" I met Bolivar one fine long morning
in Madrid, in the mouth of the Fifth Regiment.
Father, I said, are you or are you not, or who are you ?
And looking towards the Cuartel de la Montana, he said
I wake up every hundred years when the people waken." [627]

It is somewhat surprising that Professor Schlauch prefers Neruda's ideological intention and technique in advancing the Lincoln tradition or his "climactic endings." Has she read "The Long Shadow of Lincoln: A Litany" among the later poems of Carl Sandburg? To me, there is a more direct and constant appeal for action in the Sandburg poem than in the Neruda poem and the appeal is also more universal and more climactic:

"There is dust alive
with dreams of The Republic,
with dreams of The Family of Man
flung wide on a shrinking globe
    with old timetables,
    old maps, old guide-posts
    torn into shreds,
    shot into tatters,
    burnt in a firewind,
    lost in the shambles,
    faded in rubble and ashes.

There is dust alive.
Out of a granite tomb,
Out of a bronze sarcophagus,
Steps a whitesmcke ghost
Lifting an authoritative hand
In the name of dreams worth dying for,
In the name of men whose dust breathes of those dreams so worth
    dying for,
what they did being past words
beyond all smooth and easy telling.
    . . . . .
The earth laughs, the sun laughs
over every wise harvest of man,
over man looking toward peace
by the light of the hard old teaching:
'We must disenthrall ourselves.'" [628]

These are but three stanzas of the rather long poem. To me, they present wider democratic vision and greater poetic inspiration than the Neruda poem.

Mark Van Doren writes (1960) in his introduction to a volume of selected Sandburg poems: "The little poets whom the renaissance of more than forty years ago swept into oblivion had no genuine subjects." [629] This helps explain why Sandburg poetry was able to survive those years. It is attached to particular events in history and becomes an instrument of knowledge. The volume of *Complete Poems* produces a sense of the conflicts of the first half of the twentieth century; it pictures also American achievement. The critic says of the content of Sandburg poetry: "The real poet studies the world as it is: lovely, terrible, sensible. In this sense, Sandburg is a real poet, so that it is no wonder people trust him and adore him." [630]

A recent volume of American criticism of modern poetry (1960), by M. S. Rosenthal, Associate Professor of English at New York University, and Poetry Editor of *The Nation*, entitled *The Modern Poets*, deals both with British and American writers and reveals significantly the impact of two World Wars on the viewpoints of poets and critics. Today the literary critic no longer regards the early social poetry of Sandburg as brutal in comparison with the " unblinking moments of violent revelation such as T. S. Eliot and Hart Crane have shown us." The poem " Contemporary Bunkshooter " so reviled in 1916, is now, in the opinion of Professor Rosenthal, " fine, free-thinking scorn toward moral and religious pretentiousness." [631] The traumatic shock of war has brought new and even more violent attitudes toward modern life among the younger poets of the 1950's, who often present " smoking, ironic, murderous attacks on civilization " and who, in later isolated instances, offer " a dogmatic, irritable, passionate voice, not clear but troubled by its own confusions... a variety of anguished anathema-hurling, in which the poet's revulsion is expressed with monomanic frenzy." [632] Professor Rosenthal lists Yeats, Eliot and Pound as the masters of modern poetry; but he also deals in the chapter " Rival Idioms: The Great Generation " with Robinson, Frost, Williams, Stevens, Moore, Cummings, Sandburg, Jeffers, MacDiarmid and Muir; " They are," he declares, " unrivaled as a generation of begetters of new poems and of new awareness in their art; they have produced a number of strong idioms we must remark as rivaling those of Yeats, Pound and Eliot." [633]

Professor Rosenthal charges Sandburg with an " incomplete commit-ment to his art which is structurally loose... nevertheless few of us would want to do without it." He declares that Sandburg's poetry is " not too savage, not too unpleasant or difficult for contemplation; in the main his is a zestful, emphatically popular poetry—a poetry to enchant and stir a listening audience; ... his poetry is a great repository of idiomatic folk-wisdom. One can read his books, especially *The People, Yes*, with pleasure for hours just for this particular richness." [634]

Published literary criticism of Professor Rosenthal's book has given praise to his volume but has also suggested that there is ample room for disagreement with some of his evaluations of modern poets. Many people do not share his great admiration for the poetry of Pound. Professor Schlauch, in her treatise on " The Anti-Humanism of Pound," says that there are many poets who " follow snobbish modes unreflectingly, who devote themselves to elaborate skills, and to an arrogant contempt for their fellow men, thus tending to bring literary art into disrepute among ordinary people." [635] She pronounces Sandburg a true democrat.

As opposed to her view, Professor Rosenthal lays stress on the importance of style and form; he regards Sandburg as a minimal stylist lacking the transcendance of Yeats, Eliot and Pound ("whether what these writers believe they realize is always defensible in the forum is beside the question " in Professor Rosenthal's view). He concludes that Sandburg " has made his mark, but has foregone (along with Aiken, Ransom, Jeffers, Bishop and others) that ultimate expenditure of energy which can harness the past to new formal and psychological directions and thus give it renewed meaning and power... but he is idiomatically convincing..., and sees the great theme of possibility implicit in American and modern life." [636]

Sandburg's reputation in literature rests as much on his prose as on his poetry. Therefore any discussion of Sandburg and his critics would be incomplete without at least a brief consideration of estimates of his prose. The professional criticism of his prose has been much more uniformly favorable than that of his poetry.

Sandburg's first important prose work was *The Prairie Years* (1926). A few facts concerning its preparation should be presented as a preliminary to a better understanding of the criticism. Sandburg had been interested in writing on Lincoln for over twenty years before the two volumes of *The Prairie Years* were finally begun. His objective was to sketch in a brief volume the life of young Lincoln, first as a product of the prairie and then as a Springfield lawyer. He intended the book as an interpretation of the Lincoln virtues for young readers; it should contain nothing pertaining to war, and therefore would not include Lincoln as President. Sandburg's publisher, Alfred Harcourt, was interested in such a book when the two first discussed it. However, in the two years of writing, *A Boy's Life of Lincoln* grew from the anticipated 400 pages to 1000 pages. When it was taken to the publisher's office, Van Wyck Brooks, literary critic and special adviser to the publishing firm, was so deeply moved by the work that he suggested the title *Abraham Lincoln: The Prairie Years*. This book came to the attention not only of literary critics but of professional historians.

Benjamin P. Thomas, a Lincoln scholar, the author of several books on Lincoln and the author of *Portrait for Posterity*, a volume devoted to those authors who have written of Lincoln, says that scholars were at first somewhat startled by the unusual technique of Sandburg's *Prairie Years*. We have noted elsewhere that Sandburg, as opposed to the traditional historians, brought to *The Prairie Years* not only history but his skill as a poet and a journalist, and his knowledge of early American folklore and folk songs. The result is an originality of treatment unlike that of any other Lincoln biography. Sandburg spent many years in collecting his material and he set forth the pioneer influences in panoramic detail. " They were the background on which the life of Lincoln moved, had its rise and flow, and was moulder and moulded." [637] Mr. Thomas affirms that most of the historians who at first criticized Sandburg's technique came to honor him, " realizing at last that none of those who used traditional methods had been able to recapture the true feeling of Lincoln and bygone days with the power that Carl commands." [638]

The Literary Digest in 1926, in reviewing *The Prairie Years*, stated: " Carl Sandburg has produced a beautiful piece of work... in the character of Lincoln growing as a veritable product of his land, rough hewn and pioneering but with a strength of mind and body and soul that has shone with a lustre so great as to fire the imagination of everyone of us." [639]

The Swedish writer, Mrs. Anna Lenah Elgström, calls *The Prairie Years* " a gigantic chronicle of the epoch which makes this period alive to the reader. It is filled with idealism and has sections of great poetic force.

The reader sometimes feels as if he were reading a lyric ode in majestically marching strophes which lift it above a mere biography." [640]

In *The Prairie Years* Sandburg sacrificed literary perfection to literary effectiveness; if colloquialism seemed called for in the speech of the characters (all of whom, naturally, were taken from life) the author chose colloquialism to fit the occasion.

The general reading public accepted the volumes with enthusiasm; but professional historians demand documentation. While Lincoln's letters and writings and his speeches in political debates in the Illinois legislature and in Congress were authentic, Sandburg did not attempt complete document-ation for every detail of the volumes since the work was originally intended as *A Boy's Life of Lincoln*. He was very industrious in his long period of personal research; and some of the research material had come to him by word of mouth from men who had known Abraham Lincoln in Illinois and from relatives of people who had known Lincoln well in other parts of America.

After the writing of *The Prairie Years* Sandburg determined to continue with his work on the life of Lincoln. Thirteen more years of intensive research and writing, and this time of complete documentation went into the preparation of *The War* Years. Benjamin Thomas, who had offered some criticism of *The Prairie Years* from the historians' viewpoint, pro-nounced *The War Years* " invulnerable." [641]

Professor Charles A. Beard of the University of Virginia wrote: " Never yet has a history or biography like Carl Sandburg's *War Years* appeared. Few if any historians have ever labored harder in preparation for composition... an indefatigable thoroughness characterizes his pages." [642] Stephen Vincent Benét referred to the thoroughness of the massive presentation and in his appraisal declared: " To criticize it, to chip at it with a hammer would be a little like chipping at Stone Mountain." [643]

Seldom did a literary work receive the spontaneous acclaim that greeted *The War Years* by critics, historians and the academic world. All the early critics were awed by the massiveness of the work. Some reviewers mentioned a lack of system; some critics failed to see sufficient sequence; but Pro-fessor Alan Nevins sees in the volumes " a vigorous selective talent and a careful underlying plan." [644]

Many critics and readers considered this Lincoln biography the finest biography in American literature. Benjamin Thomas refers to Carl Sandburg as " an imperishable builder in the Lincoln field. But there is more than stolid permanence in his work. It quickens, impels and uplifts. He has brought Lincoln and his times alive." [645]

Next to the Lincoln biography, Sandburg's only novel, *Remembrance Rock* (1948), is his most ambitious prose work. Literary criticism of this book varies. Actually it is more history than novel. The fictional characters are created to portray the growth and development of the American Dream. One critic termed the book " less an historical novel than peopled history."[646]

Lloyd Lewis in reviewing the book for the New York *Herald Tribune* referred to it as " Carl Sandburg's ride to an American Canterbury—a long ride of 350 years with an American historical tale for every hoof beat and an adventure for every garrulous pilgrim—but he has many more riders than Chaucer." [647] The book expresses Sandburg's deep-seated conviction that in each generation, it was the plain and humble people who bore forward by difficult steps the hopes of the Pilgrim Fathers.

The book had more pattern than plot; with its symbolism, with its great length and with its multitude of characters it did not have the popular appeal for which the author had hoped and toward which he had earnestly devoted five years of careful research and writing. Every historical detail in it can be documented. Early folk ballads and folkways contribute to its atmosphere. But this work of prose lacked the vividness of the Lincoln biography in which all the characters were living people of the Civil War period. After reading *The War Years* the characters in the novel seem abstractions representing an idea; they are subordinated to the plot. It is an undertaking of high purpose, reverently written and panoramic in its sweep over time but perhaps too vast a project for one volume of fiction. The literary critic of the Cleveland *News* wrote: " One does not rise and break into cheers that this is America and we are Americans; but we put the book aside and drift into reverie that has praying in it. Or deep, unspoken thanksgiving." [648] For the trilogy is a carefully considered analysis of the spirit of the American story.

Always the Young Strangers was acclaimed by critics and general public alike. Robert E. Sherwood in reviewing it for the New York *Times* pronounced it " the best autobiography ever written by an American... By striving to tell no more than an intensely personal story, Sandburg has achieved the universality of a *Pilgrim's Progress*." [649] Differing from the involved prose of *Remembrance Rock*, the autobiography is written in a clear and informal conversational pattern, distinguished by the mobility of expression that characterized *The Prairie Years*. Pathos and humor, colorful idiom, proverbs, balladry, even a small amount of Swedish folklore and Swedish dialect are distinguishing features. The chapter " Pioneers and Old Timers" is rich in history and tradition. The volume illustrates many of the formative influences on the career of the future Lincoln biographer.

Sven Linner in the Upsala *Nya Tidning* says of *Always The Young Strangers:* " It opens a world for us which is rich and changing. It makes us acquainted with an interesting person, warm, awake, vital—Life's friend on the great prairie." [650]

The literary stature finally achieved by Sandburg has been summarized by the critic, Robert Spiller, in his volume " *Cycle of American Literature:*

" In *The People, Yes* (1936) and in the six volumes of his biography of Abraham Lincoln (1926-1939) Sandburg rose above the level of the lyric poet of scenes and men to become the epic voice of these generic American people... If America was to have an epic, this poet's life of its national hero in rhythmic and impressionistic prose comes as near to supplying the need as does any other single work in prose or verse." [651]

Thus ever since his initial recognition by Professor Wright and Harriet Monroe, Sandburg has occupied the attention of critics and has had the merit of never leaving them quite indifferent. Literary criticism of his work has shown some of the ambivalence of America itself. The lack of art the minimal amount of style, the shock-idiom that first brought so much hostile criticism of Sandburg's poetry were judgments paralleled by marks of esteem that cannot be ignored, the most important early recognition being the award of the Pulitzer Prize for Poetry for his second volume, *Cornhuskers*. Attention was drawn early to him, as a poet; and this attention was sustained in the public mind because his writing was readily available to a wider public than many collections of verse, both through the popular idiom employed, and through publication in newspapers and magazines.

In a great degree, it might be said that Sandburg at first aroused a more sympathetic reception among poets themselves than among literary critics; for much of the reaction against him could more truly be said to be a general reaction against the modern developments in poetry. To this extent, it could be labeled a traditionalist reaction, and the criticism leveled against his style and technique is to be expected and has a certain validity. On the other hand, his admirers have found new strength in his sheer vitality, in his combination of realism and idealism, in his humanitarian warmth.

Sandburg's literary reputation was greatly enhanced by *The Prairie Years* published in 1926. The overwhelming admiration of this Lincoln biography clearly influenced many readers to reassess the value of his poetry, and to revise their opinions of him as a literary figure. This admiration drew on him the attention of a vastly wider public. The publication of *The War Years* in 1939 securely established him in American literary history.

Judged on purely stylistic grounds, Sandburg as a poet does not occupy the position of more acknowledged stylists such as Robert Frost. Yet, if his success as a poet has proved anything, it is that he has succeeded in asserting his own criteria of style as a vehicle of thought; that more than any other poet living today he expresses the spiritual impulses of the American people; that more adequately than other poets he articulates the social aims and aspirations of his America. For these reasons his poetry has endured; and his image as a poet remains. This may also be due, in considerable part, to the fact that the stature he has acquired as a national figure has placed him beyond too serious harm by literary criticism. In portraying life in the United States he has aroused a warm response; and as an object of popular affection he has been transformed into something of a seer. He has become a living legend; and as legends will, his legend has carried him beyond the modest foundations on which the structure of his fame was built.

III

CARL SANDBURG AS A LIVING SYMBOL OF AMERICA

Every country with a long historical record has, within its folklore and often within its literature, legends which embody the traditions of its people. Legends in England, Scandinavia, Germany, Switzerland, France, Russia, Greece, Italy and many other countries form a part of the literary treasure of their respective peoples; and the heroes of these legends continue to live not only in literature but also in opera and in native folk songs.

Although these ancient legendary heroes and traditions are not a part of American literature, the legend-making faculty has existed in the New World. American legendry is the result of the collective energies of a new people spontaneously recording tradition and national growth; and these traditions have left an imprint on culture and literature. A portion of Lincoln's famous sense of humor derived from his knowledge of folk tales. Mark Twain owed much of his success in opening up the field of native American prose to early American folklore. The importance of folk themes is evident even in the writing of the sophisticated Henry James.

There have been men in each great period of American history who represented important events and because of this, legends were generated around them, for America has been from the time of the Pilgrims an idealistic nation; and to this new nation in a new world, beliefs, in order to stir the emotions and prove their practicality, must have a legendary root. The need for legendary roots has arisen from the people themselves. The story of Washington as the Father of His Country, as the General who brought freedom to his fledgeling nation in the New World, became one of the early American legends; the legend of Lincoln as a symbol of democracy spread through civilized nations; an Eisenhower legend will probably persist in the years to come. These are examples of heroes of American history—heroes whose deeds elevate them to lofty heights in national stature; they are symbols of national achievement.

There is another type of legendary figure—the man arising out of the everyday life of the people but becoming an out-of-the-ordinary figure achieving national significance and symbolism. Two of our greatest contemporary biographers, Douglas Southall Freeman and Carl Sandburg, have become such symbols. Dr. Freeman of Richmond, Virginia, became a student of history at an early age, and because of his great admiration for Robert E. Lee chose to model himself after the high character of the Confederate General. We are told by those who worked with Dr. Freeman, and by others who knew him well, that he became a living illustration of the famous General's personality. Professor Dumas Malone of the University of Virginia in writing of Dr. Freeman tells us that in his later years with the publication of his comprehensive four-volume biography *R. E. Lee* he "had become a legend" in Virgina, and "eventually a legendary character on the national as well as the local scene." [652] In the public mind the name of Freeman became firmly associated with that of Lee, for by right of his surpassing knowledge the author became the literary incarnation of the historic tradition which Lee personified.

The name of Carl Sandburg in his early days as a journalist became a household word for reform and change. The publication of *Chicago Poems* added to his local and regional reputation because of his criticism of civic conditions. This reputation deepened as he became a lecturer and radio speaker.

With the publication of *Abraham Lincoln: The Prairie Years*, the Lincoln legend began forming around him. In 1939, with the publication of *The*

War Years, he gained a permanent place in American historical biography, for into those four volumes had gone "the quenchless ambition of an ordered mind," [653] determined to verify and preserve the Lincoln story as its masterwork. Sandburg so closely lived with Lincoln in the long years of writing that the result of his literary companionship was an unmatched richness of detail; he produced a candid and convincing portrait of the finest traditions of a free people incorporated in the Lincoln story. In so doing, Sandburg, through the magnitude of his interpretation, became the literary embodiment of the Lincoln concept of democracy.

Americans see Sandburg as identified with his land and his people. He is representative of his age, as was Lincoln. He too, was forced to struggle with his age—as was Lincoln. Both had learned strength from struggle, from the school of difficult experience. "In the short and simple annals of the poor it seems there are people who breathe with the earth and take into their lungs and blood some of the hard and dark strength of its mystery... It may be the earth told him in her own gypsy slang one or two knacks of living worth keeping. To be organic with running wild-fire and quiet rain both at the same moment, is to be carrier of wave-lines the earth gives up only on hard usage." [654]

The Lincoln and Sandburg strengths, derived from early hardships, brought understanding and established a special bond of sympathy with a wide range of humanity; and as each grew in age and experience to face a more complex and changing America, the social concept of each broadened. Each in his individual era became intensely modern and intensely American; each became instinctive with the land, its industries, its towns, its cities, its traditions, its culture, its history. Both became dedicated to the institution of democracy.

No one would try to say that Sandburg possesses all the characteristics and experience of Lincoln. Lincoln's application to the study of law, his political genius, his career as legislator, as Congressman, as President, as Commander-in-Chief of the Union Army, his work with the War Department, with his Cabinet officials and the various offices of government, are, of course, outside the cycle of Sandburg's life experience. Nor does Sandburg possess the great self-control and calmness of spirit reflected in the story of the Lincoln personality. To Carl Sandburg Lincoln is "the incomparable" [655] and his influence on the poet-historian has been incalculable. Lincoln has been his model from the time he first read the Emancipator's words on the bronze plaque on the Main Building of Knox College in Galesburg.

Professor James G. Randall wrote of Carl Sandburg in 1952: "One must put together the statements of men all over America to have even the beginning of an appraisal of what Sandburg means in poetry, in the journalism of reporting, in the journalism of the column, in history, in biography, and in the vibrant world of American song. There occasionally arises among us one who embodies the fulfilment of American democracy, while at the same time he is the spokesman of democracy. Such a man was Lincoln, and such a man is Sandburg. In his life and achievement he stands as the proof, the very certificate, of democracy." [656]

American historians feel a fellowship with Sandburg because of his *Prairie Years* and *War Years*. Music lovers admire him for his collection and analysis of folk songs; and because in his publications of two volumes of folk songs he has preserved many early traditions which are an integral part of American culture. The academic world has shown its esteem by the thirty-two honorary doctoral degrees awarded him. The American law courts respect him for his support of democratic justice. The churches respect him because of his appeal for humanitarianism, for tolerance and for avoidance of bigotry. The attitude of the churches has been well expressed by the Reverend Alan Jenkins of the Congregational Church in Galesburg: " The secret of Sandburg's stature is essentially religious. By ' religious ' I do not mean institutional creed... A religious person, in my books, may be defined as one whose dominant desires relate to spiritual values in a context of faith. Sandburg is such a person." [657]

In his wide range of acquaintance and experience, Sandburg has attained a wisdom " knowing somewhat of both soil and seed; " [658] he has " gathered the feel " [659] of America. He has lived through three wars and two major depressions, giving of his best efforts in each instance, experiencing deeply what the American people themselves experienced; and he has become so closely identified with Lincoln and so diversely identified with America that he has become an exponent of Americanism. All of these factors have made of him a literary celebrity. The American people accept him for what he stands for, for his origin and his ways. He is one of them and his story is their own personal history, a history of their own times.

Douglas Southall Freeman in 1953 wrote of his fellow historian as follows: " Carl Sandburg is not an individual: he is an institution. At 75 he combines as does no living American the frontier and the future, the lore of yesterday and the love of today, folk music and folkways, art and sure instinct, the wisdom of the head and the deeper reason of the heart.... To know him is to have still deeper faith in America." [660]

The National Fellowship Award was presented to the aging poet-historian in Philadelphia, March 30, 1960, for his books and poetry which " have aroused the conscience of all democracy-loving citizens toward creating a human society that believes in the dignity and equality of all mankind." [661]

As we have seen in a study of his poetry Sandburg has been a cri.ic of America many times. A part of his significance in twentieth-century literature has been his condemnation of social inequalities and political wrongs. Wherever he has seen inequality his plea has been that men should free themselves from old ideas and aspire to newer ideas designed for social progress by those pioneering researchers who " pluck marvels of industry and science out of unexpected corners, who have held to a hope that each should have music and craft and personal worth." [662] Americans have learned to respect and trust him because of his humanitarianism.

Visible proof of American esteem began in 1945 when an association was formed in Galesburg under the name of Sandburg Birthplace, Incorporated, to purchase and restore the little cottage in which he was born. Donations came from all over the nation, from those in high position, from the lowly; even pennies and nickels came from school children who admired him for his *Rootabaga Stories*, for his brief lyrics such as "Fog" printed in their readers or for his nature poetry in the volume *Early Moon.*

The dedication of the birthplace as a literary shrine took place on October 7, 1946, on the anniversary of the famous Lincoln-Douglas debate in Galesburg. Sandburg, then living in North Carolina, did not attend, modestly declining to take any part in the ceremony.

On May 30, 1949, a second dedication took place—that of the Lincoln Room. After the August Sandburg family moved from the cottage to the larger Berrien Street home, the new owners built an additional room at the rear; this room had been used for storage purposes during the 1945-1946 restoration of the cottage, since there was not sufficient space for the heirlooms and antique pieces that were accumulating. Later this room was restored and presented as a gift from the State of Illinois—to be known as the Lincoln Room, in honor of Sandburg's Lincoln biography—to house it and other Sandburg writings. Appropriately this room contains authentic Lincoln possessions—an antique lamp given by the Thomas Lincoln Family to their neighbors (the Samuel Mains family) when the Lincolns left their Indiana home for Illinois; also a pitcher and platter given by Abraham Lincoln to friends in New Salem, Illinois. Many other valuable historic pieces have been sent as furnishings for the Lincoln Room.

In the birthplace itself are furnishings belonging to the Sandburg family when Carl Sandburg was a boy. Other members of the family have contributed these. Stephen Vincent Benét wrote the tribute which is placed just inside the front door:

"He came to us from the people whom Lincoln loved because there were so many of them, and through all his life, in verse and in prose, he has spoken of and for the people. A great American, we have just reason to be proud that he has lived and written in our time."

Several schools now bear the name of Sandburg, including the Levittown High School in Pennsylvania, the Robbindale High School in Minnesota, those of Elmhurst, Mundelein and Orland Park in Illinois, the Carl Sandburg Elementary School in Harvey, Illinois, and the Carl Sandburg Elementary School in Rockville, Maryland.

The University of Illinois announced, January 12, 1956, the purchase for 30,000 dollars of the private library of the poet-historian and the University directors stated that the library would be given a permanent home on the campus. This library includes the extensive collection of material on Abraham Lincoln and also many of Sandburg's manuscripts and many first editions of his books.

The year 1959 brought honors of a special nature, showing how closely this Lincoln biographer is associated with the sixteenth President in the public mind.

The combined Houses of the United States Congress invited him to address the joint session to commemorate President Lincoln, February 12, on the 150th anniversary of the Emancipator's birthday. It was the first time a man of letters had been invited to address Congress since the historian Bancroft was invited to pay tribute to Lincoln after his assassination.

A deeply appreciative audience, presided over by Vice-President Nixon (as President of the Senate) and House Speaker Rayburn, listened in perfect silence, regardless of party politics, to the 81-year-old poet and biographer. So moving was the Sandburg address that tears came to many—even to the eyes of venerable senators. The word-power of the aging poet may be gathered from portions of his speech, which was published from coast to coast in America.

" Not often in the story of mankind does a man arrive on earth who is both steel and velvet, who is as hard as rock and soft as drifting fog, who holds in his heart and mind the paradox of terrible storm and peace unspeakable and perfect.... The incomparable Abraham Lincoln born 150 years ago this day, is an approach if not a perfect realization of this character.

" In the time of the April lilacs in the year 1865, on his death, the casket with his body was carried North and West a thousand miles; and the American people wept as never before; bells sobbed, cities wore crepe; people stood in tears and with hats off as the railroad burial car passed in the leading cities of seven states ending its journey at Springfield, Illinois, the home town...

" Millions there are who take him as a personal treasure. He had something that they would like to see spread everywhere over the world. Democracy? We can't find words to say exactly what it is, but he had it. In his blood and bones he carried it. In the breath of his speeches and writings it is there. Popular government? Republican institutions? Government where the people have the say-so, one way or another telling their elected leaders what they want? He had the idea. It's there in the lights and shadows of his personality, a mystery that can be lived but never fully spoken in words....

" Perhaps we may say that the well-assured and most enduring memorial to Lincoln is invisibly there, today, tomorrow and for a long time yet to come in the hearts of lovers of liberty, men and women who understand that whenever there is freedom there have been those who fought, toiled and sacrificed for it." [663]

This was probably Carl Sandburg's most important public appearance as an interpreter of Lincoln. In addition to the members of the two houses of the United States Congress, among those present were the Chief Justice and Associate Justices of the Supreme Court, Ambassadors, Ministers and Chargés d'Affaires of foreign governments, the President's Cabinet, Generals of the Army and Admirals of the Fleet. Even the galleries were filled by a distinguished audience.

All the national radio and television networks in the United States broadcast all or part of the session either " live " or on a delayed basis; it was officially estimated that this commemorative session of Congress, through the broadcast media alone, reached more than sixty million Americans. The ceremonies were taped and carefully recorded. This means that in decades to come, perhaps after centuries, future generations will see and hear this ceremony that so impressed America in 1959. The Manchester *Guardian* stated that " never in living memory has there been an occasion in Washington comparable to this, so moving in its contrasts, so memorable in its appeal, so majestic in its inspiration." [664] One of the members of Congress wrote : " Joining a celebrated immortal of the current hour like Carl Sandburg with the most revered name in American history, especially where the relationship is that of a great biographer to his subject, provides the highest order of human drama." [665]

Among the various features of the American Exhibition in Moscow in 1959 was a gallery in which were portraits of Americans representing the democratic ideals of the United States. In this " Gallery of Great Americans " along with Jefferson, Franklin Delano Roosevelt, Wilson, Lincoln and others, was Carl Sandburg; some of his writings were also reproduced in large print on the screen.

In the same year, celebrating the sesquicentennial of Lincoln's birth, Sandburg was chosen to honor Lincoln on the field of Gettysburg. Every American knows of the importance of Gettysburg in the progress of the Civil War; and every American knows of Lincoln's dedication of the National Cemetery at Gettysburg where many thousands of Union and Confederate men had sacrificed their lives. To Americans, Gettysburg is hallowed ground. No writer has interpreted the profound significance of Lincoln's Gettysburg speech at the dedication of the National Cemetery more movingly than Carl Sandburg in *The War Years*. In impressionistic prose, a portion of that interpretation is as follows :

" He had stood that day, the world's foremost spokesman of popular government, saying that democracy was yet worth fighting for. ... He incarnated the assurances and pretenses of popular government... His outwardly smooth sentences were inside of them gnarled and tough with the enigmas of the American experiment.

" At Gettysburg the blue haze of the Cumberland Mountains had dimmed till they were a blur in a nocturne... In many a country cottage over the land, a tall old clock in a corner told time in a tick-tock delibera-tion. ... The face and dial of the clock had known the eyes of a boy who learned to read its minute and hour hands. And the boy had seen years measured off by the swinging pendulum, had grown to man size, had gone away. And the people in the cottage knew that the clock would stand there and the boy would never come again... In a row of graves of the Un-identified the boy would sleep long in the dedicated final resting-place at Gettysburg. Why he had gone away and why he would never come back had roots in some mystery of flags and drums, of national fate in which individuals sink as in a deep sea, of men swallowed and vanished in a man-made storm of smoke and steel.

" The mystery deepened and moved with ancient music and inviolable consolation because a solemn Man of Authority had stood at the graves of the Unidentified and spoken the words ' We cannot consecrate—we cannot hallow—this ground. The brave men, living and dead, who struggled

here, have consecrated it far above our poor power to add or detract. . . .
From these honored dead we take increased devotion to that cause for
which they gave the last full measure of devotion.'

" To the backward and forward pendulum swing of a tall old clock in
a quiet corner they might read those cadenced words while outside the
windows the first flurry of snow blew over the meadow, the beginnings of
winter in a gun-metal gloaming to be later arched with a star-flung sky." [666]

The " gun-metal gloaming " that was Gettysburg in 1863 would become
arched with fifty stars.

" Living in union it holds.
So long as each piece does its work
The arch is alive, singing, a restless choral. " [667]

On November 19, 1959, exactly ninety-six years after Lincoln's dedication of the National Cemetery, Sandburg spoke at Gettysburg of the
values of freedom, before an audience of many hundreds and very near
the graves of the " Unidentified." In his evocation of patriotism was his
reverent tribute to those "Unidentified" :

" When we say a patriot is one who loves his country, what kind of
love do we mean? A love we can analyze, or weigh or measure? Or is
a patriot's love of country a thing invisible, a quality, a human shade and
breath, beyond all measurement or reckoning?

" When men forget the human cost of freedom, they are in danger of
power being taken over by beasts of prey or men hollow with echoes and
vanities." [668] But he reaffirmed his confidence in the " ever renewing
vitality " of the American nation, and reaffirmed the high resolve of Lincoln's
dedicatory words that " government of the people, by the people, for the
people, shall not perish from the earth." [669]

Thus both at home and abroad Sandburg has emerged as a representative figure who has become more and more associated in the eye of the
beholder with the American image whose prophet he has been. But acts of
homage must not be confused with genuine assessment of his role and
value in American life. He represents a tradition, an evolutionary, growing
concept which has been developed through three and one-half centuries
and is still being developed. This tradition illustrates a national and humanitarian ideal which accepts fully the theory of progress and the advance of
society. Accompanying this adaptability to progress and the will to adapt,
has run the " blood-scarlet thread " of the permanent idealistic element of
the American story; together these form the touchstone against which
changes must be judged. This criterion and Sandburg's own conception
of his role, in the image of Emerson and Whitman made of him a furious,
and yet a gentle critic of his age and of its failure to live up to the best in
its tradition. This prophetic fury is the explanation of the dual nature of
his poetry of praise and criticism, of love and reproof of America. He
has held aloft a high national standard and uses it to judge his times; this
clearly reflects his aim in his portrayal of the past. Thus Sandburg's country-

men have come to associate him with the national ideal he paints; and he has himself partaken of this idealization.

The honor of standing at Gettysburg in the footsteps of the President who in 1863 " had stood as the world's foremost spokesman of popular government " memorably identifies Carl Sandburg with American democracy and with the national legend to which he has devoted a lifetime of writing.

In poetry and prose he is a voice of the American tradition of which Lincoln has been the most influential interpreter. Implicit in that tradition is the pioneering spirit of the sixteenth President as reflected in the far-reaching words of his message to Congress in 1862, which his biographer has recorded in *The War Years:*

" We can succeed only by concert.... The dogmas of the quiet past are inadequate to the stormy present. The occasion is piled high with difficulty, and we must rise with the occasion. As our case is new so must we think anew and act anew. We must disenthrall ourselves." [670]

Carl Sandburg delivering eulogy on Abraham Lincoln before a joint session of Congress on the 150th anniversary of the birth of the 16th President. In the background are Vice President Richard Nixon and Speaker Sam Rayburn. *Photograph by European Picture Service.*

BIBLIOGRAPHY

I. WORK BY SANDBURG

(a) Books written by Charles A. Sandburg

Sandburg, Charles A. *In Reckless Ecstasy.* Galesburg, Illinois. The Asgard Press, 1904. 39 pages. Introduction by Philip Green Wright.
— *The Plaint of a Rose.* Galesburg, Illinois. The Asgard Press, circa 1904. 10 pages.
— *Incidentals.* Galesburg, Illinois. The Asgard Press, circa 1905.
— *Joseffy. An Appreciation.* Galesburg, Illinois. The Asgard Press, 1910.

(b) Books by Carl Sandburg

Chicago Poems. New York: Henry Holt and Co., 1916. 183 pages.
Cornhuskers. New York: Henry Holt and Co., 1918. 147 pages.
The Chicago Race Riots. New York: Harcourt, Brace and Howe, 1919. 71 pages. Introduction by Walter Lippman.
Smoke and Steel. New York: Harcourt, Brace and Howe, 1920. 268 pages.
Rootabaga Stories. New York: Harcourt, Brace and Howe, 1922. 230 pages. Illustrations and decorations by Maud and Miska Petersham.
Slabs of the Sunburnt West. New York: Harcourt, Brace and Co., 1922. 76 pages.
Rootabaga Pigeons. Harcourt, Brace and Co., 1923. 218 pages. Illustrations and decorations by Maud and Miska Petersham.
Abraham Lincoln: The Prairie Years. New York: Harcourt, Brace and Co., 1926. Two volumes. 962 pages.
Selected Poems of Carl Sandburg. New York: Harcourt, Brace and Co., 1926. 287 pages. Edited by Rebecca West. Published the same year by Jonathan Cape, London.
Songs of America. New York: Harcourt, Brace and Co., 1926. 11 pages; a preliminary work for *The American Songbag.*
The American Songbag. New York: Harcourt, Brace and Co., 1927. 495 pages.
Good Morning, America. New York: Crosby Gaige, 1928. 251 pages.

Abe Lincoln Grows Up. New York: Harcourt, Brace and Co., 1929. 222 pages. Illustrations by James Daugherty.

Rootabaga Country. Selections from *Rootabaga Stories* and *Rootabaga Pigeons.* New York: Harcourt, Brace and Co., 1929. 258 pages.

Steichen the Photographer. New York: Harcourt, Brace and Co., 1929. 66 pages of text, 49 pages of photographs. Edition limited to 925 numbered copies signed by Carl Sandburg and Edward Steichen.

Early Moon. New York: Harcourt, Brace and Co., 1930. 130 pages. Illustrations by James Daugherty. Issued simultaneously by the Junior Literary Guild.

Potato Face. New York: Harcourt, Brace and Co., 1930. 96 pages.

Mary Lincoln, Wife and Widow. New York: Harcourt, Brace and Co., 1932. 357 pages. Documentary portion by Paul M. Angle.

The People, Yes. New York: Harcourt, Brace and Co., 1936. 286 pages.

A Lincoln and Whitman Miscellany. Chicago: Holiday Press, 1938. 33 pages. Edition limited to 250 copies.

Abraham Lincoln: The War Years. New York: Harcourt, Brace and Co., 1939. Four Volumes. 2401 pages.

Abraham Lincoln. The Sangamon Edition. New York: Charles Scribner's Sons, 1940. Six Volumes. *The Prairie Years* and *The War Years* issued as a single work. Sold by subscription only.

Bronze Wood. San Francisco: Gelber, Lilienthal Inc., 1941.

Storm Over the Land. A Profile of The Civil War Taken Mainly from The War Years. New York: Harcourt, Brace and Co., 1943. 440 pages.

Home Front Memo. New York: Harcourt, Brace and Co., 1943. 310 pages.

The Photographs of Abraham Lincoln. New York: Harcourt, Brace and Co., 1944. In collaboration with Frederick Hill Meserve. 30 pages and 96 pages of photographs.

Poems of the Midwest. Cleveland and New York: The World Publishing Co., 1946. 267 pages. Introduction by Lloyd Lewis.

The Lincoln Reader, an Appreciation. 1947. This was intended as a foreword to *The Lincoln Reader* by Paul Angle, but was received too late to be printed in the book. It was published by the Book-of-the-Month Club for its members.

Remembrance Rock. New York: Harcourt, Brace and Co., 1948. 1067 pages.

Lincoln Collector. The Story of Oliver R. Barrett's Great Private Collection. New York: Harcourt, Brace and Co., 1950. 344 pages.

Complete Poems. New York: Harcourt, Brace and Co., 1950. 676 pages.

Carl Sandburg's New American Songbag. New York: Broadcast Music Inc., 1950. 107 pages. Brief prefatory note by Bing Crosby.

Abraham Lincoln: The Prairie Years and The War Years. New York: Harcourt, Brace and Co., 1952. (A one volume edition condensed from the original six volumes, with some new material added, such as the Robert Lincoln papers unavailable to researchers until 1947; also the Lincoln letters to Judge David Davis). 747 pages.

Always The Young Strangers. New York: Harcourt, Brace and Co., 1953. Published on Carl Sandburg's 75th birthday, January 6, 1953. 445 pages.

A Lincoln Preface. Published privately in 1955 for Mr. Sandburg's friends. (Originally intended as an introduction to *The Prairie Years.)*

The Sandburg Range. New York: Harcourt, Brace and Co., 1957. 459 pages.

Wind Song. New York: Harcourt, Brace and Co., 1960. 127 pages.

Honey and Salt. New York: Harcourt, Brace and World. 1963. 111 pages.

II. A SELECTIVE BIBLIOGRAPHY OF PUBLICATIONS ON CARL SANDBURG

ANDERSON, Sherwood. "Carl Sandburg" *Bookman* LIV (Dec. 1921) 360-361.

ANGLE, Paul. *A Shelf of Lincoln Books.* New Brunswick, New Jersey: Rutgers University Press, 1946. (A critical selective bibliography of Lincolniana).

ARVIN, Newton. "Carl Sandburg" *New Republic,* LXXXVIII (Sept. 9, 1936), 119-121.

AUSLANDER, Joseph. "A poet (Sandburg) writes biography" *English Journal,* XXIX (May 1940), 347-355.

BARTON, William E. "The Abraham Lincoln of the Prairies" *World's Work,* LII (May 1926), 102-105.

BEARD, Charles A. "The Sandburg Lincoln" *Virginia Quarterly Review,* XVI (Winter 1940), 112-116.

BENET, Stephen. "Abraham Lincoln: The War Years" *Atlantic Bookshelf,* CLXIV (Dec. 1939), 20, 22.

BENSON, Adolphe B. and HEDIN, Naboth. *Americans from Sweden.* New York: J. B. Lippincott, 1950. 327-329.

BLANKENSHIP, Russell. *American Literature As an Expression of the National Mind.* New York: H. Holt, 1931. 605-613.

BRADLEY, William A. "Four American Poets" *Dial* LXI (Dec. 14, 1916) 528-530.

BRENNER, Rica. *Ten Modern Poets.* Harcourt, Brace and Co., New York, 1930.

BRICKELL, Herschel. "The Literary Landscape" *North American Review,* CCXXVI (Dec. 1928), advertising section.

Bonniers of Stockholm. "Stories of Swedish Pioneers" A collection edited by Bonniers of Stockholm. Printed in Sweden, 1948.

CHAPIN, Elsa and THOMAS, Russell. "Sandburg" *A New Approach to Poetry,* XIII (1929), 41-42, 48, 66-67, 82, 89.

COMPTON, Charles HERRICK. "Who Reads Carl Sandburg?" *South Atlantic Quarterly*, XXVIII (April, 1929), 190-200.

— *Who Reads What?* New York: Wilson, 1934, 52-69.

DALIN, Ebba. Foreword to Swedish translation of *Abraham Lincoln: The Prairie Years: The War Years.* 1944, Royal Library, Stockholm, Sweden.

DETZER, Karl William. *Carl Sandburg; A Study in Personality and Background.* New York: Harcourt, Brace and Co., 1941.

DEUTSCH, Babette. A review of "Good Morning, America" New York *Herald Tribune* (October 21, 1928), 2.

DICKINSON, Asa Don. *The Best Books of Our Time* (1901-1925). New York: Doubleday, Doren, 1928, 261-263.

DRAKE, William A. *American Criticism*, edited by William A. Drake. New York: Harcourt, Brace and Co., 1926, 194, 349.

DRINKWATER, John. "A Review of *Abraham Lincoln: The Prairie Years*" *Saturday Review of Literature*, II. (March 27, 1926), 659.

ELGSTRÖM, Anna Lenah. "Carl Sandburg" *Ord och Bild*, LIII (1944) 528-539, Stockholm, Sweden.

— *Dikter i Urval*, Tiden: Stockholm, Sweden. 1934, edited by Anna Lenah Elgström. Foreword to Swedish translation of Sandburg poems.

— "Carl Sandburg och Sverige" *Perspektiv*, (January, 1957), 8-13.

EMERSON, Dorothy. "Carl Sandburg" *Scholastic*, XXV (Sept. 22, 1934), 11, (Nov. 21, 1936), 11.

FADIMAN, Clifton. "Abraham Lincoln: The War Years" *New Yorker*, XV (Dec. 2, 1939), 114.

FLANAGAN, John T. *America Is West.* University of Minnesota Press: 1945. 30, 467.

FLETCHER, John G. *Some Contemporary American Poets.* London, Chapbook, 1920, 15-19.

GINESTIER, Paul. *Les Meilleurs Poèmes Anglais et Américains d'aujourd'hui.* Paris, S.E.D.E.S., 1958. 38, 39, 161, 164, 183.

GREGORY, Horace and ZATURENSKA, Marya. *A History of American Poetry.* New York: Harcourt, Brace and Co., 1946, 15-19, 133, 144, 145, 146, 242-251, 395, 397, 414, 416, 456, 457, 466, 467.

HANSEN, Harry. *Midwest Portraits (A Book of Memories and Friendships).* New York: Harcourt, Brace, 1923, 15-19.

— *Carl Sandburg, The Man and His Poetry.* Girard, Kansas: Handeman-Julius Co., 1925.

HATFIELD, W. W. and ROBERTS, H. D. *The Spirit of America in Literature.* New York: Century, 1931. 118, 121, 390, 558, 559, 582, 604.

HEINBERG, Aage. "Carl Sandburg — Diktare och Landbrukare". *Samtid och Framtid*, X (Jan. 1952), 21-23. In Library of University of Uppsala, Sweden.

HOLCOMB, Esther Lolita. "Whitman and Sandburg" *English Journal*, XVII (Sept. 1928), 549-555.

JONES, H. M. and LEISY, E. E. *Major American Writers*. New York: Harcourt, Brace, 1945.

JONES, Llewellyn. "Carl Sandburg: Formalist" *American Review*, Bloomington, Illinois, 1924, V 2, 256-262.

Journal of The Illinois State Historical Society (Winter, 1952). This issue is devoted entirely to Carl Sandburg.

KARSNER, David. *Sixteen Authors to One* (Intimate Sketches of Leading American Story Tellers). New York: Lewis Copeland Co., 1928, 145-155.

KREYMBORG, Alfred. *An Outline of American Poetry 1620-1930*. New York: Coward, McCann, 1929, 382-394.

LEWIS, Lloyd. *It Takes All Kinds*. New York: Harcourt, Brace, 1947, 73-81, 219-222.

LINK, (S.) Gordden. "Carl Sandburg's Philosophy of Life" *The Poetry Review*, XXI (November-December 1930), 419-427.

LINNER, Sven. "De unga främlingarna". Upsala *Nya Tidning*, Oct. 8, 1953, Uppsala, Sweden.

LOGGINS, Vernon. *I Hear America: Literature in the United States since 1900*. New York: T. Y. Crowell, 1937, 271-278.

LOWELL, Amy. *Tendencies in Modern American Poetry*. New York: Macmillan, 1917, 200-232.

— "The Poems of the Month" *Bookman* LIII (July, 1921), 404-406.

— *Selected Poems of Amy Lowell*. Boston: Houghton Mifflin, 1928, "To Carl Sandburg", 84-85.

LOWES, John Livingstone. *Convention and Revolt in Poetry*. Boston: Houghton Mifflin Co., 1926. 305.

LUCCOCK, Halford E. *American Mirror; Social, Ethical and Religious Aspects of American Literature 1930-1940*. New York: Macmillan, 1940, 28, 233-235.

LUNDBERG, Holger. "Carl Sandburg" *American Scandinavian Review*, XXVI (March, 1938), 49-50-51.

LUNDKVIST, Arthur. *Diktare och Avslöjare i Amerikas Moderna Litteratur*. Nordisk Rotogravyr: Stockholm, 1942, Kooperativa forbundets bokfarling, Stockholm.

MIMS, Edwin Abingdon. *Christ of the Poets*. Nashville, Tennessee: Cokesbury Press, 1948, 225-227.

MONROE, Harriet. *A Poet's Life; Seventy Years in a Changing World*. New York: Macmillan, 1938. 190, 312, 314, 322, 335, 342, 350, 351, 464, 471.

— "Carl Sandburg" *Poetry*, XXIV (Sept., 1924), 320.

MONTGOMERY, Elizabeth. *Story Behind Great Stories*. New York: McBride, 1947. 88-91.

NASH, J. V. "Carl Sandburg: An American Homer" *Open Court*, XLIV (Oct., 1939), 633-639.

PATTEE, Fred Lewis. *The New American Literature, 1890-1930*. New York, London: Century Co., 1930. 278-283.

PHELPS, William Lyon. *The Advance of English Poetry in the Twentieth Century*. New York: Dodd, Mead, 1918, 289-291.

"Pulitzer History Award" *Saturday Review of Literature*. XXII (May 11, 1940), 13.

ROSENFELD, Paul. "Carl Sandburg" *Bookman*, LIII (July, 1921), 389-396.

— *Port of New York; Essays on Fourteen American Moderns*. New York: Harcourt, Brace, 1924, 65-81.

ROSENTHAL, M. L. *The Modern Poets*. New York: Oxford Press, 1960. 19, 152-156, 159, 200.

SCHELLING, Felix E. *Appraisements and Asperities as to Some Contemporary Writers*. Philadelphia: J. B. Lippincott, 1922. 73-78.

SCHLAUCH, Margaret. *Modern English and American Poetry*. London, Watts, 1956. 115, 119, 159, 192.

SHERMAN, Stuart P. *Americans*. New York: Scribner's, 1922. 239-245.

— *The Genius of America*. New York: Scribner's, 1923. 235.

— "Review of Abraham Lincoln: The Prairie Years." *Books* (New York *Herald Tribune*), (Feb. 7, 1926), p. 1.

SHERWOOD, Robert Emmet. "Review of Abraham Lincoln: The War Years." New York *Times Book Review* (Dec. 3, 1939), p. 1.

SIMON, Charlie May. *Lays of The New Land*. New York: Dutton, 1943. 187-198.

SOSKIN, William. "Review of *Remembrance Rock*" *Saturday Review of Literature*, XXXI (Oct. 9, 1948), 14-15.

SPILLER, Robert E. *Cycle of American Literature*. New York: Macmillan Co., 1955, p. 236.

SPILLER, Robert E.; THORP, Willard; JOHNSON, T. H.; CANBY, Henry Seidel. *Literary History of the United States*. New York: Macmillan, 1948. pp. 716, 863, 1120, 1174, 1181-1184, 1296, 1359, 1377, 1394, 1395, 1398, 1426.

STOVALL, Floyd. *American Idealism*. Norman, Oklahoma: University of Oklahoma Press, 1943. 196-197, 198-200.

TAUPIN, René. *L'Influence du Symbolisme Français sur la Poésie Américaine*. Paris: H. Champion, 1929, pp. 302; 66, 196, 253, 266, 279, 284.

THOMAS, Benjamin, P. *Portrait for Posterity: Lincoln and His Biographers*. Rutgers University Press, New Jersey, 1947, XVII, 285-301.

THOREN, Arne. "A Midnight Visit with Carl Sandburg" *American Swedish Monthly*, L (May, 1956), 9-10.

UNTERMEYER, Louis. " Strong Timber " *Dial* LXV (Oct. 5, 1918), 263, 264.

— *American Poetry Since 1900.* New York: Holt, 1923. 67-87.

UNTERMEYER, Louis. *Modern American Poetry*, New York: Harcourt, Brace and Co., 1936; 13, 15, 16, 18, 21, 91, 235-250, 437, 528, 571.

VAN DOREN, Carl. *Many Minds*, New York: Knopf, 1924; 136-150.

VAN DOREN, Mark. " Carl Sandburg " *Nation*, CXXVII (Oct. 31, 1928) 456, 457.

WEIRICK, Bruce. *From Whitman to Sandburg in American Poetry.* New York: Macmillan, 1924; 210-221.

WEST, Rebecca. *Selected Poems of Carl Sandburg.* New York: Harcourt, Brace and Co., 1926. Introduction.

WILKINSON, Mrs. Marguerite Ogden. *New Voices; An Introduction to Contemporary Poetry.* New York: Macmillan, 1928. 180-182, 217-218, 303-304.

YUST, Walter. " Carl Sandburg, Human Being " *Bookman*, LII (Jan., 1921), 285-290.

NOTES

[1] PARRINGTON, Louis, *Beginnings of Critical Realism in America*, New York: Harcourt, Brace, 1930, pp. 7-10.

[2] SANDBURG, Carl. *Always the Young Strangers*, p. 16.
Much of the information concerning the first twenty years of Carl Sandburg's life has been derived from *Always the Young Strangers* published by the author in 1953. The volume is autobiographical, covering, however, only his boyhood and young manhood.

[3] SANDBURG, Carl. *Always the Young Strangers*, p. 428.

[4] Ibid., pp. 58-59.

[5] Ibid., p. 357.

[6] Ibid., p. 211.

[7] Ibid., p. 375.

[8] Ibid., p. 379.

[9] Ibid., p. 381.

[10] Ibid., p. 377.

[11] SANDBURG, Carl. Introduction to *Always the Young Strangers*, p. 11.

[12] SANDBURG, Carl. *Always the Young Strangers*, p. 390.

[13] Ibid., p. 394.

[14] Ibid., p. 423. Information from Lombard College records pertaining to the enrollment of Charles August Sandburg was kindly supplied to the writer of this thesis by L. W. Elder, Curator of Memorabilia of Knox College with which Lombard was merged in 1930. A personal visit to Knox College in the interest of Sandburg research yielded some information. A personal interview with Mrs. John E. George and kind letters from her have been of great assistance.

[15] SANDBURG, Carl. Introduction to volume of *Complete Poems*, p. xxviii.

[16] LOWELL, Amy. *Tendencies in Modern American Poetry*, pp. 230, 232.

[17] WEIGEL, John C., is the author of this paragraph which was printed in the Knox College *Siwasher*, October 1934; reprinted in the *Journal of the Illinois State Historical Society*, Winter 1952, p. 315.

[18] WRIGHT, Quincy (son of Philip Green Wright). "Lombard Memories," p. 307 of *Journal of the Illinois State Historical Society*, Winter 1952.

[19] *Journal of the Illinois State Historical Society*, Winter 1952, p. 316.

[20] Ibid., p. 318.

[21] Ibid., p. 318.

[22] Ibid., p. 318.

[23] Ibid., p. 309.

[24] Ibid., p. 312.

[25] Ibid., pp. 313, 314.

[26] Ibid., p. 314.

[27] Ibid., p. 311.

[28] DETZER, Karl William. *Carl Sandburg; A Study in Personality and Background*, p. 63.

[29] SANDBURG, Charles August. *In Reckless Ecstasy*, privately printed in the home of Philip Green Wright in 1904. But a copy of the little volume is carefully preserved in the Rare Book Room of the Library of Congress, Washington, D.C. It is now a collector's item. Only 50 copies of it were printed in 1904.

[30] SANDBURG, Charles A. *In Reckless Ecstasy*, p. 10.

[31] Ibid.

[32] Ibid., p. 11.

[33] Ibid.

[34] Ibid.

[35] DETZER, Karl William. *Carl Sandburg; A Study in Personality and Background.*

[36] HAGEDORN, Hermann. *Roosevelt Family of Sagamore Hill*, Macmillan, 1954, p. 306.

[37] *Journal of the Illinois State Historical Society*, Winter 1952; p. 314.

[38] DETZER, Karl William. *Carl Sandburg; A Study in Personality and Background*, pp. 76-80.

[39] MONROE, Harriet and HENDERSON, Alice C. *The New Poetry*, p. XLII.

[40] SANDBURG, Carl. *Complete poems*, p. 3.

[41] UNTERMEYER, Louis. *Modern American Poetry*, p. 16.

[42] SANDBURG, Carl. *Complete Poems*, Preface, pp. XXIV, XXV, XXVIII.

[43] Ibid., p. 10.

[44] Ibid., p. 51.

[45] Ibid., p. 56.

[46] SANDBURG, Charles A. *In Reckless Ecstasy*, p. 17.

[47] SANDBURG, Carl. *Complete Poems*, pp. 79 to 84.

[48] Ibid., p. 85.

[49] Ibid., p. 80.

[50] Ibid., p. 139.

[51] Ibid., p. 150.

[52] Ibid., p. 178.

[53] Ibid., p. 168.

[54] Ibid., p. 207.

[55] Ibid., p. 168.

[56] Ibid., p. 194.

[57] Ibid., p. 307

[58] Ibid., p. 313.

[59] LOWELL, Amy. *Tendencies in Modern American Poetry*, pp. 230, 232.

[60] LOWELL, Amy. *Selected Poems of Amy Lowell*, pp. 84, 85.

[61] SANDBURG, Carl. *The Sandburg Range*, p. 91.

[62] Ibid., p. 101.

[63] Rupert Hughes incorporated three Sandburg poems in his *Free Verse Songs:* " Lost " (a poem of nine lines depicting the fog and mist and boats of the harbor of Chicago), " Bricklayer Love " and " Prayers of Steel."
" Prayers of Steel " was also set to music by Walter Buckman. The nobility of its theme, the humility of the author, the beauty of metaphor and religious devotion contained in the lines endowed it with such merit that it was among those Sandburg poems translated into Swedish and published in Stockholm in 1934.
Another poem which has been set to music for a baritone solo (the music by Arthur Prentice Van Iderstine) is the brief verse of seven lines entitled " Nocturne in a Deserted Brickyard." The exultant lyricism of the long poem " Prairie " is one of its striking characteristics. Because of the quality of the lines and their inspiring subject matter, " Prairie " has been set to music by Lucas Foss, as a secular cantata for a full chorus of mixed voices, with soprano, alto, tenor and bass soli and orchestra.

The delicately symbolic lines of " Under the Harvest Moon " have been set to music by Charles Naginsky; the forthright practicality of " Omaha " by the musician Ernest Bacon; " Come on Superstition " by Elmer Russ; and the strong, powerful lines of " Upstream " have been transcribed to two musical settings by two different composers, Marie Travers and Albert Hay Marlotte.

Sandburg poems were sung by the Metropolitan Opera star, Rose Brampton, when she appeared in concert at McMillen Auditorium of Columbia University, in New York City, February 22, 1948. The Sandburg selections which were sung were " The Wind Sings Welcome in Early Spring," " Tawny Days " and " Great Memories."

64 SANDBURG, Carl. *Complete Poems*, p. 157.

65 SANDBURG, Carl. *Always The Young Strangers*, p. 242.

66 SANDBURG, Carl. *Complete Poems*, pp. 324, 325.

67 Ibid., p. 335.

68 Ibid., p. 333.

69 Ibid., p. 335.

70 Ibid., p. 336.

71 Ibid.

72 WHITMAN, Walt. *The Poetry and Prose of Walt Whitman*, edited by Louis Unter-meyer, New York; Simon and Schuster, 1949, pp. 562, 563.

73 SANDBURG, Carl. *Complete Poems*, pp. 345, 346.

74 Ibid., p. 346.

75 DETZER, Karl William. Carl Sandburg; *A Study in Personality and Background*, p. 181.

76 SANDBURG, Carl. *Complete Poems*, p. 437.

77 Ibid., Preface, p. XXIII.

78 Ibid., p. 615.

79 Ibid., p. 616.

80 Ibid., pp. 616, 617.

81 *The Nation*. Oct. 31, 1926. Article by Mark Van Doren, p. 457.

82 *Journal of the Illinois State Historical Society*, Winter 1952, p. 376.

83 Raleigh *News and Observer*. Article by Elsie Pinckney, June 1946.

84 SANDBURG, Carl. *Complete Poems*, pp. 626, 627.

85 This statement was made personally by Mr. Sandburg to the writer of this thesis.

86 SANDBURG, Carl. *Wind Song*, p. 127.

87 Ibid., p. 65.

88 Ibid., Preface.

89 Asheville *Citizen-Times*. March 27, 1955. Article by Carl Fleming.

90 Cincinnati *Enquirer*. June 1, 1958. Article by Frankie Sharp.

91 *Look*, July 10, 1956, p. 95.

92 SANDBURG, Carl. *Home Front Memo*, p. 12.

93 SANDBURG, Carl. *Abraham Lincoln: Prairie Years and War Years* (one-volume edition), p. 148.

94 SANDBURG, Carl. *Home Front Memo*, p. 31.

95 SANDBURG, Carl. *Complete Poems*, p. 521.

96 Ibid., p. 524.

97 *Journal of the Illinois State Historical Society*, Winter 1952, p. 299.

98 SANDBURG, Carl. "Abraham Lincoln : The Soil and the Seed," in *Literary History of the United States*, edited by Spiller, Thorp, Johnson, Canby, pp. 778-786.

99 SANDBURG, Carl. *Abraham Lincoln: The War Years*, vol. IV, p. 192.

100 Ibid., vol. II, p. 446.

[101] SANDBURG, Carl. *Abraham Lincoln: The War Years*, vol. IV, pp. 95, 96.

[102] Ibid., vol. IV, p. 387.

[103] *Literary History of the United States;* edited by SPILLER, THORP, JOHNSON, CANBY; p. 372.

[104] SANDBURG, Carl. *Always the Young Strangers*, p. 230.

[105] EMERSON, Ralph Waldo. " The American Scholar." From *American Poetry and Prose* edited by Norman Foerster, New York : Houghton, 1934, pp. 381, 384.

[106] Ibid., p. 388.

[107] SANDBURG, Carl. *Wind Song* (1960), p. 51.

[108] EMERSON, Ralph Waldo. *Essays*, New York : Burt, 1900, vol. II, pp. 51-55.

[109] Ibid., p. 74.

[110] Ibid., pp. 81, 82.

[111] SPILLER, Robert E. *The Cycle of American Literature*, p. 236.

[112] DICKINSON, Emily, in *Modern American Poetry* edited by Louis Untermeyer, p. 88.

[113] Ibid., p. 87.

[114] SANDBURG, Carl. *Complete Poems*, p. 49.

[115] Ibid., p. 670.

[116] SANDBURG, Carl. *Complete Poems*, p. 73.

[117] SANDBURG, Carl. *Complete Poems*, Preface, p. xxv.

[118] THOREAU, Henry David. In *Masterpieces of American Poets*, edited by Mark Van Doren, Garden City Publishing Co., 1936, p. 246.

[119] SANDBURG, Carl. *Complete Poems*, p. 33.

[120] WHITTIER, John G., in *Masterpieces of American Poets*, edited by Mark Van Doren, Garden City Publishing Co., 1936, p. 166.

[121] *Literary History of the United States*, edited by SPILLER, THORP, JOHNSON & CANBY, p. 916.

[122] WHITMAN, Walt. From the Untermeyer Edition of *The Poetry and Prose of Walt Whitman*, New York : Simon and Schuster, 1949, p. 530.

[123] SANDBURG, Carl. *Complete Poems*, pp. 184, 185.

[124] WHITMAN, Walt. " The Poet and His Prefaces," Untermeyer Edition of *The Poetry and Prose of Walt Whitman*, New York : Simon and Schuster, 1949, pp. 520, 521.

[125] WHITMAN, Walt. " Eidolons." Untermeyer Edition of *The Poetry and Prose of Walt Whitman*, New York : Simon and Schuster, 1949, p. 80.

[126] WHITMAN, Walt. "Poetry Today in America." Untermeyer Edition of *The Poetry and Prose of Walt Whitman*, New York : Simon and Schuster, 1949, p. 567.

[127] WHITMAN, Walt. "Ventures on an Old Theme." Untermeyer Edition of *The Poetry and Prose of Walt Whitman*, New York : Simon and Schuster, 1949, p. 889.

[128] SANDBURG, Carl. In the Sandburg *Foreword* to the special edition of Whitman's *Leaves of Grass* published in 1921, New York : The Modern Library.

[129] WHITMAN, Walt. "Democratic Vistas," Untermeyer Edition of *The Prose and Poetry of Walt Whitman*, New York : Simon and Schuster, 1949, p. 819.

[130] SANDBURG, Carl. *Abraham Lincoln: The Prairie Years*, vol. II, p. 4.

[131] HUGO, Victor. *Les Feuilles d'Automne*, Paris : Classiques Larousse, pp. 46, 47.

[132] SANDBURG, Carl. *Complete Poems*, p. 134.

[133] HUGO, Victor. *Derniers Recueils Lyriques*, Paris : Larousse, p. 108.

[134] SANDBURG, Carl. *Complete Poems*, p. 113.

[135] Ibid., p. 646.

[136] Ibid., Preface, p. xxiv.

[137] LANSON, Gustave. *Histoire de la Littérature Française*, Paris : Hachette, 1912, p. 177.

[138] UNTERMEYER, Louis. *Modern American Poetry*, quoting T. S. Eliot, p. 21.

[139] VILLON, François. *Œuvres;* in Edition Garnier, (Paris), p. 140.

[140] Ibid., p. 127.

[141] SANDBURG, Charles A. *In Reckless Ecstasy.* The Invocation at the end of the volume.

[142] SANDBURG, Carl. *Early Moon*, Preface.

[143] SANDBURG, Carl. *Complete Poems*, pp. 109, 110.

[144] Ibid., p. 669.

[145] SANDBURG, Charles A. *In Reckless Ecstasy*, p. 24.

[146] SANDBURG, Carl. *Complete Poems*, pp. 667-668

[147] PEALE, Norman Vincent. *Guideposts*, February 1955, p. 2.

[148] SANDBURG, Carl. *Home Front Memo*, p. 313.

[149] SANDBURG, Carl. *Complete Poems*, pp. 80, 81.

[150] Ibid., pp. 130, 131.

[151] Ibid., p. 364.

[152] Ibid., p. 221.

[153] Ibid., p. 552.

[154] Ibid., p. 365.

[155] Ibid., p. 81.

[156] Ibid., p. 366.

[157] Ibid., p. 432.

[158] Ibid., p. 311.

[159] Ibid., p. 433.

[160] Ibid., p. 366.

[161] SANDBURG, Carl. *Wind Song*, p. 25.

[162] SANDBURG, Carl. *Complete Poems*, p. 83.

[163] Ibid., pp. 80, 81.

[164] Boston *Herald*, June 13, 1955.

[165] SANDBURG, Carl. *Complete Poems*, p. 80.

[166] Ibid., p. 80.

[167] Ibid., p. 81.

[168] Ibid., pp. 79-85.

[169] TEGNER, Esaias. *Frithiof's Saga*, translated into English by Henry Wadsworth Longfellow. In Longfellows' *Complete Poetical Works*, Cambridge Edition, Houghton-Mifflin & Co., 1893, p. 598.

[170] SANDBURG, Carl. *Complete Poems*, p. 83.

[171] Ibid., p. 84.

[172] Ibid., p. 79.

[173] Ibid., p. 79.

[174] Ibid., p. 80.

[175] EMERSON, Ralph Waldo. *Essays*, New York : Burt, 1900, vol. II, p. 74.

[176] LAGERLÖF, Selma. *The Story of Gösta Berling*, Boston : Little, 1940, p. 35.

[177] EMERSON, Ralph Waldo. *Essays*, New York : Burt, 1900, vol. II, p. 215.

[178] Ibid., vol. II, p. 216.

[179] Ibid., vol. II, p. 233.

[180] SANDBURG, Carl. *Complete Poems*, p. 80.

[181] Ibid., pp. 80-83.

[182] Ibid., p. 83.

— 235 —

EMERSON, Ralph Waldo. Harvard Phi Beta Kappa Address, 1837. "The American Scholar." From *American Poetry and Prose (A Book of Readings)*, edited by Norman Foerster, New York : Houghton, Mifflin, 1934, p. 385.

[184] SANDBURG, Carl. *Complete Poems*, p. 83.

[185] Ibid., p. 85.

[186] Ibid., p. 85.

[187] WHITMAN, Walt. From *The Poetry and Prose of Walt Whitman*, edited by Louis Untermeyer, New York : Simon and Schuster, 1949, p. 891.

[188] SANDBURG, Carl. *Complete Poems*, p. 256.

[189] Ibid., p. 126.

[190] Ibid., p. 138.

[191] Ibid., p. 96.

[192] Ibid., p. 255.

[193] Ibid., p. 305.

[194] Ibid., p. 428.

[195] Ibid., p. 423.

[196] Ibid., p. 87.

[197] Ibid., p. 355.

[198] Ibid., p. 355.

[199] Ibid., p. 81.

[200] Ibid., p. 81.

[201] Ibid., pp. 3-4.

[202] Ibid., p. 6.

[203] Ibid., pp. 8, 9.

[204] Ibid., p. 7.

[205] Ibid., p. 23.

[206] Ibid., p. 17.

[207] Ibid., pp. 31, 32.

[208] Ibid., p. 31.

[209] Ibid., p. 31.

[210] Ibid., pp. 65, 66.

[211] Ibid., p. 4.

[212] Ibid., p. 5.

[213] Ibid., p. 10.

[214] Ibid., pp. 67, 75.

[215] Ibid., p. 5.

[216] Ibid., p. 69.

[217] Ibid., p. 564.

[218] Ibid., p. 271.

[219] Ibid., p. 271.

[220] Ibid., p. 272.

[221] Ibid., pp. 271, 272.

[222] Ibid., p. 272.

[223] Ibid., pp. 272, 276.

[224] Ibid., p. 275.

[225] Ibid., pp. 276, 277.

[226] Ibid., pp. 275, 276.

[227] Ibid., pp. 277, 278.

228 SANDBURG, Carl. *Complete Poems*, p. 280.
229 Ibid., p. 280.
230 Ibid., p. 280.
231 Ibid., p. 281.
232 Ibid., p. 281.
233 SANDBURG, Carl. *Abraham Lincoln: The Prairie Years*, vol. I, p. 353.
234 Ibid., pp. 353, 354.
235 SANDBURG, Carl. *Complete Poems*, p. 232.
236 Ibid., pp. 282, 283.
237 Ibid., p. 121.
238 Ibid., p. 320.
239 Ibid., pp. 228, 229.
240 Ibid., p. 368.
241 Ibid., p. 364.
242 Ibid., p. 233.
243 Ibid., p. 323.
244 Ibid., p. 663.
245 Ibid., pp. 320, 322.
246 Ibid., p. 597.
247 Ibid., p. 162.
248 Ibid., p. 3.
249 Ibid., p. 172.
250 Ibid., p. 172.
251 Ibid., p. 92.
252 Ibid., p. 272.
253 Ibid., p. 281.
254 Ibid., pp. 154, 155.
255 Ibid., p. 152.
256 EMERSON, Ralph Waldo. Harvard Phi Beta Kappa Address, 1837, "The American Scholar." From *American Poetry and Prose (A Book of Readings)* edited by Norman Foerster, New York: Houghton, Mifflin, 1934, p. 384.
257 SANDBURG, Carl. *Complete Poems*, p. 12.
258 Ibid., pp. 278, 279.
259 Ibid., p. 161.
260 Ibid., p. 116.
261 Ibid., p. 105.
262 EMERSON, Ralph Waldo, *Essays* (" Politics "), New York: Burt, 1900, p. 239.
263 SANDBURG, Carl. *Complete Poems*, p. 596.
264 LERNER, Max. *America as a Civilization*, Simon, Schuster, 1957, pp. 362 to 371.
265 EMERSON, Ralph Waldo. *Essays*, New York: Burt, 1900, vol. II, pp. 242, 243, 253.
266 *Poetry and Prose of Walt Whitman*, Untermeyer; Simon, Schuster, 1949, p. 857.
267 SANDBURG, Carl. *The Sandburg Range*, p. 59.
268 *Poetry and Prose of Walt Whitman*, Untermeyer; Simon, Schuster, 1949, p. 523.
269 SANDBURG, Carl. *Complete Poems*, p. 375.
270 Ibid., p. 374.
271 Ibid., p. 377.
272 Ibid., p. 121.
273 Ibid., p. 86.

[274] SANDBURG, Carl. *Complete Poems*, p. 130.
[275] SANDBURG, Carl. *Remembrance Rock*, pp. 132, 133.
[276] Ibid., p. 112.
[277] Ibid., p. 112.
[278] Ibid., p. 147.
[279] Ibid., p. 148.
[280] Ibid., pp. 329, 330.
[281] Ibid., pp. 201, 202.
[282] Ibid., p. 265.
[283] Ibid., pp. 277, 278.
[284] SANDBURG, Carl. *Complete Poems*, p. 486.
[285] SANDBURG, Carl. *Remembrance Rock*, pp. 21, 22.
[286] Ibid., pp. 351 and 368.
[287] Ibid., p. 462.
[288] Ibid., pp. 530, 531.
[289] Ibid., p. 534.
[290] Ibid., p. 537.
[291] SANDBURG, Carl. *Home Front Memo*, p. 271.
[292] Ibid.
[293] SANDBURG, Carl. *Remembrance Rock*, p. 578.
[294] SANDBURG, Carl. *Complete Poems*, pp. 622-623.
[295] Ibid., p. 623.
[296] Ibid., p. 623.
[297] SANDBURG, Carl. *Home Front Memo*, pp. 261, 262.
[298] SANDBURG, Carl. *Complete Poems*, pp. 330, 331.
[299] SANDBURG, Carl. *Always the Young Strangers*, p. 357.
[300] SANDBURG, Carl. *Abraham Lincoln: The Prairie Years*, vol. I, pp. 117 and 124.
[301] Ibid., vol. II, pp. 197, 198.
[302] SANDBURG, Carl. *Complete Poems*, p. 625.
[303] Ibid., p. 521.
[304] Ibid., p. 609.
[305] SANDBURG, Carl. One-volume edition of *The Prairie Years and the War Years*, p. 330.
[306] SANDBURG, Carl. *Complete Poems*, p. 625.
[307] Ibid., pp. 563, 564.
[308] Ibid., p. 521.
[309] Ibid., p. 522.
[310] Ibid., p. 522.
[311] Ibid., p. 523.
[312] SANDBURG, Carl. *Abraham Lincoln: The War Years*, vol. II, p. 531.
[313] Ibid., vol. II, p. 498.
[314] Ibid., vol. I, pp. 520, 521, 523, 526.
[315] Ibid., p. 520.
[316] Ibid., p. 517.
[317] SANDBURG, Carl. *Remembrance Rock*, pp. 987, 988.
[318] SANDBURG, Carl. *The War Years*, vol. IV, p. 202.
[319] SANDBURG, Carl. *Always the Young Strangers*, p. 148.
[320] Ibid., p. 405.

— 238 —

[321] SANDBURG, Carl. *Always the Young Stangers*, pp. 413, 414, 415.

[322] Ibid., p. 416.

[323] Ibid., p. 421.

[324] SANDBURG, Carl. *Complete Poems*, p. 331.

[325] Ibid., p. 470.

[326] SAINTE-BEUVE. *Pensées et Maximes*, rassemblées par Maurice Chapelan, p. 386, (Paris : Grasset, 1955).

[327] SANDBURG, Carl. *Complete Poems*, pp. 5, 6.

[328] Ibid., p. 6.

[329] Ibid., p. 14.

[330] Ibid., pp. 69, 70.

[331] Ibid., p. 113.

[332] Ibid., p. 16.

[333] HANSEN, Harry. *Carl Sandburg: The Man and His Poetry*, Little Blue Book No. 814, p. 50.

[334] SANDBURG, Carl. *Complete Poems*, p. 67.

[335] Ibid., p. 68.

[336] Ibid., pp. 256, 257.

[337] Ibid., p. 257.

[338] Ibid., p. 26.

[339] Ibid., p. 33.

[340] Ibid., p. 279.

[341] Ibid., p. 616.

[342] Ibid., p. 10.

[343] Ibid., p. 124.

[344] *Journal of the Illinois State Historical Society*, Winter 1952, p. 352.

[345] Asheville *Times*, March 27, 1955. Article by Karl Fleming.

[346] SANDBURG, Carl. *Complete Poems*, p. 208.

[347] Ibid., p. 236.

[348] Ibid., p. 209.

[349] Ibid., p. 107.

[350] Ibid., p. 107.

[351] Ibid., p. 37.

[352] Ibid., p. 38.

[353] Ibid., pp. 140, 141.

[354] Ibid., p. 145.

[355] Ibid., pp. 144, 145.

[356] Ibid., p. 143.

[357] Ibid., p. 145.

[358] Ibid., pp. 143, 146.

[359] SANDBURG, Carl. *Home Front Memo*, pp. 302, 309.

[360] SANDBURG, Carl. *Complete Poems*, p. 147.

[361] SANDBURG, Carl. Photostatic copy of his European N.E.A. reports published November 1918.

[362] Ibid., published December 28, 1918.

[363] Ibid., January 17, 1919.

[364] Ibid., January 23, 1919.

[365] Ibid., January 1919.

366 SANDBURG, Carl. Photostatic copy of his European N.E.A. reports published January 6, 1919.

367 PASTERNAK, Boris. *Dr. Zhivago*, New York : Pantheon, 1960, p. 202.

368 Ibid., p. 362.

369 SANDBURG, Carl. *Complete Poems*, p. 285.

370 Ibid., p. 288.

371 Ibid., p. 288.

372 Ibid., p. 169.

373 Ibid., p. 194.

374 SANDBURG, Carl. *Home Front Memo*, p. 45.

375 Ibid., p. 45.

376 SANDBURG, Carl. *Complete Poems*, pp. 606, 607.

377 Ibid., p. 599.

378 Ibid., p. 570.

379 *Literary History of the United States*, edited by SPILLER, THORP, JOHNSON, CANBY, p. 1300.

380 SANDBURG, Carl. *Complete Poems*, p. 484.

381 Ibid., p. 484.

382 Ibid., p. 484.

383 Ibid., p. 485.

384 Ibid., p. 555.

385 Ibid., p. 483.

386 Ibid., pp. 559, 560.

387 Ibid., p. 455.

388 Ibid., p. 547.

389 Ibid., p. 449.

390 Ibid., p. 564.

391 Ibid., p. 520.

392 Ibid., p. 577.

393 Ibid., p. 471.

394 Ibid., p. 142.

395 Ibid., p. 143.

396 Ibid., pp. 462, 463.

397 Ibid., p. 617.

398 Ibid., p. 616.

399 Ibid., p. 614.

400 ELIOT, T. S. *On Poetry and Poets* (Quotation by Eliot from Charles Péguy writing of Hugo), New York : Farrar, Straus, 1956, p. 201.

401 SANDBURG, Carl. *Complete Poems*, p. 574.

402 Ibid., p. 455.

403 EMERSON, Ralph Waldo. *Essays*, New York : Burt, 1900, vol. II, p. 55.

404 SANDBURG, Carl. *Complete Poems*, p. 617.

405 Ibid., p. 194.

406 SANDBURG, Carl. *Home Front Memo*, p. 37.

407 Ibid., pp. 59, 60.

408 Ibid., pp. 123-126.

409 Ibid., p. 181.

410 SANDBURG, Carl. *Complete Poems*, p. 638.

411 SANDBURG, Carl. *Home Front Memo*, p. 311.

412 SANDBURG, Carl. *Complete Poems*, p. 589.

413 SANDBURG, Carl. *Home Front Memo*, p. 309.

414 *Journal of the Illinois State Historical Society*, Winter 1952, p. 378.

415 SANDBURG, Carl. *Remembrance Rock*, p. 1052.

416 *Poetry and Prose of Walt Whitman*. Untermeyer. Simon, Schuster, 1949, p. 555.

417 SANDBURG, Carl. " Chicago Dynamic." This portion in *Life*, Nov. 4, 1957, p. 107. The entire speech is available in the Rare Book Room in the Library of Congress in Washington where a copy is presently kept.

418 SANDBURG, Carl. *Complete Poems*, p. 176.

419 SAINTE-BEUVE. Quotation used by Whitman. *Poetry and Prose of Walt Whitman*, edited by Louis Untermeyer, New York : Simon and Schuster, 1949, p. 555.

420 SANDBURG, Carl. *Complete Poems*, p. 51.

421 SANDBURG, Carl. " Chicago Dynamic " Speech. Also *Complete Poems*, p. 597.

422 SANDBURG, Carl. *Complete Poems*, p. 646.

423 SANDBURG, Carl. Lincoln Birthday Memorial Speech before the two Houses of Congress in Washington. Reprinted in Washington *Evening Star*, February 12, 1959.

424 SANDBURG, Carl. In *Better Homes and Gardens*, April 1959, pp. 56, 57.

425 SANDBURG, Carl. *Home Front Memo*, p. 342.

426 Washington *Evening Star*, Jan. 5, 1958.

427 Ibid., July 29, 1957, Article by Bernie Harrison.

428 SANDBURG, Carl. *Home Front Memo*, p. 294. Also in *Always the Young Strangers*, p. 304.

429 SANDBURG, Carl. *Remembrance Rock*, p. 1054.

430 EMERSON, Ralph Waldo. *Essays*, New York : Burt, 1900, vol. II, p. 56.

431 SANDBURG, Carl. *Complete Poems*, p. 592.

432 Ibid., p. 347.

433 Ibid., p. 591.

434 Ibid., p. 591.

435 Ibid., p. 578.

436 *The Poetry and Prose of Walt Whitman*, edited by Louis Untermeyer, New York : Simon and Schuster, 1949, p. 496 and p. 563.

437 JONES, Llewellyn. *First Impressions*, New York : Knopf, 1925, p. 59.

438 SANDBURG, Carl. *Complete Poems*, pp. 29, 31.

439 *Poetry and Prose of Walt Whitman*, Untermeyer. Simon, Schuster, 1949, p. 83.

440 Ibid., p. 334.

441 MONROE, Harriet. In *Poetry*, May 1916, pp. 320-325.

442 SANDBURG, Carl. *Complete Poems*, pp. 120, 121.

443 Ibid., p. 625.

444 Ibid., p. 455.

445 SANDBURG, Carl. *The Sandburg Range*, p. 61.

446 SANDBURG, Carl. *Complete Poems*, p. 528.

447 Ibid., p. 165.

448 SANDBURG, Carl. *Early Moon*, Preface.

449 Ibid., Preface.

450 WORDSWORTH, William, in the Preface to *Lyrical Ballads*, published by Wordsworth and Coleridge.

451 *Modern American Poetry*, edited by Louis Untermeyer, pp. 145, 146.

452 Ibid., p. 162.

— 241 —

[453] Robinson, Edwin Arlington. *Collected Poems,* New York: The Macmillan Company, 1939, p. 66.
[454] ROSENFELD, Paul. *Port of New York.* (Essays on 14 American Moderns.), p. 8.
[455] SANDBURG, Carl. *Home Front Memo,* p. 151.
[456] *Modern American Poetry,* edited by Louis Untermeyer, p. 144.
[457] SANDBURG, Carl. *Complete Poems,* p. 87.
[458] Ibid., p. 56.
[459] SANDBURG, Carl. *Home Front Memo,* p. 31.
[460] *Modern American Poetry,* edited by Louis Untermeyer, p. 164.
[461] Ibid., p. 166.
[462] Ibid., p. 165.
[463] Ibid., p. 165.
[464] *Masterpieces of American Poets,* edited by Mark Van Doren, p. 214.
[465] Ibid.
[466] *Modern American Poetry,* edited by Louis Untermeyer, p. 231.
[467] SANDBURG, Carl. *Complete Poems,* p. 88.
[468] *Modern American Poetry,* edited by Louis Untermeyer, pp. 221, 222.
[469] Ibid., p. 213.
[470] Ibid., p. 215.
[471] Ibid., p. 231.
[472] Catel, Jean. " Lettres Américaines " in *Revue de la Quinzaine,* March 15, 1920.
[473] *Modern American Poetry,* edited by Louis Untermeyer, p. 233.
[474] *Life,* Dec. 1, 1961, p. 474.
[475] Ibid.
[476] WHITMAN, Walt. In *The Poetry and Prose of Walt Whitman,* edited by Louis Untermeyer, New York: Simon and Schuster, 1949, pp. 480, 481, 482.
[477] SANDBURG, Carl. *Complete Poems,* pp. 184, 185.
[478] Ibid., Preface, p. xxiv.
[479] ELIOT, T. S. *The Four Quartets* (" East Coker "), Faber edition, p. 30.
[480] *Literary History of the United States,* edited by SPILLER, THORP, JOHNSON, CANBY, p. 725.
[481] ELVIN, Lionel. *Introduction to the Study of Literature,* London: Sylvan, 1949, p. 220.
[482] JONES, H. M. and LEISY, E. E. *Major American Writers,* p. 23.
[483] KRUTCH, Joseph Wood. In *The American Scholar,* Summer 1959, p. 378.
[484] MACLEISH, Archibald. In *The Atlantic Monthly,* March, 1959, pp. 43-45.
[485] SANDBURG, Carl. *Complete Poems,* Preface, p. xxiv.
[486] SANDBURG, Carl. *Home Front Memo,* pp. 258, 259.
[487] ROSENTHAL, M. L. *The Modern Poets,* p. 183.
[488] SANDBURG, Charles A. *In Reckless Ecstasy,* p. 19.
[489] SANDBURG, Carl. *Home Front Memo,* p. 35.
[490] SANDBURG, Carl. *Complete Poems,* p. 614.
[491] *The Pathfinder,* October 23, 1946.
[492] SANDBURG, Carl. *Complete Poems,* p. 537.
[493] Ibid., 607.
[494] Ibid., 606.
[495] Ibid., p. 562.
[496] Ibid., p. 617.

[497] SANDBURG, Carl. Speech at Madison Square Garden, August 19, 1941, in *Home Front Memo*, pp. 38, 39, 40.

[498] *Literary History of the United States*, edited by SPILLER, THORP, JOHNSON, CANBY, pp. 1183, 1184.

[499] SANDBURG, Carl. *Complete Poems*, p. 605.

[500] SANDBURG, Carl. *Home Front Memo*, p. 268.

[501] SANDBURG, Carl. *Remembrance Rock*, p. 277.

[502] SANDBURG, Carl. *Abraham Lincoln: The War Years*, Foreword, p. ix.

[503] SANDBURG, Carl. *Home Front Memo*, pp. 268, 269.

[504] SANDBURG, Carl. *Complete Poems*, pp. 464, 465.

[505] Ibid., p. 582.

[506] Ibid., p. 479.

[507] ARLAND, Marcel. *Anthologie de la Poésie Française*, Paris : Stock, 1956, p. 675.

[508] New York *Times*, June 1, 1952.

[509] ELIOT, T. S. *On Poetry and Poets*, New York : Farrar, Straus, 1956, p. 51.

[510] SANDBURG, Carl. *Complete Poems*, p. 616.

[511] Ibid., p. 437.

[512] SCHLAUCH, Margaret. *Modern English and American Poetry*, p. 115.

[513] Ibid., p. 117.

[514] BLANKENSHIP, Russell. *American Literature*, p. 613.

[515] SANDBURG, Carl. *The Prairie Years*, vol. I, p. 451.

[516] Ibid., pp. 47, 49.

[517] Ibid., p. 76.

[518] SANDBURG, Carl. *The Prairie Years*, vol. II, p. 67.

[519] WHITE, William Allen. In *Sandburg Range*, p. 348.

[520] SANDBURG, Carl. *The War Years*, in the Foreword, p. VII.

[521] Ibid., vol. II, pp. 332, 333.

[522] Ibid., vol. IV, p. 239.

[523] Ibid., p. 351.

[524] Ibid., p. 377.

[525] Ibid., p. 387.

[526] Ibid., pp. 387 and 399.

[527] *Journal of the Illinois State Historical Society*, Winter, 1952, p. 340.

[528] FADIMAN, Clifton. In *The New Yorker*, December 2, 1939, p. 114.

[529] SANDBURG, Carl. *Home Front Memo*, p. 11, quoting the Reverend O. B. Frothingham.

[530] Ibid.

[531] *Journal of the Illinois State Historical Society*, Winter, 1952, p. 361.

[532] RANDALL, James G. *Lincoln The President*, vol. I, Preface.

[533] AMES, Mary Clemmer. *My Ten Years in Washington*, Chicago : Lloyd, 1874, p. 242.

[534] RANDALL, Ruth Painter. *Mary Lincoln*, Boston : Little, 1953, Preface.

[535] SANDBURG, Carl. *Mary Lincoln: Wife and Widow*, p. 138.

[536] SANDBURG, Carl. *Always the Young Strangers*, pp. 286, 287.

[537] SANDBURG, Carl. *Remembrance Rock*, inside of jacket cover.

[538] Ibid., pp. 21, 22.

[539] SANDBURG, Carl. *Remembrance Rock*, pp. 1007, 1008.

[540] Ibid., p. 1067.

[541] Ibid., p. 30.

[542] *Journal of the Illinois State Historical Society*, Winter 1952, p. 347.

[543] SANDBURG, Carl. *Complete Poems*, Preface, p. XXIV.

[544] WEST, Rebecca. *Selected Poems of Carl Sandburg*, Introduction.

[545] A group of young Swedish poets—among them Martinson, Kjellgren, Lundkvist and Asklund.

[546] *Twentieth Century Scandinavian Poets*, edited by Martin Allwood, p. 343.

[547] Ibid. Published by Kooperativa forbundets bokförlag, Stockholm, 1950.

[548] Ibid., p. 235.

[549] SANDBURG, Carl. *Complete Poems*, p. 168.

[550] *Twentieth Century Scandinavian Poets*, edited by Martin Allwood, p. 260.

[551] Ibid., Published by Kooperativa forbundets bokförlag, Stockholm, 1953, p. 258.

[552] Ibid., p. 253.

[553] LAGERLÖF, Selma. *The Wonderful Adventures of Nils*, pp. 86, 91.

[554] *Twentieth Century Scandinavian Poets*, edited by Martin Allwood, p. 255.

[555] Upsala *Nya Tidning*, August 10, 1953, criticism by Sven Linner.

[556] Upsala *Nya Tidning*, April 20, 1950.

[557] *Samtid och Framtid*, vol. 10, Jan. 1953, pp. 21-23; criticism by Aage Heinberg.

[558] Ibid.

[559] Upsala *Nya Tidning*, Aug. 10, 1953, literary criticism by Sven Linner.

[560] HUTCHENS, John K. In New York *Herald Tribune* Review, Jan. 1953 — also on p. 255 of *The Sandburg Range* by Carl Sandburg.

[561] Upsala *Nya Tidning*, Aug. 10, 1953.

[562] CATEL, Jean. " Lettres Américaines " in *Revue de la Quinzaine*, March 15, 1920.

[563] GINESTIER, Paul. *Les Meilleurs Poèmes Anglais et Américains d'aujourd'hui*, Preface.

[564] Ibid., p. 38.

[565] VERHAEREN, Émile. *Les Villes Tentaculaires*, Mercure de France: Paris, 1949, p. 13.

[566] GINESTIER, Paul. *Les Meilleurs Poèmes Anglais et Américains d'aujourd'hui*, p. 163.

[567] Ibid., p. 165.

[568] VERHAEREN, Émile. *Les Villes Tentaculaires*, Mercure de France: Paris, 1949, p. 163.

[569] Vienna Publishers of *Abraham Lincoln: Das Leben Eines Unsterblichen* by Carl Sandburg. Zsolnay, Paul, on jacket cover.

[570] DRIMMEL, Heinrich. In Introduction to *Abraham Lincoln: Das Leben Eines Unsterblichen*, by Carl Sandburg. Vienna, Zsolnay, 1958.

[571] Ibid.

[572] SHERRILL, Henry K. Letter on file in Pack Memorial Library, Asheville, North Carolina.

[573] DRIMMEL, Heinrich. In Introduction to *Abraham Lincoln: Das Leben Eines Unsterblichen*, by Carl Sandburg. Vienna, Zsolnay, 1958.

[574] JARRELL, Randall. " Poets, Critics and Readers ", in *The American Scholar*, Summer 1959, p. 288.

[575] SAINTE-BEUVE, Charles Augustin. *Pensées et Maximes*, Paris: Grasset, 1955, p. 207.

[576] LEWIS, Lloyd. Quoting from The Boston *Transcript*, in his introduction to Carl Sandburg's volume *Poems of The Midwest*, p. 16.

[577] Ibid., p. 17.

[578] Ibid.

[579] *The Bookman*, Jan. 1921, p. 285. Article by Walter Yust.

— 244 —

[580] *Modern American Poetry*, edited by Louis Untermeyer, pp. 15, 16 of Preface.

[581] Ibid.

[582] Ibid.

[583] Ibid.

[584] LEWIS, Lloyd, Quoting from the Boston *Transcript*, in his introduction to Carl Sandburg's volume *Poems of The Midwest*, p. 17.

[585] Ibid.

[586] SANDBURG, Carl. *Complete Poems*, p. 48.

[587] MONROE, Harriet. In *Poetry*, May, 1916, p. 320.

[588] *The Bookman*, January, 1921, p. 285. Article by Walter Yust.

[589] Ibid.

[590] *The American Scholar*, Summer 1959, p. 376. Article by Joseph Wood Krutch.

[591] ELVIN, Lionel. *Introduction to the Study of Literature*, London : Sylvan Press, 1949, vol. I, p. 187, quoting D. H. Lawrence.

[592] LEWIS, Lloyd; quoting H. L. Mencken in the introduction to Carl Sandburg's volume *Poems of The Midwest*, p. 19.

[593] West, Rebecca. In the introduction to her publication *Selected Poems of Carl Sandburg*, pp. 26, 27, 28.

[594] Ibid.

[595] Ibid.

[596] JONES, Llewellyn. In *American Review*, vol. IV, pp. 54, 55.

[597] LINK, Gordden. In *The Poetry Review*, vol. XXI, p. 423.

[598] *Literary History of the United States*, edited by SPILLER, THORP, JOHNSON, CANBY, p. 1395.

[599] Ibid., p. 1396.

[600] ELGSTRÖM, Anna Lenah. *Dikter i Urval*, Preface.

[601] LUNDKVIST, Arthur. *Diktare och Anslöjare I Amerikas Moderna Litteratur*, 1942, Nordysk Rotogravyr, Stockholm.

[602] Upsala *Nya Tidning*, Aug. 10, 1953. Criticism by Sven Linner.

[603] Ibid., Aug. 10, 1953.

[604] ARNAVON, Cyrille. *Histoire Littéraire des États-Unis*, Paris : Hachette, 1953, p. 361.

[605] Ibid.

[606] Ibid.

[607] UNTERMEYER, Louis. *Modern American Poetry*, p. 16.

[608] ARNAVON, Cyrille. *Histoire Littéraire des États-Unis*, Paris : Hachette, 1953, p. 362.

[609] EMERSON, Ralph Waldo. *Essays*, New York : Burt, 1900, vol. II, p. 86.

[610] *Literary History of the United States*, edited by SPILLER, THORP, JOHNSON, CANBY, p. 1181.

[611] ARNAVON, Cyrille. *Histoire Littéraire des États-Unis*, Paris : Hachette, 1953, p. 362.

[612] VAN DOREN, Mark. In *Carl Sandburg — Harvest Poems*, Harcourt, Brace, p. 6.

[613] ARNAVON, Cyrille. *Histoire Littéraire des États-Unis*, Paris : Hachette, 1953, p. 362.

[614] GINESTIER, Paul. *Les Meilleurs Poèmes Anglais et Américains d'aujourd'hui*, p. 38.

[615] SANDBURG, Carl. *Complete Poems*, Preface, p. XXIII.

[616] GINESTIER, Paul. *Les Meilleurs Poèmes Anglais et Américains d'aujourd'hui*, p. 38.

[617] SCHLAUCH, Margaret. *Modern English and American Poetry*, p. 114.

[618] SCHLAUCH, Margaret. *Modern English and American Poetry*, p. 115.

[619] Ibid.

[620] Ibid., p. 117.

[621] *Wisdom*, August, 1959, p. 26.

[622] *Poetry and Prose of Walt Whitman*, Untermeyer. N.Y., Simon, Schuster, 1949, p. 65.

[623] Ibid., p. 191.

[624] SANDBURG, Carl. In *Better Homes and Gardens*, April, 1959, p. 57.

[625] SANDBURG, Carl. *Home Front Memo*, p. 33.

[626] SCHLAUCH, Margaret. *Modern English and American Poetry*. p. 119.

[627] Ibid., pp. 119, 120.

[628] SANDBURG, Carl. Complete Poems, pp. 636, 637.

[629] Van Doren, Mark. In *Carl Sandburg-Harvest Poems*, Harcourt, Brace, p. 5.

[630] Ibid., pp. 6, 9.

[631] ROSENTHAL, M. L. *The Modern Poets*, pp. 154, 155.

[632] Ibid., pp. 267, 272.

[633] Ibid., p. 104.

[634] Ibid., pp. 152, 155, 156.

[635] SCHLAUCH, Margaret. *Modern English and American Poetry*, p. 121.

[636] ROSENTHAL, M. L. *The Modern Poets*, pp. 154, 19, 159.

[637] THOMAS, Benjamin P. *Portrait for Posterity*, p. 28.

[638] THOMAS, Benjamin P. In *Journal of the Illinois State Historical Society*, Winter 1952, p. 339.

[639] *Literary Digest*, May, 1926.

[640] ELGSTRÖM, Anna Lenah. In *Ord och Bild*, 1953, pp. 528-539.

[641] In *Journal of the Illinois State Historical Society*, Winter, 1952, p. 340.

[642] Ibid., p. 363.

[643] THOMAS, Benjamin P. *Portrait for Posterity*, quoting Stephen Vincent Benét, p. 300.

[644] *Journal of the Illinois State Historical Society*, Winter, 1952, p. 363.

[645] Ibid., p. 340.

[646] BUTCHER, Fanny. In Chicago *Sunday Tribune*. Reprinted in a brochure on Carl Sandburg published by Harcourt, Brace & Co., 1949, p. 9.

[647] LEWIS, Lloyd. In New York *Herald Tribune*. Reprinted in above-mentioned brochure, p. 5.

[648] HOWARD, N. R. In Cleveland *News*, reprinted in the Harcourt, Brace & Co., brochure, pp. 26, 27.

[649] SHERWOOD, Robert E. On p. 255 of *Sandburg Range* by Carl Sandburg.

[650] LINNER, Sven. In Upsala *Nya Tidning*, Aug. 10, 1953.

[651] SPILLER, Robert. *Cycle of American Literature*, p. 236.

[652] MALONE, Dumas. In the Introduction to vol. VI of *George Washington* by Douglas Southall Freeman, New York: Scribner, 1954.

[653] Ibid.

[654] SANDBURG, Carl. *The Prairie Years*, vol. I, p. 49.

[655] SANDBURG, Carl. In his speech before Congress, printed in the Washington *Evening Star*, Feb. 13, 1959.

[656] *Journal of the Illinois State Historical Society,* Winter, 1952, p. 329.

[657] *Wisdom,* The Encyclopedia Americana Edition, Aug. 1959, p. 25.

[658] SANDBURG, Carl. In his chapter of the *Literary History of the United States,* edited by Spiller, Thorp, Johnson, Canby; p. 786.

[659] SANDBURG, Carl. *Complete Poems,* p. 523.

[660] FREEMAN, Douglas Southall. In a printed tribute in the Rare Book Room of the Library of Congress.

[662] Washington *Evening Star,* March 12, 1960.

[662] Ibid., p. 608.

[663] Ibid., Feb. 13, 1959.

[664] Report of the Committee on Arrangements on the Lincoln Commemoration Ceremony in the 86th Congress, Feb. 12, 1959; p. 29; House Document No. 211.

[665] Ibid., p. 31.

[666] SANDBURG, Carl. *The War Years,* vol. II, pp. 476, 477.

[667] SANDBURG, Carl. *Complete Poems,* p. 452.

[668] Washington *Evening Star,* Nov. 20, 1959.

[669] Ibid.

[670] SANDBURG, Carl. *The War Years,* vol. I, p. 621.

Further information concerning the publications of the above-mentioned literary critics who have written on the prose and poetry of Carl Sandburg may be found in the bibliography.

INDEX